Very interesting
book

P9-CQF-582

LOST IN SHANGRI-LA

LOST IN
SHANGRI-LA

A TRUE STORY OF
SURVIVAL, ADVENTURE,
AND THE MOST INCREDIBLE
RESCUE MISSION OF
WORLD WAR II

MITCHELL
ZUCKOFF

HARPER
An Imprint of HarperCollins*Publishers*
www.harpercollins.com

HarperCollins books may be purchased for educational, business, or sales
promotional use. For information, please write: Special Markets Department,
HarperCollins Publishers, 10 East 53rd Street, New York, NY 10022.

Designed by Fritz Metsch

Library of Congress Cataloging-in-Publication Data has been applied for.

ISBN: 978-0-06-198834-9 (Hardcover)
ISBN: 978-0-06-209358-5 (International Edition)

11 12 13 14 15   OV/RRD   10 9 8 7 6 5 4

CONTENTS

A Note to the Reader   XI

1   MISSING   I

2   HOLLANDIA   5

3   SHANGRI-LA   19

4   *GREMLIN SPECIAL*   31

5   EUREKA!   44

6   CHARMS   58

7   TARZAN   71

8   GENTLEMAN EXPLORER   80

9   GUILT AND GANGRENE   92

10 EARL WALTER, JUNIOR AND SENIOR   104

11 UWAMBO   115

12 WIMAYUK WANDIK, AKA "CHIEF PETE"   128

13 COME WHAT MAY   141

14 FIVE-BY-FIVE   152

15 NO THANKSGIVING   162

16 RAMMY AND DOC   173

17 CUSTER AND COMPANY   181

18 BATHTIME FOR YUGWE   195

19 "SHOO, SHOO BABY"   204

20 "HEY, MARTHA!"   217

21   PROMISED LAND   232

22   HOLLYWOOD   243

23   GLIDERS?   255

24   TWO QUEENS   268

25   SNATCH   285

EPILOGUE: After Shangri-La   298

Cast of Characters   317

Acknowledgments   322

Notes on Sources and Methods   327

Notes   329

Select Bibliography   368

Index   371

A NOTE TO THE READER

NEAR THE END of World War II, a U.S. Army plane flying over the island of New Guinea crashed in an uncharted region inhabited by a prehistoric tribe.

In the weeks that followed, reporters raced to cover a tale of survival, loss, anthropology, discovery, heroism, friendship, and a near-impossible rescue mission. Their stories featured a beautiful, headstrong corporal and a strapping, hell-bent paratrooper, stranded amid bone-through-the-nose tribesmen reputed to be headhunters and cannibals. They told of a brave lieutenant grieving the death of his twin brother; a wry sergeant with a terrible head wound; and a team of Filipino-American soldiers who volunteered to confront the natives despite knowing they'd be outnumbered more than a thousand to one. Rounding out the true-life cast were a rogue filmmaker who'd left Hollywood after being exposed as a jewel thief; a smart-aleck pilot who flew best when his plane had no engine; and a cowboy colonel whose rescue plan seemed designed to increase the death toll.

Front pages blazed with headlines about the crash and its aftermath. Radio shows breathlessly reported every development en route to an astonishing conclusion.

But the world was on the brink of the Atomic Age, and a story of life and death in the Stone Age was soon eclipsed. In time, it was forgotten.

I came across an article about the crash years ago while searching newspaper archives for something else entirely. I set it aside and found what I thought I was looking for. But the story nagged at me. I began doing what reporters call "collecting string"— gathering pieces of information wherever possible to see if they might tie together.

News reports and official documents can talk about the past, but they can't carry on a conversation. I dreamed of finding someone who'd been there, someone who could describe the people, places, and events firsthand. More than six decades after the crash, I located the sole surviving American participant, living quietly on the Oregon coast with vivid memories and an extraordinary story.

That discovery, and the interviews that followed, led to an explosion of string that wove itself into a tapestry. Among the most valuable items was a daily journal kept during the weeks between the crash and the rescue attempt. A lengthy diary surfaced, along with a trove of priceless photographs. Three private scrapbooks followed close behind, along with boxes of declassified U.S. Army documents, affidavits, maps, personnel records, military bulletins, letters, and ground-to-air radio transcripts. Relatives of more than a dozen other participants supplied more documents, photos, letters, and details. Perhaps most remarkably, the trail led to several thousand feet of original film footage of the events as they unfolded.

Next came a trip to New Guinea, to learn what had become of the place and the natives; to find old men and women who'd witnessed the crash as children; and to hike to the top of a mountain where pieces of the plane still rest, along with the bones and belongings of some of those who died there.

As I write this, on my desk sits a melted piece of metal from the plane that resembles a gnarled human form. It's a tangible reminder that, as incredible as this story seems, every word of it is true.

—MITCHELL ZUCKOFF

LOST IN SHANGRI-LA

1

MISSING

ON A RAINY day in May 1945, a Western Union messenger made his rounds through the quiet village of Owego, in upstate New York. Just outside downtown, he turned onto McMaster Street, a row of modest, well-kept homes shaded by sturdy elm trees. He slowed to a stop at a green, farm-style house with a small porch and empty flower boxes. As he approached the door, the messenger prepared for the hardest part of his job: delivering a telegram from the U.S. War Department.

Directly before him, proudly displayed in a front window, hung a small white banner with a red border and a blue star at its center. Similar banners hung in windows all through the village, each one to honor a young man, or in a few cases a young woman, gone to war. American troops had been fighting in World War II since 1941, and some blue-star banners had already been replaced by banners with gold stars, signifying a loss for a larger gain and a permanently empty place at a family's dinner table.

Inside the blue-star home where the messenger stood was Patrick Hastings, a sixty-eight-year-old widower. With his wire-rim glasses, his neatly trimmed silver hair, and the serious set of his mouth, Patrick Hastings bore a striking resemblance to the new president, Harry S. Truman, who'd taken office a month earlier upon the death of Franklin Delano Roosevelt.

A son of Irish immigrants, Patrick Hastings grew up a farm

boy across the border in Pennsylvania. After a long engagement, he married his sweetheart, schoolteacher Julia Hickey, and they'd moved to Owego to find work and raise a family. As the years passed, Patrick rose through the maintenance department at a local factory owned by the Endicott-Johnson Shoe Company, which churned out combat boots and officers' dress shoes for the U.S. Army. Together with Julia, he reared three bright, lively daughters.

Now, though, Patrick Hastings lived alone. Six years earlier, a fatal infection had struck Julia's heart. Their home's barren flower boxes were visible signs of her absence and his solitary life.

Their two younger daughters, Catherine and Rita, had married and moved away. Blue-star banners hung in their homes, too, each one for a husband in the service. But the blue-star banner in Patrick Hastings's window wasn't for either of his sons-in-law. It honored his strong-willed eldest daughter, Corporal Margaret Hastings of the Women's Army Corps, the WACs.

CORPORAL MARGARET HASTINGS OF THE WOMEN'S ARMY CORPS, PHOTOGRAPHED IN 1945. (PHOTO COURTESY OF C. EARL WALTER JR.)

Sixteen months earlier, in January 1944, Margaret Hastings had walked into a recruiting station in the nearby city of Binghamton. There, she signed her name and took her place among the first generation of women to serve in the U.S. military. Margaret and thousands of other WACs were dispatched to war zones around the world, mostly filling desk jobs on bases well back from the front lines. Still, her father worried, knowing that Margaret was in a strange, faraway land: New Guinea, an untamed island just north of Australia. Margaret was based at a U.S. military compound on the island's eastern half, an area known as Dutch New Guinea.

By the middle of 1945, the military had outsourced the delivery of bad news, and its bearers had been busy: the combat death toll among Americans neared 300,000. More than a 100,000 other Americans had died noncombat deaths. More than 600,000 had been wounded. Blue-star families had good reason to dread the sight of a Western Union messenger approaching the door.

On this day, misery had company. As the messenger rang Patrick Hastings's doorbell, Western Union couriers with nearly identical telegrams were en route to twenty-three other star-banner homes with loved ones in Dutch New Guinea. The messengers fanned out across the country, to rural communities including Shippenville, Pennsylvania; Trenton, Missouri; and Kelso, Washington, and to urban centers including New York, Philadelphia, and Los Angeles.

Each message offered a nod toward sympathy camouflaged by the clipped tone of a military communiqué. Each was signed by Major General James A. Ulio, the U.S. Army's chief administrative officer. Patrick Hastings held the pale yellow telegram in his calloused hands. It read:

THE SECRETARY OF WAR DESIRES ME TO EXPRESS HIS DEEP REGRET THAT YOUR DAUGHTER, CORPORAL HASTINGS, MARGARET J., HAS BEEN MISSING IN DUTCH NEW GUINEA, THIRTEEN MAY, '45. IF FURTHER DETAILS OR OTHER INFORMATION ARE RECEIVED YOU WILL BE PROMPTLY NOTIFIED. CONFIRMING LETTER FOLLOWS.

When Owego's newspaper learned of the telegram, Patrick Hastings told a reporter about Margaret's most recent letter home. In it, she described a recreational flight up the New Guinea coast and wrote that she hoped to take another sightseeing trip soon.

In mentioning the letter, Patrick Hastings's message was clear: he feared that Margaret had gone down in a plane crash. But the reporter's story danced around that worry, offering vague optimism instead. "From the wording of the [telegram] received yesterday," the reporter wrote, "the family thinks that perhaps she was on another flight and will be accounted for later."

When Patrick Hastings telephoned his younger daughters, he didn't sugarcoat the news or hold out false hope about their sister's fate. Outdoing even the military for brevity, he reduced the telegram to three words: Margaret is missing.

HOLLANDIA

ELEVEN DAYS BEFORE the messenger appeared at her father's door, Margaret Hastings awoke as usual before dawn. Already the moist tropical heat had crept under the flaps of the cramped tent she shared with five other WACs. She dressed alongside her tentmates in the regulation khakis she'd cut down to match her petite frame. At first, Margaret wrote to a friend back in Owego, the uniforms "fit me like sacks." But after a few failed alteration efforts, she boasted in the letter, "I got hold of a pair of men's

TENTS FOR MEMBERS OF THE WOMEN'S ARMY CORPS IN HOLLANDIA, DUTCH NEW GUINEA, DURING WORLD WAR II. (PHOTO COURTESY OF U.S. ARMY.)

trousers that were miles too big for me, and used the material. They really turned out quite well, considering."

The date was May 13, 1945. It was Sunday, so the bugler had the day off from his usual 5:30 a.m. reveille. Not that Margaret could sleep in. The workweek was seven days long at Base G, a sprawling U.S. military installation built around the town of Hollandia, on Dutch New Guinea's northern coast. By eight o'clock Margaret was due at her post, a metal desk with a clackety typewriter where daily she proved that war wasn't just hell, it was hell with paperwork.

Margaret was thirty years old, lithe and beautiful. She had alert blue eyes, alabaster skin, and long, light brown hair she wore in a stylish figure-eight bun. At just under five-foot-two and barely a hundred pounds, she still fit her high school wardrobe and her teenage nickname, Little Girl. But Margaret's size was deceiving. She carried herself with style, shoulders back and chin up, the lasting effects of drama club performances, violin lessons, and what her youngest sister called a feisty, "take-charge" nature. She met strangers with a sidelong glance and a half smile that dug dimples beneath her high cheekbones. Somewhere between sly and sexy, the look suggested that Margaret had a secret that she had no intention of sharing.

As a girl growing up in Owego, Margaret bicycled to the local swimming hole, hitchhiked when she wanted to explore beyond the village, did well in school, and read books under the covers late at night. As she grew older and prettier, she became one of the most sought-after girls in town. She enjoyed the attention but didn't depend on it. Margaret considered herself an independent young woman who, as she put it, "drank liquor, but not too much" and "liked the boys, but not too much."

Even after her younger sisters married, Margaret held out beyond the limit of her twenties. Being single at thirty didn't bother her, but it made her unusual: the average marrying age for women of her generation was twenty-one. She wasn't interested in the men of Owego, but she didn't blame them, either. "To tell the truth," she told an acquaintance, "I'm not sure I go for the kind of man who's supposed to make a good husband."

After graduating from high school and bouncing through several jobs, Margaret found work as a secretary at a local factory owned by Remington Rand, a company that turned steel into everything from typewriters to .45-caliber pistols. She liked the work, but it bothered her that she'd never been farther from home or anywhere more exciting than Atlantic City. It sounded corny, but Margaret wanted to see the world, serve her country, and find out what she was made of. Joining the Women's Army Corps gave her the chance to do all three.

AS MARGARET GOT ready for work, families across the United States were preparing for Mother's Day—the fourth time the holiday had fallen during World War II. This time, though, a mother's love wasn't the only cause for celebration. Five days earlier, Germany had surrendered unconditionally. Reports were trickling out that Adolf Hitler had killed himself in his bunker. Other Nazi leaders were in custody. Concentration camps were being liberated, their horrors fully exposed. After a terrible toll of "blood, toil, tears, and sweat," victory had finally arrived in Europe. In fact, May 13, 1945, marked five years to the day since British prime minister Winston Churchill had uttered that phrase to rouse his countrymen for the fight ahead.

To mark the once-improbable success of the war in Europe, the dome of the U.S. Capitol building, which had been blacked out since Pearl Harbor, again gleamed under the glow of floodlights. Congress unanimously endorsed President Truman's declaration of May 13, 1945, as not just Mother's Day but also "A Day of Prayer." As Truman put it: "The western world has been freed of the evil forces which for five years and longer have imprisoned the bodies and broken the lives of millions upon millions of free-born men." House Speaker Sam Rayburn hailed the news in Europe but added two somber notes. He lamented the passing of President Roosevelt weeks before V-E Day. Then he noted that the war wasn't over: "I am happy but also sad, because I cannot help but think of those thousands of our boys who are yet to die in the far-flung Pacific islands and the Far East in order that victory may come to our armies, and that the glory of America may be upheld and peace and an ordered world may come to us again."

News from the Pacific was encouraging, though fierce engagements continued there. For the previous six weeks, ferocious fighting had been under way on the island of Okinawa, which American generals intended to use as a springboard for an invasion of Japan, if necessary. Few relished that idea, yet optimism ran high. That morning, *The New York Times* declared that final victory was assured, whether by negotiated surrender or outright defeat. The paper told its readers, "It will be a busy summer for the Japanese enemy, and Hirohito can be confident that the 'softening-up' period, now started, will be followed by lethal blows."

That confident inevitability might have been plain to editors of the *Times* and to policy makers in Washington. But the war in the Pacific remained a moment-by-moment struggle. Between sunrise and sunset on May 13, 1945, more than 130 U.S. fighters and bombers would attack troops, trains, bridges, and other Japanese "targets of opportunity" in southern and eastern China. Ten B-24 Liberators would bomb an underground hangar on a dot of land called Moen Island. Nine other B-24s would bomb an airfield on a lonely speck in the northern Pacific called Marcus Island. On Borneo, B-24s would bomb two airfields. To the east, B-25 Mitchell bombers and P-38 Lightning fighters would support ground forces on Tarakan Island. The U.S. 7th Marine Division would burst through Japanese defenses on Okinawa to capture Dakeshi Ridge. In the Philippines, the 40th Infantry Division would capture Del

Monte Airfield, and bombers and fighters would pound targets on Luzon Island.

Those were the major events of the day, to be catalogued, analyzed, and recounted in countless books and films about the Big War. Another incident on May 13, 1945, would escape the notice of historians and Hollywood: a C-47 transport plane carrying two dozen officers, soldiers, and WACs would disappear during a flight over the mountainous jungles of New Guinea.

AFTER ENLISTING, MARGARET spent nearly a year in basic training, at Fort Oglethorpe in Georgia, and at Mitchel Field on Long Island, New York. She learned to march in formation, abandon ship, wear a gas mask, read a map, scrub a latrine, maintain proper hygiene, and live by endless military rules. In December 1944, having risen from private to corporal, she shipped out to New Guinea, a place as different from Owego as imaginable.

Located between Australia and the equator, New Guinea was a largely uncharted tropical island roughly twice the size of California. At fifteen hundred miles long and nearly five hundred miles wide at its center, it was the world's second-largest island, after Greenland. On a map, New Guinea resembled a prehistoric bird taking off from Australia or a comedian's rubber chicken. But resemblances can be misleading; there was nothing funny about the place.

The island was a gift-box assortment of inhospitable environments. Much of the coastline featured barely habitable lowlands, swamps, and jungles. In the great middle were soaring limestone mountains covered by impenetrable rain forests and topped by snow or rocky outcroppings. The New Guinea terrain was so forbidding that the most common experience for its inhabitants was isolation. Pockets of humanity carved out small places to survive, fighting with anyone who came near and often among themselves. As a result, the island evolved into a latter-day Babel.

U.S. MILITARY MAP OF NEW GUINEA DURING WORLD WAR II, WITH HOLLANDIA
ON THE NORTHERN COAST AT ROUGHLY THE MIDPOINT OF THE ISLAND. THE MAP-
MAKER WAS UNAWARE OF A LARGE VALLEY 150 MILES SOUTHWEST OF HOLLANDIA,
IN THE MOUNTAIN RANGE THAT CROSSES THE ISLAND'S MIDSECTION. (U.S. ARMY
MAP.)

New Guinea's natives spoke more than one thousand languages,
or about one-sixth of the world's total—despite accounting for
less than one-tenth of one percent of the global population.

Inhabited by humans for more than forty thousand years,
New Guinea passed the millennia largely ignored by the rest of
the world. Lookouts on European ships caught sight of the island
early in the sixteenth century. A racially single-minded explorer
named it for an African country, Guinea, ten thousand miles away,
because the natives he saw on the coast had black skin. For another two centuries, New Guinea was left mostly to itself, though
trappers stopped by to collect the brilliant plumes of its birds of
paradise to make hats for fashionable Sri Lankan potentates. In
the eighteenth century, the island became a regular landing spot
for French and British explorers. Captain Cook visited in 1770.
Scientists followed, and the island drew a steady stream of field

researchers from around the globe searching for discoveries in zoology, botany, and geography.

In the nineteenth century, New Guinea caught the eye of traders seeking valuable raw materials. No precious minerals or metals were easily accessible, but the rising value of coconut oil made it worthwhile to plant the flag and climb the palm trees along the coastline. European powers divided the island in half, and the eastern section was cut in half again. Over the years, claims of sovereignty were made by Spain, Germany, the Netherlands, and Great Britain. Nevertheless, even well-educated westerners had a hard time finding the island on a map.

After World War I, New Guinea's eastern half was controlled by Britain and Australia. The island's western half was controlled by the Netherlands—and was henceforth known as Dutch New Guinea, with Hollandia as its capital. World War II drew unprecedented attention to the island because of its central location in the Pacific war zone.

Japan invaded in 1942, planning to use New Guinea to launch attacks on Australia, just over a hundred miles away at the closest point. In April 1944 U.S. troops executed a daring strike called "Operation Reckless" that scattered the Japanese troops and won Hollandia for the Allies. The Americans turned it into an important base of their own, and General Douglas MacArthur, Supreme Commander of Allied Forces in the Southwest Pacific, built his headquarters there before moving on to the Philippines.

IN NEW GUINEA as elsewhere, Margaret Hastings and other WACs filled strictly noncombat roles, as expressed by their slogan, "Free a Man to Fight." An earlier motto, "Release a Man for Combat," was scratched because it fed suspicions among the WACs' detractors that their secret purpose was to provide sexual release for soldiers in the field. MacArthur wasn't among those critics. He liked to say the WACs were "my best soldiers" because they worked harder and groused less than male troops. Eventually, more than 150,000 women served as WACs during World War II, making them the first women other than nurses to join the U.S. Army.

Margaret arrived in Hollandia eight months after the success of Operation Reckless. By then, little of the war's bloody drama was playing out in that corner of the Pacific. Thousands of Japanese troops remained armed and in hiding on the island, but few were believed to be in the immediate vicinity of Hollandia. Nevertheless, sentries patrolled the sea of tents and one-story headquarters buildings on the base. WACs were routinely escorted under armed guard, and women's tents were ringed by barbed wire. One WAC explained that the ranking woman in her tent was given a sidearm to keep under her pillow, with instructions to kill her tentmates, then herself, if Japanese troops attacked. New Guinea natives also raised concerns, though the ones nearest Hollandia had grown so comfortable with the Americans they'd call out, "Hey Joe— hubba, hubba—buy War Bonds." Australian soldiers who'd received help from the natives during battles with the Japanese nicknamed them "Fuzzy Wuzzy Angels."

Some WACs thought the safety precautions' real aim was to protect them not from enemies or natives but from more than a hundred thousand U.S. soldiers, sailors, and airmen in and around Hollandia. Some of those fighting boys and men hadn't seen an American woman in months.

Almost immediately upon her arrival in Hollandia, Margaret became a focus of lovelorn soldiers' attentions. "I suppose you have heard about blanket parties," she wrote to a friend in Owego in February 1945. "I know I did and was properly shocked. They are quite the thing in New Guinea. However, they are not as bad as they seem and anyway, nothing can be done on a blanket that can't be done in the back seat of a car.

"You see, we have no easy chairs and Jeeps are not too easy to sit in. So you just take your beer, or at the end of the month when the beer is all gone, your canteen of water and put it in a Jeep and ride all around until you find some nice place to relax. The nights are lovely over here and it's nice to lay under the stars and drink beer and talk, or perhaps go for a swim. . . . With the surplus of men over here, you can't help but find some nice ones. I have had no difficulty along that line at all."

Far from home, Margaret indulged her adventurous impulses. "One night," she wrote, "six of us went out in a Jeep without any top and drove all over the island. We traveled on roads where the bridges had been washed away, drove through water, up banks, and almost tipped over about ten times." The letter didn't give away military secrets, only personal ones, so it slipped untouched past the base censors.

Margaret's regular double-date partner was a pretty brunette sergeant named Laura Besley. The only child of a retired oil driller and a homemaker, Laura hailed from Shippenville, Pennsylvania, ninety miles from Pittsburgh, a town so small it would've fit comfortably inside Owego. Laura had spent a year in college, then worked as a typist for the Pennsylvania Labor Department before enlisting in the WACs in August 1942.

Laura was taller and more full-figured than Margaret, but otherwise the two WACs were much alike. Laura was thirty-one and single, with a reputation among her family for being a "sassy" young woman who did as she pleased.

WHEN THEY WEREN'T working, blanketing, or joyriding, Margaret, Laura, and the other WACs made their quarters as plush as possible. "It is really quite homelike, and I am lucky enough to be in with five exceptionally nice girls," Margaret wrote another friend in Owego. They furnished their twelve-foot-square canvas home with small dressing tables made from boxes and burlap. They sat on chairs donated by supply officers who hoped

SERGEANT LAURA BESLEY OF THE
WOMEN'S ARMY CORPS. (PHOTO COUR-
TESY OF GERTA ANDERSON.)

the gifts would translate into dates. A small rug covered the concrete pad that was the floor, mosquito netting dangled over their cots, and silky blue parachute cloth hung as decoration from the tent ceiling.

A single bulb illuminated the tent, but a kind lieutenant named John McCollom who worked with Margaret's boss gave Margaret a double electric socket. The coveted device allowed her to enjoy the luxury of light while she ironed her uniforms at night. Quiet and unassuming, John McCollom was one of a pair of identical twins from Missouri who served together in Hollandia. He was single and couldn't help but notice Margaret's good looks, yet he didn't try to parlay the gift into a date. That made Margaret appreciate it all the more.

The wildlife of New Guinea wasn't so unassuming. Rats, lizards, and hairy spiders the size of coffee saucers marched boldly into the WACs' tents, and mosquitoes feasted on any stray arm or leg that slipped out from under the cots' protective netting. Even the precautions had vivid side effects. Bitter-tasting Atabrine tablets warded off malaria, but the pills brought on headaches and vomiting, and they turned soldiers' and WACs' skin a sickly shade of yellow.

A lack of refrigeration meant most food came three ways: canned, salted, or dehydrated. Cooking it changed the temperature but not the flavor. WACs joked that they'd been sent to the far reaches of the South Pacific to "Get skinny in Guinea."

To top it off, Hollandia was paradise for fungus. The weather varied little—a mixture of heat, rain, and humidity—which left everyone wet and overripe. Margaret showered at least twice a day using cold water pumped from a mountain stream. Still, she perspired through her khakis during the boiling hours in between. She relied on Mum brand deodorant, as well as "talcum, foot powder, and everything in the books in order to keep respectable," she wrote in a letter home. "It is a continuous effort to keep clean over here. There are no paved roads and the dust is terrible, and when it rains there is mud."

An American military officer described Hollandia vividly: "There was 'jungle rot'—all five types. The first three were interesting to the patient; the next two were interesting to the doctor and mostly fatal to the patient. You name it—elephantiasis, malaria, dengue fever, the 'crud'—New Guinea had it all. It was in the water in which you bathed, the foliage you touched—apparently the whole place was full of things one should have cringed from. But who has time to think when there are enemy snipers hanging dead, roped to their spotter trees; flesh-eating piranhas inhabiting the streams; lovely, large snakes slithering nearby; and always the enemy."

Yet there was great beauty, too, from the lush mountains to the pounding surf; from the sound of the wind rustling through the leaves of coconut palms to the strange calls and flamboyant feathers of wild birds. Margaret's tent was some thirty miles inland, near Lake Sentani, considered by its admirers to be among the world's most picturesque bodies of water. Small islands that looked like mounds of crushed green velvet dotted its crystalline waters. On long workdays, Margaret relieved her tired eyes by looking up from her desk to Mount Cyclops, its emerald flank cleaved by the perpetual spray of a narrow waterfall. She described the sight as almost enough to make her feel cool.

Mostly, though, Hollandia was a trial. The WACs' official history singled out Base G as the worst place in the war for the health of military women: "The Air Surgeon reported that 'an increasing number of cases are on record for nervousness and exhaustion,' and recommended that personnel be given one full day off per week to relieve 'nervous tension.' "

Margaret's boss took such warnings to heart, and he searched for ways to ease the stress among his staff.

MARGARET WAS ONE of several hundred WACs assigned to the Far East Air Service Command, an essential if unglamorous supply, logistics, and maintenance outfit known as "Fee-Ask." Just as in civilian life, Margaret was a secretary. Her commanding officer was Colonel Peter J. Prossen, an experienced pilot and Fee-Ask's chief of maintenance.

The early hours of May 13, 1945, were quiet in the big headquarters tent at Fee-Ask. Colonel Prossen spent part of the morning writing a letter to his family back home in San Antonio, Texas: his wife Evelyn, and their three young children, sons Peter Jr. and David, and daughter Lyneve, whose name was an anagram of her mother's.

Prossen was thirty-seven, stocky, with blue eyes, a cleft chin, and thick brown hair. A native of New York from an affluent family, he graduated from New York University in 1930 with an engineering degree. After working in private industry for a few years, he joined the military so he could fly.

Prossen had spent most of his children's lives at war, but his elder son and namesake knew him as a warm, cheerful man with a love of photography. He'd sing "Smoke Gets in Your Eyes" loudly and out of tune while his wife played flawless piano. After visits home, Prossen would fly over their house and tip his wings to say good-bye.

In a letter to his wife a day earlier, addressed as always to "My dearest sweetheart," Prossen commented on the news from home, counseled her to ignore slights by his sister, and lamented how long it took for photos of their children to reach him. He told her to save the stuffed koalas he'd shipped home until their baby daughter's second birthday. He asked her to watch the mail for a native ax he'd sent home as a souvenir.

A dozen years in the military hadn't diminished Prossen's tenderness to his family. He sent his wife love poems and heart-filled sketches on Valentine's Day, and he yearned for them to be reunited. Despite

COLONEL PETER J. PROSSEN WITH HIS SONS, DAVID AND PETER JR. (PHOTO COURTESY OF PETER J. PROSSEN JR.)

the harsh conditions he endured in Hollandia, Prossen commiserated sincerely with his wife about the hardships of gas rationing and caring for their children without him there.

The morning of May 13, 1945, for Mother's Day, he wrote to Evelyn in his crabbed handwriting: "My sweet, I think that we will be extra happy when we get together again. Don't worry about me. . . . I am glad that the time passes fairly quickly for you—hope it does till I get home. Then I want it to slow down."

Later in the letter, Prossen described a poem he'd read about two boys playing "make-believe." It made him wistful for his own sons. Sadness leaked through his pen as he wrote that their son Peter Jr. would make his First Communion that very day without him: "I'll bet he is a nice boy. My, but he is growing up." Prossen signed off, "I love you as always. Please take good care of yourself for me. I send all my love. Devotedly, Pete."

Lately, Prossen had been anxious about the toll Dutch New

Guinea was taking on the hundred or so men and the twenty-plus WACs serving directly under him. He wrote to his wife that he tried to relieve the pressures shouldered by junior officers, enlisted men, and WACs, though he didn't always succeed. "I lose sight of the fact that there is a war going on and it's different," he wrote. "My subordinates are also depressed and been here a long time." He wanted to show them that he valued their labors.

Prossen wheedled pilots flying from Australia to bring his staff precious treats: Coca-Cola syrup and fresh fruit. Lately, he'd offered even more desirable rewards—sightseeing flights up the coastline. One of those pleasure jaunts had featured prominently in Margaret's most recent letter to her father.

On this day, May 13, 1945, Colonel Peter Prossen had arranged the rarest and most sought-after prize for his staff, one certain to boost morale: a trip to Shangri-La.

3

SHANGRI-LA

A YEAR EARLIER, in May 1944, Colonel Ray T. Elsmore heard his copilot's voice crackle through the intercom in the cramped cockpit of their C-60 transport plane. Sitting in the cockpit's left-hand seat, Elsmore had the controls, flying a zigzag route over and through the mountainous backbone of central New Guinea.

Elsmore commanded the 322nd Troop Carrier Wing of the U.S. Army Air Forces. On this particular flight, his mission was to find a place to build a landing strip as a supply stop between Hollandia, on New Guinea's northern coast, and Merauke, an Allied base on the island's southern coast. If that wasn't possible, he at least hoped to discover a more direct, low-altitude pass across the Oranje Mountains to make it easier to fly between the two bases.

The copilot, Major Myron Grimes, pointed at a mountain ahead: "Colonel, if we slip over that ridge, we'll enter the canyon that winds into Hidden Valley."

Grimes had made a similar reconnaissance flight a week earlier, and now he was showing Elsmore his surprising discovery. Later, a rumor would spread that Grimes's first flight over the place he called Hidden Valley was a happy accident by an amorous man. Grimes was late for a hot date in Australia, the wags said, and he took a daring shortcut across New Guinea to avoid the long flight around the coastline. It was a good story, but it wasn't true; Grimes had been flying a routine reconnaissance mission.

On his return from that first flight, Grimes claimed to have found a mostly flat, verdant valley some 150 air miles from Hollandia, in a spot where maps used by the Army Air Forces showed only an unbroken chain of high peaks and jungle-covered ridges. Mapmakers usually just sketched a string of upside-down Vs to signify mountains and stamped the area "unknown" or "unexplored." One imaginative mapmaker claimed that the place Grimes spotted was the site of an "estimated 14,000-foot peak." He might as well have written, "Here be dragons."

If a large, uncharted tabletop valley really existed in the jigsaw-puzzle mountain range, Colonel Elsmore thought it might make a good spot for a secret air supply base or an emergency landing strip. Elsmore wanted to see this so-called Hidden Valley for himself.

ON GRIMES'S SIGNAL, Elsmore pulled back on the C-60's control wheel. He guided the long-nosed, twin-engine plane over the ridge and down into a canyon. Easing back the plane's two throttle levers, he reduced power and remained below the billowing white clouds that shrouded the highest peaks. Pilots had nightmares about this sort of terrain. An occupational hazard of flying through what Elsmore called the "innocent white walls" of clouds was the dismal possibility that a mountain might be hiding inside. Few pilots in the Army Air Forces knew those dangers better than Elsmore.

At fifty-three years old, energetic and fit enough to pass for a decade younger, Elsmore resembled the actor Gene Kelly. The son of a carpenter, he'd been a flying instructor during World War I, after which he'd spent more than a decade delivering airmail through the Rocky Mountains. He'd also earned a law degree from the University of Utah and served as a deputy county prosecutor. With the second world war looming, Elsmore returned to mili-

tary service before Pearl Harbor
and was assigned to the Philippines. When the war started,
he immediately proved his
worth. In March 1942, when
General MacArthur, his family, and his staff were ordered to
flee the besieged island of Corregidor in Manila Bay, Elsmore
arranged MacArthur's evacuation flight to the safety of Australia. Later he became director
of air transport for the Southwest Pacific, delivering troops
and supplies wherever MacAr-

COLONEL RAY T. ELSMORE. (PHOTO
COURTESY OF B. B. MCCOLLOM.)

thur needed them in New Guinea, the Philippines, the Dutch
East Indies, Borneo, Australia, and the western Solomon Islands.

As Elsmore and Grimes flew deeper into the canyon, they could
see the walls growing steeper and narrower, steadily closing in on
the plane's wingtips. Elsmore steered around a bend, trying to stay
in the middle of the canyon to maximize clearance on both sides
of the sixty-five-foot wingspan. Straight ahead he saw a horrifying
sight: a sheer rock wall. Elsmore grabbed both throttle levers. He
began to thrust them forward, trying to gain full power as he prepared to veer up and away. But Grimes urged otherwise.

"Push on through," the major said. "The valley is just beyond."

Surveying the situation with only seconds to spare, traveling at
more than two hundred miles per hour, Elsmore chose to trust his
twenty-four-year-old copilot. He followed Grimes's instructions,
slicing his way over the onrushing ridge and just beneath the over-
hanging clouds.

Safely in the clear, Elsmore saw a break in the puffy clouds,
framing the vista like a heavenly vision. Spread out before them

was a place their maps said didn't exist, a rich valley Elsmore later called "a riot of dazzling color." The land was largely flat, giving him a clear view of its full breadth—nearly thirty miles long and more than eight miles wide at its widest point, running northwest to southeast. Surrounding the valley were sheer mountain walls with jagged ridges rising to the clouds.

At the southeastern end, a river entered the valley by cascading over a cliff. The cocoa-colored river, more than a hundred feet wide in spots, snaked through the valley, interrupted by occasional rapids. At the valley's northwestern end, the river disappeared into an enormous hole in a mountain wall that formed a natural grotto, its upper arch some three hundred feet above the ground. Much of the valley was carpeted by tall, sharp kunai grass, waist-high in spots, interrupted by occasional stands of trees.

Even more remarkable than the valley's physical splendor were its inhabitants: tens of thousands of people for whom the Stone Age was the present day.

PEERING DOWN THROUGH the cockpit windows, Elsmore and Grimes saw several hundred small, clearly defined native villages. Surrounding the native compounds were carefully tended gardens, with primitive but effective irrigation systems, including dams and drainage ditches. "Crops were in full growth everywhere and, unlike the scene in most tropic lands, the fields were literally alive with men, women, and children, all hard at work," Elsmore marveled.

Men and boys roamed naked except for hollowed-out gourds covering their genitals; women and girls wore only low-slung fiber skirts. Mesmerized by the scene below him, Elsmore watched the natives scatter at the sight and sound of the roaring airplane, "some crawling under the sweet potato vines and others diving into the drainage ditches." Pigs wandered around the compounds, and Elsmore caught sight of a few brown dogs lazing about.

A NATIVE VILLAGE PHOTOGRAPHED FROM THE AIR BY COLONEL RAY T. ELSMORE.
(PHOTO COURTESY OF C. EARL WALTER JR.)

At the edges of large, open fields, Elsmore noticed spindly towers made from lashed-together poles rising some thirty feet or more above the valley floor. Each tower had a platform for a sentry near the top, and some towers had small grass roofs, to shelter the sentries from the sun. Elsmore pushed the control wheel forward to guide the plane lower for a better look. He guessed, correctly, that they were watchtowers to guard against marauding enemies. As the C-60 flew on, the thrumming noise of its twelve-hundred-horsepower engines bounced off the valley floor and mountain walls. Frightened sentries abandoned their posts, climbed down the towers, and ran to nearby huts. Elsmore saw wooden spears more than fifteen feet long leaning against those huts.

Elsmore snapped a few photographs, focusing on the people and their huts, some of them round like toadstools or thatched-roof "igloos," he thought, and others long and narrow like boxcars. "The panorama of these hundreds of villages from the air is one of the most impressive sights I have ever seen," Elsmore wrote after-ward.

He and Grimes had a mission to complete, so Elsmore pulled back on the control wheel and roared up and out of the valley. He pointed the plane southeast and flew some two hundred miles to another potential site for a landing strip, in an area called Ifitamin.

SEVERAL DAYS LATER, Elsmore wrote a secret memo on his findings to his commanding officer, General George C. Kenney, America's top airman in the Pacific during World War II. The memo described the survey flights and paid special attention to the valley and the people in it. Major Grimes had called his dis-covery Hidden Valley, but in the memo Elsmore referred to it in less poetic terms. He called it the Baliem Valley, using the name of the river that flowed through it.

One concern Elsmore expressed to General Kenney about building a landing strip was the reaction of the natives. "There is no access into this valley . . . except by air, and for that rea-son very little is known of the attitude of the natives. It is known that there are headhunters in many of the adjacent regions and there is a suspicion that the natives in the Baliem Valley may also be unfriendly," he wrote. Also in the memo, Elsmore issued an ominous warning to fellow pilots who might follow him there. He described at length how treacherous it could be to fly through the cloud-covered entrance pass into the valley, especially "for a pilot unfamiliar with this canyon."

As it turned out, by any name Hidden Valley or Baliem Valley was unsuitable for a military landing strip. At a mile above sea level, surrounded by mountains reaching thirteen thousand feet and higher, it was too dangerous and inaccessible. Also, there was a better alternative. Elsmore learned that an Australian missionary had found the natives at Ifitamin to be friendly and eager to be put to work. That fit Elsmore's plan perfectly. "Not only were we anxious to avoid incidents and bloodshed"—believed to be a strong possibility with the natives of Hidden/Baliem Valley—"but we wanted to employ native labor on the construction project."

Although the valley could serve no military purpose, news of its discovery spread quickly around Hollandia and beyond. Interest heightened when Elsmore began telling people that he thought the valley's inhabitants looked much taller and larger than any other New Guinea natives he'd seen. By contrast, he described the natives at Ifitamin as "pygmy type."

Elsmore's impressions contributed to fast-spreading stories, or more accurately, tall tales, that Hidden Valley was populated by a previously unknown race of primitive giants. Some called them black supermen—handsome models of sinewy manhood standing seven feet tall. Soon the natives were said to be headhunters and cannibals, savages who practiced human sacrifice on stone altars. The pigs the natives raised were said to be the size of ponies. The bare-breasted native women were said to resemble the curvaceous pinup girls in soldiers' barracks, especially the exotic, sarong-wearing actress Dorothy Lamour, whose hit movies included "The Jungle Princess." The only difference was that the valley women were described as "Dorothy Lamours in blackface."

In time, the stories multiplied, largely because no one could contradict any claim, no matter how outlandish. And it seemed as though the stories would remain unchallenged. No one in Hollandia had any reason to hike a hundred and fifty miles past untold Japanese troops in hiding, over mountains, and through swamps and jungles. And no planes could safely land in the valley—the ground was too soft, uneven, and grassy for a natural runway, and helicopter blades couldn't generate enough lift in the thin, high-altitude air to clear the surrounding mountains. Above all, the soldiers at Base G had a war to fight, not an anthropological expedition to mount.

Still, the valley captivated Elsmore. He asked around among

Dutch and Australians whom he considered to be experts on New Guinea and found no evidence that any outsider had ever set foot in the valley. As far as the U.S. Army was concerned, then, Colonel Ray T. Elsmore was the Christopher Columbus of Hidden Valley, while Grimes's role was downgraded to "co-discoverer."

As the stories spread, sightseers clamored to see Hidden Valley with their own eyes. Overflights became a perk for officers, WACs, and enlisted men. Some returned with exciting stories of natives firing arrows and throwing spears at their planes. The more adventurous among them dreamed of touching the valley floor, even if it meant crash landing. "I suppose I would have regretted it," a lieutenant named William J. Gatling Jr. wrote to his family in Arkansas, "but I feel I would have liked to have been forced down simply to get a good first-hand idea of the whole area. Flying over was like holding candy just out of reach of a baby."

Gatling's letter continued, "Quite a number of us were skeptical of what we had heard before we made the trip but our skepticism had all vanished by the time we returned. Some will and some will not believe this story. . . . Beyond what has been observed from the air, it is believed nothing first-hand is known of these primitive people and their habits and customs. Sealed as they are in their Hidden Valley, they appear to be wholly self-supporting and self-sufficient. It is possible, of course, that they have some hidden footpath out of there, but such has not been located from the sky. Even if they could leave their valley, they would face a 150-mile trek through almost impenetrable rainforest-type jungle to reach the Pacific coast in the north, or would encounter 150 miles of impassable, unexplored swamp extending between them and the Arafura Sea to the south."

After describing all he'd seen during his flight, Gatling concluded his letter home with a philosophical thought: "Probably after the war the Dutch government will send an expedition into the valley or missionaries may penetrate it, so until then the natives . . . will know nothing of the white man except that he flies a big bird that makes lots of noise. Who knows, maybe they are much better off the way they are. At any rate, I am sure if they knew of the turmoil in which we are now engaged, they would be much happier to stay ignorant of the 'civilized' world."

COLONEL ELSMORE MADE frequent flights over the valley, photographing it from every angle and making observations and suppositions about its inhabitants. On one flight he saw more than three hundred natives assembled on a grassy field. Divided into two groups, they were armed with spears, bows, and arrows, their bodies slathered with ceremonial war paint. Elsmore pushed the control wheel forward, forcing the plane into a dive, and buzzed low over the field. The warriors ran off, suspending their battle at least temporarily.

The press got wind of the valley, and Elsmore agreed to a fly-over by two veteran war reporters, George Lait and Harry E. Patterson. Lait, in particular, had a lot to live up to. His father was Jack Lait, the pugnacious editor of the *New York Mirror*, who as a reporter in 1934 had filed an exclusive, on-scene story describing how the FBI gunned down bank robber John Dillinger. At thirty-eight, George Lait was on the way to matching his old man. As a swashbuckling correspondent for the International News Service, he palled around with legendary reporter Ernie Pyle and gossip columnist Walter Winchell; he was knocked out cold in London when shrapnel hit his helmet during the Blitz; and he was blown out of a car seat by a German bomb. He'd shot pheasants with England's King George VI, spent eighteen months with the British Eighth Army, and qualified as a paratrooper with the U.S. Army's 11th Airborne. Another reporter once said of him: "As a war correspondent, George was an inspired writer, fighter and souvenir collector. Where other correspondents might liberate a pistol or a helmet, George liberated machine guns, bazookas, tanks, and once had to be persuaded not to put the snatch on a Messerschmitt. It was a big war, George said, and he wanted something big to prove it."

A man on his way to having seen it all, George Lait admitted that he'd never seen anything quite like the valley. After returning from the flight with Elsmore, he filed a dispatch rich in description though tinged with racial and cultural condescension:

> Skimming less than 100 feet over the valley floor, one was able to identify among the native crops banana trees, a water plant (swamp taro), extensive patches of the native sweet potato or yam, and a waist-high plant closely resembling tobacco.
>
> Of animals, only a few dogs and pigs were seen. The pigs, staple meat food throughout New Guinea and religiously revered by most natives of the island, appeared exceptionally large and well kept, and of two varieties—an all-black or dark brown species, and a black and white variety, the latter growing to immense size.
>
> When the plane first roared over the valley, crowds of natives ran from their houses and vanished into the standing crops or clumps of trees. But after flying down the valley several times, their child-like curiosity seemed to overcome their fear of the motors—they cautiously emerged to watch the soaring plane.

Harry Patterson's story of the flight emphasized drama and intrigue: "Even today, weeks after the discovery that has the whole South Pacific buzzing with speculation, no white man and probably no regular native has set foot in the lost valley. . . . It is pretty well-known in this part of the world that most of the New Guinea savages were either cannibals or head hunters." Patterson quoted Colonel Elsmore describing the valley natives as "taller, more finely built and lighter-skinned than the usual New Guinea fuzzy-wuzzies."

The colonel, fancying himself an amateur geologist as well as a cockpit anthropologist, speculated that the natives' ancestors came to the valley "hundreds or thousands of years ago." Wrote Patterson: "He thinks that after they settled in this mountain paradise an earthquake or some tremendous upheaval trapped them in the valley."

As impressed as they were by what they'd seen, Lait and Patterson were disappointed by the name Hidden Valley. Determined to rechristen it, they thought back several years to the Frank Capra movie *Lost Horizon* and its source, a 1933 James Hilton novel about a mysterious, peaceful utopia isolated from a war-weary world.

Hilton's story revolves around the crash of a small plane into a Tibetan mountain. The survivors, one of them a woman, are rescued by monks who guide them to a bucolic valley where the inhabitants' lives are long and happy, a land where moderation and tolerance reign supreme. In time, the survivors must choose whether to remain forever in the valley or return to the outside world, knowing that they might never be able to return.

Often read as an adventure tale, Hilton's book is really a meditation on finding peace and preserving humanity in a world spiraling toward self-destruction. Hilton saw "civilization" trapped in a ruinous cycle, careening from one war to the next, each more deadly and destructive than the last. In a long exchange between two main characters, *Lost Horizon* anticipated a global war of unimaginable proportions. More than a decade before the first atom bomb, Hilton feared a future in which "a single-weaponed man might have matched a whole army."

Describing one especially wise character, Hilton wrote: "He foresaw a time when men, exultant in the technique of homicide, would rage so hotly over the world that every precious thing would be in danger, every book and picture and harmony, every treasure garnered through two millenniums, the small, the delicate, the defenseless—all would be lost."

Hilton's frightening prediction didn't escape notice. President Roosevelt quoted that passage from *Lost Horizon* in a 1937 speech in Chicago. Four years before Pearl Harbor, Roosevelt used Hilton's horrifying vision to warn that, in defense of civilization, America might find itself forced to quarantine aggressive nations bent on unleashing a global storm. Roosevelt's warning had proved prescient.

It's no wonder, then, that a pair of veteran war correspondents looked wistfully on a fertile valley, sealed from the outside world, its natives ignorant of Nazis and kamikazes, and thought of the name that Hilton had given his fictional paradise. Never mind the reports of headhunters and cannibals, of spears and arrows, of watchtowers and sentries and battles among neighbors. Never mind the possibility that the native world glimpsed by Colonel Elsmore and Major Grimes wasn't peaceful at all, but a window into a shared human inheritance, one that suggested that the very nature of man was to make war.

Those questions could wait for another day, perhaps until someone from outside entered the valley and met the natives. In the meantime, George Lait and Harry Patterson bestowed a new name on New Guinea's Hidden Valley: they called it Shangri-La.

4

GREMLIN SPECIAL

THE VALLEY'S NEW name took hold.

Elsmore's unit formed a "Shangri-La Society" for pilots and passengers fortunate enough to fly over it. Each society member received a comically ornate certificate on parchment paper that looked like a hard-earned diploma, complete with blue-and-yellow ribbons affixed by a gold foil seal. Signed by Elsmore and one of his subordinates, the certificates were personalized with the society member's name and the date of his or her special flight. The certificates also included the valley's precise longitude and latitude, so society members could find their way back, unlike visitors who left Hilton's Shangri-La.

Reporters couldn't get enough of Elsmore—one dubbed him the "leading authority on the valley and its people"—and the colonel lapped it up. After Lait and Patterson, other correspondents clamored to visit the valley, and Elsmore usually obliged. Some who didn't see it for themselves but interviewed Elsmore or Grimes took flights of fancy. One desk-bound reporter gushed about the valley's beauty and called it "a veritable Garden of Eden." Then he interviewed Elsmore about fears of headhunters. The colonel played up the danger, with a wink. Elsmore told the reporter that he might drop a missionary into the valley by parachute to show that "we come as friends and mean no harm. But I'm afraid it would more likely be a case of 'head you lose.' "

The quotable colonel told a correspondent for The Associated Press that when the war ended, he wanted to be the first white man to step foot in the valley and make contact with, in the reporter's phrase, the "long-haired, giant natives." Elsmore said his plan was to land in a glider, "fully equipped with bargaining trinkets, also weapons if they won't bargain, food and the necessary material for swiftly setting up an airstrip so that transport planes can follow in."

The AP story appeared in U.S. newspapers on Sunday, May 13, 1945—the same day that Corporal Margaret Hastings's boss, Colonel Peter Prossen, began rounding up members of the Fee-Ask maintenance division for a trip to Shangri-La.

FOR OFFICIAL PURPOSES, Prossen described the flight as a "navigational training" mission. The truth—a Mother's Day sightseeing joyride—wouldn't look nearly as good in a military flight log. Although he'd taken his staff on similar recreational flights up and down the New Guinea coast, this would be Prossen's first trip to Shangri-La.

Margaret was at her desk when the invitation came. She had a date after work with a soldier she'd been seeing regularly, a handsome sergeant from Pennsylvania named Walter "Wally" Fleming. He'd managed to get the keys to a Jeep, so they planned a drive to a secluded beach for an ocean swim. Yet Margaret had been desperate to visit Shangri-La since arriving at Fee-Ask five months earlier. Confident that she'd be back in time for her date, she leaped at Prossen's offer.

The letter Prossen wrote that morning to his wife apparently put him in a mood to chat about home. He stopped by Margaret's desk and shared amusing news from his wife's last letter, laughingly telling Margaret that the family's new dog—a mutt that his son Peter Jr. had named Lassie—was somehow winning prizes at local dog shows.

Margaret rushed to clear Prossen's desk of work by noon. She wolfed down a lunch of chicken, with ice cream for dessert, abandoning her usual practice of savoring each cold spoonful.

Prossen arranged for a truck to take Margaret and eight other WACs to the nearby Sentani Airstrip, named for the lake of the same name, while the men invited on the flight walked or hitched rides there. When the passengers arrived, they found Prossen, his copilot, and three crew members mingling outside a fully fueled transport plane, its engines warming and propellers spinning. In civilian life, the plane was a Douglas DC-3, but once enlisted in the war effort it became a C-47 Skytrain, a workhorse of the wartime skies, with more than ten thousand of them deployed at Allied bases around the world.

Nearly sixty-four feet long, with a wingspan of more than ninety-five feet, the C-47 cruised comfortably at 175 miles per hour. At full throttle it theoretically could fly 50 miles per hour faster. It had a range of about 1,600 miles, or about five times as far as the round-trip that Prossen had planned. Most C-47s had

C-47 IN FLIGHT DURING WORLD WAR II. (PHOTO COURTESY OF U.S. ARMY.)

twin twelve-hundred-horsepower Pratt & Whitney engines. Some had guns, but Prossen's plane was unarmed. C-47s weren't flashy, and they weren't especially fast, but they were as reliable as Buicks and stable in flight. If troops or matériel were needed somewhere, a C-47 could be counted on to get them there. Pilots spoke fondly of their signature smell, a bouquet of leather and hydraulic fluid.

Consolidated Aircraft Corporation had built Prossen's plane in 1942 at a cost to the military of $269,276. Upon its arrival in Hollandia, the plane had been painted in camouflage colors to blend with the jungle if spotted from above by an enemy fighter or bomber. One problem: if the C-47 went down in the dense New Guinea jungle, its paint job would make it nearly impossible for searchers to spot.

To the Army Air Forces, Prossen's plane was serial number 42-23952. In radio transmissions, it would be identified by its last three numbers, as 952. C-47s were often called "Gooney Birds," especially in Europe, and individual planes earned their own monikers from their captains and crews. Around the Sentani Airstrip, Prossen's plane was affectionately called *Merle*, though its better-known nickname was the *Gremlin Special*.

The name was ironic at best. Gremlins were mythical creatures blamed by airmen for sabotaging aircraft. The term was popularized by a 1943 children's picture book called *The Gremlins*, written by a young Royal Air Force flight lieutenant destined to become a world-famous author: Roald Dahl. In Dahl's story, the tiny horned beasties were motivated to make mechanical mischief as revenge against humans, who'd destroyed their primeval forest home to build an airplane factory.

AT TWO O'CLOCK in the afternoon it was time to go. As the passengers lined up outside the *Gremlin Special*, Prossen told them to expect a three-hour tour.

"Let the girls in first," Prossen said, "and then fill it up with any enlisted men and officers who want to go."

One enlisted man, especially keen to see Shangri-La, grumbled, "Hey, that's showing partiality." Prossen ignored the soldier's complaint.

One after another, the nine WACs climbed into the plane through a door near the tail, with Margaret first in line. Once inside, she found bucket seats with their backs against the inner walls of the cabin, so the passengers on one side of the plane would look across a center aisle at the passengers on the other side.

Like a child playing musical chairs, Margaret ran up the aisle toward the cockpit. She plopped into the bucket seat closest to the pilots, certain she'd picked a winner. But when she looked out the window, she didn't like the view. The C-47's forward cabin windows looked down onto the wings, making it difficult if not impossible to see directly below. Determined to make a full aerial inspection of Shangri-La, Margaret jumped up, did a quick about-face, and ran back down the aisle toward the tail. She grabbed the last seat on the plane's left side, near the door she'd used to come aboard. The view was perfect.

Close behind Margaret was her close friend and double-date partner, Laura Besley. The attractive sergeant sat directly across from Margaret, in the last seat on the plane's right side. The center aisle of the plane was so narrow that the toes of their shoes almost touched. Margaret caught Laura's eye and winked. They were certain to have quite a story to tell at their next blanket party.

Sitting next to Laura Besley was Private Eleanor Hanna, a vivacious, fair-skinned farm girl from Montoursville, Pennsylvania. At twenty-one, the curly-haired Eleanor had an older brother in the Army Air Forces and a younger brother in the U.S. Navy. Her father had served in the ambulance corps in World War I, and had spent time in a German prisoner-of-war camp. Eleanor had a reputation around Fee-Ask for singing wherever she went.

"Isn't this fun!" she yelled over the engines.

On Eleanor Hanna's wrist dangled a decidedly nonmilitary

adornment: a souvenir bracelet made from Chinese coins strung together with metal wire. She owned at least two others just like it.

Also on board was Private Marian Gillis of Los Angeles, the daughter of a newspaper publisher. An amateur pilot, she'd already lived a whirlwind life, including fleeing from Spain with her mother at the outbreak of the Spanish Civil War. Nearby was Sergeant Belle Naimer of the Bronx, the daughter of a retired blouse manufacturer. She was still grieving the death of her fiancé, an Army Air Forces lieutenant killed months earlier when his plane went down in Europe.

Another WAC searching for a seat was Sergeant Helen Kent of Taft, California. A widow, she'd lost her husband in a military plane crash. Bubbly and fun-loving despite her loss, Helen had joined the WACs to help relieve her loneliness. Her best friend at the base, Sergeant Ruth Coster, was supposed to accompany her on the flight, but Ruth was swamped with paperwork for planes that General MacArthur wanted flown to the Philippines. Ruth had urged Helen to go ahead and, upon her return, tell her what it was like. Ruth would join the "Shangri-La Society" another day.

BEST FRIENDS SERGEANT RUTH COSTER (LEFT) AND SERGEANT HELEN KENT GOOFING AROUND FOR THE CAMERA. RUTH WANTED TO JOIN HELEN ABOARD THE *GREMLIN SPECIAL* BUT HAD TOO MUCH WORK. (PHOTO COURTESY OF DONA CRUSE.)

Three more WACs climbed aboard: Sergeant Marion W. McMonagle, a forty-four-year-old widow from Philadelphia with no children; Private Alethia M. Fair, a divorced fifty-year-old telephone operator from Hollywood, California; and Private Mary M. Landau, a single thirty-eight-year-old stenographer from Brooklyn.

Behind them came Colonel Prossen, trailed by his copilot, Major George H. Nicholson Jr. of Medford, Massachusetts. Nicholson was thirty-four, a student of the classics who'd graduated from Boston College, then received master's degrees from Harvard, in the arts, and Boston University, in education. After several years on the home front in the infantry reserve, during which he taught junior high school, Nicholson joined the Army Air Forces to earn his silver pilot's wings. He'd only been overseas for four months, during which he'd served under Lord Mountbatten, the Supreme Allied Commander in Southeast Asia, before transferring to Dutch New Guinea.

Four days earlier, George Nicholson had skipped a "Victory in Europe" party at the Fee-Ask Officers' Club. He spent the night alone in his tent, writing a remarkable letter to his wife, Alice, a fellow schoolteacher he'd married days before reporting for active duty.

In neat script, with a historian's sense of scale and a poet's lyric touch, Nicholson marked the Allied victory over Germany by composing a vivid fifteen-page narrative of the war in Europe and Africa. His words swept armies across continents, navies across oceans, warplanes across unbounded skies. He channeled the emotions and prayers of families on the home front, and the fear and heroism of soldiers, marines, sailors, and airmen on the front lines. He tracked the American military's rise from a hodgepodge of ice-cream-eating schoolboys to a juggernaut of battle-tested warriors. He moved Allied men and machines through crushing blows at Dieppe, in France, and the Kasserine Pass, in Tunisia. He roused them to victory on North African soil against the hardened German tank units in the battle of El Guettar. He drove them on to Salerno and "Bloody Anzio," in Italy.

Nicholson gained momentum, just as the Allies had, as he ap-

MAJOR GEORGE H. NICHOLSON. (PHOTO COURTESY OF JOHN MCCARTHY.)

proached the beaches of Normandy on D-Day. He wrote as if he'd been there: "Then the morning twilight was stabbed by the flashes of ships' guns pounding the invasion coast, and the air was rocked by the explosions of shells from the guns and bombs from the planes. Rockets traced fiery arcs across the sky. The choppy waters of the Channel made many of the troops seasick in the assault boats. German artillery plowed into the water, plowed often into assault boats and larger vessels, blowing them to destruction. Mines exploded with tremendous shock. Beach and boats drew closer. Fear gripped the men but courage welled from within them. The ramps were let down, the men waded through obstacle-strewn water, they reached the beaches. The invasion had begun."

Four pages later, Nicholson described American troops crossing the Rhine into Germany, American flyers driving the feared pilots of the Luftwaffe from the sky, and Allied forces squeezing the Third Reich by the throat to force its surrender. "We may have been soft, but we're tough now," he wrote. "The battle is the payoff. We beat them into submission."

Only at the very end did the letter turn personal, as Nicholson expressed his guilt and questioned his own manhood for not having served in Europe with the U.S. Eighth Air Force. Addressing his wife directly, Nicholson confessed: "This is illogical, I admit, but a man is scarcely a man when he does not desire to pitch in when the combat involves his country and his loved ones. Do not think harshly of me, darling. The proof lies in action; I would have liked to go to the Eighth, but I never requested it."

Having unburdened himself, Nicholson signed off: "Darling, I love you." Then, for the first time in fifteen pages of commanding prose, he repeated himself. "I love you."

ALONG WITH PROSSEN and Nicholson came the plane's three other crew members, Staff Sergeant Hilliard Norris, a twenty-three-year-old flight engineer from Waynesville, North Carolina, and two privates, George Newcomer of Middletown, New York, a twenty-four-year-old radio operator, and Melvin Mollberg of Baudette, Minnesota, the assistant engineer.

Mollberg, known to his friends as "Molly," was a muscular, handsome twenty-four-year-old farm boy with thick blond hair and a crooked grin. He was engaged to a pretty young woman from Brisbane, Australia, where he'd been stationed before arriving in Hollandia a month earlier. Mollberg was a last-minute substitute on the *Gremlin Special* crew. The assistant engineer whose name initially came up on the duty roster was Mollberg's best friend, Corporal James "Jimmy" Lutgring, with whom Mollberg had spent nearly three years in the Fifth Air Force in the South Pacific.

CORPORAL JAMES "JIMMY" LUTGRING (LEFT) AND HIS BEST FRIEND, PRIVATE MELVIN MOLLBERG, WHO REPLACED LUTGRING ON THE CREW OF THE *GREMLIN SPECIAL*. (PHOTO COURTESY OF MEL LUTGRING.)

But Lutgring and Colonel Prossen didn't get along. The source of the tension wasn't clear, but it might have traced back to Lutgring believing that Prossen had played a role in denying him a promotion to sergeant. Lutgring didn't want to spend his Sunday afternoon flying on the colonel's crew, even if it meant missing a chance to see Shangri-La. Mollberg understood. He volunteered to take his pal Jimmy's place on the flight.

Next came the ten male passengers: two majors, a pair of captains, three lieutenants, two sergeants, and a corporal.

Among the enlisted men was Tech Sergeant Kenneth Decker of Kelso, Washington. A wiry, laconic draftsman in the command's engineering department, Decker had worked in his father's furniture store before the war. He'd been in New Guinea for several months, after being stationed in Australia for more than two years. The flight was a special treat for Decker: he was celebrating his thirty-fourth birthday. On the other hand, seeing

TECH SERGEANT KENNETH DECKER.
(PHOTO COURTESY OF U.S. ARMY.)

Corporal Margaret Hastings on the plane wasn't necessarily a pleasure for Decker. Weeks earlier, Decker had asked her on a date, only to get shot down. A flight over Shangri-La separated by a few seats seemed about as close to Margaret as he'd ever get.

Another passenger was Herbert F. Good, a tall, forty-six-year-old captain from Dayton, Ohio. Good had survived service in World War I, after which he'd married and returned home to life as an oil salesman and a leader in his Presbyterian church. Then war called again, so again he went.

At the end of the line were identical twins, John and Robert McCollom, twenty-six-year-old first lieutenants from Trenton, Missouri. They were nearly indistinguishable, with sandy blond hair, soulful blue eyes, and lantern jaws. One small difference: John was five-foot-six, and Robert was a shade taller, a fact that Robert used to tease his "little" brother. Known to friends and family as "The Inseparables," the twins had clung to each other as toddlers after their mother left them, their older brother, and their father. As eight-year-olds, they'd dressed in matching outfits and idolized aviator Charles Lindbergh for his solo nonstop flight across the Atlantic. When the twins came home from third grade and gushed about their teacher, Miss Eva Ratliff, their father, a railroad station manager, decided to meet her. John, Robert, and their older brother soon had a stepmother.

The McCollom twins had become Eagle Scouts together. They'd been sports fanatics together, though they were better rooters than players. They'd joined the Reserve Officers' Training Corps together and roomed together as aerospace engineering students at the University of Minnesota, where they'd worked long hours to pay tuition while managing the school's hockey team. They could only afford one set of books, so they'd shared them. Though alike in most ways, Robert McCollom

TWINS JOHN AND ROBERT MCCOLLOM SHARING A SCOOTER AS TODDLERS. (PHOTO COURTESY OF B. B. MCCOLLOM.)

was quieter, more introverted, while John was the outgoing twin. Robert was always known as Robert, while John was often called "Mac."

The McCollom twins' first test apart had come two years earlier, on May 5, 1943, when Robert married a young woman he'd met on a blind date, Cecelia Connolly, known by her middle name, Adele. In a wedding photo published in a local newspaper, both McColloms are in uniform; the only way to tell them apart is by Adele's winsome smile in Robert's direction. After the wedding, Robert, Adele, and John became a threesome, spending evenings together at the Officers' Club. The McColloms earned their pilot's licenses together in the service, and with the exception of a brief period apart, were stationed together at several bases stateside. Six months before the flight to Shangri-La, they were sent overseas together to New Guinea.

Six weeks before the Mother's Day flight, Adele McCollom gave birth to a girl she and Robert named Mary Dennise and called Dennie. Robert McCollom had yet to see his new daughter.

LIEUTENANTS JOHN (LEFT) AND ROBERT MCCOLLOM. (PHOTO COURTESY OF B. B. MCCOLLOM.)

The McCollom twins wanted to see Shangri-La through the same window of the *Gremlin Special*, but they couldn't find two seats together. Robert McCollom walked toward the cockpit and slipped into an open seat near the front. John McCollom saw an empty seat next to Margaret Hastings, the second-to-last spot on the plane's left-hand side, near the tail.

Margaret knew John McCollom from his regular visits to Colonel Prossen's office. She also remembered how months earlier he'd outfitted her tent with a double electric socket.

"Mind if I share this window with you?" he asked.

Margaret shouted her assent over the engines.

The *Gremlin Special* was full. On board were twenty-four members of the U.S. military, most of them from the Fee-Ask maintenance division. Nine were officers, nine were WACs, and six were enlisted men. As the door closed, Margaret noticed that the soldier who'd complained about Prossen's WACs-first rule wasn't among them.

5

EUREKA!

AT 2:15 P.M., with Colonel Peter Prossen at the controls, the *Gremlin Special* rumbled past the palm trees lining the runway at the Sentani Airstrip and lifted off into a clear blue sky. As the plane passed over Lake Sentani, the passengers twisted in their seats for a look at the shimmering blue waters and the green hills that rolled down to the lake's edge. Prossen guided the plane toward the Oranje Mountains, setting a course directly toward the valley. He announced over the intercom that it would take fifty-five minutes to get there.

A WAC sitting near the cockpit chanted, "Oh, what is so rare as a June day in May?" The WAC on the way to Shangri-La was invoking a medieval knight's quest for the Holy Grail. Her chant quoted the sentiment if not the exact words of a century-old epic poem, *The Vision of Sir Launfal*, by James Russell Lowell, which asked, "And what is so rare as a day in June?" Just as appropriate were other lines of the poem, which read:

> *Joy comes, grief goes, we know not how;*
> *Everything is happy now,*
> *Everything is upward striving;*
> *'Tis as easy now for the heart to be true,*
> *As for grass to be green or skies to be blue.*

Glued to the window, Margaret looked down through puffy white clouds. She thought the lush jungle below looked as soft as green feathers that would cushion a fall from even that great height. In the distance, the passengers could see snow-topped Mount Wilhelmina, named for the Dutch queen, at 15,580 feet the highest peak in the range.

John McCollom was more curious about the *Gremlin Special*'s altitude and directional heading. He estimated that they were flying at about seven thousand feet, and he learned from the crew that they were on a heading of 224 degrees, or due southwest from the base. That course would take them to the northwest end of Shangri-La, to the narrow pass through the mountains discovered a year earlier by Major Grimes.

AS THEY CRUISED toward the valley, Colonel Prossen made a fateful decision: he unbuckled his seat belt and walked back into the cabin. The point of the trip, after all, was to let his staff know that he cared about them and their morale. This was a bonding opportunity, a chance for them to see Shangri-La together. Yet in light of the uncharted mountains, the changeable weather, and the relative inexperience of his copilot, Major George Nicholson, Prossen's move from the pilot's seat was ill-advised.

Both Prossen and Nicholson were making their first flights to Shangri-La. All they knew about the treacherous entrance through the mountain pass was

COLONEL PETER J. PROSSEN. (PHOTO COURTESY OF PETER J. PROSSEN JR.)

what they'd read or heard from other pilots. By leaving the cockpit and trusting the most difficult part of the flight to his copilot, Prossen was underestimating the risks or disregarding them altogether. Moreover, with Prossen occupied by administrative tasks in his Fee-Ask job, and with Nicholson new to New Guinea, it's not clear how often, if ever, they'd previously flown together. Perhaps most troubling of all was that Prossen disregarded Colonel Ray Elsmore's warning, after his initial flight to Shangri-La, about the dangers that would confront "a pilot unfamiliar with this canyon."

The C-47 had seat belts for passengers, but when the socializing started after takeoff, at least some were unfastened. Most of the passengers were members of Prossen's maintenance division at Fee-Ask, so they knew each other and fell into easy conversation. Prossen joined the camaraderie, standing in the narrow radio compartment that separated the cockpit from the passenger cabin.

Looking into the cockpit, John McCollom noticed that Sergeant Helen Kent had walked forward from the cabin. The curvaceous WAC had plopped into the left-hand seat left vacant by Prossen, to enjoy an unobstructed view out the front windshield. Next to her, the copilot, Major Nicholson, was alone at the controls.

Nearly an hour into the flight, the *Gremlin Special* sneaked over a ridge, dropped several hundred feet, and entered a narrow valley that was an offshoot of the main valley that was their destination. The plane flew at about sixty-five hundred feet above sea level, or some thirteen hundred feet above the valley floor. Jungle-covered mountains flanked the *Gremlin Special* on both sides. Nicholson eased the control wheel forward, which lowered the elevators on the C-47s tail. The tail rose and the nose tipped downward. He guided the *Gremlin Special* down to an altitude of about one thousand feet above the valley floor. The drop continued. Soon they were flying at less than four hundred feet over the ground.

"Eureka!" cried an overeager WAC.

The passengers whirled around to the windows and saw a small native village—a cluster of mushroom-shaped huts with thatched roofs, surrounded by carefully marked, well-tended fields of sweet potato. Margaret was thrilled, but something was missing. It occurred to her that the village seemed empty. She didn't see any natives. Not realizing that this was only a small settlement in a side valley—the huge valley of Shangri-La was another ten to fifteen miles ahead—she felt cheated.

Turning to John McCollom, she complained, "I want to come again!"

McCollom wasn't listening. His head was turned sharply to the left as he stared into the cockpit. Looking through the windshield, he saw clouds dead ahead. Through the whiteness, he saw snatches of dark green jungle covering a mountain he estimated at twelve or thirteen thousand feet. In the parlance of pilots, the cloud had a rock in it.

McCollom's body stiffened. "Give her the gun and let's get out of here," he shouted toward the cockpit.

Margaret and some of the other passengers thought he was joking. But Major Nicholson knew it was no joke; he'd already recognized the risk.

As a licensed pilot, McCollom knew that the first rule of mountain flying was always to be in a position to turn. But this valley was too narrow for Nicholson to even try. That left only one option. Nicholson gripped the control wheel and pulled sharply back. With Colonel Prossen standing in the radio compartment, and Sergeant Helen Kent still enjoying the view from the pilot's seat, the young major was on his own.

Nicholson pointed the plane's nose skyward, desperate to clear the fast-approaching ridge. McCollom watched Nicholson thrust the throttles forward, applying full power to climb. As Nicholson strained to gain altitude, McCollom spun around to look out the window by his seat. Through holes in the clouds he glimpsed trees below, their highest branches reaching up toward the belly of the *Gremlin Special*. He was certain that the clouds obstructed Nicholson's view out the front windshield. That meant the copilot was not only flying without the aid of his more experienced superior, Colonel Prossen, but he was also guiding the plane blind, relying on the instrument panel arrayed before him. That, and gut survival instinct.

NO ONE WHO wasn't inside the cockpit could say with certainty what had brought the *Gremlin Special* and its twenty-four passengers and crew to this perilous moment. A mechanical malfunction—the work of gremlins—was possible, though that appears highly unlikely. More likely was a combination of factors that included Prossen leaving the cockpit, errors by Nicholson, and the inherent difficulty of flying into the valley called Shangri-La.

Based largely on what John McCollom witnessed and what happened next, it appears that Nicholson, who'd learned to fly only three years earlier, grew momentarily disoriented or misjudged the situation when he flew low through the small valley. But the threat to the *Gremlin Special* might have been exaggerated by conditions beyond Nicholson's control.

As Nicholson fought to gain altitude, a powerful gust of wind might have swept down on the C-47. Turbulent air was common in canyons and narrow valleys. Winds rushed over one edge and raced down to the valley floor, creating downdrafts, then raced back up the other side, creating updrafts. Sudden, short-lived updrafts and downdrafts often appeared without warning. The high-altitude valleys and canyons of New Guinea were especially treacherous. One reason was the ragged terrain. Another was a tendency toward rapid changes in air temperatures, a result of jungle heat rising into the cumulus clouds that routinely formed over and around the peaks in mid-afternoon.

If a downdraft did occur at that moment, the twenty-four people aboard the *Gremlin Special* might have been in mortal danger no matter who was at the controls. In fact, an official military account of the flight suggested that "a sudden down-draft of air current" apparently stymied the pilots' effort to gain altitude. However, the account was incomplete. It made no mention of Prossen's absence from the cockpit or the apparent mistakes by Nicholson.

AS NICHOLSON STRUGGLED and McCollom worried, Margaret felt no sense of danger. She'd been so engrossed in the sight of the native huts that she hadn't even noticed that Colonel Prossen had given his seat to Helen Kent and was standing outside the cockpit. Margaret felt the nose of the plane rise, but she was unaware that Nicholson was flying alone. She thought that Prossen was merely gaining altitude, intending to fly them through a high pass between the mountains that she'd glimpsed earlier.

At the controls, Nicholson couldn't make the plane bend to his wishes. The *Gremlin Special* began to shear the tops of giant tropical evergreens, their limbs and leaves scratching and smacking and cracking against the plane's camouflage-painted, sheet-metal skin. Even if Prossen grasped what was happening, as he surely must have, he had no time to race back to his seat, evict Helen Kent, and take over.

Still, Margaret remained calm. Her confidence in her boss was so complete that for a split second she thought that Prossen was showing them some fancy maneuvers. She figured that he'd buzzed the treetops to give his passengers a thrill—flying "flat on the deck," as pilots called it.

John McCollom knew better. He grabbed Margaret's arm.

"This is going to be darn close," he told her, "but I think we can get over it."

His optimism was misplaced. Shortly after three o'clock in the afternoon on Sunday, May 13, 1945, Major George Nicholson's desperate struggle to gain altitude ended. The distance between the C-47 and the unforgiving terrain closed to zero. To the ear-splitting din of metal twisting, glass shattering, engines groaning, branches snapping, fuel igniting, bodies tumbling, lives ending, the *Gremlin Special* plunged through the trees and slammed into the jungle-covered mountainside.

THE CABIN CRUMPLED forward toward the cockpit. The walls of the fuselage collapsed as though sucked inward. Both wings ripped away. The tail section snapped off like a balsa-wood toy. Flames shot through the wreckage. Small explosions rang out like gunshots. Black smoke choked off the light. The air grew bitter with the stench of burning metal, burning leather, burn-ing rubber, burning wires, burning oil, burning clothes, burn-ing hair, burning flesh.

One small mercy was that Nicholson had managed to point the nose of the plane skyward in his attempt to clear the ridge, so the C-47 hit the mountain at an upward angle instead of head-on. As a result, although fire rushed through the cabin, the *Gremlin Special* didn't explode on impact. Anyone not immediately killed or mortally wounded might stand a chance.

When the plane burrowed through the trees, John McCollom flew across the center aisle, from the left side of the plane to the right. He lurched forward by momentum, turning somersaults as he fell. He momentarily blacked out. When he came to, he found himself on his hands and knees halfway up the cabin toward the cockpit, surrounded by flames. Driven by instinct, he searched for an escape route. He saw a flash of white light where the tail had been. The roof of the cabin had flattened down like a stepped-on tin can, so he couldn't stand. He crawled toward the light, landing on the scorched earth of the mountain jungle, disoriented but with barely a scratch.

McCollom began to comprehend the horror of what had happened. He thought about his twin brother and the twenty-two others on board—all trapped inside and dead, he believed. As he rose to his feet outside the broken plane, he told himself: "This is a heck of a place to be, 165 miles from civilization, all by myself on a Sunday afternoon."

WHEN THE *GREMLIN SPECIAL* HIT THE MOUNTAIN, Margaret bounced through the cabin like a rubber ball. Her first impulse was to pray. But that felt like surrender, and Margaret wasn't the surrendering type. She grew angry. She knew it wasn't rational, but as she tumbled she took it personally, indignant that her dreamed-of trip to Shangri-La had been spoiled by a plane crash. And she still hadn't seen any natives.

When she stopped tumbling and regained her senses, Margaret found herself lying on top of a motionless man. Her fall had been cushioned by his body. She tried to move, but before he died the man had somehow wrapped his thick arms around her. Whether he'd tried to save her or simply grabbed on to whatever was closest to him wasn't clear. Either way, Margaret was locked in a dead man's grip. She felt flames licking at her face, feet, and legs. The air filled with the acrid scent of sizzling hair. Again Margaret thought of relaxing, giving up. Then her fury returned, and with it her strength.

She pried loose the man's hands and began to crawl. She had no idea whom she was leaving behind or which way she was heading—back toward the missing tail or ahead toward the crushed cockpit and into the inferno. As she crawled toward her hoped-for salvation, she didn't see anyone else moving or hear anyone speaking or moaning inside the burning cabin. Whether by luck or divine intervention, she chose the right direction for escape.

Margaret stumbled out the torn-open rear end of the fuselage onto the jungle floor.

"My God! Hastings!" called John McCollom, who'd come out the same way less than a minute earlier.

Before Margaret could answer, McCollom heard a WAC scream from inside the plane: "Get me out of here!"

The *Gremlin Special* was now fully aflame. McCollom doubted it would explode, but he wasn't sure. Without hesitating, the Eagle Scout–turned–Army lieutenant scrambled back inside, crouching beneath the smoke and fire, avoiding and ignoring the heat as best he could. He inched his way along, following the WAC's pleading voice.

"Give me your hand!" he ordered.

A moment later, Margaret watched as McCollom led out her friend Laura Besley. McCollom placed the WAC sergeant on the fire-seared ground, turned around, and headed back inside the burning fuselage.

He fought his way through the smoke toward Private Eleanor Hanna, who'd sat next to Laura Besley, directly across from him and Margaret. Eleanor had been badly burned, far worse than Margaret or Laura. Her hair still crackled with burning embers when he carried her out.

By now, McCollom's hands were scorched and his hair was singed from rescuing the two WACs. Otherwise, remarkably, he remained unhurt. Still, he couldn't go back for a third rescue mission—the fire raged higher and hotter, and one explosion after another echoed from inside the wreckage. He doubted anyone inside could still be alive.

Startled by a movement, McCollom looked up and saw a man walk woozily toward him from around the right side of the plane. Any hope that it was his twin brother quickly faded. He recognized Sergeant Kenneth Decker—McCollom supervised Decker's work in the drafting room of the Fee-Ask maintenance department. Decker was on his feet, but dazed and badly hurt. Margaret saw a bloody gash several inches long on the right side of Decker's forehead, deep enough to expose the gray bone of his skull. Another cut leaked blood on the left side of his forehead. Burns seared both legs and his backside. His right arm was cocked stiffly from a broken elbow. Yet somehow Decker was on his feet and moving zombielike toward them.

"My God, Decker, where did you come from?" McCollom asked.

Decker couldn't answer. He would never regain any memory of what happened between takeoff at the Sentani Airstrip and his deliverance into the jungle. Later, McCollom would find a hole on the side of the fuselage and conclude that Decker had escaped through it, though he also thought it possible that the sergeant had been catapulted through the cockpit and out through the windshield.

As he walked unsteadily toward McCollom and Margaret, Decker repeatedly muttered, "Helluva way to spend your birthday."

Margaret thought he was talking gibberish from the blows he'd taken to the head. Only later would she learn that Decker was born on May 13, 1911, and this really was his thirty-fourth birthday.

Turning back to the three surviving WACs, McCollom saw Margaret standing fixed in place, apparently in shock. He set aside his hollowness, his feelings of unspeakable grief at being alone for the first time in his life. The situation was clear. McCollom was the least injured among the five survivors, and though he was only a first lieutenant, he outranked Decker and the three WACs. McCollom steeled himself and assumed command.

He snapped: "Hastings, can't you do something for these girls?"

Laura Besley and Eleanor Hanna were lying next to each other on the ground where McCollom had placed them. Margaret knelt by Eleanor. The bubbly young WAC private from rural

Pennsylvania didn't seem to be in pain, but Margaret knew it was too late to help her. The fire had seared off all her clothes, leaving Eleanor with vicious burns over her entire body. Only her cherubic, fair-skinned face was unscarred.

Eleanor looked up with pleading eyes and offered Margaret a weak smile.

"Let's sing," she said. They tried, but neither could make a sound.

Laura Besley was crying uncontrollably, but Margaret and McCollom couldn't understand why. She seemed to have suffered only superficial burns.

McCollom heard someone yell. He scrambled around the right side of the plane to a spot where he could see Captain Herbert Good lying on the ground. McCollom knew that he was the reason that Good was aboard the *Gremlin Special*. That morning, McCollom had bumped into Good at the base in Hollandia. Affable as always, McCollom asked Good, a member of General MacArthur's staff, whether he had afternoon plans. Good was free, so McCollom invited him to join in the fun on a trip to Shangri-La.

Captain Good looked unhurt, so McCollom beckoned him to join the other survivors. Good didn't seem to hear him, so McCollom started fighting through the smoldering undergrowth in his direction. Decker followed, not fully alert but instinctively wanting to help or to stay close to McCollom. Maybe both.

As they edged closer to Good, flames exploded from fuel tanks in the torn-off wings, which had remained close to the fuselage. When the flames subsided, McCollom rushed to Good. But it was too late—Good was dead. McCollom never learned whether he'd been killed by the explosion or from previous injuries suffered in the crash. When McCollom reached Good's body, he learned why the captain hadn't moved when McCollom first called: his foot was tangled in the roots of a tree.

There was nothing they could do for the Ohio husband, church leader, oil salesman, and World War I survivor. They left Good's body where it fell, hunched on the ground amid brush and branches a few feet from the wrecked plane, his head tilted awkwardly to one side. Good's right arm, bent at the elbow, reached downward toward the moist ground.

No one else emerged alive from the C-47 *Gremlin Special*, bound for Shangri-La on a Sunday-afternoon pleasure flight.

Gone was Colonel Peter J. Prossen, who'd begun that day worried about his wife and children in Texas and his staff in Dutch New Guinea. In a few days, the letter he'd written that morning would arrive in San Antonio—his family would receive Mother's Day greetings from a dead man.

Gone was the copilot, Major George H. Nicholson Jr., a Massachusetts junior high school teacher who days earlier had written so eloquently to his wife about battles in Europe that he'd never seen.

THE BODY OF CAPTAIN HERBERT GOOD, PHOTOGRAPHED APPROXIMATELY TWO WEEKS AFTER THE CRASH. (PHOTO COURTESY OF U.S. ARMY.)

Gone was WAC Sergeant Helen Kent of Taft, California, who'd left behind her dear friend Ruth Coster. When she learned what happened, a devastated Ruth would find it tragically appropriate that Helen had died in the pilot's seat, just as Helen's husband Earl had perished when his plane went down eighteen months earlier over Europe.

Gone, too, was Sergeant Belle Naimer of the Bronx, who joined her fiancé as a casualty of a wartime air crash. Gone were four other WACs: Sergeant Marion W. McMonagle of Philadelphia; Private Alethia M. Fair of Hollywood, California; Private Marian Gillis of Los Angeles; and Private Mary M. Landau of Brooklyn.

Gone were the plane's three enlisted crew members: Sergeant Hilliard Norris of Waynesville, North Carolina; Private George R. Newcomer of Middletown, New York; and Private Melvin "Molly" Mollberg of Baudette, Minnesota, who'd volunteered to take his best friend's place on the flight crew.

Gone were the male passengers: Major Herman F. Antonini, twenty-nine years old, of Danville, Illinois; Major Phillip J. Dattilo, thirty-one, of Louisville, Kentucky; Captain Louis E. Freyman, who would have turned twenty-nine the next day, of Hammond, Indiana; First Lieutenant Lawrence F. Holding, twenty-three, of Raleigh, North Carolina; Corporal Charles R. Miller, thirty-six, of Saint Joseph, Michigan; and Corporal Melvyn Weber, twenty-eight, of Compton, California.

Flames cremated the bodies inside the *Gremlin Special*, making the wreckage a funeral pyre and a mass grave for the passengers and crew killed inside the cockpit and cabin.

Yet amid the ashes, a gold wedding ring with a white inlay somehow survived intact. Inscribed on the inside of the band were two sets of initials, "CAC" and "REM," and a date, "5-5-43." Two years before the crash, John McCollom had stood on a church altar as his sister-in-law, Cecelia Adele Connolly—CAC—slipped it onto the finger of Robert Emert McCollom—REM.

When the ring was discovered years later inside the wreckage, it provided final proof of John McCollom's agonizing realization during those first minutes in the mountain jungle. After twenty-six inseparable years, gone was First Lieutenant Robert E. McCollom.

6

CHARMS

MOURNING WOULD WAIT. As McCollom and Decker stood over Captain Good's body, the exploding fuel tanks spread the fire closer to the three surviving women, threatening to trap them in a ring of flames.

Margaret saw the impending danger. She yelled to McCollom, who was still being shadowed by the woozy Decker: "Lieutenant McCollom, we have to get out of here. We're going to be surrounded by fire if we don't."

Even as he hurried, searching for a path to safety, McCollom fought to maintain composure. No one under his command would panic. He responded calmly: "You're all right."

Margaret saw a small rock ledge at the edge of a cliff, some twenty yards down the jungle-covered mountain from the wreckage. She clawed her way toward it. From the sky, the rain forest had looked to Margaret like an inviting green cushion, but now on the ground she discovered it was something else entirely—a botanist's dream and a crash survivor's nightmare.

Covering its rocky, muddy, uneven floor was a snarling mesh of giant ferns, vines, shrubs, fallen tree trunks, and spongy mosses, always wet. Thorns and spines and saw-toothed leaves ensnared her legs and tore her clothes and skin. Huge rhododendron bushes filled the spaces where light shone through a multilayered canopy of leaves. Above her head was a jumble of trees—giant eucalyptus, banyan, palm, bamboo, yoli myrtle, scrub oak, pandanus, tropical chestnut, soaring araucaria pines, evergreen casuarina, and hundreds of other species—some more prominent at higher altitudes, some at lower, the tallest of them reaching more than a hundred feet into the sky.

Gnarled webs of thick woody vines, heavy beards of lichen, spindly climbers, and aptly named strangler figs knitted the trees to one another and hung from branches like beaded curtains. Orchids sprouted everywhere, in hundreds of species, with flaming colors and strange, erotic shapes. The lush flora created a luxuriant bouquet, as the jungle carried out its endless cycle of birth, growth, decay, death, and new birth.

In the skies and the trees were hawks, owls, parrots, rails, swifts, flycatchers, warblers, and perhaps the most wondrous avian creatures in Shangri-La: color-drenched birds of paradise. The jungle had no predatory mammals, but rodents and small marsupials scurried in the underbrush. Salamanders, lizards, and snakes worthy of Eden, notably a python that grew to fifteen feet or more, represented the reptile kingdom.

Many of the natural wonders had never been seen by anyone other than natives. Margaret could have discovered new species simply by reaching out her hand. But in a diary Margaret began to keep shortly after the crash, she admitted that she was too preoccupied to appreciate the show. "Everything in the jungle had tentacles," she wrote, "and I was too busy fighting them to enjoy nature."

AS MARGARET CLIMBED over the fat trunk of a tree mowed down by the plane, it dawned on her that she wasn't wearing shoes—they'd either been blown off or burned away. She stopped in her tracks, sat down on the tree's jagged stump, and took stock. She pulled off her half-socks to inspect her feet. Her right foot was badly cut and bleeding. To her surprise, her left sock didn't have a mark on it, but the bottom of her left foot was burned—heat had passed through the fabric to sear her skin. Both legs had deep burns, and her right hand was cut and bloody. The left side of her face was blistered from the heat.

Margaret pulled off her khaki shirt. After that came her cotton bra. For a moment she was as topless as the native women she'd hoped to see. She put her shirt back on, buttoning it to the very top, as though readying herself for inspection during basic training back at Fort Oglethorpe. She tore the bra in half and tried to bandage her feet, but it did little good. Margaret unbuttoned her pants, slipped them down her burned legs, and set them aside. She bent over and pulled off the mud-brown rayon underwear that was standard issue for WACs—white underwear was banned by the military, out of fear that it would attract enemy bombers when hanging to dry on jungle clotheslines. Margaret pulled her pants back on over her naked bottom. She intended to use the panties' silky fabric to make bandages for herself and the other survivors.

As she finished dressing, Margaret saw McCollom leading the way down the rough path she'd followed minutes beforehand, carrying Eleanor Hanna on his back, her arms draped over his shoulders. Eleanor's clothes had been burned off, but somehow her Chinese coin bracelet still dangled from her wrist. On the way down, McCollom lost his footing, slipped, and landed awkwardly on a small tree. He picked himself up, brushed himself off, and pulled Eleanor onto his back once more. McCollom had emerged from the crash unhurt, but he had just suffered his first injury: a broken rib. He told no one.

Ken Decker and Laura Besley trailed close behind. When all five survivors were together, Margaret still wasn't thinking clearly. Although she'd removed her underpants to make bandages, she immediately forgot about that plan. She asked McCollom for a handkerchief, which she used to wrap her lacerated hand, binding it tight to stem the bleeding.

As they walked on, Decker tried to help McCollom with Eleanor Hanna. When they reached the ledge Margaret had seen, the five of them sat there, catching their breath, collecting themselves, and thinking about what had happened—to them, to their friends, and in McCollom's case, to his beloved twin. They were about nine thousand feet above sea level, and as they sat there, the late-afternoon temperature began to fall. Rain followed, and they learned firsthand why the jungle was called a rain forest. Small trees gave them some cover, but after a short time their clothes soaked through to their skin, chilling them to the bone and compounding their misery.

After a brief rest, McCollom and Decker left the three women on the ledge and climbed back up toward the wreckage. McCollom's Eagle Scout survival training kicked into gear. He hoped to find supplies to build a shelter, and also food, clothing, and weapons. He had a lighter and a small pocketknife he carried everywhere, but those wouldn't be much use if they ran into the giant, spear-carrying natives they'd expected to see only from the air.

McCollom recalled that one of the plane's crew members carried a .45-caliber pistol. He'd also noticed that the plane carried blankets, jugs of water, and crates of Cracker Jack–size boxes of K-rations. The ready-to-eat meals might include entrées such as ham and cheese, or beef and pork loaf; hard biscuits or crackers; bouillon cubes; instant coffee; powdered lemon drinks; heat-resistant chocolate bars; hard candy; and small packs of cigarettes, books of matches, and chewing gum. Some K-rations might contain one of the greatest military luxuries of all: toilet paper.

But when McCollom and Decker reached the plane, they discovered that none of those items could be salvaged. The cockpit and much of the cabin were still on fire. Fed by the plane's fuel, the wreckage would burn until the middle of the next day. The fire guaranteed that nothing would be left intact that hadn't already been destroyed by a series of explosions following a two-hundred-mile-per-hour crash into a tree-covered mountain. As McCollom surveyed the scene, he understood that in one sense they'd been lucky. On one side of the wreckage was a fifteen-foot boulder; if they'd hit the rock head-on, no one would have survived.

Another piece of relatively good news was that the *Gremlin Special*'s tail section, after separating on impact, hadn't caught fire or exploded. The tail rested at an odd angle by a ravine, jammed against a tree stump and swathed in vines at the edge of a steep drop. The jagged opening where the tail had torn away from the rest of the plane pointed upward toward the sky, like the hungry mouth of a baby bird.

McCollom climbed up to the tail's opening and pulled himself inside. He found a duffel bag with a bright yellow, self-inflating life raft, two heavy tarpaulins designed as covers for the open raft, and a few basic supplies. He tossed the bag outside and climbed out. He inflated the life raft and took inventory of the supplies. He counted several small tins of water and a first-aid kit with bandages, a few vials of morphine, vitamins, boric acid to disinfect wounds, and sulfathiazole tablets to fight infection. The only food was Charms, fruit-flavored hard candies made from sugar and corn syrup that were a staple of soldiers' rations. McCollom found a signaling mirror and, even better, a signal pistol he could use to draw the attention of searchers. There was just one problem: he couldn't find any flares.

McCollom and Decker hauled the life raft and the supplies over toward the ledge. Along the way, the raft snagged on something sharp and deflated. When they reached the WACs, they cleaned and bandaged their wounds and gave them shots of water to wash down the anti-infection tablets. McCollom put the flattened life raft under Laura Besley and Eleanor Hanna and covered them with a tarpaulin. As he tucked them in, Eleanor smiled. Again, she said, "Let's sing." McCollom gave her morphine, hoping it would help her to sleep.

The ledge was too small for all five survivors to stretch out, so Margaret and the two men moved a few yards away to another ledge. Exhausted, they wrapped themselves in the second tarpaulin. A pack of cigarettes had survived the crash in McCollom's pocket, so he flicked his lighter and they shared a few drags in silence. As darkness fell, they could see through the hanging vines and thick foliage that the plane was still aflame. They huddled together, bracing for a cold, wet night.

Several times that first night in the jungle, they heard a plane overhead and caught a glimpse of signal flares. But they had no way to let the searchers know they were alive under the thick canopy. Margaret wasn't even sure the lights were flares; they were so far off she thought they might be lightning. They talked hopefully about rescue. Privately, McCollom had already begun wondering if they'd have to hike all 150-plus miles back to Hollandia.

Now and then, in the inky black night, the jungle erupted with noises that sounded to the survivors like the yaps and barks of wild dogs.

THE NEXT MORNING, Monday, May 14, McCollom rose first and went to check on Eleanor Hanna and Laura Besley. As he knelt by the injured WACs, what he found didn't surprise him. He returned to the ledge where he'd slept beside Margaret Hastings and Ken Decker.

"Eleanor's dead," he said quietly.

McCollom went back to the other ledge and carefully wrapped the body in a tarpaulin. They had no tools for burial, and no energy to try, so he laid the remains of Eleanor Hanna at the base of a nearby tree.

The silence was broken by Laura Besley, who'd sat next to

Eleanor on the plane and slept beside her all night: "I can't stop shaking," she said.

Hurt and in shock, chilled and wet, thirsty and hungry, sore and tired, Margaret and Decker realized that they were shaking, too.

They couldn't do anything about Eleanor, and there was little they could do for themselves or each other. McCollom resolved to ration their water, so they each took a few sips with a vitamin pill and a few Charms to tide them over. Their shaking continued.

After their paltry breakfast, McCollom and Decker returned to the plane. Back in the tail section, they found two cots, another life raft, two more large yellow tarps and one small one, two compasses, a heavy cotton flying suit, more first-aid kits, a signaling mirror, and seventeen cans of water, each one containing about one cup of liquid. Decker dug into a tool kit and brought out a roll of black electrical tape and a pair of pliers. They carried their bounty back to the ledge.

Laura's crying and shaking continued, though she didn't complain of being in pain. McCollom gave her the flight suit for warmth and told her to lie on one of the cots. She was thirsty and wanted water, but each time she drank, she'd spit it up. She looked fine, and her burns seemed superficial. McCollom feared that she'd suffered internal injuries.

Margaret took a closer look at her legs and discovered rings of burned skin, three to six inches wide, around each calf. To her surprise, they weren't as painful as they looked. That wasn't the case with her bandaged feet, which hurt more with every step on the jungle floor. She worried that she wouldn't get far on burned feet covered by cotton bandages. Margaret asked Laura if she could borrow her shoes while Laura rested. Laura gave them to her.

In Margaret's diary, written in secretarial shorthand on scraps of paper and cardboard from their supplies, she confessed that she didn't want to return her friend's shoes. Later, upon rewriting and expanding the diary, she wrote: "Secretly, I wondered if—without shoes—I would ever be able to keep up with the others. I would have to give Laura's shoes back to her before we started down the mountain. I was frightened that I would never be able to make it through the jungle in feet covered only by half sox and a layer of cotton bandage."

The survivors had felt confident that search planes would be dispatched when the *Gremlin Special* failed to return to Sentani Airstrip as scheduled. That belief had been confirmed the night before when they heard a plane flying somewhere above them. But McCollom knew they'd never be visible in their current location. Their plane was a demolished, camouflage-painted speck in a dense swath of trees and vines. Still visible on the detached tail section was a five-pointed white star—the signature emblem of a United States military plane. But the leaves and fronds overhead made it impossible to see except from a short distance. From the air, the star was as inconsequential as a flower petal in the ocean.

Smoke from the wreckage might help to place the survivors' location, but only if searchers spotted it before the flames died. Complicating matters was the fact that although Prossen's flight plan listed his destination as Shangri-La, the *Gremlin Special* had crashed into a mountain miles from the pass that led into the valley. No one back in Hollandia could have known that. Alone at the controls and consumed by trying to keep the plane aloft, Nicholson didn't place a Mayday call. In fact, no radio communication had been exchanged between the plane and ground controllers at the base after Prossen took off from the Sentani Airstrip.

Decker's wristwatch had fared better than his skull, so they knew how slowly time was passing. At about eleven o'clock on Monday morning, less than twenty-four hours after the crash, they heard the distinctive sound of an airplane engine. McCollom grabbed the signaling mirror he'd found in a life raft and worked it furiously to flash snatches of sunlight skyward. It was no use. The engine sound grew faint as the plane flew away.

Still, McCollom considered it a hopeful sign. "Don't worry," he assured his companions. "I don't know how, but they'll get us out."

Mist settled over the mountain by mid-afternoon, and with it came steady rain. They talked about their families, and Margaret dreaded to think how her father back home in Owego would take the news that her plane had crashed and she was missing. Margaret told her diary she felt relieved that her mother had been spared the anxiety of learning that her eldest daughter was lost in Dutch New Guinea. It was the first time she'd felt at peace with her mother's death.

MARGARET'S MIDDLE NAME was Julia, her mother's first name. Margaret's youngest sister believed that Margaret was their mother's favorite. In a school essay, Margaret described her mother as "the sweetest, kindest and the most lovable little woman who ever lived. My father, my two younger sisters and I all lived at home, and she was the very hub of our existence. At fifty-five she was a tiny woman, with silvery white hair, pink and white skin, fine features—much prettier than any of her daughters."

In the essay, Margaret described how she'd learned from a doctor that her mother was seriously ill and would live no more than a year. "Onto my shoulders, so unaccustomed to responsibility, was thrown suddenly the problem of deciding how this crisis should be met. Should I tell my younger sisters, my father and my mother's brothers and sisters? For days I debated the question pro and con, and finally decided to act in the way which would cause Mother the least unhappiness. I was sure she didn't want to die— not when she was having so much fun for the first time in her life. I didn't feel sure that I could rely on my sisters to act normally if they knew the truth, so I told only my father. To this day I don't know whether I was right or wrong, but the decision was mine to make, and I did what I thought best."

Her mother died three months later.

AT ABOUT THREE that afternoon, the four remaining survivors felt exhausted from their injuries, the lack of food, and the little sleep they'd managed the night before. They set up the two cots.

Margaret and Laura shared one, pulling a tarp over themselves and hugging tightly to keep from falling off. Margaret lay there, trying to sleep while at the same time listening for search planes overhead. Laura couldn't stop tossing, so McCollom gave her morphine and tucked the tarp tightly around her. Margaret's eyes burned from fatigue, and she was eager to sleep, but even after the morphine Laura remained restless. Her squirms on the narrow cot kept Margaret awake.

Hanging in the air was a rhetorical question Laura had posed to McCollom as he'd tucked her in. Looking up from the cot, she'd asked: "Everyone else is dead and we're very lonely, aren't we?"

Eventually, Margaret drifted into a fitful sleep. When she awoke around midnight, she felt an unexpected stillness. Laura had stopped fidgeting. Margaret put her hand on Laura's chest. Nothing. She searched her friend's neck for a pulse. Again nothing.

Margaret screamed: "Please, McCollom, please come. Laura has died!"

Roused from much-needed sleep, McCollom suspected that Margaret was overreacting. Clearly Laura was hurt, and her inability to keep down water was a bad sign. But he thought her injuries weren't life-threatening. Decker was doubly sure, and he didn't hide his annoyance.

"Don't be a dope, Hastings," Decker replied. "She's all right."

McCollom walked to the cot and felt Laura's hands. Doubt

crept into his mind. He searched in vain for a pulse. Margaret was right.

Without a word, McCollom lifted Laura Besley's body from the cot. He wrapped her remains in one of the tarps and placed it alongside Eleanor Hanna's body at the foot of a tree.

Even in their grief Margaret and McCollom knew how fortunate they'd been. Margaret had changed seats for a better view, and McCollom had boarded too late to sit alongside his brother. They ended up in the last two seats on the left side of the plane. They lived. Laura Besley and Eleanor Hanna, who'd sat across from them, died.

"I ought to have cried," Margaret wrote in her diary. "I ought to have felt some kind of terrible grief for this dear friend. But all I could do was sit on the cot and shake. I couldn't even think that Laura was dead. I just sat there and shook and all I could think was: 'Now the shoes belong to me.' "

The death toll had reached twenty-one. The survivors of the *Gremlin Special* were down to three: John McCollom, a stoic twenty-six-year-old first lieutenant from the Midwest who'd just lost his twin brother; Kenneth Decker, a tech sergeant from the Northwest with awful head wounds who'd just celebrated his thirty-fourth birthday; and Margaret Hastings, an adventure-seeking thirty-year-old WAC corporal from the Northeast who'd missed her date for an ocean swim on the New Guinea coast. McCollom was the youngest of the

MARGARET HASTINGS AFTER THE CRASH. (PHOTO COURTESY OF B. B. MCCOLLOM.)

three, but he held the highest rank and suffered the fewest injuries. Combined with his quiet competence, those qualities made him the group's natural leader.

The three survivors had known each other casually around the base, but were hardly close friends. As they rested in the shadow of their burning plane, they considered themselves no more than comrades and acquaintances who'd shared a horrible experience. For the time being, they'd follow protocol and call each other by rank, last name, or both, as in "Sergeant," "Decker," or "Sergeant Decker," as opposed to Ken or Kenneth.

But women in the military were still a novelty, and calling a woman by her last name didn't always come naturally. Unless McCollom was giving her an order or Decker was needling her, "Corporal Hastings" soon became "Maggie." The truth was, she preferred to be called Margaret—she hated the nickname Maggie. But she never complained or corrected them.

After wrapping Laura Besley's body, McCollom returned to

JOHN MCCOLLOM AFTER THE CRASH. (PHOTO COURTESY OF B. B. MCCOLLOM.)

KENNETH DECKER AFTER THE CRASH. (PHOTO COURTESY OF B. B. MCCOLLOM.)

Margaret, who'd remained fixed on the cot. He lit a cigarette and handed it to her. Then he sat next to her to share it. She wrote in her diary: "No night will ever again be as long as this one."

As the hours passed, McCollom lit several more cigarettes, the smoldering orange tip moving back and forth between them in the darkness. He remained with her on the cot until dawn. They didn't speak.

7

TARZAN

ON ONE TRIP between the rock ledge and the wreckage, McCollom climbed a tree and surveyed the area. He saw what looked like a clearing several miles away. Using a compass he'd found in the plane's detached tail, McCollom plotted a course they could follow to reach it. With his companions' injuries festering, and with little water and no food but hard sucking candies, they'd need to get to the clearing as soon as Margaret and Decker felt strong enough to hike there.

Plane crash survivors are usually told to remain with the wreckage to increase their likelihood of being found. But the usual rules rarely applied in New Guinea. McCollom recognized that if they remained where they were, hidden under the jungle canopy, they faced certain death. Even if they reached the clearing, the likelihood of rescue seemed slim.

NEW GUINEA'S JUNGLES were boundless cemeteries of unmarked military graves. In April 1944, when the wife of a missing Army Air Forces pilot sought information about her husband's prospects, an officer wrote back with unusual candor: "It is necessary to cross high mountain ranges on practically every flight made on the island. Thick jungle growth goes right up to the tops of the peaks and entire squadrons could completely disappear under this foliage. No matter how thorough the search is, the possibility of locating the plane is rather remote. We have had numerous other instances of like nature and no word has come concerning those crews or airplanes. The weather and terrain account for more [downed] airplanes than combat flying."

More than six hundred American planes had crashed on the island since the start of the war, some in combat but many from rough weather, mechanical failures, pilot error, uncharted mountains hiding in clouds, or some combination. Hundreds more planes from Japan, Australia, Great Britain, New Zealand, and the Netherlands had crashed on New Guinea, as well. Some were located after they went down, but many were concealed by the emerald green rain forests. By 1945, New Guinea was home to more missing airplanes than any country on earth.

Two and a half years earlier, in November 1942, a severe downdraft struck an American C-47 delivering troops and supplies to another part of the island. The plane crashed into a mountain at nine thousand feet, into conditions almost identical to those encountered by the survivors of the *Gremlin Special*. Search planes flew one sortie after another, but found no trace of the C-47, which was nicknamed the *Flying Dutchman*.

Seventeen of the twenty-three men aboard survived the crash, though some had severe injuries. When no rescuers arrived, eight men felt fit enough to try to walk out of the jungle. They split up, leaving the crash site in two groups of four. On the fifth day of their trek, the first group came to a narrow gorge with a fast-moving river. They couldn't cross, so they tried to ride logs down the rapids. Two drowned. The other two eventually met friendly natives, who guided them from village to village. After thirty-two arduous days, they arrived at an Allied base. The second group had an easier time. They received help from natives after ten days, and within a month all four were safely out of the jungle.

The reappearance of survivors from the *Flying Dutchman* triggered a new search for the injured men left behind, but that failed, too. As a last-ditch effort, a reward was offered to any natives who discovered the wreck. More than sixty days after the crash, a group of natives came across a cluster of decaying bodies and a lone survivor, a U.S. Army chaplain described in one account as "blind from malnutrition and so light that he 'felt like a baby.'" Around him was a bare semicircle of dirt—near the end of his ordeal, he'd sustained himself by eating mountain moss within his reach. The natives offered him cooked banana, but he died in their arms. They left his body, but brought back his Bible as proof that they'd located the *Flying Dutchman*.

Long after, searchers returned to the wreck and found a rear cargo door where the survivors had kept a makeshift diary written in charcoal. The first entries were simple reports with an almost military tone. Each entry was a few words long, noting when the crash occurred, when each group of healthy survivors left, how the remaining men had tried to launch a balloon to attract searchers, and what food they'd found and eaten. The rationing of one chocolate bar and a single can of tomato juice took up five days' worth of entries.

After a while, when food, tomato juice, and cigarettes were gone, the entries scratched on the cargo door turned personal, revealing hope, fear, and occasional flashes of grim humor. On Friday, November 27, 1942, seventeen days after the crash, an entry read: "Buckets full [of] water this morn . . . still got our chin up." Two days later: "Boy we're getting weak." But the diarist added, "Still have our hope." The next day: "Still going strong on imaginary meals." On Monday, December 7, the anniversary of Pearl Harbor, the entry read: "Year ago today the war started. Boy, we didn't think of this then." Two days later, a month after the crash: "Just thirty days ago. We can take it but it would be nice if someone came." A week later, as thoughts turned to Christmas: "Running out of imaginary meals. Boys shouldn't be long in coming now—6 more shoping [sic] days." Six days later:

"Tonite is Christmas eve. God make them happy at home." Six days later: "Johnnie died today."

The entries petered out after two more days, seven weeks after the crash. The final entry noted that it was New Year's Eve. The three remaining survivors signed their names: Pat, Mart, and Ted. Days later, the natives found the wreckage. The last man to die—the blind, malnourished, moss-eating chaplain, down to his last breaths—was Captain Theodore Barron, known to his friends as Ted.

AT DAYLIGHT ON Tuesday, May 15, 1945, the second day after the *Gremlin Special* crash, McCollom announced that he'd changed his mind. They couldn't wait for Margaret and Decker to feel stronger before starting their trek to the clearing he'd spotted from the tree.

With soiled and soggy bandages on their burns, McCollom feared, his companions would get worse before they got better. Already they moved slowly, as though swimming through honey, a side effect of their injuries, sleeplessness, empty stomachs, and the thin air more than a mile above sea level. A native would have considered the rain forest a mess hall overflowing with fruits and roots, birds and small mammals, but for the survivors it was as mysterious as a menu in Mandarin. The only nourishment they trusted was their hard candy Charms.

McCollom assembled most of their supplies in one of the remaining yellow tarpaulins. He packed a smaller one for Decker and gave Margaret a pail that he'd found in the plane's tail. Rattling around in it were her day's rations: two tins of water and a few cellophane-wrapped Charms.

McCollom returned to Laura Besley's body for a grisly but necessary task. He unwrapped the tarp and removed the flight suit he'd given her for warmth. Just as Margaret had shortened her uniforms when she'd first arrived in Hollandia, McCollom used his pocket knife to slice twelve inches of fabric from each cuff so Margaret could wear the flight suit without tripping over herself.

When McCollom brought her the suit, Margaret knew that it came from the body of her good friend and double-date partner. But she was glad to have it, just as she knew that wearing Laura's shoes might be the difference between life and death. Margaret still had the rayon underwear she'd stripped off after the crash, intending to make bandages. Now she tore the panties in half and used the fabric to cover the burns on her legs, so the rough flight suit wouldn't scrape against her charred skin.

Later, writing in her diary, Margaret wished that before they left the crash site they'd said a prayer, built a cross, or laid some kind of marker for the twenty-one friends, comrades, and McCollom's twin. Even a moment of silence would have made her feel better about their departure. But at the time, their only focus was on reaching a place where they might be spotted from the air.

THE DETACHED TAIL SECTION OF THE *GREMLIN SPECIAL*. (PHOTO COURTESY OF U.S. ARMY.)

"LET'S GO," MCCOLLOM ORDERED his two-person squad. He took the lead, Margaret followed close behind, and Decker brought up the rear.

They first had to climb up from the ledge where they'd spent the previous two nights and make their way past the wreckage. The growth was so thick that they made the most progress by crawling on their hands and knees. In a few places, a wrong step would mean a fall into a rocky ravine. In others, it would mean a deadly plunge over a cliff. It took an exhausting half hour just to get twenty-five yards past the plane.

Margaret tried to tie back her hair, which fell halfway down her back. But it was no use. It kept getting caught in the clawing vines and branches that surrounded them. They repeatedly had to halt their crawl-march to untangle it. In desperation, Margaret shook loose her hair and declared: "Please, McCollom, hack it off."

The lieutenant used his pocket knife to saw through chunks of Margaret's thick hair, dropping the cuttings where they stood. After working his way around Margaret's head, McCollom fashioned what Margaret called "a rather sad, three-inch 'feather' bob." They started out again, but still the jungle tore at her.

"For goodness sake, McCollom, I've got to get rid of this hair!" she yelled.

McCollom cut it even shorter.

Margaret's burns made each step painful. Decker, worse off, still unsteady from his head injury, moved stiffly but never complained.

As they inched through the mud and brush on the jungle floor, the trio stumbled upon what Margaret considered a miracle: a dry creek bed, or gully, that formed a narrow path down the mountain. Calling it miraculous mostly reveals how difficult the jungle was by contrast. The gully angled sharply downward, in some places forcing them to climb, slide, or jump down the rocky slope. The footing was unstable even along the flatter sections of the path, with loose stones that slid out from under them. In other places they had to climb over boulders and old tree trunks. But it was a trail nonetheless.

"It is foolish to think that we could have cut our way out of that dense, clinging jungle with a pocket knife, our only weapon," Margaret wrote in her diary. "The gully promised two things: a foothold in the jungle, precarious though it was, and eventual water."

Even as they followed the creek bed, the survivors had to stop and rest every half hour. After two breaks they noticed trickles of icy water draining into the gully from tiny mountain creeks. At first, they were delighted. Margaret and Decker, aching with thirst, announced that they intended to fill their stomachs as soon as the water became deep enough to collect. McCollom warned against it, worrying that waterborne germs would torture their bowels. But they were too excited to listen. In no time, the tributaries grew larger and they had more water than they wished for. It rose over their shoe tops and kept rushing into the gully, threatening to sweep them down the mountain with the swift-moving stream.

They navigated the rougher spots by sliding along on their bottoms, getting soaked in the process. In the steepest places, waterfalls cascaded from two to ten feet down. The jungle bordered closely on both sides of the gully, so fallen logs rested in some of the waterfalls. Whenever possible, they used those logs as ladders or poles to climb down. When no logs were available, McCollom led the way, climbing down the falls hand over hand, the water pouring over his head. He stood at the bottom, under the rushing water, as Margaret made her way down far enough to stand on his shoulders. She slid into his arms, and McCollom placed her in shallower water past the falls. When she was safe, he returned to help Decker.

They came to a twelve-foot waterfall, too high and too steep to try McCollom's shoulder trick. Margaret and Decker rested at the side of the stream, while McCollom fought his way into the encroaching jungle to search for a way around. But the growth was especially thick there, so he returned with a new idea.

McCollom grabbed a thick vine that hung from a tree alongside the falls. After testing it with his weight, he held tight to the vine, took a running jump, and swung over and beyond the falls. When he cleared the cascading water, he let himself down at the bottom. He tossed back the vine and told the others to follow.

Margaret didn't hesitate. She grabbed the vine and launched herself into space. When she cleared the falls, McCollom caught her as she let go of the vine. Next came Decker, who followed suit.

When he was safely beside them, the sergeant deadpanned with a western drawl: "Damned if I ever thought I'd understudy Johnny Weissmuller." Decker's mention of the vine-swinging movie star who played Tarzan made Margaret smile, though she overlooked the obvious implication: that made her Jane.

As they trudged onward, Margaret felt worse with each step. She was cold, wet, and exhausted. Her whole body ached. Tears welled in her eyes, but it was a point of pride with her not to cry.

From time to time they heard search planes overhead. As the thrum of each plane's engines grew closer, McCollom frantically worked the signal mirror. But he knew that the foliage canopy made the effort useless. Still, the sound alone was enough to revive their confidence that the Army Air Forces wouldn't give up.

McCollom's plan was to hike until early afternoon, then set up camp when the daily mist and rain rolled in. But the jungle bordering the stream was so relentless they couldn't find a spot on the bank large enough to stretch out. They kept moving until they could go no farther, eventually settling on a location that was far from ideal.

McCollom placed one tarp on the sodden ground and draped the other tarp over them as a cover. They ate a few Charms, then bunched together to keep warm as they slept. McCollom slid between Decker and Margaret, so he could care for them both if needed. Decker thought McCollom displayed "the old mother hen instinct," but he appreciated it and kept quiet.

Their campsite slanted sharply toward the stream, and several times during the night the trio rolled in a heap down the bank into the icy water. Each time they dragged out the tarps and their soggy selves and tried again to sleep.

Also disturbing their sleep was something they'd seen earlier in the day. While walking through the stream, they noticed an unmistakable sign that they weren't alone: outlined in the mud was a fresh human footprint. Further evidence of the natives came as they huddled under the tarps: they heard strange barking sounds in the distance.

AS FAR AS the three survivors knew, they were the first outsiders to trek through this part of New Guinea's mountainous rain forest. But they were mistaken. That distinction belonged to a wealthy amateur American zoologist who seven years earlier had led an expedition to New Guinea in search of undiscovered flora and fauna.

One unfortunate result of that 1938 expedition was an act of deadly violence. The question now was whether that legacy would threaten the three survivors of the *Gremlin Special*.

8

GENTLEMAN EXPLORER

DURING THE YEAR before the *Gremlin Special* crash, Colonel Ray Elsmore had basked in public acclaim as the valley's self-styled discoverer. Unbeknownst to him or anyone else in the U.S. Army, Elsmore was the New Guinea equivalent of Antarctic explorer Robert Falcon Scott. After believing that he'd snowshoed through virgin territory to the South Pole, Scott learned that his rival Roald Amundsen had beaten him there. In other words, Elsmore was the second outsider to discover Shangri-La, third if he counted Major Myron Grimes.

The valley's true Western discoverer was Richard Archbold, a young man who enjoyed the good fortune of having been born exceedingly rich. And unlike Elsmore and Grimes, Archbold had visited the valley on the ground.

Archbold's inherited wealth flowed from his grandfather, John D. Archbold, a president of Standard Oil and a partner of John D. Rockefeller. The family's millions guaranteed that Richard Archbold would never be required to work a traditional job. This was convenient, as he was never much of a traditional student. As a boy, skinny, shy, and socially awkward, with piercing eyes and a brusque manner, Archbold bounced among several private schools, including one in Arizona where his favorite subject was camping. He took classes at Hamilton College in upstate New York and at Columbia University in Manhattan without staying long enough at either school to collect a degree.

One subject to which Archbold applied himself was the great outdoors. In 1929 Archbold's father, hoping to set Richard on a productive path, agreed to help finance a joint British, French, and American research expedition to Madagascar. The elder Archbold had one condition: along with his money came his underachieving twenty-two-year-old son. The expedition's organizers were delighted by the cash but not quite sure what to do with young Archbold, who'd reached adulthood as a tall, thin, moderately handsome man with a shock of wavy black hair, a thick mustache, and a partiality for bow ties.

After initially planning to use Archbold as a photographer, one of the expedition's senior scientists suggested, "Why don't you collect mammals?" So he did.

Archbold practiced collecting at the family's Georgia estate—something akin to a big game hunter preparing for a safari at a zoo—and learned from his many mistakes. But once in Madagascar, he stoically suffered the bites of land leeches and mosquitoes, the many discomforts of camp life in the wild, and the stigma among serious scientists of being the rich kid along for the ride. Along the way, he found his calling as a biological researcher.

Upon his return from Madagascar, Archbold learned that his father had died. He collected his inheritance and with it a Manhattan apartment on Central Park West. He took a low-level job down the street, as a research associate in the mammal department at the American Museum of Natural History, where his grandfather had been a major benefactor.

Working in an office across the hall on the museum's fifth floor was a young ornithologist from Germany named Ernst Mayr, who later became a legend in evolutionary biology. Archbold's new acquaintance encouraged him to focus on the wilds of New Guinea, where Mayr had spent months studying bird life. Archbold put his inheritance to work by organizing, funding, and leading several major expeditions there under the auspices of the museum. From

the outset, his plan was nothing less than "a comprehensive biological survey of the island." Unlike Mayr, who'd done his work
among small groups of scientist-explorers, Archbold assembled a
veritable research army to attempt the ambitious task.

Archbold enjoyed notable success on his first two New Guinea
journeys, one begun in 1933 and another in 1936, as he and his
well-funded teams reached previously unexplored territory and
supplied the New York museum with numerous new plant and
animal species. But Archbold grew frustrated by the logistical
challenges posed by the enormous island, not least of which were
the inhospitable terrain and the lack of native pack animals. Na-
poleon said armies march on their stomachs; the same could be
said for large, exotic scientific expeditions. Archbold's journeys in
New Guinea depended on efficient supply lines, which meant that
someone or something needed to carry tons of provisions to explorers cut off from civilization for months on end.

In the absence of horses, mules, oxen, or camels, and in light of
the impossibility of using trucks in the roadless interior, human
bearers were the only land-based option. But Archbold learned
that New Guinea natives couldn't be relied upon. One reason was
fear, not of the explorers but of each other. The island's innumer-
able tribes and clans were usually at war with one another, so the
instant a native bearer left his home territory, he had reason to fear
death at the hands of a neighbor.

Archbold concluded that the best way to conquer New Guinea,
scientifically at least, would be with air support. He became a pilot
and began buying airplanes. In early 1938, he purchased the largest privately owned airplane in the world—the first commercial
version of a U.S. Navy patrol bomber known as a PBY. With a
wingspan of more than one hundred feet, a yawning cargo bay,
and a range exceeding four thousand miles, Archbold's PBY fit
his needs perfectly. Its greatest appeal was the PBY's design as
a "flying boat." Fitted with pontoons, it could take off and land

on bodies of water, including the high-altitude lakes and rivers of New Guinea. Archbold added special navigation and communications equipment, then named his plane after a native word for a powerful storm: *Guba*. With *Guba* at his disposal, Archbold could ferry supplies, personnel, and specimens wherever needed, making possible his third and most ambitious expedition to New Guinea.

Archbold obtained approval and support from the Dutch government, which controlled the area he wanted to explore. The government's motivation was that the expedition would provide authorities in the Netherlands with deeper knowledge about their colony, including not just the flora and fauna in Archbold's sights but also the people and the resources hidden within.

In April 1938 Archbold's team established a base camp in Hollandia with nearly two hundred people, including scientists from the American Museum of Natural History; seventy-two Dyak tribesmen brought from the neighboring island of Borneo as bearers; two cooks; a backup pilot; a navigator; a radioman; and two mechanics. The Dutch government contributed nearly sixty soldiers, including a captain and three lieutenants. Also on hand, courtesy of the Dutch, were thirty political prisoners—anticolonial activists, mostly—pressed into duty as "convict carriers."

EXPLORER RICHARD ARCHBOLD IN 1938, STANDING ON THE *GUBA* AFTER LANDING IN WHAT WAS THEN KNOWN AS CHALLENGER BAY IN HOLLANDIA. (PHOTO COURTESY OF ARCHBOLD BIOLOGICAL STATION.)

The expedition focused on collecting mammals, birds, plants, and insects at a range of altitudes—from sea level to the barren twelve-thousand-foot peaks in the least-studied area of New Guinea, the north slope of the Snow Mountains, one of several ranges in the island's interior. With *Guba*, the Dyak bearers, and the convicts carrying supplies to keep them fed, Archbold and his team of scientists gathered a trove of remarkable specimens, including tree-climbing kangaroos, three-foot-long rats, and a previously unknown songbird with a flycatcher beak. But nothing was as startling as what they encountered on the morning of June 23, 1938.

ARCHBOLD WAS PILOTING *Guba* toward Hollandia after a reconnaissance flight when the plane broke through thick clouds surrounding the three-mile-high mountain named for Dutch Queen Wilhelmina. Ahead, Archbold saw a wide, flat, heavily populated valley that appeared nowhere on his maps and was unknown except to its inhabitants. He estimated that the valley was roughly forty miles long by ten miles wide. Later, adopting patrician nonchalance and the detached language of science, he downplayed his shock and called it "a pleasant surprise."

A Dutch soldier on board *Guba* called the area a *Groote Vallei*, or Grand Valley, and Archbold declared that that would be its name.

He initially placed the population at sixty thousand people, though in fact it was perhaps double that, including natives who lived in the surrounding mountains. Even at Archbold's estimate, that was enough people to immediately establish the valley as the most densely populated area in all of Dutch New Guinea. Archbold's discovery was comparable to a botanist in 1938 searching for bumblebees in the American Midwest and stumbling upon Kansas City, Kansas.

It almost defied belief. New Guinea was remote, but hardly unknown. Explorers had penetrated large parts of the island's interior on foot, and mountaineers had climbed its highest peaks. Separate expeditions in 1907, the early 1920s, and 1926 came close to Archbold's Grand Valley and made contact with some traveling natives, but they never found the valley itself. One group of explorers, the Kremer expedition of 1921, reached a nearby area called the Swart Valley. The anthropologist Denise O'Brien, who studied the Swart Valley some forty years later, wrote that when they first encountered Kremer and his team, the natives "were puzzled as to why the light-skinned men, who must really be ghosts or spirits, had no women with them. Finally they decided that the spirits' women were carried in containers, containers that the spirits also used for carrying and cooking food. Sometimes the spirit women came out of the containers, and to the (natives) they looked like snakes as they slithered along the ground, but to the spirit men they looked like women." The natives' overall reaction, O'Brien wrote, was fear, compounded by a severe epidemic of dysentery after the explorers left.

Even if land-based surveyors missed the valley, surely a military or commercial pilot should have spotted an area of three hundred or so square miles filled with hundreds of villages, inhabited by tens of thousands of men, women, and children—not to mention pigs. Yet some of the world's most celebrated aviators missed it. In July 1937, a year before Archbold's discovery, Amelia Earhart flew over part of New Guinea as she attempted to circumnavigate the globe. Her last known stop was at an airstrip in the town of Lae, at New Guinea's eastern edge, after which her plane disappeared somewhere in the Pacific. But she, too, never saw the Grand Valley.

By the late 1930s, most anthropologists believed that every significant population center on the planet had been discovered, mapped, and in most cases modernized to some degree by missionaries, capitalists, colonizers, or a combination of the three. No one doubted that pockets of undisturbed aborigines still roamed the rain forests of the Amazon and elsewhere. But the people of Archbold's Grand Valley were stationary farmer-warriors, living in clearly defined villages, in a wide-open area, covered only by the clouds above. A hundred thousand people, hiding in plain sight. Sixty years later, mammalogist Tim Flannery, an authority on the natural wonders of New Guinea, declared that Archbold's find represented "the last time in the history of our planet that such a vast, previously unknown civilization was to come into contact with the West."

One explanation is that an unusual combination of forces kept the valley off the map. When Archbold described his find for *National Geographic* magazine, an editor there tried to make sense of it, writing, "Forestation is so heavy and terrain so rugged that earlier explorers passed on foot within a few miles of the most thickly populated area without suspecting the existence of a civilization there." The surrounding mountains played an important role as well, discouraging flights overhead and commercial incursions by land. The lifestyle of the valley natives helped, too. They were self-sufficient farmers, as opposed to hunter-gatherers who might travel far and wide to feed themselves and obtain needed goods. Their stay-at-home tendency was cemented by their wars, which ensured that most spent their lives within short, relatively safe distances of their huts.

WHEN ARCHBOLD FIRST saw the valley, rough weather prevented him from changing course or dipping *Guba* low for a better look. But in the weeks that followed, he flew several reconnaissance missions, photographing the valley and sending pigs and their owners running for cover—just as Colonel Elsmore's flights would do six years later.

Archbold's chief botanist, L. J. Brass, described what they saw from the air: "The people were living in compact, very orderly and clean, fenced, walled or stockaded villages of about three or four to about fifty houses. Dwellings were of two types, built with double walls of upright split timbers, grass-thatched, and without floors. The men's houses were round, ten to fifteen feet in diameter, with dome-shaped roofs; the women's houses were long and narrow. The everyday dress of the men consisted of a penis gourd, and perhaps a hair net of looped string. The women affected either short skirts of pendent strings, worn below the buttocks, or an arrangement of cords around the thighs, and always one or more capacious carrying nets hung over the back from the forehead. As arms and implements they had bows, arrows of several kinds, spears, stone adzes, and stone axes."

Archbold seemed only mildly interested in the people, but he was fascinated by their farming methods. Unlike all other known tribes on New Guinea, natives of the valley grew sweet potatoes—their staple food—in clearly defined plots of land, with labyrinthine drainage ditches and surrounding walls. Archbold said it reminded him fondly of the farm country he'd seen on holiday in central Europe.

Archbold's assistants established a camp some fifteen miles west of the valley on a body of water called Lake Habbema, where *Guba* could set down and take off. One day, two natives presented themselves to the outsiders. "One was evidently a man of some importance," Archbold wrote. "The other, who was younger, perhaps a bodyguard, remained very much on the alert. They squatted on their haunches, their backs toward home, their bows and arrows handy, while we sat down on the camp side of them."

Archbold gave the two men beadlike cowrie shells—small, pearly white, naturally smooth shells that were widely used as currency and jewelry in Africa and elsewhere. He plied them with sugar, cigarettes, and dried fish. The two men accepted the gifts, but after a polite period of time handed them back, a gesture that Archbold interpreted "as a sign of independence." He noted, however, that the more senior man did accept a few draws from the cigar of the senior Dutch officer on the expedition, a captain named C. G. J. Teerink. After a fifteen-minute visit, the two natives left the explorers' camp.

Subsequently, Archbold dispatched two exploration teams, each consisting of Dutch soldiers, convict carriers, and Dyak tribesmen trained to collect flora and fauna. The teams, one led by Captain Teerink and the other by a lieutenant named J. E. M. Van Arcken, started their treks at opposite ends of the valley, so they'd meet roughly in the middle.

In August 1938 the two teams marched through the valley's high grasses, past one village after another. If the outsiders had been tribesmen from other parts of the valley, such an incursion likely would have been greeted with spears and arrows. But the white explorers and their bearers were so strange and exotic, so far removed from the day-to-day warfare among the tribes, they were met by little more than curiosity from the native men and shyness from the women and children. The explorers saw signs that the natives practiced cannibalism, but the heavily armed Dutch army troops felt they had nothing to fear.

Occasionally some tribesmen would discourage the explorers from traveling to the next village—placing sticks in their path, pantomiming the firing of arrows, and standing arm in arm as a human blockade. Language barriers prevented Captain Teerink or Lieutenant Van Arcken from getting a full explanation, but the acts seemed to Teerink more protective than hostile. The natives apparently didn't want their new acquaintances to be harmed by enemies who lived in the next village.

That pattern remained in place until an incident that involved a band of natives and the exploration team led by Lieutenant Van Arcken.

On August 9, 1938, as Van Arcken's patrol neared the Baliem River in the valley's center, they were met by tribesmen "in large numbers" carrying spears and bows and arrows. "We apparently were not to be trusted because we had come from the direction of enemy territory," Van Arcken wrote in his daily log. He defused the confrontation with a few cowrie shells. Later that night four natives came into his camp, asking to sleep among the soldiers. "These gentlemen were sent packing," Van Arcken wrote, "after a shot in the air to scare them off."

The next day, Van Arcken found that the patrol's trail had been "closed off with tree branches, behind which some youths with spears took cover." His troops brandished their weapons, and the young natives fled. As the column of soldiers moved forward, bringing up the rear were two soldiers, one of them a corporal named Pattisina. Van Arcken wrote that two natives grabbed Pattisina from behind. When the other lagging soldier came to Pattisina's aid, one of the natives "wanted to spear the corporal with his lance, whereupon said native was shot by the corporal." In short, Van Arcken's report revealed that Pattisina had killed a native, and the official version was that he'd done so in self-defense.

Captain Teerink, the highest-ranking Dutch officer on the expedition, didn't buy the explanation. Teerink, who was leading the other patrol, wrote a critical addendum to Van Arcken's report that suggested he held a more humane view of the natives: "In my view, this fatal shot is to be regretted. Corporal Pattisina should have fired a warning shot first. It has been my experience that with tribes like this, a warning shot is usually sufficient. It is requested that you issue instructions to this effect to your men."

EVEN BEFORE HE returned to the United States, Archbold published articles about the expedition in *The New York Times* and elsewhere. In March 1941 he wrote a long piece for *National Geographic Magazine*. In it, he described a number of encounters with natives, most of them friendly though a few laced with tension. He seemed most surprised when his expedition passed villages and the natives paid them little mind: "Here the natives seemed to take our party for granted. Some stood by and watched the long line of carriers file by, while others, digging in the gardens of rich black earth, did not even look up."

But in none of his accounts did Archbold describe what the natives must have considered the most awful moment of the outsiders' visit.

Four years after the shooting, in June 1942, Archbold finally acknowledged that an incident had occurred between the natives and Van Arcken's patrol that day near the river. But the way he described it and the publication he chose guaranteed that the significance would be overlooked. Writing in the *Bulletin of the American Museum of Natural History*, Archbold described how on August 10, Van Arcken's patrol encountered a trail barricaded with branches and guarded by men with spears: "Here occurred the one incident of the whole expedition where more than a show of force was necessary." Without stopping to explain what he meant, much less acknowledge and discuss the gunshot death of a native, Archbold forged ahead to report the time of day that the patrol reached the river and the precise width of the river's floodplain.

Van Arcken took an even more misleading approach when he created the first known map of the valley. On it, he drew an arrow to the spot of the August 10, 1938, confrontation and wrote: "Location where one native died due to a lance attack." Unless a map reader knew better, Van Arcken's note seemed to suggest that the explorers had witnessed a fatal duel between two natives.

Elsewhere in Archbold's report to the museum, he outlined his overall philosophy where natives were concerned. There he whitewashed the shooting entirely: "In venturing into an unknown area, the kind of reception the natives will extend is unpredictable. Certain it is that natives in general tend to be more friendly toward a large, well-armed party than toward a small, weak one. Our parties inland were usually of the former category and no unpleasant incidents of importance arose in our contacts with the people."

Archbold apparently had no interest in determining whether the natives considered the Grand Valley's first fatal gunshot to be "unpleasant" or an "incident of importance."

ARCHBOLD'S EXPEDITION AND his writings about the valley went unnoticed by Colonel Elsmore. When initially told about Archbold after the crash of the *Gremlin Special*, Elsmore brushed it off, certain that his Hidden Valley, his Shangri-La, was distinct from Archbold's Grand Valley. After all, New Guinea was so huge and unexplored, who could say how many isolated, undiscovered valleys might still exist?

But Grand Valley and Shangri-La were one and the same. And the first known contact between its natives and the outside world had been marked by blood.

9

GUILT AND GANGRENE

AFTER SEEING THE native footprint, the three survivors spent what Margaret called "this aching, miserable night" on the sloped, muddy banks of the mountain creek. Soggy and exhausted from their repeated rolls into the cold water, they woke in the dim predawn light on Wednesday, May 16, to resume their trek toward the clearing that McCollom had spotted farther down the slope.

As Margaret tried to stand, pain racked her body, and with it came fear. Overnight, her joints had stiffened, and the burned skin on her legs had tightened around her muscles. The burns choked off blood flow, starving healthy flesh. It hurt to even think about walking and sliding farther downstream. She couldn't straighten up. She wrote in her diary, "My legs were so stiff they were a sickening sight."

A quick inspection showed that infection had set in. She downplayed the gory details in her diary—the oozing pus, the blue-black hue of dead tissue. But she had a sickening idea of the causes and the dangers of what she described as "big, evil-smelling, running sores."

New Guinea teemed with bacteria, and the microscopic organisms were feasting on the stagnant blood in her poorly dressed wounds. The combination of burned flesh, unsanitary conditions, and swarming bacteria was a recipe for gangrene. Unless treated, the dread condition meant the death of a damaged body part and ultimately an entire body. Gangrene comes in two varieties, wet and dry. Both are awful, but wet gangrene is worse. Dry gangrene usually appears gradually as a result of blocked blood flow through the arteries. Decades of smoking might lead to dry gangrene and the slow death of a smoker's feet. That wasn't Margaret's worry. Her infected injuries were ripe for fast-moving, fast-killing wet gangrene. The longer her wounds went untreated, the greater the chance that her legs would have to be amputated. Even that radical step might not be enough. Wet gangrene can lead to the blood infection called sepsis. In the jungle, sepsis is fatal. The only question is whether it takes its victim in hours or days.

Margaret steeled herself and struggled upright onto her tender feet. She walked in agony, back and forth on the inclined bank, trying to loosen her joints and get limber enough to continue the journey. She glanced at Decker, knowing that he must have been in at least as much pain. She admired how stoic he remained.

McCollom looked at his two companions. He felt responsibility for them, but more than that. Respect and growing admiration. Affection, too. During all the walking, all the sliding downstream, all the discomforts, Decker hadn't complained once about his gaping head wound or his other injuries. And this petite WAC corporal—by now McCollom thought of her affectionately as Maggie—had turned out to be much tougher than he'd expected. Not only was she soldiering on with gangrenous wounds on her legs and hand, but the burns on the left side of her face had darkened. It occurred to him that other WACs he'd known, as well as some male soldiers, wouldn't have survived half of what she'd already been through.

Yet as their injuries worsened and infections took hold, McCollom could see his companions' strength ebbing. He felt certain that both already suffered from full-blown wet gangrene, and he feared that if the search planes didn't find them soon, he'd be the only one left alive.

McCollom wouldn't reveal it to Margaret or Decker, but he was fighting back fear. Later he explained, "We were in what was thought to be headhunter territory, we had no medical supplies, no shelter. We were in the middle of nowhere. I knew my twin brother was dead in the wreckage. I had to take care of the others. I didn't want to think about being out there all by myself, so I did what I could as much for myself as for them."

Though determined to save Margaret and Decker, McCollom made a private resolution: if the searchers gave up before spotting them, he would somehow find a navigable river and build a raft, or if need be, keep walking. He'd float or walk all the way to the ocean a hundred and fifty miles away, if that's what it took to get out of there. He'd return to Hollandia, and after that to his family. He couldn't save his brother, but he was determined to save himself and keep watch over his brother's infant daughter.

He'd do everything in his power to help Decker and Margaret. But if gangrene got the best of them, McCollom would go it alone.

BREAKFAST WAS WATER and more Charms, still their only food on the third day after the crash. They separated the candies by color, eating the red ones until they tired of them, moving on to yellow, and so on. Decker jokingly called the color-by-color approach a good way to vary their diet. They had cigarettes, but McCollom's lighter was dry and their matches were wet. As they prepared to resume their trek, rolling their supplies into the yellow tarpaulins, their thoughts turned to coffee.

"I'd love to be back in the mess hall having some of that delicious battery acid," Decker said.

"Me, too!" Margaret said. She didn't understand why, but despite not eating since her lunch of chicken and ice cream three days earlier, she didn't feel especially hungry.

The stream bank was too steep for them to walk on, and the jungle foliage gave no quarter. They gingerly stepped down the eight-foot bank, back into the mountain stream, to resume their soaking march. Again they clambered over fallen logs and slid on their bottoms down waterfalls.

"By this time my feet, my leg and my cut hand were infected," Margaret wrote in her diary. "We were all in the last stages of exhaustion, and now the nightmare of yesterday commenced all over again."

Tears filled her eyes as Margaret fought to keep up. Her feet throbbed with each step. Decker hung back with her. McCollom marched on, eager to reach the clearing. He got so far ahead they lost sight of him.

Margaret teetered on the edge of panic.

"McCollom has gone off and left us, and he's got all the food," she cried to Decker. "And we're going to starve to death." She plopped down in the stream. It was the closest she'd come to giving up since the thought of surrender flickered through her mind in the burning plane.

Decker, usually the quiet man among the three, had heard enough. He wheeled around like a red-faced drill sergeant. Margaret wouldn't quote his full tirade to her diary, but she sheepishly admitted that he called her "a piker" and "a quitter." Whether he did it as a motivating technique or in real anger, Decker had found the exact right words.

"I got so mad I wanted to kill him," she wrote. "But I got on my feet and stumbled downstream once more. Pretty soon we caught up with McCollom."

Margaret wasn't someone who easily admitted that she was wrong, but almost immediately she felt regret. McCollom had been steadfast and strong, guiding and helping them even as he suppressed his emotions about his brother's death, which Margaret suspected hurt more deeply than her burns. She told her diary: "It shames me to the core to think that even in hysteria, I doubted him for a moment."

BACK IN HOLLANDIA, the *Gremlin Special*'s failure to return to the Sentani Airstrip had sent shock waves through Fee-Ask headquarters. The plane's absence and the lack of radio communication almost certainly meant a crash, and a crash meant a search. From the outset, the mindset at Fee-Ask was a rescue mission, aimed at finding survivors, as opposed to a recovery effort, aimed at returning remains to families.

As a unit on a large air base, Fee-Ask had almost unlimited access to pilots and planes. The fact that the missing crew and passengers were colleagues, friends, and subordinates of the Fee-Ask brass made it doubly certain the search organizers would have whatever they needed. Raising the ante further were nine special circumstances: the WACs on board.

There's no evidence to suggest that Colonel Ray Elsmore and the other officers at headquarters would have been any less aggressive if everyone aboard was male. But transport planes crashed regularly during the war with no notice from the press. Elsmore, savvy about the ways of reporters, must have known that the WACs aboard the *Gremlin Special* would attract special interest.

SEVERAL HUNDRED U.S. women had already died in World War II, but the numbers are fuzzy in part because some were civilians working with the Red Cross and other relief organizations, and some died in transit to war zones and in accidents on U.S. soil. Of the women who died serving noncombat military roles, many were nurses, including decorated heroes such as Lieutenant Aleda Lutz, a U.S. Army flight nurse who took part in nearly two hundred missions. In November 1944 she was aboard a

C-47 hospital plane evacuating wounded soldiers from a battle-field in Italy when it ran into rough weather and crashed, killing everyone aboard. Thirty-eight U.S. military women who died were members of the Women's Auxiliary Ferrying Squadron, the WAFS, and the Women Airforce Service Pilots, the WASPs, who flew military aircraft on noncombat missions to keep male pilots fresh and available for battle.

Each death of a woman in World War II drew attention, but in most cases the deaths came singly or in pairs. Exceptions included six nurses killed by German bombing and strafing of a hospital area during the battle on Anzio. And just two weeks before the *Gremlin Special* crash, six nurses were among twenty-eight crew members killed when a Japanese kamikaze pilot slammed into the U.S. Navy hospital ship *Comfort* off Leyte Island, between Guam and Okinawa.

The base at Hollandia had suffered only one previous WAC death, in February 1945, when a private from West Virginia drowned while swimming in the Pacific. On the day before her burial, her distraught friends wanted to honor her by flying the WAC flag—a banner of gold and green satin, with a fringe at the edge, its center adorned by the profile of the Greek war goddess Pallas Athena. No such flag existed anywhere in New Guinea. As one Hollandia WAC put it, the materials needed to make one were "as out of their reach as a handful of icicles." Regardless, a group of WACs stayed awake past four in the morning, fashioning a flag from Australian bed-sheets, colored with dyes made from yellow Atabrine antimalaria tablets and red Merthiolate antiseptic ointment pilfered from the infirmary. For the image of Pallas Athena, they used green India ink from the drafting department. For a fringe, they used old para-chute cords. Bleary-eyed, they finished in time for the funeral. They ignored their flag's blotchy colors and irregular size, its makeshift fringe and rough edges, saluting proudly as it waved in the warm breeze for their lost friend.

That was the reaction to the death of one drowned Hollandia WAC. Now nine Hollandia WACs were missing and feared dead in the island's wild interior.

AFTER THE *GREMLIN SPECIAL* missed its estimated return time, calls were made to Allied landing strips throughout the region to see if Colonel Prossen and Major Nicholson had unexpectedly landed the C-47 elsewhere. That proved fruitless, so Fee-Ask planners hauled out their admittedly inadequate maps and divided the island into sectors where the pilots might have made what they euphemistically called "a forced landing."

Though hampered by incessant rain, airborne searchers spent three days scouring those sectors. In all, twenty-four planes took part—a squadron of C-47s, a C-60 transport plane, and a flock of heavy bombers, including B-24 Liberators, B-25 Mitchells, and a B-17 Flying Fortress. A volunteer crew member on one of the search planes was Corporal James Lutgring, hoping against hope that he might rescue his best friend, Melvin Mollberg, who'd taken his place on the *Gremlin Special*.

Overseeing the rescue effort was Colonel Elsmore, who knew the area around the Shangri-La Valley better than anyone else in the U.S. military.

AT AROUND ELEVEN Wednesday morning, May 16, after five hours of trudging through the stream, McCollom climbed up the eight-foot bank.

"Come on," he called, "this is it."

Decker scrambled up, dragging Margaret behind him. On flat ground at the top, she fell face-forward onto the earth, unable to take another step. Decker and McCollom went ahead while she crawled after them on her hands and knees. A half hour later, she reached the spot fifty yards from the stream where Decker and McCollom lay panting on the ground. Margaret sprawled next to them, catching her breath. Feeling the warmth of the sun's rays, she noticed that for the first time in days she could see a wide expanse of sky. They'd reached their goal, a clearing in the rain forest atop a small knoll.

Within minutes, the survivors heard the roar of four powerful engines. They looked up to see a B-17 bomber, its unmistakable shape silhouetted high overhead against the blue sky. The trio waved to draw its attention, but the pilot of the Flying Fortress flew away without spotting them. They rested and ate what passed for lunch, disappointed by the near miss but heartened by the sight of the plane.

An hour later, either the same B-17 or another just like it made another pass over the clearing. This time McCollom wasn't taking any chances. He jumped to his feet.

"Get out the tarps!" he shouted.

McCollom and Decker raced to untie their supplies and spread out the yellow tarpaulin covers they'd salvaged from the *Gremlin Special*'s life rafts. The B-17, with Captain William D. Baker at the controls, was flying over the jungle at high altitude. Along with his usual crew, Baker had brought along an unusual passenger for a heavy bomber: Major Cornelius Waldo, the Catholic chaplain at the Hollandia base.

Margaret worried that the pilot would miss them again and declare that sector of the mountain fully searched, with no sign of wreckage or survivors. She begged her companions to hurry.

Just when it seemed to the survivors that the B-17 was about to fly away, Captain Baker turned the big bomber and circled back over the clearing. Still, Baker gave none of the traditional signs that he'd seen them. McCollom called to the sky:

"Come on down, come on down and cut your motors," he cried. "Cut your motors and dip your wings."

Margaret chimed in: "I know they see us, I know they do."

Decker added a note of optimism: "They see us by now."

Even though Baker was flying high above the clearing, he couldn't mistake the survivors for any natives that might be around. One obvious distinction was that all three wore clothing. But the real giveaway was the tarp. Less than five minutes after the survivors spotted the B-17, the B-17 returned the favor. Baker raced his engines. He dipped his wings.

They'd been found.

McCollom had made the right call when he'd ordered them to leave the crash site and march down the mountain and through the icy stream. As one pilot experienced in jungle searches described it, "An airplane going into the trees makes a very small gash in a limitless sea of green." By leading them to a clearing and laying out the bright yellow tarpaulin, McCollom had given them a shot at being rescued.

Later, a funny thought struck him: a life raft designed for ocean survival had saved them in the middle of a jungle.

UNBEKNOWNST TO THE survivors, they weren't alone. Hiding in the nearby jungle was a group of native men and boys from a nearby village, among them a boy named Helenma Wandik. "I watched them," he recalled. "I saw them in the clearing, waving."

BARELY ABLE TO stand just a short time earlier, now Margaret, McCollom, and Decker jumped up and down. They danced and screamed and waved their weary arms. For the first time since they'd sat in the *Gremlin Special*, they laughed.

Baker wagged the B-17's wings again to be sure they'd seen him. He logged their position by longitude and latitude, then had his crew drop two life rafts as markers as close as possible to the clearing. With a violent thunderstorm moving toward the valley, no more flights could be made at least until morning. As Baker flew out of sight, heading toward the island's northern coast, he radioed a message to the Sentani Airstrip: three people in khaki, waving, spotted in a small clearing on the uphill side of a forested ridge, about ten air miles from the valley floor.

"We'll probably be back in Hollandia by Sunday," said Decker, who by then had dropped back to the ground.

"Hollandia, here I come," Margaret replied.

She wrote in her diary that she planned a do-over for having stood up her swimming date, Sergeant Walter Fleming. In her daydream, Wally would sit adoringly at her hospital bedside, holding her hand and telling her how brave she'd been. Knowing that she'd be teased, she didn't share that vision with McCollom or Decker.

Meanwhile, Decker displayed a dry wit. Affecting a glum tone, he told McCollom, "I suppose one of us will have to marry Maggie and give this adventure the proper romantic ending."

McCollom joined the act. He appraised the injured, worn, and tired WAC. After looking her up and down, he delivered the punch line: "She'll have to put on more meat before I'm interested."

Margaret puffed herself up and defended her injured pride: "I wouldn't marry you if you were the last man in the world. I'm going to marry Decker!"

Decker, who'd been turned down by Margaret for a date weeks before their flight, wouldn't give her the last word. But stumped for a snappy comeback, he blurted: "The hell you are!"

Relieved, they sat together on the ground and wondered how long it would take until more planes returned with supplies. Above all, Margaret wanted real food, so they could throw away "the damn hard candy."

AS THE SURVIVORS lounged and chatted in the clearing, the thought occurred to Margaret that the jungle hadn't spontaneously stopped growing there. Someone had painstakingly cut down the trees and dragged out the shrubs. They were sprawled in a mountainside garden of sweet potato, or *camote*, mixed with a smattering of wild rhubarb.

Eventually, the garden's owner or owners would come to tend or harvest it, and that could mean trouble. But returning to the stream wasn't an option, and neither was leaving the place where they'd been spotted by the B-17. They'd hunker down and pray for the best. Maybe the gardeners lived far away and only rarely visited this particular field. They had no choice but to wait and hope.

Their wait didn't last long.

An hour after the B-17 flew off, the jungle came alive. They heard the sounds they'd thought were the yaps and barks of a far-away pack of dogs.

"Do you hear something funny?" Decker asked.

The sounds grew closer. The creatures making them were human.

The survivors had no idea how they'd fight off wild dogs. But they preferred that prospect to the seven-foot flesh-eating, head-hunting, human-sacrificing natives they'd expected to see only from the air, through the windows of the *Gremlin Special*.

Their assets and weaponry consisted of a lanky sergeant with painful burns and gaping head wound, an undersize WAC with gangrenous burns, and a hungry lieutenant with a broken rib and a Boy Scout knife. It wouldn't be much of a fight.

It seemed to Margaret that more voices joined the strange chorus. The survivors told each other optimistically that maybe the yapping was the noise that native children made when they played. Or maybe the people making the sounds would continue on their way in the jungle and pass them by altogether. But Margaret worried that the rising number of voices meant that "the signal had spread that a tasty dinner was waiting in the camote patch."

Still they saw no one, even as the sound was upon them. No longer did it seem to come from everywhere. It rose from the far edge of the garden clearing, across a gully some twenty-five yards away.

The jungle rustled and shook. As the survivors stared helplessly in that direction, their fears took human form: dozens of nearly naked black men, their eyes shining, their bodies glistening with soot and pig grease, their hands filled with adzes made from wood and sharpened stone, emerged from behind the curtain of leaves.

10

EARL WALTER,

JUNIOR AND SENIOR

GOOD NEWS RACED through the ranks at Fee-Ask.

Word that Captain Baker had spotted survivors in the jungle near the Shangri-La Valley sent Colonel Elsmore and his Hollandia staff into high gear. Baker had only seen three khaki-clad people in the clearing, but his B-17 was only over the area for a few minutes, flying at high altitude. He couldn't communicate with the people he saw, and he didn't spot any wreckage. There was room for optimism. If three were alive, why not all twenty-four?

Maybe Colonel Prossen had somehow been able to set down the *Gremlin Special* intact in an emergency landing. Maybe the three survivors that Baker saw were an advance party, and others who'd been aboard the C-47 were hurt but alive at the crash site. Or maybe they'd split up, as the *Flying Dutchman* survivors had done, with some heading in another direction in search of help.

Those hopes found expression in material form. Elsmore's team assembled what one observer called "enough equipment to stock a small country store." Supply crews attached cargo parachutes to crates filled with essentials such as ten-in-one food rations, blankets, tents, first-aid kits, two-way radios, batteries, and shoes. Having spotted what looked like a WAC on the ground, they included less conventional jungle survival necessities including lipstick and bobby pins. Not knowing how many among the crew and passengers had survived, the would-be rescuers assembled enough provisions to feed, clothe, and temporarily house all twenty-four.

Excitement aside, Elsmore and his command staff knew they faced a serious problem: They had no idea how to reach the survivors, and worse, they had no idea how to get them back to Hollandia. If there'd been a way to land a plane in Shangri-La and take off again, Elsmore almost certainly would have done so already. He probably would have brought reporters along, to record him subduing or befriending the natives, possibly both, perhaps while planting a flag with his family crest to claim the valley as his sovereign territory.

Dutch and Australian authorities, who'd been in contact with Elsmore throughout the search, offered help and expertise outfitting an overland trek. But that idea was nixed when it became apparent that such an expedition would require scores of native bearers and an undetermined number of troops to defend against hostile tribes and thousands of Japanese soldiers hiding in the jungles between Hollandia and the survivors. Even more problematic than the cost in manpower and equipment, it might take weeks for marchers to reach the valley, and by then any survivors might be dead from their injuries or at the hands of natives or enemy troops. Even if the crash victims survived the wait, they might lack the strength for a month-long march over mountains and through jungles and swamps back to Hollandia.

Helicopters were raised as a possibility, but were almost as quickly shot down. As far as the Fee-Ask planners knew, helicopters wouldn't be able to fly at the necessary altitudes—the air was too thin for their blades to generate the necessary lift to carry them over the Oranje Mountains.

Still under consideration were rescue pilots from the U.S. Navy who could land a seaplane on the Baliem River. Also on the drawing board were plans worthy of Jules Verne involving lightweight planes, blimps, gliders, and U.S. Navy PT boats that could operate in shallow water and might reach the interior by river. If a submarine had been available or remotely feasible, someone on Elsmore's team no doubt would have suggested that, too.

But every idea had logistical flaws, some worse than others, so a rescue plan would have to wait. Elsmore's immediate concern was getting the survivors help on the ground. Presumably some were wounded, so they needed medical care. Equally urgent, considering the stories about the natives, the survivors needed protection. One solution would be to drop in a team of heavily armed paratroopers, soldiers as well as medics, who wouldn't mind—or at least wouldn't fear—being horribly outnumbered by presumably cannibalistic native "savages."

One challenge would be finding volunteers for such a mission. A bigger problem would be availability. Infantry-trained paratroopers were in the thick of the fight. As far as Elsmore and his staff knew, none were anywhere near Hollandia.

The Southwest Pacific region hosted two storied airborne units, the 503rd and the 511th Parachute Infantry Regiments. Both had played major roles in the Pacific war, most notably and heroically in the Philippines. Three months earlier, in February 1945, the 503rd had recaptured the island of Corregidor and helped General MacArthur make good on his promise to return to the Philippines. That same month, on the island of Luzon, the 511th had carried out a lightning raid twenty-four miles behind enemy lines that freed more than two thousand American and Allied civilians, including men, women, and children, from the Los Banos Internment Camp.

Both airborne regiments were still committed to combat in the Philippines, and winning the war took precedence over fetching a handful of survivors from a sightseeing crash in the New Guinea jungle.

When it looked as though they'd run out of paratrooper options, an idea struck one of Elsmore's planners, a bright young officer named John Babcock.

Before the war, Babcock taught biology and chaired the sci-

ence department at a private military high school in Los Angeles. When the United States entered the war in December 1941,
he traded his chalk for the rank of lieutenant colonel in the U.S.
Army. His science background led to his assignment as Fee-Ask's
chemical warfare officer.

A few weeks before the crash, Babcock learned that one of
his former students was based in Hollandia. Babcock knew two
things about this particular young man: C. Earl Walter Jr. First,
he'd been expelled from school as a troublemaker, and second, he
was now an infantry-trained paratrooper, frustrated about being
stuck in Hollandia.

C. EARL WALTER Jr.'s boyhood revolved around his father, C.
Earl Walter Sr.

Most of that boyhood was spent
in the Philippines, where the elder
Walter had moved his wife and
toddler son from Oregon to take
a job as a lumber company executive. Before the boy was nine, his
mother fell ill with malaria. She
returned to the United States for
treatment, but she so missed her
husband and son that she took the
next boat back to the Philippines.
She died several months later.

That left just C. Earl Walter,
senior and junior. Neither cared
for the name Cecil, so both went
by Earl. In the midst of the Depression, father and son lived on
the southern Philippines island of
Mindanao, in a big house with a

CAPTAIN C. EARL WALTER JR. (PHOTO
COURTESY OF C. EARL WALTER JR.)

full-time cook and a couple of native houseboys who saw to their every need. The younger Earl Walter had a small horse and his own little boat, and lots of friends who lived in the barrio near his home. He was smart, but with so many distractions and a busy father, school was a low priority. So low, in fact, that for two years Earl Junior didn't attend. He preferred to go with his father into the wild reaches of the island on lumber surveying trips. His favorite boyhood memory came from one of those trips.

"We had been hiking all day, and we found this little glade in the forest, and there was a little creek that had formed a pool," Walter recalled. "So he and I took our clothes off and we got in the water and splashed around just to get rid of the sweat. We were both naked, and when we got out of the water, it was so funny because the natives were standing two or three deep around the pool. Dad asked our guide what that was all about, and he said, 'They're just curious to see if you're white all over.' "

By the time he was fourteen, the tall, handsome white boy with wavy brown hair, blue-gray eyes, and a well-off father was even more of a curiosity, especially among the local girls. And vice versa. "At that age you're old enough to wonder about women," Walter explained. "You wonder what it's like."

Walter's father saw where things were headed, and he didn't like the direction. Above all, he worried that his only child wasn't getting much of an education. He had remarried after his wife's death. His new wife's mother, who lived in Portland, Oregon, was willing to take charge of Earl Junior. Among other benefits, the move would give the boy a chance to catch up to his American peers in school. It's possible that Earl Senior had other concerns, too. Even before Pearl Harbor, the elder Walter feared a Japanese invasion. "When I was growing up with Dad, he used to say, 'I'm going to put a machine gun over there, and a machine gun over there, and when the Japs come, we'll be ready for them.' "

Earl Junior returned to the States, first to his stepgrandmother's house and then to the care of his paternal grandmother, who did her best to spoil him. His father decided that a firmer hand was needed: "I think Dad felt that I needed a military school to go to, and that might straighten me out."

Earl Junior shipped out to the Black-Foxe Military Institute in Los Angeles, a high-toned private academy complete with a polo team. Located between the Wilshire Country Club and the Los Angeles Tennis Club, Black-Foxe provided a useful place for movie stars to stash their wayward sons. At various times, the Black-Foxe student body boasted the sons of Buster Keaton, Bing Crosby, Bette Davis, and Charlie Chaplin. Chaplin's son Sydney once described Black-Foxe as "a sleep-away school for the sons of Hollywood rich people."

There, Earl Junior grew into his full height of six-foot-four and became an All-American swimmer, backstroking his way onto a record-setting relay team. One class he especially liked was biology, which meant that he skipped it less often than the others. His biology teacher was a future U.S. Army lieutenant colonel named John Babcock.

For the most part, Earl Senior's get-tough plan backfired. Earl Junior wasn't a malicious teen, but he found endless ways to avoid studying: "It didn't straighten me out. In fact, I learned more bad habits there than I did anywhere."

His stepmother had made the mistake of setting up a generous allowance to ease the transition into a new school. Black-Foxe administrators controlled the money, but Earl found a clever way around that barrier. Drawing on his school account, he spent lavishly at the school store on notebooks and other supplies. Then he'd sell them for half price to other students, for the cash. Even with the discounts, "I had more money than I knew what to do with."

"What kind of trouble did I get into? Well, I was always looking for female companionship," the younger Earl Walter recalled. "I had a bosom buddy named Miller, and we'd go to downtown Los Angeles, just hitchhike down to the bars. If you had money in those days and you were tall enough, they served you liquor. So I'd always have a couple of gin drinks. There was one area of L.A. where the burlesque shows were. Miller and I liked to look at naked women, so that's where we'd go."

Black-Foxe decreed that young Earl was a "bad influence" on the other boys and kicked him out. He returned to his grandmother's house and finished high school in Portland. By then he was nearly twenty. "I heard that quite a few parents told their girls to stay away from Earl Walter because, what the hell, I was old enough to chase women and liked it."

One girl he dated introduced him to her friend Sally Holden. Her mother wasn't keen on Earl, but Sally was. "She was a beautiful gal," he said, "and we mutually fell in love. Once we started going steady, I had no interest in anybody else."

EARL SPENT TWO semesters at the University of Oregon before being drafted in August 1942, when he was twenty-one. He went to officer candidate school and underwent parachute training at Fort Benning, Georgia. Just before he was about to ship out for the European front, as a junior officer in the infantry, Army Lieutenant C. Earl Walter Jr. received unexpected news about his father. The last he'd heard from Earl Senior was a letter in 1941, just before Pearl Harbor, in which his father wrote that he'd "most likely stay on in the islands in the event that war came."

As a U.S. territory, the Philippines sent a resident commissioner to Washington to represent its interests, without a vote, in Congress. At the time, the resident commissioner was Joaquin Miguel "Mike" Elizalde, a member of one of the Philippines' richest families. The Elizaldes held an interest in the lumber company where the elder Earl Walter was an executive. Mike Elizalde learned that Earl Senior had followed through on his plan to remain in the Philippines when war came. Rather than surrender and face internment or death, or try to flee to Australia or the United States, Earl Senior took to the jungles of Mindanao. There he led a resistance force of Filipino guerrilla fighters. Earl Senior's bravery earned him praise, medals, and the rank of major in the U.S. Army, on his way to being commissioned a lieutenant colonel.

A book about a fellow guerrilla leader in the Philippines described the elder Walter as a "tough, no-nonsense warrior" and "a leathery man in his fifties . . . ready with his fists." It said he'd been honored for bravery under fire in World War I and picked up where he left off during World War II. Walter and his guerrilla troops "mounted as vicious a close-in infantry action as men have fought"—ambushing Japanese soldiers along a coastal road and patrolling the streets of Japanese garrison towns at night.

Mike Elizalde, the Philippines' resident commissioner in

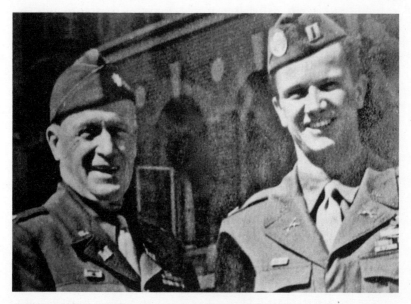

C. EARL WALTER, SENIOR AND JUNIOR. (PHOTO COURTESY OF C. EARL WALTER JR.)

Washington, sent word to the younger Walter to let him know that his father was alive, well, and fighting the Japanese. Walter told one of his commanding officers at the time that Elizalde "gave me enough information of my father to at least stop my fears for his safety and make me proud of his work."

The news about his father had another effect: C. Earl Walter Jr. lost interest in battling Germans and Italians in Europe. In a report filed at the time, a lieutenant colonel quoted Walter as saying that he didn't know many specifics of his father's guerrilla fighting, but it was "enough to make me envy the type of work he was doing."

With help from Elizalde, Lieutenant Walter volunteered for a special commando and intelligence unit, the 5217th Reconnaissance Battalion, made up almost entirely of Filipino-American volunteers. The idea was to insert Filipino-American soldiers onto one of the Japanese-held islands by submarine or parachute, under the theory that they could immediately blend in among the native civilians. Once there, members of the unit would organize guerrilla operations and direct supply drops for resistance fighters. That sounded ideal to C. Earl Walter Jr.

Having grown up in the Philippines, Walter knew the culture and the Visayan dialect, which made him an ideal officer for the 5217th. As a qualified paratrooper, he was a natural to establish a jump school for the battalion outside Brisbane, Australia, known as Camp X. Best of all, when he got to the Philippines, he could fight alongside his father. That was the plan, at least.

After marrying Sally, Walter shipped out in early 1944 and got to work turning members of the 5217th Recon into qualified paratroopers—occasionally with amusing results. The U.S. Army used large parachutes, and many of the Filipino-American soldiers weighed less than a hundred and twenty pounds. After jumping, they'd float around in the air currents. "This one little guy kept yelling, 'Lieutenant, I'm not coming down!' " Eventually he did, and afterward one of Walter's sergeants fitted smaller men with weighted ammunition belts to speed their descent.

In July 1944, upon his arrival in the South Pacific, Walter filled out a duty questionnaire for officers. He immediately sought a "special mission" in the Philippines prior to the anticipated Allied invasion. He explained his reasoning more fully in a long, bold memo to his new commanding officer. In it, he detailed his upbringing in the Philippines and his knowledge of the islands and its languages, and described his father's work and his own ambitions. "In short," he wrote, "I have an intense hatred for the Jap and came to this theater hoping to join a combat parachute unit and do my bit in their extermination."

Later in the memo, Walter wrote that he would perform to the best of his ability in a noncombat intelligence or propaganda mission, but only if he were denied a posting in the heart of the action. Though he had yet to fire a shot in anger, Walter believed he knew how he would react if and when the opportunity arose. Despite his discipline and training, Walter wrote, he might not be able to restrain his trigger finger in a noncombat assignment. "My only desire is that I be given a job which would involve possible contact with the enemy, as I am afraid my liking for combat with the Jap might run away with itself when it should be curbed."

His thirst for battle notwithstanding, Walter's unit was left out of the invasion of the Philippines and MacArthur's return to the islands in October 1944, which came some three months after Walter had appealed for a role in the fight. Even as the battle for control of the Philippines continued, Walter and his men remained at ease. Ill at ease would be more accurate.

While suppressing his frustration and biding his time for a meaningful assignment, Walter worked with members of the battalion who were secretly brought to the islands by submarine for intelligence missions. One submarine trip was to the island of

Mindanao, and Walter went along. When he arrived at the land-ing place, he climbed out of the sub to find a surprise: his father was waiting there to greet him. Walter was thrilled—he hadn't seen Earl Senior for seven years, since he'd been sent to the United States to finish high school far from the Filipinas.

But his happiness was short-lived. The elder Walter told his son that he didn't want him taking part in more secret missions, by submarine or any other conveyance. Earl Senior also said that he intended to let higher-ups in the U.S. Army know his wishes. As far as C. Earl Walter Sr. was concerned, the Allies would have to win the war without the help of C. Earl Walter Jr.

11

UWAMBO

WHEN CAPTAIN BAKER and his B-17 crew reported seeing three survivors in a jungle clearing, they didn't mention any natives nearby. Even if they'd spotted the tribesmen approaching Margaret, McCollom, and Decker from the surrounding jungle, they couldn't have done anything about it. They weren't about to start shooting, they couldn't land, and they had neither paratroopers nor weapons to drop to the trio.

The *Gremlin Special* survivors were on their own, and they were about to experience a first encounter with the people of Shangri-La.

MARGARET, MCCOLLOM, AND DECKER had crash-landed in a world that time didn't forget. Time never knew it existed.

In their isolation, the people of this so-called Shangri-La followed an idiosyncratic path. They had tamed fire but hadn't discovered the wheel. They caked their bodies with clay when mourning but had never developed pottery. They spoke complex languages—the verb that meant "hit" or "kill" could be inflected more than two thousand ways—but had a single word to describe both time and place: *O*. Their only numbers were one, two, and three; everything beyond three was "many." In a world awash in color, they had terms for only two: *mili*, for black, maroon, dark browns, greens, and blues; and *mola*, for white, reds, oranges, yellows, light browns, and reddish purples.

They ornamented themselves with necklaces and feathers but created no lasting works of art. They believed the moon was a man and the sun was his wife, but they ignored the stars that hung low in the night sky. Four hundred years after Copernicus declared that the earth revolved around the sun, people in and around the Baliem Valley thought the sun revolved around them. They believed it crossed the sky by day, spent the night in a sacred house, then traveled underground to its starting place at dawn. The moon had a house of its own.

They feared the ghosts of their ancestors but worshipped no gods. They were gentle with children but hacked off girls' fingers to honor dead relatives. They treated pigs as family—women nursed piglets when needed—but slaughtered them without remorse. They built thirty-foot-tall watchtowers, but their only furniture was a funeral chair for the dead. They grew strong tobacco but never distilled their crops into liquor. They practiced polygamy, but men and women usually slept apart. They valued cleverness but not curiosity. Loyalty had special significance. To greet close friends and relations, they said *Hal-loak-nak*, "Let me eat your feces." Its true meaning: "I will do the unthinkable for you."

The sixty thousand or so natives in the main valley, and tens of thousands more in the surrounding areas, organized themselves into communities consisting of small fenced villages or hamlets. Most had thirty to fifty people living communally in huts arranged around a central courtyard, though larger villages might have several times that number. Men of the hamlet usually slept together in a round hut that was generally off-limits to women. Women lived with children in other round huts and worked together in a long, oval cooking house. Pigs lived in the huts, too, so they would not wander at night or be stolen by enemies.

When they referred to themselves, the natives of the valley might say they were *ahkuni*, or people. Their enemies were *dili*. Sometimes they'd identify themselves by the name of their neighborhood or clan, or by the name of the big man, or *kain*, who held sway over the military confederation to which their neighborhood belonged. They might describe themselves in relation to the river that wound through the valley: *Nit ahkuni Balim-mege*, or "We people of

DANI TRIBESMEN, PHOTOGRAPHED BY EARL WALTER IN 1945. (PHOTO COURTESY OF B. B. MCCOLLOM.)

the Baliem." Although they were members of the Yali or the Dani tribe, tribal affiliation was less important than neighborhood, clan, and alliance loyalties. Different clans and neighborhoods within the same tribe were often enemies, and Yali and Dani people routinely crossed tribal lines to fight shared enemies.

A walk of a few minutes to an hour might take a resident of any one hamlet to ten or fifteen similar hamlets that comprised a neighborhood. Several neighborhoods that joined together for war made a confederation, and several confederations constituted an alliance of four to five thousand people. Native wars, called *wim*, were fought between alliances. Despite shared language, ethnicity, and culture, alliances nurtured deep, long-standing hostilities toward one another, the original source of which was often unknown. They had always been enemies, and so they remained enemies.

Indeed, hostility between alliances defined the natives' lives. If

covered by a glass roof, the valley would've been a terrarium of human conflict, an ecosystem fueled by sunshine, river water, pigs,
sweet potatoes, and war among neighbors.

Their ancestors told them that waging war was a moral obligation and a necessity of life. Men said, "If there is no war, we will
die." War's permanence was even part of the language. If a man
said "our war," he structured the phrase the same way he'd describe an irrevocable fact. If he spoke of a possession such as "our
wood," he used different parts of speech. The meaning was clear:
ownership of wood might change, but wars were forever.

When compared with the causes of World War II, the motives
underlying native wars were difficult for outsiders to grasp. They
didn't fight for land, wealth, or power. Neither side sought to repel
or conquer a foreign people, to protect a way of life, or to change
their enemies' beliefs, which both sides already shared. Neither
side considered war a necessary evil, a failure of diplomacy, or an
interruption of a desired peace. Peace wasn't waiting on the far side
of war. There *was* no far side. War moved through different phases
in the valley. It ebbed and flowed. But it never ended. A lifetime of
war was an inheritance every child could count on.

In the Baliem Valley, the inexhaustible fuel for war was a need
to satisfy spirits or ghosts, called *mogat*. The living built huts for
them, so the spirits would have a place to rest and a hearth to light
their tobacco. The living also designed rituals to please them, believing that the *mogat* could choose to either help or hurt them,
so they had best be kept happy. When a person died in war, his
or her friends and family sought to mollify his or her spirit. That
required killing a member of the hated enemy—a male warrior, a
woman, an elder, even a child. It could happen on the battlefield
or in a raid on a sweet potato patch. Until the spirit was satisfied,
the survivors believed that their souls were out of balance, and the
mogat of the fallen would torment them with misfortune. Once
they settled the score, they'd celebrate with dancing and feasting.

Sometimes those rituals included cooking and eating the flesh of their enemies. While the successful warriors and their families celebrated, their enemies cremated their dead, held elaborate mourning rituals, and began plotting a turn of events. Because combatants on both sides shared the same spiritual beliefs, one side or the other always had a death to avenge, a retaliatory killing to plan, a ghost to placate. An eye for every eye, ad infinitum.

Pacifying ghosts was the main rationale for war, but it wasn't the only one. In an isolated valley where people enjoyed generally good health and abundant food and water, a place with temperate climate and no seasons, where nothing seemed to change, war animated communities and bound people to one another. It satisfied a basic human need for festival. War deaths and their resulting funerals created obligations and debts, shared enmities and common memories. Occasionally war led to changes among allies, which freshened everyone's outlook, for good or ill. War also had a practical benefit for some: warrior deaths meant fewer men, which allowed male survivors to take multiple wives without creating villages filled with unhappy bachelors.

DANI TRIBESMEN, PHOTOGRAPHED BY EARL WALTER IN 1945. (PHOTO COURTESY OF B. B. MCCOLLOM.)

The practice of war in the valley was as unusual as its principles. Battles were arranged by calling out an invitation to the enemy across a no-man's-land. If the enemy declined, everyone went home. They fought only by day, to prevent mischievous night spirits from getting involved. They canceled battles in bad weather, lest the rain smear their war paint. Their war whoop wasn't a predator's cry but the hoot of a cuckoo dove. They put feathers in their hair but not on their arrows; when fired, the arrows traced jagged patterns, like birds in flight. During breaks in battle, warriors lounged, sang, and gossiped. They knew details about their enemies' lives, and hurled insults across the front lines. A nasty remark about an enemy's wife might reduce both sides to belly laughs. Then they'd pick up their spears and try again to kill one another.

Because success in war was seen as necessary for the well-being of the community, men who succeeded in battle gained social standing. Skilled warriors had access to more potential wives. This was especially valuable in a culture in which married couples routinely abstained from sex for up to five years after the birth of a child. But it would be wrong to overstate the link between war, polygamy, and abstinence. For many men, war was its own reward, a source of pleasure and recreation, a platform on which to find excitement and camaraderie. A sporting good time, with a reasonable chance of injury or death. Paradoxically, when villagers were not waging war, life tended to be serene, punctuated by occasional conflicts over pig theft and marital discord. Among friends and family, the most common way of coping with conflict wasn't violence but avoidance—one party would simply move away.

War had few apparent benefits for women. It hung over every journey a woman's male kin made from their village and each trip she and her daughters made to the gardens or to the brine pools to collect salt, where an enemy raiding party might set upon them.

War shaped children from their earliest memories. Boys' education and play involved mimicking male elders waging war and staging raids. Toys were small bows with arrows made from bamboo or long stalks of grass. Grass arrows routinely found their way into boys' eyes, leaving them half blind but no less eager to grow into warriors. For girls, war meant having the upper halves of one or more fingers chopped off each time a close relative was killed, to satisfy the dead person's ghost. By the time a girl reached marrying age, her hands might be all thumbs. An anthropologist who followed the *Gremlin Special* survivors into the valley years later described the process: "Several girls are brought to the funeral compound early on the second day. One man, the specialist in this practice, is waiting for them. First he ties off a girl's arm with a tight string above the elbow. Then he smashes her elbow down on a rock or board, hitting the olecranon process, the 'funny bone,' in order to numb the nerves in the fingers. Someone holds the girl's hand on a board, and the man takes a stone adze and with one blow he cuts off one or two fingers at the first joint."

Making war and appeasing spirits wasn't all the native people did. They built huts and watchtowers, grew sweet potatoes and other vegetables, tended pigs, raised families, and cooked meals. Most of the hard work fell to the women. Men built homes and watchtowers and tilled gardens, which left plenty of time to spare. They devoted that time and energy to war—planning it, fighting it, celebrating its victories, mourning its losses, and planning it anew. In between, they talked about it, sharpened their weapons, pierced their noses so pig tusks would fit into the holes and make them look fierce, and wrapped greasy orchid fibers around their arrows to cause infections if the wounds weren't immediately fatal. They also spent endless hours scanning for enemy movements from the watchtowers on the edge of the vast no-man's-land that separated their homes and gardens from their enemies' identical homes and gardens.

When the anthropologist Margaret Mead learned about the people of the Baliem Valley, she saw a connection between "the distant past and the future towards which men are moving." She wrote: "These are clearly human beings, like ourselves, entrapped in a terrible way of life in which the enemy cannot be annihilated, conquered, or absorbed, because an enemy is needed to provide the exchange of victims, whose only possible end is another victim. Men have involved themselves in many vicious circles, and kingdoms and empires have collapsed because they could find no way out but to fall before invaders who were not so trapped. Here in the highlands of New Guinea there has been no way out for thousands of years, only the careful tending of the gardens and rearing of children to be slain."

By evoking the name of the peaceful paradise in *Lost Horizon*, war correspondents George Lait and Harry E. Patterson had indulged in a calculated fantasy. Their readers longed for a Shangri-La after a daily diet of war news. Yet the reporters couldn't have dreamed up a more ironic name if they'd tried. The Baliem Valley was a beautiful and extraordinary place, but it was no heaven on earth.

COLONEL ELSMORE'S SPECULATION about earthquakes notwithstanding, no one knew how people had come to live in the valley or how long they'd been there. One possibility was that they were descendants of people who'd lived on the island's coast and were driven inland by subsequent arrivals. Equally mysterious was the source of their beliefs and customs.

Yet clues to the past could be found in oral myths told around their fires. The first lines of a Dani creation myth, translated by an outsider, were: "In the beginning was The Hole. Out of The Hole came the Dani men. They settled in the fertile lands around The Hole. Then came pigs. The Dani took the pigs and domesticated them. Next came women, and the Dani took the women." People who lived near the agreed-upon location of The Hole called themselves *iniatek*, the originals.

Another myth described how, after leaving The Hole, humans became separate from other creatures of the valley. At first, the myth explained, humans came out of The Hole with birds, bats, insects, reptiles, and forest mammals. The assembled creatures asked the first man, called Nakmatugi, to differentiate among them. He organized them by type and gave them individual identities. At first he placed the birds and men together. But the birds thought otherwise, so they flew off and left their brothers on the ground.

The natives' belief in an ancient link between man and birds was a recurring theme. The myth of Bird and Snake describes the two creatures arguing about death, immortality, and the fate of mankind. Snake insisted that men should return from the dead, just as snakes could shed their skins and be reborn. But Bird said men should stay dead, like fallen birds, and other birds would smear mud on themselves to mourn. To decide which belief would prevail, Bird and Snake had a race. Bird won, so men, like birds, must die. People took the fable to heart. Women smeared their bodies with mud when mourning, and the weapons, ornaments, and other trophies taken from enemies killed in battle were called "dead birds."

In the natives' myths, mankind's early existence in the valley never featured an earthly paradise or a Garden of Eden. Violent death and hostile alliances dated to the beginning of time. When people emerged from The Hole, one myth claimed, a fight broke out and killings occurred. The victims' families joined forces and said, "Let us take revenge on our enemy together." They did, and when the enemy retaliated, the cycle of war never stopped.

The people of the valley also had a legend called Uluayek. It told of spirits that lived in the sky over the valley, and of a vine that hung down to the ground. Long ago, according to the Uluayek legend, the valley people and the sky spirits climbed up and down the vine to visit one another. Some said the sky spirits had long hair and light skin and eyes. Some said they had hairy arms they kept covered. No one knew for sure, because the spirits had stolen pigs and women, and the people of the valley had cut the vine, ending contact. The Uluayek legend claimed that one day the sky spirits would replace the vine and climb down again.

The spirits' return would herald the End of Days.

THE CLUSTER OF huts the *Gremlin Special* passengers saw shortly before the crash was a village the natives called Uwambo. When the plane first roared overhead, the villagers—members of the Yali tribe—were busy with their daily chores. The sound of the low-flying plane sent them ducking for cover in their sweet potato fields or running to hide in the surrounding jungle, which is why Margaret didn't see any natives near the huts.

The people of Uwambo had seen planes before, especially during the previous year, as Colonel Elsmore and other pilots made regular flights over their homes. Still, the natives didn't know what to make of them. Westerners speculated that the natives thought the planes were giant birds, but the people of Uwambo knew how birds soared and turned and rushed through the sky, silent except for song or cry. Planes didn't look or move or sound like birds. Some native children thought they might be large men with their arms spread. Few if any imagined that they carried people inside.

One thing the natives knew for certain was the sound the planes made. They used their word for noise, *ane*, pronounced "ah-nay," and attached suffixes—*woo* or *kuku*—that approximated the engines' drone. Planes entered the native language as *anewoo* or *anekuku*.

As the passengers aboard the *Gremlin Special* looked through the windows searching for natives, a Yali boy named Helenma Wandik watched the *anewoo* from his hiding place in the jungle. He would always remember that this particular *anewoo* seemed to be flying especially low to the ground. His cousin, a teenage girl named Yunggukwe Wandik, who'd recently been given her first pig, was working in the sweet potato gardens when she saw it. Fearful, she fell to the ground and grabbed the legs of a woman working alongside her.

Both Helenma and Yunggukwe thought the *anewoo* circled twice in the little valley, then pointed its nose toward a place they called the Ogi ridge, near a mountain stream they called the Mundi. Neither saw it plow into the trees, but Helenma wondered why he heard thunder on such a clear day.

WHEN IT GREW dark the night of the crash, the people of Uwambo saw flames coming from the place on the Ogi ridge where the *anewoo* had disappeared. A village leader named Yaralok Wandik crept through the jungle along the spine of the ridge to see what was happening. As he approached, he caught wind of a strange smell. When he reached the edge of the crash site, he watched unseen from the jungle. He saw creatures that resembled people, but they didn't look like any people he'd ever seen. The skin on their faces was light, and they had straight hair. The skin on their bodies was strange. They had feet but no toes. Only later would he learn that coverings called clothing shielded their skin and that footwear called "shoes" encased their toes.

Yaralok left without being spotted. When he returned to Uwambo, he told no one what he'd seen. Several other men did the same. Among them were Nalarik Wandik, whose first name meant "Getting Lost," and Inggimarlek Mabel, whose name meant "Nothing in His Hands." Another man, Pugulik Sambom, went up, too, and among the natives he was perhaps the most disturbed by what he'd seen. Yet at first none of them spread the news about the creatures who seemed to have come from the wrecked *anewoo*.

Their silence fit a cultural idiosyncrasy among the Yali: the bearer of bad news risked being blamed for it. Rather than spread the word about what they knew, the men kept silent. They joined the rest of their hamlet as the frightened people gathered half-ripe sweet potatoes and fled into the jungle.

The next day, Yaralok returned to the crash site and saw what he thought were three men and one woman, though in their odd coverings he couldn't be sure. One man—likely Decker—had a covering on his head that reminded Yaralok of the light-colored markings on the head of a bird. He thought he saw them carrying a body away from what remained of the *anewoo*. He heard popping noises and the sound of small explosions. After watching awhile he crept off again, certain they were spirits from the sky.

To a Yali farmer-warrior from Uwambo, that explanation fit perfectly. Since boyhood, he'd heard the Uluayek legend, which anticipated the return of spirits whose rope to the valley floor had been cut. The legend described these creatures from the *anewoo* perfectly—light skin, long hair, light eyes, arms covered. The *anewoo* made sense, too. In the absence of a rope, the sky spirits had found another way down to the valley. Still, Yaralok was in no rush to share his conclusions.

As his nephew Helenma explained, "Something cataclysmic was happening. He didn't want to create panic or be blamed. These were spirits. The legend said long-haired people would come down from the sky. They were horrified. This could be the End Times. It was something they had been talking about and hearing about for generations."

After other villagers began talking about the flames they'd seen in the jungle, Yaralok broke his silence. To his relief, no one blamed him. They were too busy worrying what the visitors' arrival might portend. One village leader, Wimayuk Wandik, listened especially closely to Yaralok's story.

One option for the people of Uwambo was to welcome the spirits, even if their arrival meant the end of their world as they knew it.

The other option, more natural to a warlike people, was to kill them.

12

WIMAYUK WANDIK, AKA "CHIEF PETE"

THE NATIVE MEN approaching the survivors, residents of Uwambo and nearby villages, had all danced to celebrate the deaths of foes. They'd grieved the loss of family and friends as casualties of war. Some had shed blood in battle and drawn the blood of their enemies. Some had taken a life, or several. All could recount where those deaths had occurred and the names of their fallen foes. Some might have butchered dead enemies and tasted human flesh as a spoil of victory.

"When we killed somebody we'd have a victory dance," said Helenma Wandik, who was a boy at the time. He accused his enemies, a clan called the Landikma, of eating the entire bodies of battle victims. He considered that barbaric. By contrast, Helenma Wandik said, his people only ate the hands of their enemies, severed after death and cooked in a pit with hot rocks.

The bad news, then, was that at least some of the bogeyman stories that Margaret, McCollom, and Decker had heard about the natives eating the flesh of their enemies were true. The nearly naked, adze-wielding men who emerged from the jungle had no qualms about killing. And they had every reason to consider it wise to strike first at strangers.

The natives sorted the world into three useful categories of people: themselves, their allies, and their enemies. They lived or cooperated with the first two. They routinely tried to kill, and avoid being killed by, the third. Margaret, McCollom, and Decker obviously didn't belong to the first two categories. But they also didn't resemble the natives' usual enemies. The survivors didn't know it, but their best hope would be if the people of Uwambo continued to think they were spirits.

One piece of good fortune for Margaret, McCollom, and Decker was that the Yali people of Uwambo weren't among the natives who'd come into contact with the Archbold expedition. They owed no payback to appease the spirit of the man killed by gunshot seven years earlier.

STANDING IN THE native sweet potato garden, separated by a gully and ten thousand years of what's commonly called progress, the survivors and the natives waited for someone to make the first move.

In every immediate way, the natives had the upper hand. They outnumbered the survivors by more than ten to one. They were healthy and well fed. None suffered burns, head injuries, or gangrene. None had lived for three sleep-deprived days on sips of water and hard candy. Their sharpened stone adzes made a joke of McCollom's Boy Scout knife.

Beyond Shangri-La, of course, the situation was different.

By conventional measures of wealth, education, medicine, and technological achievement, the world represented by Margaret, McCollom, and Decker far surpassed the natives' Shangri-La. Yet looked at another way, the survivors' civilization hadn't advanced all that far from the culture of the Stone Age warriors wearing penis gourds. The crash survivors were parts of a military machine engaged in the largest and deadliest war in history, one that was about to become far deadlier.

As the survivors faced the natives, American political leaders were considering the use of a new super weapon, a bomb that could level a city and plunge any survivors into a primitive existence.

The bomb's makers were still uncertain whether it would work, but if it did, it would eerily fulfill the warning in *Lost Horizon* of a future in which "a single-weaponed man might have matched a whole army."

Albert Einstein once said, "I do not know with what weapons World War III will be fought, but World War IV will be fought with sticks and stones." Viewed in that light, the people of Shangri-La were the most advanced warriors on earth.

At the moment, though, Margaret wasn't thinking about the moral and practical relativity of modern and traditional warfare. She stared at the men with the stone-and-wood axes, their dark skin glistening from a coating of pig grease. As she waited for orders from McCollom, a thought ran through her mind: how awful to have survived a plane crash only to end up in a native stew.

AFTER THE B-17 stopped waggling its wings and flew off, Mc-Collom had relaxed for the first time since the crash. Now, as the natives approached, he leaped back into action, barking orders at his companions.

"We haven't any weapon," he told Margaret and Decker, wisely discounting the value of his little knife. "There is nothing we can do but act friendly. Smile as you've never smiled before, and pray to God it works."

McCollom told them to hold out their hands with their remaining Charms—they were sick of the candies by then, anyway. He added his knife to the paltry peace offerings.

"Stand up—and smile," McCollom said.

For the previous hour, since their discovery by the search plane, Margaret and Decker had been sitting in the dirt of the garden clearing. Exhausted and in pain, Margaret was unsure she could stand again. But with McCollom commanding her to rise, she struggled to her feet, as did Decker.

McCollom watched as the natives began to line up behind a

fallen tree, perhaps twenty-five yards from where the survivors stood. By McCollom's count there were about forty of them, all adult males. Margaret, possibly exaggerating in her fright, put the number at more like one hundred. Over their shoulders they carried what she called "wicked-looking stone axes." At least one carried a long spear.

Margaret felt her hand shaking, rattling the Charms like dice. As she put it, "The bottom had long since dropped out of my stomach." She wrote in her diary: "Black heads began to pop out from behind jungle trees. 'Smile, damn it!' rasped McCollom. We smiled. Oh, we smiled to high heaven. We smiled for our lives. We smiled and held out the candy and the jackknife and then we waited as the black men advanced."

McCollom heard one of his companions darkly muse: "Well, maybe they'll feed us before they kill us." He didn't recall who said it, but it sounded like Decker.

The noises the survivors had thought resembled dogs yapping stopped. After a brief pause, the silence was replaced with what Margaret called "an excited and frantic jabbering, accompanied by much gesturing. We couldn't tell whether that was a good sign or bad. We could only fasten the smiles on more securely."

A gully separated the survivors' clearing and a knoll at the edge of the jungle where the natives emerged. A long, fallen tree served as a bridge across the gully. An older man stepped forward. He was wiry and alert, naked except for a necklace with a narrow piece of shell that hung over his sternum and a penis gourd more than a foot long that pointed toward the sky. McCollom and the others took him to be the chief.

He beckoned the survivors forward toward the log bridge. No one moved. He waved them toward him again, more forcefully this time.

"I think we ought to go," McCollom said. "We'd better humor them."

Margaret didn't move. Her feet and legs hurt so badly that she could barely stand. She was sure she'd fall off the slippery log. But that wasn't her only hesitation. She despaired at the thought that, having survived the crash and the march down the mountain, and having just been spotted by a rescue plane, she was being asked to deliver herself to men she thought were savages and, worse, cannibals.

"Honest, McCollom, I can't walk it," she said, "Truly, I can't."

"I know, Maggie," he replied. He considered the situation briefly then decided: "Let 'em come to us."

The survivors used their candy-filled hands to motion the natives toward them. After a brief discussion with his troops, the native leader stepped alone onto the log. McCollom thought it wise to meet him halfway, man to man. If McCollom felt afraid, he'd never admit it. As he inched forward on the log, he called back to Margaret and Decker, demanding that they keep smiling.

The natives on the other side of the gully continued talking and staring at the survivors, until they again fell quiet. "Their silence seemed a thousand times more sinister and threatening than their yapping or their chatter," Margaret wrote. She and Decker stretched their arms forward to more submissively offer their gifts.

The two leaders edged closer on the log bridge. When they met in the middle, McCollom reached out and grasped the native's hand. He pumped it like a cross between a politician, a car salesman, and a long-lost relative.

"How are you? Nice to meet you!" McCollom said repeatedly.

In Margaret's recollection, the native was the one who held out his hand first, and McCollom, "weak with relief, grabbed it and wrung it."

Either way, McCollom turned the leader's attention to the smiling candy-bearers: "Here! Meet Corporal Hastings and Sergeant Decker."

Regardless of who had extended his hand first, the tension was broken, and now both groups were smiling at each other. The native leader shook hands with Margaret and Decker, and in no time the rest of the natives followed suit. Margaret described the moment in her diary: "There on the knoll we held as fine a reception as any ever given by Mrs. Vanderbilt," she wrote. "The black man who never had seen a white man and the white man who never before had met a savage on his own ground understood each other. The smiles had done it."

As her fear ebbed, Margaret sensed that the natives weren't fierce. They seemed shy, perhaps even afraid of the three bedraggled intruders. When she asked Decker if he thought the same thing, he shot back: "Shh, don't tell 'em so!"

McCollom nicknamed his handshake partner "Pete," after a college classmate. The survivors didn't know that "Pete" and his fellow villagers thought they were spirits from the sky. And they never learned "Pete's" real name.

"PETE" WAS WIMAYUK WANDIK, a leader though not a "chief" in Uwambo.

Wimayuk had listened closely to his clansman Yaralok Wandik describe what he saw at the crash site. Although his name meant "Fearful of War," Wimayuk was more cautious than afraid. He'd been in many battles, and he knew the cost of war—his younger brother Sinangke Wandik had been mortally wounded in battle. He and Yaralok Wandik shared the responsibility of calling the men of Uwambo to fight. It was a role he didn't take lightly.

He told his son Helenma Wandik, the second of his five children, that he acted warmly to the creatures he thought were sky spirits because of the way he'd learned the Uluayek legend. Although the spirits' return meant the end of an era, Wimayuk

JOHN MCCOLLOM WITH WIMAYUK
WANDIK SEVERAL WEEKS AFTER THE
CRASH. (PHOTO COURTESY OF B. B.
MCCOLLOM.)

Wandik believed that something good could come of it. He hoped the new era might be better for his people.

Also, Wimayuk Wandik was a man willing to be flexible when an opportunity presented itself. He and his fellow villagers were traders, regularly walking twenty or so miles from their homes to the Baliem Valley lands of the Dani tribe, the heart of what the outsiders called Shangri-La. They exchanged feathers from birds of paradise, string, and bows and arrows for cowrie shells, pigs, and tobacco. If a battle happened to break out while they were trading, they'd join the fight on the side of their trading partners, even if they had no beef with the enemy. It was good for business, and good fun, too. When he found the survivors smiling and offering gifts in the clearing he called Mundima—the place of the Mundi River—Wimayuk saw an opportunity to befriend the spirits.

ALTHOUGH MARGARET CONTINUED to refer to the natives as "savages" in her diary, she realized how much fiction had circulated around Hollandia about the natives:

> Far from being seven feet tall, they averaged from five feet four inches to five feet seven inches in height. And certainly, only on close observation, they didn't look very fierce. They were black

as the ace of spades and naked as birds in feathering time. Their clothing consisted of a thong around their waists, from which a gourd was suspended in front and a huge triple leaf hung tail-like in back. Some wore bracelets above their elbows. There were two kinds of bracelets. Those woven of fine twigs and those made of fur. . . . All but Pete, the chief, wore snoods suspended from their heads and hanging far down their backs. At least they looked like snoods. They seemed to be made of heavy string, like a shopping bag, and they were certainly the New Guinea counterpart of a shopping catch-all. In these snoods, the natives tucked anything they had to carry. After all, they didn't have any pockets.

Margaret wrinkled her nose at the powerful, musky scent of sweat mixed with the ash-blackened pig grease the natives smeared on their bodies: "Pete and his boys certainly needed baths and a lot of rosewater," she wrote. "The breeze was coming from the wrong direction, and I prayed they would get tired of staring soon and go home."

The feeling was mutual, at least about the odor. Wimayuk and Yaralok told their children that the spirits carried a terrible smell. Considering the gangrenous sores on Margaret and Decker, combined with their unwashed days in the jungle, all three survivors almost certainly reeked.

Margaret recoiled at the swarms of flies that hovered around the natives' cuts and scratches. She marveled at the "biggest, flattest feet any of us had ever seen." The survivors thought all the natives at the edge of the jungle were adults, but during the handshakes and greetings Margaret noticed that a group of boys had followed the men—they'd hung back until friendly relations were established.

As the greetings continued, a native started a fire—splitting open a stick and quickly rubbing a rattan vine to make a spark—

to cook sweet potatoes, which the natives called *hiperi*. McCollom bent down and pulled up a plant he thought looked like the rhubarb he'd grown in a garden back home in Missouri. He wiped off the dirt, bit into the stalk, and felt smoke shoot from his ears.

"That's the hottest damn stuff I ever tasted!" McCollom said later. He spit it out—sending the natives into peals of laughter. All except one.

The unamused native began protesting to "Pete" in a way that the survivors interpreted to mean that they'd trampled through his personal garden. Margaret felt afraid of the man, whom she called "Trouble Maker." But "Pete" stepped in.

"The native who had the garden," McCollom recalled, "he apparently started griping to the chief, and the chief, in effect turned around and said, 'Shut up.' And from then on we were friends."

THE UNHAPPY MAN was almost certainly Pugulik Sambom. His objections, according to Yaralok's daughter Yunggukwe, weren't about the ruined crops but about the survivors themselves.

MARGARET HASTINGS WITH A NATIVE CHILD. (PHOTO COURTESY OF B. B. MCCOL-LOM.)

"Pugulik was yelling at everyone that something bad would happen because of the spirits," she said through an interpreter. "He said, 'They're spirits! They're spirits! They're ghosts! Don't go in there with them.' "

Yunggukwe watched as Pugulik paced back and forth on a fallen log, more scared than angry, repeating his warning that the strangers were *mogat*, spirits or ghosts, and certain to bring bad tidings. The woman whose legs Yunggukwe had grabbed in the field when the *Gremlin Special* flew overhead was Pugulik's wife, Maruk, whose name meant "Bad." Maruk echoed her husband's warnings. Fortunately for the survivors, the Wandiks outnumbered the Sambom and welcomed them, spirits or not.

THE SURVIVORS TRIED to get the natives to take McCollom's knife as a gift. They encouraged them to try the Charms.

"They handled the jackknife curiously," Margaret wrote. "We tried to show them that the candy was to eat. We would open our mouths, pop in a piece of hard candy, smack our lips and look rapturous—though we had come to hate it like poison. Apparently they didn't understand us. So we thought we would give the candy to some boys of ten or twelve who had accompanied Pete and his men. But when we started to feed the kids, 'Trouble Maker' danced up and down and shrieked until we backed off in a hurry."

Alarmed, Margaret dug into her pocket for her compact. She popped it open and showed "Pete" his image. Delighted, Wimayuk Wandik passed the mirror from man to man. "If ever anything was calculated to make friends and influence savages, it was that cheap red enamel compact from an Army PX," she wrote. "These naked strangers beamed and gurgled and chattered like magpies over a sight of their own faces."

"Maggie," Decker told her, "you ought to write home to the missionaries to stock up on compacts."

———

PHYSICALLY AND EMOTIONALLY exhausted, her burned legs and feet throbbing, Margaret dropped back down to the ground. A group of natives circled around her, squatting on their haunches and staring. Using her compact, Margaret took stock of herself and understood their curiosity.

She wrote in her diary that not only was she the first white woman the natives had seen, she was "the first black-and-white person they had ever seen." Burns from the crash had darkened the left side of her face, while the right side was unmarked. Her eyebrows and eyelashes had been singed, and her nose seemed swollen. McCollom's jungle salon treatment didn't help—short tufts of Margaret's once-lustrous hair stood at attention all over her head. She didn't know it, but even more interesting to the natives were her bright blue eyes.

As she stared at the natives and the natives stared back, Margaret felt relief. Soon it spread into affection. "At the moment, I could not have loved Pete and his followers more dearly if they had been blood brothers," she wrote. "They had turned out to be a race of Caspar Milquetoasts"—the name of a mild-mannered comic book character—"in black face instead of head hunters or cannibals. I was duly grateful."

McCollom brought "Pete" to Margaret and Decker to show him their injuries. The native leader nodded solemnly. Margaret detected sympathy in his reaction.

"He looked again and muttered, 'Unh, unh, unh,' over and over again. We knew he was trying to tell us he was sorry and wanted to help. The only native word we ever picked up was 'Unh, unh, unh' repeated over and over," Margaret wrote. In fact, *unh* wasn't a word in the Yali or Dani language. It was a murmur, a local equivalent of a polite listener in English saying "Hmmm" to express interest.

"Pete" examined the gash in Decker's scalp. He stepped in close and blew into the cut. Margaret made light of it: "For the first and only time, I thought Decker was going to faint. Old Pete then came over to me and blew on my legs and hand. And I thought I would faint. Pete undoubtedly had the world's worst case of halitosis."

"Decker and McCollom and I came to the conclusion," Margaret continued, "that the blowing of the chieftain's breath on a wound was probably some native cure-all custom, like laying on of hands in other parts of the world. But Decker and I didn't appreciate the honor."

The survivors' conclusion about the practice was close, but it failed to capture the full significance of the moment. Margaret and Decker had just received a remarkable gift, one that signified that the people who'd found them hurt and hungry in a sweet potato patch wanted nothing but for them to survive.

WHEN A YALI or Dani man is wounded in battle, the physical damage is almost a secondary concern. More worrisome is the possibility that the injury might dislodge the essence of his being, his *etai-eken*, or "seeds of singing." A better translation: his soul.

Among people of the valley who enjoy good physical and spiritual health, the *etai-eken* are believed to reside in the upper part of the solar plexus, just below the front arch of the ribs. The native leader's shell necklace, hanging as it did at just that spot, might well have been placed there to protect his *etai-eken*. Under pain or duress, the *etai-eken* are believed to retreat from the front part of the chest to a person's back. Such a move is a spiritual calamity, a threat to an individual's well-being that demands urgent action.

First, a specialist removes any remnants of the arrow or spear that caused the wound. Then he makes several incisions in the victim's stomach to drain what the natives call *mep mili*, or "dark blood," which is believed to cause pain and sickness. Next comes the more essential treatment. A person who is either close to the wounded warrior or especially skilled in the healing arts speaks directly to the man's *etai-eken*. He coaxes the soul matter back to its proper place, blowing and whispering special pleadings in the victim's ear. He also blows directly on the wounds.

A short time earlier, the survivors had feared that they'd be killed and eaten by Wimayuk Wandik, the native they called "Pete." Now he was tending to their souls.

BY MID-AFTERNOON THE survivors were bushed, but the natives were so fascinated by the sky spirits that they showed no sign of leaving. Then, around four o'clock, the cold nightly rains arrived. The natives gathered up the cooked sweet potatoes— "They took the chow with them!" Decker complained—but left the knife, the compact, and the hard candy behind. It would be another starving night for the survivors.

The trio found a smooth spot of cleared ground, laid out one tarp, used the other as a cover, and went to sleep, "too weak to do much and too happy to care," Margaret wrote. They'd scratched their way through the mountain jungle to a clearing, been spotted by a search plane, and made friends with the natives. Margaret summed it up with understatement: "It had been a big day."

When she awoke in the middle of the night, she sensed that someone was hovering over her. Before she could scream, she recognized a man's face: "Pete."

"It was as plain as day that he was worried about us and had come back to see how we were. He hovered over us like a mother hen. I woke up McCollom. He took a good look at Pete and said, 'Holy smoke! We've got a guardian.'"

Later, when she compared notes with McCollom and Decker, Margaret learned that whenever one or the other woke that night, he saw Chief Pete/Wimayuk Wandik watching over them.

13

COME WHAT MAY

BY NOVEMBER 1944, Earl Walter and sixty-six jump-qualified members of the 5217th Reconnaissance Battalion were sweating out the war in "strategic reserve," stuck in steamy but peaceful Hollandia, Dutch New Guinea. The closest thing to excitement came when their battalion was renamed the 1st Reconnaissance Battalion (Special), known as the 1st Recon. The new name did nothing to change their idle fate. Neither did Walter's promotion from lieutenant to captain.

As months passed, Allied forces under General MacArthur kept busy retaking the islands of the Philippines—one after another, from Leyte to Luzon, Palawan to Mindanao. As the fight progressed, paratroopers from the 503rd and 511th regiments carried out their dangerous and heroic missions on Corregidor and Luzon.

All the while, Walter and his men yearned to get out of the heat of Hollandia and into the fire of war. Their battalion's devil-may-care motto was *Bahala na!* a phrase from the Tagalog dialect of the Philippines that can be translated as "Come what may!" The more time passed without a mission, the more it seemed like a taunt. The problem, as Walter and his men saw it, was that nothing came their way.

While awaiting orders in Hollandia—some eighteen hundred miles southeast of Manila—Walter's men pressed him for news.

With families and roots in the Philippines, they wanted the honor and the satisfaction of driving the enemy from their homeland. They craved payback for more than two years of Japanese occupation. They wanted revenge for the Bataan Death March of 1942, during which Japanese troops killed or brutalized thousands of captured Filipino and American soldiers along a forced hundred-mile march to a prison camp. Newspapers had detailed the atrocities, fueling a combustible mix of fear and hatred of the Japanese, perhaps nowhere more so than among the men in Walter's unit. One of them, Corporal Camilo "Rammy" Ramirez, had experienced the horrors at Bataan firsthand before making a daring escape.

Walter tried to boost morale and conditioning, leading grueling runs around Hollandia to keep his men's legs strong for parachute landings. Yet privately, Walter feared it was a waste of time. He worried that he'd spend his life saying, "Nothing much," when asked what he'd done in the war.

"My men would come to me and say—I was a lieutenant then—'Lieutenant, when in hell are we going to get to the Philippines?' " Walter recalled. "And I'd say, 'As soon as I can get us there.' " One hindrance, at least from Walter's perspective, was that the Japanese were retreating faster than expected, potentially making unnecessary his unit's unique language, intelligence, and parachute skills.

Walter proposed one combat task after another to his superiors, to no avail. Showing some moxie, he tried to cut through the U.S. Army bureaucracy by drawing up plans for a behind-enemy-lines parachute drop. He shared the plans with an acquaintance—a lieutenant who happened to be the son of General Courtney Whitney, who oversaw guerrilla resistance in the Philippines and was MacArthur's closest confidant.

When that gambit didn't spark a response, on March 13, 1945, Walter took the next step and wrote a blunt letter directly to General Whitney. In it, Walter complained about being idle and fairly pleaded for combat duty in the Philippines. If that wasn't possible, he wrote, he wanted to be reassigned to a fighting unit in Europe or anywhere at all before it was too late and the war was already won.

"As you know, Sir," Walter wrote the general, "I came to this theater at my own request, in fact I worked hard for the assignment, but now I find that my efforts were in vain." After making his case, he acknowledged that he'd violated protocol and jumped multiple levels in the chain of command by sending the letter. "In closing may I add that I admit I have stepped over the line but I am afraid this is a trait I inherited from my father."

Whitney seemed to admire Walter's pluck. He responded two weeks later with a letter filled with praise and encouragement. The brigadier general gently explained to the young officer that matters more pressing than personal ambition—however courageous or well-intentioned—took priority in the effort to reclaim the Philippines. Whitney urged Walter to keep his men ready to invade Japan, and offered flattery and morale-building suggestions. "The work of the Battalion and the preparation of your parachutists for active service has been brilliant," the general wrote. "Your leadership in this latter field has been cause for much satisfaction on the part of every staff officer of this Headquarters. . . . My advice to you is to do all possible to keep your men in trim and keep patient a little longer. I am sure that your desire for an opportunity to employ these men in the manner for which they have been trained will be fully satisfied in the campaigns which yet lie ahead."

Whitney's letter cheered Walter. He wrote the general in response: "I took the liberty of reading it to my parachutists, and to the man they were overjoyed, and their morale has climbed to a new high. They are all very anxious to do their part, and the work given us, no matter how difficult, I can guarantee will be a complete success. The men will be kept in trim and when our turn comes we will be ready. Thank you for giving the hopes of my officers and men a new foundation and I can easily say for all, you can count on us for anything."

General Whitney returned his attention to the war. Weeks passed with no further word on a role for the 1st Recon, and Walter's excitement ebbed. He grew frustrated to the point of distraction. He became convinced that his father had followed through with the threat he'd made at the submarine landing site. Earl Senior, Walter believed, had voiced concerns about his son's safety, and by doing so had sidelined the paratroopers of the 1st Recon.

"I was an only son, an only child, and I think my dad worried," Walter explained. "My dad was strong enough in the guerrilla movement, and known well enough by people in the Army, that when he said, 'I don't want you using my son overtly,' they listened."

Whether his father had such power is unclear. No records exist to confirm that Earl Senior raised objections to his son's participation in risky duty. But the fact remained that in May 1945, as Captain C. Earl Walter Jr. approached his twenty-fourth birthday, the war seemed to be winding down, and he and his unit were men without a mission.

THE MEN WHO SERVED under Walter in the 1st Recon had a right to be equally upset. Perhaps more so. Every soldier of Filipino descent had followed a difficult road to service in the American military.

The roots of the tangled relationship between Filipinos and Americans dated back nearly fifty years, to 1898 and the Treaty of Paris, which marked the end of the Spanish-American War. The treaty gave the United States control over the Philippines, much to the chagrin of the Filipino people, who ached for independence after three centuries under Spanish rule. But America was feeling its imperialist oats as a world power. President William McKinley declared in his famous if sometimes disputed quote that it was the United States' duty to "educate the Filipinos, and uplift and Christianize them."

Within weeks of the treaty, American and Filipino patrols traded fire on the outskirts of Manila, triggering a forty-one-month clash that became known as the Philippine-American War, the most overlooked conflict in United States history. Before it was over, the United States had suffered more than four thousand combat deaths. The Philippines lost perhaps five times as many soldiers, as well as more than one hundred thousand civilians who died from famine and disease. President Theodore Roosevelt declared victory on July 4, 1902, and the Philippines became a U.S. territory, though skirmishes continued for years. Atrocities by American soldiers were whitewashed, and Roosevelt's secretary of war congratulated the military for conducting "a humane war" in the face of "savage provocation" by "a treacherous foe."

The next three decades saw an influx of Filipino immigrants to the United States, with a majority of the newcomers heading to California and Hawaii. At the same time, a mutually beneficial trading relationship developed across the Pacific. One resource the Americans especially valued was hardwood, which is how C. Earl Walter Sr. came to manage a lumber company in Mindanao. But for many Filipinos, the United States was hardly welcoming. Anti-Filipino sentiment ran high, and Filipinos experienced racially motivated attacks and legal restrictions against owning land. Antimiscegenation laws in western states prevented them from marrying white women. For most, economic opportunities were limited to field work, service occupations, manual labor, and jobs in canneries and factories.

Meanwhile, the drive for independence for the Philippines continued. In 1934 President Franklin D. Roosevelt signed a law establishing a ten-year transition period, at the end of which the Philippines would have its own U.S.-style democracy. Until then, new immigration by Filipinos would be severely limited, and repatriation laws would pressure Filipinos living in the United States to return to the islands.

Then came December 8, 1941. One day after Pearl Harbor, Japan launched a surprise air-and-land attack on the Philippines, centered on the island of Luzon. The outnumbered Filipino and American forces, under General MacArthur's command, quickly withdrew to the Bataan Peninsula and the island of Corregidor, at the entrance to Manila Bay. The U.S.-Philippine forces surrendered in April 1942, and with help from none other than Colonel Ray Elsmore, MacArthur escaped to Australia to begin plotting his return. Surviving American and Filipino troops and the Filipino people weren't so fortunate; they suffered through the Bataan Death March and a brutal occupation.

News of the attacks on Pearl Harbor and the Philippines made Filipinos in the United States eager to fight the Japanese. By then, more than a hundred thousand transplanted Filipinos lived in Hawaii and on the U.S. mainland. But they were in a strange limbo. They were legal U.S. residents, but they weren't eligible for citizenship, so they could neither be drafted nor volunteer for military service.

Individually and through their representatives in Washington, Filipinos petitioned Roosevelt, his secretary of war, and members of Congress for the right to fight. Some wanted to serve for practical reasons, such as the opportunities and benefits they expected would come to veterans after the war. But more spoke of vengeance. Although the United States had been attacked by air at Pearl Harbor, the Philippines had been invaded. Sounding like a colonial recruit in the Revolutionary War, one Filipino volunteer declared, "Life is so small a property to risk as compared to the fight incurred for the emancipation of a country from . . . foul, ignominious, barbaric, inhuman treatments."

Within weeks of the Japanese invasion, Roosevelt signed a

law that allowed Filipinos to join the U.S. military. This led to the creation of the 1st Filipino Battalion, which from the outset was expected to help in the battle to retake the islands through overt and covert action. By May 1942, more than two thousand men of Filipino descent had volunteered. So many new recruits volunteered that the battalion was upgraded to the 1st Filipino Regiment. Soon after, the U.S. Army created a 2nd Filipino Regiment. Eventually, more than seven thousand men of Filipino descent served in the two regiments. Roosevelt rewarded their fervor by making Filipino soldiers in the U.S. military eligible for citizenship, and several thousand took the oath.

An American reporter who caught up with the Filipino-American troops a few months after their induction described them with unreserved admiration: "The men of this Filipino regiment are taking the business of sudden death seriously. Their American officers have commended their amazing conscientiousness and ardor, and have encouraged them to add a purely Filipino fillip to the orthodox warfare methods. In simulated jungle fighting, these sons and grandsons of guerrilla warriors . . . like to creep close to the enemy with bayonets tightly gripped in their mouths, and then jump at him, wielding their bayonets as if they were their native bolos."

In spring 1944, the 2nd Filipino Regiment was merged into the 1st Filipino Regiment and sent overseas as the 1st Filipino Infantry Regiment. Its members made it to the Philippines in February 1945. In one battle on Samar Island, the regiment reported killing 1,572 Japanese soldiers while losing only five of its men. In May 1945, while Walter and his men were still in Hollandia awaiting an assignment, the 1st Filipino Infantry Regiment moved into heavy combat against the Japanese on Leyte Island.

A FEW WEEKS before the crash of the *Gremlin Special*, Walter was invited to lunch by his former military school teacher, Lieutenant Colonel John Babcock. In the officer's mess hall, Babcock listened as Walter told him about the Filipino paratroopers he'd trained for behind-enemy-lines missions. Walter poured out his exasperation at being stuck in New Guinea, unable to find a way into action.

Babcock had taught classes at Black-Foxe Military Institute for six years before joining the Army Air Forces, so he knew when a boy became a man. Walter's transformation couldn't have escaped his notice. Walter still had the slim-hipped, broad-shouldered build of the All-American swimmer he'd been at school. But the class-cutting, undisciplined boy who sold half-price notebooks to classmates to finance visits to strip clubs had become a sober, determined captain in the airborne infantry. If he listened closely, Babcock also must have recognized that Walter was determined to prove to his father, and to himself, that he could lead troops into danger and back out again.

Babcock and Walter left the lunch with a promise to meet again. But before they had the chance, Babcock became involved in planning the rescue of survivors from the *Gremlin Special* crash. He learned that Colonel Elsmore believed that no paratroopers were available in Hollandia.

"When Babcock heard that," Walter recalled, "he said, 'I've got just the people to go in there and get them out.' "

A PARACHUTE DROP into Shangri-La wasn't a combat posting or an intelligence assignment, at least not in a conventional sense. But compared to endless, apparently pointless physical training in Hollandia, it more than fit the bill. When Babcock told him what was happening, Walter leaped at the opportunity. He didn't know what his father would say about the mission, and since the elder Walter was somewhere behind enemy lines in the Philippines, the younger Walter wouldn't worry about asking. Babcock relayed word of Walter's interest up the chain of command.

A series of hastily arranged meetings followed, during which Walter met Elsmore and other senior officers coordinating the search and rescue effort. The meetings were straightforward enough, devoted largely to making certain that Walter understood the situation and the dangers that he and his men would face.

When he'd absorbed the warnings, Walter returned to the tents occupied by his unit. His men gathered around him, the tallest among them a full head shorter than their captain. Even before he began to speak they bustled with excitement, sensing that—at least for some—their months of waiting were over.

When they settled down, Walter explained the situation. Word of the crash had spread throughout the sprawling base, but news of survivors was still trickling through the unreliable pipeline of fact, rumor, and gossip. Walter announced that the paratroopers of the 1st Recon had been chosen for a special mission—to protect survivors of the *Gremlin Special* crash on the

CAPTAIN C. EARL WALTER JR. (BACK ROW, CENTER) AND THE MEMBERS OF THE 1ST RECONNAISSANCE BATTALION OUTSIDE THEIR "CLUB BAHALA NA" IN HOLLANDIA. (PHOTO COURTESY OF C. EARL WALTER JR.)

ground and eventually lead them to safety. He needed ten volunteers to join him, including two medics. But before taking names, he delivered a four-part warning.

First, Walter told them, the area they'd be jumping into was marked "unknown" on maps, so they'd have nothing but their wits and their compasses to guide them.

Second, the two medics would parachute as close as possible to the survivors, into a jungle so thick it would be what Walter called "the worst possible drop zone." He and the eight other volunteers would drop onto the floor of the Shangri-La Valley some twenty to thirty air miles away. There, they'd establish a base camp with the goal of eventually leading the medics and any survivors from the crash site down to the valley.

Third, if they survived the jumps, their band of eleven men would confront what Walter described as "a very good possibility that the natives would prove hostile." Their squad would have the advantage in terms of weapons, but they could expect to be outnumbered by hundreds to one in any confrontation.

Walter saved the worst for last: Fourth, no one had a plan, even a rough one, to get them out of the valley. They might have to hike some one hundred and fifty miles to either the north or south coast of New Guinea, through some of the most inhospitable terrain on earth, with crash survivors who might be hurt and unable to walk on their own. Complicating matters, if they hiked north they'd go through an area "known to be the domain of headhunters and cannibals." If they hiked south, they'd pass through jungles and swamps occupied by perhaps ten thousand Japanese troops who'd been hiding since the Allies captured New Guinea's coastal areas.

Walter didn't mention it, but if they did have to trek their way to the coast, he'd choose to face the Japanese rather than the headhunters. Death seemed a strong possibility either way, but at least they'd go into the fight with a clear idea how Japanese soldiers would react to a group of American paratroopers. Also, unlike the natives, the Japanese wouldn't have home-field advantage. Maybe best of all, being horribly outnumbered by Japanese troops while leading his men in jungle warfare would mean that Walter had followed in his father's footsteps.

As Walter stood before his men, he recognized that each one had his own reasons for being there, whether revenge, patriotism, opportunity, or all three. One quality he knew they had in common was desire. All had volunteered for military service, after which they'd all volunteered for reconnaissance work and paratrooper training. Now Walter was testing them again.

When Walter finished his litany of warnings, he waited a beat, then asked for volunteers. As Walter recalled it, every member of the parachute unit raised his hand. Then each one took a step forward. Walter swelled with pride.

"Bahala na," several said, voicing the battalion's motto. *Come what may.*

14

FIVE-BY-FIVE

AFTER ANOTHER FITFUL night, the survivors awoke at dawn—
Thursday, May 17—still weary, cold, wet, and hungry. Knowing
that more search planes would return to the spot where Captain
Baker tossed out the life rafts as markers, they ate some of their
remaining candies and talked about being rescued. Unaware of
the technical limits, McCollom predicted that the Army Air
Forces would use a helicopter to pluck them from the jungle and
whisk them back to Hollandia in no time. The only obstacles he
anticipated were the trees, but he considered that a minor incon-
venience. "We can clear enough space for it to land," he told the
others.

They spotted the first plane around nine that morning—a
C-47. For the first time, Margaret, McCollom, and Decker could
see what the *Gremlin Special* must have looked like from the natives' perspective before it crashed.

When the plane was over the clearing, a cargo door opened
to deliver its payload: wooden supply crates attached to big red
cargo parachutes. Margaret watched as the first chute blossomed
in the sky like a huge, upside-down tulip. The crate swayed in the
breeze before landing about a hundred yards from the clearing.
McCollom and Decker plunged into the jungle to retrieve it, while

Margaret stayed behind on the relative high ground of the little knoll. She kept busy by taking note of where subsequent chutes and boxes landed.

The two men took a while to drag the crate out, but when Decker and McCollom returned, they bore a prize more precious than food: a portable FM radio that could be used to transmit and receive messages. It was almost certainly a rugged, waterproof thirty-five-pound two-way radio the size of a small suitcase. Developed by Motorola for the Army Signal Corps, the device could be carried on a soldier's back, hence its immortal nickname, the "walkie-talkie." Its design was a milestone that contributed to a revolution in portable wireless communication, but to the survivors its value was immediate and immense.

"McCollom swiftly set it up," Margaret told her diary. "The plane was still circling overhead, and Decker and I were in a true fever as we watched it and then McCollom."

Holding the radio's telephone-like mouthpiece near his lips, McCollom felt emotions welling up that he'd suppressed since crawling out of the burning plane. For the first time since the death of his brother, he found himself too choked up to speak. He had to swallow hard, twice, before his voice returned. "This is Lieutenant McCollom," he croaked finally. "Give me a call. Give me a call. Do you read me? Over."

The answer came back swiftly and clearly. "This is *three-one-one*," said the plane's radio operator, an affable New Yorker named Sergeant Jack Gutzeit, following Army Air Forces protocol by identifying himself by his plane's last three serial numbers. "*Three-one-one* calling *nine-five-two*"—the final serial numbers of the *Gremlin Special*.

Using radio lingo to describe the strength and clarity of a signal, Gutzeit said: "I read you five-by-five"—a perfect connection.

Tears flowing, Margaret looked at her two comrades. Her

companions. Her friends. She saw that McCollom and Decker were crying, too. They were still marooned in the jungle, but they no longer felt quite so alone. Now they had a lifeline to home, or at least a lifeline to a Brooklyn accent aboard a U.S. Army plane circling overhead.

Regaining his composure, McCollom briefly described the *Gremlin Special* flight, the crash, and the aftermath. In doing so, he delivered the heartrending news that Gutzeit would need to relay to his superiors, for dispersal through the ranks and beyond: no other survivors.

The first hopes dashed would be in Hollandia, among the friends and comrades of the twenty-one lost passengers and crew, including Ruth Coster, awaiting word about Helen Kent, and James Lutgring, praying for the safety of his pal Melvin Mollberg. From there, word would spread via Western Union telegrams to blue-star families throughout the United States. Formal letters of sympathy would follow.

A U.S. ARMY flight surgeon aboard the plane named Captain Frank Riley asked McCollom to report their condition. Margaret and Decker knew that their burns had turned gangrenous, and their other injuries were infected or nearly so. Margaret described herself and Decker in her diary as "almost too weak to move."

McCollom wasn't sure what to say, so he looked to them for an answer.

"Tell 'em we're fine," Margaret said.

Decker agreed: "Tell 'em we're in good shape. There's nothing they can do, anyway."

McCollom followed their orders. Only later would they reveal the full extent of their wounds.

The plane, piloted by Captain Herbert O. Mengel of St. Petersburg, Florida, continued to circle overhead. Radioman Jack

Gutzeit told the survivors that a plan was being drawn up to rescue them, but nothing was firmly in place. First, they intended to drop medics by parachute as soon as possible. In the meantime, he assured them, "We're dropping plenty of food. Everything from shrimp cocktails to nuts." Whether Gutzeit was exaggerating about the delicacies wasn't clear, but the survivors never found shrimp in the jungle.

WHEN THE PLANE flew off, the survivors saw that the natives had returned.

"There on the knoll across from us were Pete and his chums," Margaret wrote. "They were squatted on their haunches, grinning and watching us like an audience at a Broadway play." She counted her blessings, with a touch of condescension: "The natives, who might easily have been head-hunters, stood about and watched us with childish pleasure."

The natives made a small fire to warm themselves in the morning chill, and they sat around it, contentedly smoking stubby green cigars. Margaret, McCollom, and Decker looked on with envy. They had cigarettes in their pockets, but McCollom's lighter was spent and their matches were wet. His spirits lifted by the conversation with the men on board the C-47, McCollom told the others, "I think I'm going over and borrow a cup of sugar from the neighbors." He cadged a light, then shared the flame with Margaret and Decker.

"The natives smoked on their knoll and we smoked on ours," Margaret wrote. "No peace pipe ever tasted better."

Margaret began to fantasize about "the luscious Spam and K-rations probably awaiting us within a stone's throw." Despite her hunger, she told her friends, there were certain foods she wouldn't savor: "One is canned tomatoes and the other is raisins," she said. "When I was little I ate myself sick on both, and now I can't stand the sight of either."

McCollom answered: "I could eat the tomatoes, can and all, if I could get 'em."

He rose and marched off in search of the supplies. Margaret appreciated McCollom's endurance and leadership. She was even more impressed by the man shadowing him through the jungle.

"Decker was emaciated, his eyes like burnt holes in a blanket," she wrote. "We knew he was hurt, but just how gravely we were not to discover for a few more hours. How Decker got to his feet I shall never know. But he did, and staggered uncomplainingly after McCollom, determined to do his share of the work."

Although McCollom explained during the radio conversation that there were only three survivors, the C-47 had been packed optimistically, with supplies for two dozen. Their orders were to drop the supplies, and Captain Mengel and his crew had no intention of disobeying. The sky over Shangri-La filled with cargo parachutes.

While Decker and McCollom went off in search of supplies, Margaret worried that the natives might collect boxes of rations she saw falling on the other side of a nearby hill. "I decided to scout that situation," she wrote. "It was excruciating to stand on my burned, infected legs. So part of the way I crawled on my hands and knees. When my infected hand hurt too much, I would sit down and bounce along on the ground."

When she reached the other side of the hill, Margaret was stunned to see a split-rail fence that she thought looked straight out of the Old West. Just beyond it was a native compound. She wrote:

It was an odd and fascinating New Guinea housing project, with one large section and several smaller ones mushroomed around it. The huts were round, with bamboo sides and thatched roofs, and seemed to be at least semi-attached to each other. As for the roofs, they were alive with natives, all craning their jet-black necks for a better look at me. I could see a large-sized hole in one thatched roof. A hunch and a sinking feeling hit me simultaneously. I knew that one of our packages of supplies had gone through one roof. I was right, too, McCollom discovered later. I wondered if the natives were angry about this, or if they might go on the warpath because one of their houses was damaged. But they just stood and stared, entranced by the free show I made. So I decided to leave well-enough alone and go back to my own knoll.

THE CRATE THAT crashed through the roof did no harm beyond requiring new thatchwork. But another crate, dropped without a parachute, permanently embittered one resident of Uwambo toward the sky spirits in her midst.

Yaralok's daughter Yunggukwe, a girl on the cusp of womanhood, had recently become the owner of her first pig. This milestone, and the possession itself, was of immense importance to a Yali girl. So great was the pig's value to Yunggukwe—emotionally as well as, eventually, gustatorily—that its worth could only be exceeded by two pigs.

That morning, she tied her pig to a stake outside her hut, thinking it would be safe there. But when the supply plane roared over Uwambo, the pig had nowhere to run. To save parachute cloth, some of the boxes containing unbreakable items such as tents were pushed freefall out the C-47's cargo door, and such was the case with a crate dropped this day.

There was no evidence of intent, but no pinpoint bombing raid during the war found a mark more squarely. It landed on Yunggukwe's pig, killing it instantly and striking with such force that the animal shattered into pieces. Yunggukwe never received an apology or compensation, and she neither forgot nor forgave.

"That was my own pig that died," she said angrily sixty-five years later.

———————

MARGARET CRAWLED BACK to the clearing just as McCollom and Decker returned from the jungle, "grinning like apes." In their arms were half a dozen cans of the only food they could find: tomatoes and tomato juice.

"Come on, Maggie," Decker said. "Be a big girl now and eat some tomatoes."

She forced down four mouthfuls before quitting. Watching Decker and McCollom gorge themselves on the fleshy fruit, she grew so angry she demanded that they return to the jungle to find her something else to eat. They headed in the direction where they thought the parachutes landed, but turned up only a half dozen "jungle kits" filled with Atabrine pills for malaria, ointments for wounds, water purification tablets, and bags to collect water from streams or lakes. Also inside were jungle knives, mosquito nets, bandages, and gauze. The only food in the kits was chocolate bars. Margaret felt only slightly better about the chocolate than the tomatoes. "By this time I was almost as sick of candy as I was of tomatoes," she wrote.

Again Margaret marveled at Decker's fortitude. Determined to do his part, he gathered the water bags and went to fill them in the icy stream. "He was gone so long I began to worry about him," Margaret wrote. "It took every ounce of his strength to get back to our knoll, and when he reached us he just sagged gently onto the hard earth."

McCollom, meanwhile, was worried about his companions. He decided the time was overdue to tend more thoroughly to their wounds. On McCollom's orders, Margaret rolled up her pants to expose the wide rings of burns around her calves. Left untended for four days, they oozed pus and reeked of dying flesh. The burns and cuts on both her feet had turned gangrenous, as had part of her hand.

"Decker and McCollom looked at me, and I knew they were

CREW MEMBERS ABOARD A C-47 PREPARE TO DROP SUPPLIES TO THE SURVIVORS OF THE *GREMLIN SPECIAL* CRASH. (PHOTO COURTESY OF C. EARL WALTER JR.)

alarmed. Suddenly I was in terror, lest I lose my legs," she told her diary. She fought to remain in control, fearing that letting down her guard might trigger a spiral into panic. She helped McCollom to apply an ointment they'd found in the jungle kits, after which he wrapped her wounds in gauze.

Even without looking in her little mirror, Margaret knew that she was filthy and unkempt, almost unrecognizable from the eager, take-charge WAC who cared about her appearance and spent nights tailoring her khakis so they'd fit her petite figure. Decker, in what was becoming his usual blunt way, didn't hold back.

"Maggie, you are certainly a sad sack," he said.

McCollom wisely kept his mouth shut, but even that wasn't enough to spare him her wrath. Margaret looked at the two of them—equally dirty, with four days' growth of beard on their hollowed cheeks. She shot back: "Neither one of you are exactly Van Johnsons," she said, referring to the actor whose all-American good looks landed him heroic roles in MGM war movies.

After Margaret it was Decker's turn for triage. The gash on his forehead was deep and oozing. Wimayuk Wandik's breath might have salved his soul, but it did nothing to heal the wound. Margaret and McCollom worried that any attempt to treat it without sterile tools and proper medicine might only make matters worse, so they left it alone. They took the same approach with what appeared to be a broken right elbow, focusing instead on Decker's one seemingly less urgent complaint. Several times during the previous days, Decker had mentioned discomfort caused by his pants sticking to his backside. They thought the cause might be burns from the crash, but the fabric was neither torn nor scorched, so they didn't believe the burns to be serious. Now McCollom ordered Decker to drop his trousers and lie facedown on the ground.

"What we saw horrified us both," Margaret wrote, "and made us realize for the first time what pain Decker had been suffering in silence."

His buttocks and the back of his legs were laced with angry burns that had turned horribly gangrenous. Margaret found the sight sickening. Frightening, too. From the look on his face, so did McCollom. They didn't want to upset Decker, so they said nothing and went to work trying to gently wipe away ruined skin. They cleaned the area as much as they could and applied a generous coating of ointment.

Decker had no idea how he'd been burned. One possibility was that he fell against a piece of scalding metal during the crash. The result would've been the same as ironing pants while still wearing them: the trousers would be fine, and the skin underneath would be destroyed.

Decker accepted the treatment with stoicism until McCollom covered the burns on his bottom with a large, triangular bandage that resembled a diaper. "That momentarily broke Decker's spirit," Margaret wrote. As much as possible, they'd all maintained a gallows humor since the crash, ribbing each other and themselves to boost morale and seal their camaraderie. Decker's bandage could have been an easy source of jokes, but the others knew better. "We were all silently worried and trying not to let the other fellow know it," Margaret wrote. Fearing that her legs would have to be amputated, and that Decker's infections would fatally poison his blood, she wrote: "We were all wondering if the medics would reach us in time."

AFTER THE INFIRMARY session, McCollom ordered both patients to lie down and remain still. All three stayed close together, listening for the planes they hoped would drop the promised medics before nightfall. But clouds rolled in and the weather turned foul by two o'clock that afternoon. A heavy mist settled on the valley and on the survivors' hopes. They knew that no paratrooper medics would dare jump into such soup, especially because hidden beneath the mist was a thick jungle in which to get tangled or impaled. They could do nothing but spread out the tarps and try to keep warm.

By nightfall, only McCollom could get around on his feet. Decker could barely move, worn out from his injuries, his exertions, and his embarrassment. Margaret felt equally bad. She told her diary that, despite his obvious exhaustion, McCollom patiently ministered to her "as if I were a baby."

She felt helpless, too sick and too weak to walk. All she could do was pray. She told her diary that she'd never prayed so hard in her life.

15

NO THANKSGIVING

AFTER EVERY PARATROOPER in the 1st Recon volunteered to jump into Shangri-La despite the dire warnings, Captain Earl Walter chose ten of his troops. He immediately picked his right-hand man, Master Sergeant Santiago "Sandy" Abrenica, whom Walter considered a good friend and the best soldier he'd ever met. Abrenica was thirty-six, whippet-thin, with dark, deep-set eyes and a wary expression. Born on Luzon in the Philippines, Abrenica immigrated alone to the United States in 1926, when he was seventeen, declaring that his intended address was a YMCA in Seattle. As a civilian he'd worked as a gardener, and as a hobby he raced model airplanes.

Next Walter needed two medics who he thought might have the toughest job of all. They'd be parachuting into a dense jungle to treat the survivors, while the rest of the unit jumped into a flat, mostly treeless area of the Shangri-La Valley some thirty miles away to establish a base camp. After talking to his men and leafing through their service records, he picked Sergeant Benjamin "Doc" Bulatao and Corporal Camilo "Rammy" Ramirez. Both Doc and Rammy were good-natured, with easy smiles—Rammy's was more distinctive, as it revealed two front teeth made of gold. Otherwise they were entirely different. Doc Bulatao was quiet, shy almost, while Rammy Ramirez had the gift of gab and an outsize personality for a man who stood just five-foot-one.

Like Abrenica and most other enlisted men in the 1st Recon, the thirty-one-year-old Bulatao was single and had immigrated to the United States as a young man. A farm worker before the war, Bulatao joined the 1st Filipino Regiment in California before being assigned to Walter's unit.

Rammy Ramirez's route to Hollandia was more circuitous and more perilous. Born in the city of Ormoc on the island of Leyte, Ramirez enlisted ten months before the war. He was assigned to the Philippine Scouts, a unit of the U.S. Army consisting of native Filipinos who served in the islands under American command. When the Japanese invaded the Philippines after Pearl Harbor, Ramirez was part of the overmatched, undersupplied force that held out against the enemy, hunger, and dysentery for more than four months on the Bataan Peninsula. After Filipino and American troops surrendered in April 1942, Ramirez endured the Bataan Death March, suffering not only from his captors' brutality and the lack of food and water but also from malaria and dengue fever. Only a daring gambit spared him from a prisoner-of-war camp.

At a temporary holding area, Ramirez noticed a hole at a corner of a fence that had been patched with barbed wire. "I said to myself, 'I will get through there,' " he recalled. The next night, he waited until a Japanese guard set down his rifle and appeared to doze off at his post. "So I roll, little by little, towards the gap in the barbed wire." He tried to pry apart the patch to enlarge the opening but couldn't find the strength—"It's kind of hard, because I am small, you know." As he crawled through, his shirt snagged; razor wire ripped a gash in his side.

"About ten feet from the barbed wire were bushes, lots of bushes and trees. So I went toward the bushes when I got out. I didn't even notice that I cut myself." He was about a hundred and fifty yards from the fence, running through the woods, when he heard gunfire behind him—"boom, boom, boom, boom, boom!"

Later Ramirez learned that Japanese guards had opened fire when other prisoners tried to follow him through the hole. "I kept running, and my head was really pounding—the fever, malaria fever and dengue fever mixed."

Ramirez dragged himself to a nearby house, where sympathetic residents gave him clothes to replace his uniform. He hid his dog tags in his shoe, avoided main roads, and headed toward Manila, an "open city," supposedly safe from bombing by either side. He saw an ambulance and hitched a ride to a hospital, but everyone there was evacuating to a medical ship bound for Australia. Manila was blacked out, but he found his way to the pier and saw the ship silhouetted in the moonlight. He talked his way on board and curled up in a warm spot on the deck amid scores of sick and wounded.

After a month recovering in a Sydney hospital, Ramirez regained his strength just as the 1st Filipino Regiment was arriving in Australia. He was still officially attached to the U.S. military, so it seemed a natural fit. "They discharged me from the hospital and put me with them."

In time, he was assigned to medical, commando, and paratrooper training in Brisbane as part of the 5217th Reconnaissance Battalion, the predecessor to the 1st Recon, under the command of Captain Walter. Now twenty-six, with a scar for life from his escape, Rammy Ramirez wanted to help Margaret, McCollom, and Decker to make their own getaway.

Walter was especially glad to have Ramirez on the team. "I just liked his gung-ho attitude. He was happy." Other medics, including Bulatao, were more experienced treating patients, "but they weren't as free and easygoing as Rammy was. I felt the two survivors that were badly injured . . . needed someone that was kind of happy and a good talker, and was not the least bit hesitant about talking back and forth."

"That's how I picked those two for the jump," Walter said. "I

CAPTAIN C. EARL WALTER JR. WITH
CORPORAL CAMILO "RAMMY" RAMIREZ
(LEFT) AND SERGEANT BENJAMIN "DOC"
BULATAO. (PHOTO COURTESY OF C. EARL
WALTER JR.)

picked 'em mainly because Ben was the most qualified and Rammy had the most guts."

After Abrenica, Bulatao, and Ramirez, Walter filled out his parachute infantry team with seven of his most senior and capable enlisted men: six sergeants—Alfred Baylon, Hermenegildo Cao-ili, Fernando Dongallo, Juan "Johnny" Javonillo, Don Ruiz, and Roque Velasco—and a corporal, Custodio Alerta.

In civilian life, they'd been gardeners and kitchen workers, farmhands and laborers, familiar with the slights and discrimination routinely experienced by Filipinos in America. Now they were U.S. soldiers, volunteering to parachute into uncharted territory to protect and rescue three comrades. When Walter was choosing his squad, neither he nor his men knew that the first natives who made contact with the survivors were friendly. All they knew were Walter's warnings: no maps, no safe drop zone, no predicting the natives' response, and no exit plan. Yet all they wanted to know was how soon they could jump into Shangri-La.

Walter spoke again with Colonel Elsmore and Colonel T. R. Lynch, deputy commander of Fee-Ask, who was deeply involved in the search and rescue effort. In an earlier meeting, Lynch made clear to Walter that he'd be given wide latitude in terms of choosing which men to use and how best to carry out the mission. Walter quoted Lynch as saying, "It's gonna be your operation. You're en-tirely responsible." Walter understood Lynch to mean that if it went horribly wrong, if a live WAC, a live lieutenant, or a live sergeant came back dead, or if his ten paratroopers failed in any way, Walter would shoulder the blame. His answer: *Bahala na.*

After meeting with the brass, Walter joined a flight crew for several reconnaissance passes over the valley, the crash site, and the survivors' clearing. Then he spoke again with his superiors. "We figured out just how they were going to get us in there," Walter recalled. "I was very concerned because I knew we had to parachute in there. It was the only way. The territory north of the valley was inhabited by headhunters, we figured, and south of the valley were Japanese troops. So there's no way to get in there by foot unless you wanted to get into a firefight, and I wasn't the least bit interested in exposing us to that."

Walter instructed his men to pack supplies and parachutes. None of them had jumped since leaving their training base in Brisbane months earlier, so he arranged for each to make one or two practice jumps in Hollandia. "That was a mess because the only place they found that we could use was kind of a swampy area," Walter said. "The men and I laughed about it afterward, but we sure as hell didn't at the time. We were in what they called kunai grass"—with sharp edges, each blade several feet high. "It was very thick and almost one hundred percent coverage. We'd take two or three steps and then purposely fall forward to make an indent in the grass, and then we'd take two or three steps and fall again. A mess."

Walter went back to his medics and asked, "Do you really want to do this?"

"I remember both of them saying, 'Yes, sir. We want to do this because they need us.' "

"I know they do," Walter told his men. "I can't do it. You can, because you know what to do medically."

Later, Walter said of the moment: "This, to me, is one of the things I want people to think about. They didn't have to do this. They wanted to."

Walter noted in a journal that it was his twenty-fourth birthday, Friday, May 18, 1945. Having finally found himself engaged in a real mission, he was too busy and too distracted to celebrate. After his last practice jump, he returned to camp, packed parachutes, and went to bed.

ON THEIR SIXTH day in Shangri-La, the survivors spent the morning waiting for the comforting sound of the approaching supply plane. When the 311 appeared, the sky filled with parachutes slowing the descent of wooden crates. When the survivors made contact with the plane's crew by walkie-talkie, they warned that however bad the terrain looked from the sky, it was even worse on the ground.

In her diary, Margaret wrote that she told the crew: "Don't let anyone jump in here if it means he'll be killed. I'd rather die right here than have anyone killed trying to get me out." McCollom and Decker felt the same. "We had seen enough of death and tragedy," she wrote. "God knows we wanted to live, but not at the expense of someone else."

Their fears for the paratroopers would remain with them for at least another day. The mist rolled in early, shrouding the jungle and the surrounding ridges. That made it impossible to fly safely over them, much less jump into the cloudy mess.

When the plane was out of sight, McCollom traipsed into the jungle in search of cargo. "I could no longer move at all," Margaret wrote, "and Decker was so white and feverish that McCollom sternly ordered him to stay in camp. Flesh had melted away from all of us, even McCollom."

On successive trips, McCollom brought back a package filled with pants and shirts, but only in a size small enough to fit Margaret. She was grateful, though she wished he'd also found panties and bras to replace the underwear she'd removed five days earlier to make bandages. On another outing, he found enough thick blankets to fashion two makeshift beds in their jungle infirmary. He made one for Margaret and the other for him and Decker to share. That night, fleas in the blankets tormented Decker but ignored McCollom, which annoyed Decker even more.

Returning to their knoll after another trip, McCollom shouted, "Eureka! We eat!" In his arms were boxes of ten-in-one rations.

"Food, real food, at last, after almost six days," Margaret wrote. She confessed that her stomach ached from hunger, and the men admitted the same despite having gorged on the tomatoes without her. As McCollom pried open the packages, Margaret's spirits soared: "It was such a beautiful sight: sliced bacon in cans, canned ham and eggs, canned bacon and eggs, canned meat, canned hash and stews, the makings of coffee, tea, cocoa, lemonade and orange-ade, butter, sugar, salt, canned milk, cigarettes, matches, and even candy bars for dessert."

All three chose cans of bacon and ham, and each hastily worked little key openers to reveal the tasty-under-the-circumstances innards. As they dug into their cold breakfasts, the survivors gave no thought to making a fire. For one thing, all the nearby wood was saturated from the relentless rains. "Even more important," Margaret wrote, "even McCollom was too far gone physically to do anything that took an extra, added effort."

Despite how hungry she'd been, Margaret felt stuffed after only a few bites. She stopped eating before she'd finished one small can, realizing that a steady diet of Charms, water, and a few mouthfuls of tomatoes had shrunk her already small stomach.

As they waited for the medics, the survivors' anxiety grew about Margaret's and Decker's injuries. The ointments and gauze they'd found in the supply crates had done nothing to slow the spread or the flesh-killing power of gangrene. After they ate, Mc-

Collom did what he could to tend to their wounds. He removed the dressings on Margaret's legs, releasing the nauseating stench of infection. McCollom tried to ease off the bandages, but they were stuck to the burned skin. He closed his eyes, knowing the pain he'd have to cause Margaret by ripping them off.

"Honest, Maggie, this hurts me worse than it does you," he told her.

Within an hour the fresh bandages he'd applied were drenched with foul-smelling pus. They repeated the excruciating process. Margaret wrote: "I tried not to show my growing terror that I would lose both legs, but it was mounting in me like a tide, and sometimes I thought I would pass out with fear."

Margaret's fears deepened when she tried to help McCollom treat Decker. The gangrene on his legs and backside had grown worse during the previous twelve hours. "He was in great pain and we knew it, although he had never said a word," she wrote. "He lay on his stomach all day with a kind of exhausted patience and pain."

In the afternoon, the native leader they called Pete returned with his greatest show of trust yet: a woman whom Margaret took to be his wife. The couple stood on the knoll across from the survivors' camp and beckoned them over. Neither Margaret nor Decker could walk, so McCollom went alone. The two leaders shook hands and tried to communicate, with little success. At breaks where a response seemed appropriate, McCollom murmured, "Uhn, uhn, uhn," just as he'd heard the natives do when the two groups met. The conversation didn't progress much beyond that.

Elsewhere in her diary, Margaret wrote of the natives: "They would chatter like magpies to us. We would always listen carefully, from time to time muttering, 'Uhn, uhn, uhn.' They would be delighted, like the bore to whom you keep saying, 'Yes, yes, yes' during long-winded conversation. 'Uhn, uhn, uhn,' we would say as the natives chattered. They would beam at us and then talk twice as fast."

As McCollom spoke with his counterpart, Margaret sized up the native woman. Margaret was pleased to find that the first woman she'd seen up close in Shangri-La was "shorter than my five-feet, one-and-one-half inches." A woven bag hung down her back, suspended from a string handle draped over her head. She stood "mother naked," other than what Margaret described as "a queer New Guinea g-string woven of supple twigs" that somehow remained in place on her hips.

Unknown to Margaret, the woman's name was Gilelek. Despite the practice of polygamy that would have allowed Pete/Wimayuk Wandik to take more than one wife, she was his one and only.

"She and all her jungle sisters under the skin were the most graceful, fleet creatures any of us have ever seen," Margaret wrote. "And they were shy as does."

THE COUPLE LEFT, and in the late afternoon the survivors settled into their blanket beds. Less than an hour later, Wimayuk and a large group of his followers returned. It appeared as though his wife had approved of the strangers, and had reminded him that his obligation to guests went beyond kindness.

"They held out a pig, sweet potatoes and some little green bananas, the only fruit we ever saw," Margaret wrote.

"They want to give us a banquet," McCollom said. "Maggie, if our lives depend upon it, I cannot get up and make merry with the natives."

"Amen," said Decker.

If the feast had been offered a day earlier, the survivors would have been thrilled. "But tonight," Margaret wrote, "for the first time in days, our stomachs were full of Army rations, and we were bushed." They used sign language to explain as politely as possible that they were too tired, too sick, and too full to appreciate another meal.

By declining the dinner, Margaret, McCollom, and Decker had

A NATIVE COUPLE IN A DANI VILLAGE, PHOTOGRAPHED IN 1945. (PHOTO COURTESY OF C. EARL WALTER JR.)

effectively canceled what would have been the first Thanksgiving in Shangri-La. The man they called Pete would have filled the role of Chief Massassoit, and the survivors would have played the Pilgrims.

More significant, they unknowingly missed a chance to become bonded to the natives through one of the tribe's most important community rituals: a pig feast. As an anthropologist later explained: "It is the remembrance of pigs which holds . . . [this] society together. At every major ceremony pigs are given from one person to another, and then killed and eaten. But they leave behind memory traces of obligations which will be paid back later; when this happens, the people will create new obligations. And so the network of the society is constantly refurbished by the passage of pigs. A single man in his lifetime is bound to his fellows by the ties of hundreds and perhaps thousands of pigs which he and his people have exchanged with others and their people."

Despite the deep symbolism of their offer, the natives took no apparent offense at the survivors' refusal to share a pig.

"Pete, who must have had a wonderfully understanding heart in that wiry black body, comprehended at once," Margaret wrote. "He tucked the pig more firmly under his arm. He ordered his men, who had started a fire by some magic known only to them, to put it out. Then he clucked over us reassuringly and herded his followers home."

The survivors burrowed into their beds and went to sleep, feeling sated and relatively warm and comfortable for the first time since leaving Hollandia. In what Margaret called "the irony of an evil fate," they were awakened several hours later by a sudden cloudburst. Margaret's nest of blankets, arranged on low ground, became a woolly swamp. The bed on higher ground shared by McCollom and Decker was wet, but not soaked. Margaret ordered them to make room, and she crawled in alongside them.

"Lord," said McCollom in mock protest, "are we never to get rid of this woman?"

They huddled together against the cold and wet through the night, talking now and again under the blankets about helicopters, medics, and being rescued.

16

RAMMY AND DOC

FLYING IN A C-47 over the survivors' clearing, Earl Walter was sweating.

The plane carrying him and the medics Rammy Ramirez and Doc Bulatao took off from the Sentani Airstrip around 8:00 a.m., Saturday, May 19. During several passes over the intended drop zone, it looked more treacherous than Walter remembered from his first view, two days earlier. Adding to his concern was the unpredictability of the mountain winds. Already he'd dropped five wind dummies—weighted bundles used to assess turbulence—without any benefit. "The reason I dropped five," he explained, "is because every one of them changed direction, so I had no idea" which way the winds would blow the medics.

Walter pushed the medics' equipment out of the cargo door over the jungle near the survivors' campsite, so they wouldn't have to carry the supplies the entire way from the landing area. The cargo drops provided no more useful information about the wind conditions. As he watched the dummies and the equipment crates spin and twist in the shifting currents, Walter kept his fears to himself.

"I never told Ben or Rammy because, well, it wouldn't have done any good," Walter said. "I mean, it didn't make any difference. We knew we had to put two people in there, no matter what."

The young captain knew that Bulatao and Ramirez were about to become what paratroopers call "human wind dummies." If they'd been officers like Walter rather than enlisted men, they would have earned the more formal moniker "turbulence testers." Either way, the swirling winds added another danger to an already frightening jump.

Walter's biggest worry was the drop zone itself, an area of four-foot-high brush, jagged rocks, and sharp-topped tree stumps that looked as though it had been the scene of a recent lightning fire. "I can remember flying over there at roughly a couple of hundred feet because I wanted to get down and see what it looked like," he said. "And it looked like hell. Pardon the expression, but it did. I mean, there'd been fires, there were rock formations, stumps, trees that had been broken or whatever. I don't remember ever hearing about a drop zone like that." An ideal landing area was flat and soft, wide open, with little or no breeze; this was the opposite.

Reluctantly, Walter chose the area because it was within two miles of the survivors' campsite, and it was better, though not much, than parachuting into a full-fledged jungle. Jumping into the campsite itself wasn't an option because it was too small a target.

Walter's plan called for the medics to exit the plane only a few hundred feet above the ground, to reduce the chance that they'd drift miles from where the survivors desperately needed their help. But improving the odds for the survivors meant increasing the risks for Bulatao and Ramirez.

Cords called static lines ran from their parachute packs to an anchor cable inside the plane. If everything went as intended, the lines would ensure that their chutes would deploy automatically after the men stepped out the door and were clear of the plane. But jumping so close to the ground meant that they'd have no time to deploy a reserve parachute if their main chutes failed. The mountain altitude added to the peril. They were more than eight thousand feet above sea level, which meant the air would be thin and they'd fall faster. They'd have little opportunity to steer themselves away from trees or other hazards by pulling on the nylon straps that linked their harnesses to the cords leading to the parachutes' umbrella-like canopies.

A light man in thin air with a twenty-eight-foot-diameter parachute might descend at a rate of fifteen feet per second. If that rate held true, from the time they left the plane, Ramirez and Bulatao would be on the ground—or stuck in a tree, or impaled on a jagged stump, or lost in a rocky gorge—in less than thirty seconds. That is, if the winds didn't spin them around, tangle their lines, and turn their parachutes into narrow "streamers." Without a reserve chute, a streamer meant almost certain death.

Walter and the pilot conferred about wind speed and direction, then agreed on what they thought would be the best approach. Both knew their calculations were only slightly more useful than expert guesses.

Ramirez and Bulatao rose from their seats and did the paratrooper shuffle to the jump door to keep from losing their balance with their heavy loads. Walter "stood them in the door"—paratrooper lingo for preparing to jump—and again checked their resolve.

He shouted over the engines and the wind: "Are you ready?"

In unison, Ramirez and Bulatao answered: "Yes, sir!"

Describing the scene more than sixty years later, Walter's eyes misted with pride.

The medics leaped into the void, one after the other, their parachutes opening as intended and filling with air. At first, they seemed to be headed toward an area below the clearing where Walter thought they could make a relatively safe landing. Then the winds shifted again, blowing them off course.

————

MARGARET, MCCOLLOM, AND Decker awoke that morning anticipating the medics' arrival. "It was patent to all of us now—though we never once mentioned it—that Decker might die and I would surely lose my legs unless the medical paratroopers reached us immediately," she wrote.

All three were "wet, miserable and aching" from the rainstorm the night before as McCollom served her and Decker cold breakfast rations. Their ears pricked up at the sound of the plane, and McCollom manned the radio. "They told us the two medical paratroopers were aboard," she wrote, "and would jump two miles down the valley as soon as the plane had discharged its 'chute cargo of pup tents, ponchos, blankets, more medical supplies and food."

A radio operator on the plane assured them the medics would be taking care of them within forty-five minutes. When McCollom relayed the message, Margaret rattled her lips in a Bronx cheer. McCollom and Decker joined in. "We had some intimate knowledge of the jungle by this time," Margaret wrote, "and we knew that even over a native trail it would take hours for the medics to make the two-mile hike."

The survivors watched as two small figures left the plane and their parachutes mushroomed in the sky. A single thought crossed Decker's mind: "God bless you." He considered the medics to be "the difference between life and death for us."

When they lost sight of the paratroopers, Margaret wrote, they knew there was nothing they could do but wait and pray. "I said more 'Our Fathers' and 'Hail Marys' in the next two hours than ever before in my life."

Watching from the plane's open jump door, Walter did the same.

ON THE WAY down, struggling against the wind in a futile effort to get back on course, Camilo "Rammy" Ramirez gained a more complete understanding of what he'd volunteered himself into. "We were about a hundred feet above the jump zone," he recalled. "I could see the stumps and the rocks. I said to myself, 'There's all this—it's dangerous.' So I tried to face away from the wind. I tried to pilot the parachute toward the woods, where I could see no rocks in there. I missed the stumps, but I did not miss the rock."

He stumbled as he landed, painfully wrenching his left ankle. After discarding his parachute, Ramirez examined his ankle and was relieved to find that the bone wasn't broken and he wasn't bleeding. Doc Bulatao landed safely nearby. That was the good news.

Immediately upon the medics' landing, they were surrounded by natives. Ramirez reached for his rifle, a semiautomatic M-1 carbine with an eighteen-inch barrel and a fifteen-round clip. "The natives have spears, and bow and arrows," Ramirez said. "And I had my carbine cocked, in case somebody acted to throw the spear, or bow and arrow."

Out stepped a native man Ramirez called "the chief of that village"—Wimayuk Wandik, whom the medics would soon know as Pete. They didn't understand each other's language, but using hand signs and body English, Ramirez explained himself. "I expressed my mission. That an airplane crashed. Catch on fire. I'm here to help."

Wimayuk nodded. He called over a group of boys and instructed them to lead the two medics to Mundima, the place by the river Mundi where the survivors were camped. "We followed them, just like rabbits, through the jungle," Ramirez said. Hobbled by his twisted ankle, Ramirez couldn't keep up with the nimble barefoot boys, who hopped from stump to stump, scampered across fallen logs wet with moss, and saw trails where anyone else would have seen none. Bulatao hung back with his friend. After several hours of losing and regaining sight of the boys, trekking through, over, and around the ferns and vines and trees, they arrived at the clearing.

Margaret, McCollom, and Decker rose to shake hands with the medics. "When I got close to them," Ramirez said, "Margaret was crying. She hugged me, and I kept smiling." Margaret recorded the scene in her diary:

When I spotted them down the native trail, I couldn't keep the tears back any longer. They spilled out of their own volition and poured down my one blistered cheek and my one good cheek. Leading the way and limping slightly was Corporal Rammy Ramirez, medical technician. Rammy had a heart of gold, we came to know, and a smile of the same hue. Even as he came limping up the trail, his face was split in a wide, warm smile, and his two gold front teeth shone resplendently. Rammy was better for morale than a thousand-dollar bill. I felt better just looking at him through my tears. Sergeant Ben Bulatao, medical technician, brought up the rear. When the sergeant walked into camp, there arrived to take care of us one of the most kind and gentle men God ever put on earth. . . . I want to say right now that when better men are born, they will undoubtedly be Filipinos. If ever they or their islands need aid or a champion, they only have to send a wire to enlist me in the cause.

Rammy rummaged through the jungle, gathering the supplies Walter had tossed from the plane. Favoring his bad ankle, he "hopped around on one foot like a cheerful sparrow," Margaret wrote. He built a fire, pulled up a dozen or so sweet potatoes to roast, and boiled water. He shaved pieces of chocolate into a canteen cup and made hot chocolate—the survivors' first warm drink in nearly a week.

"It was heavenly," Margaret wrote. "We gulped down the first cup like ravenous animals, and then held them out for more." By the next morning, Rammy and Doc would be waking them with the rich aromas of hot coffee and fried bacon.

They wolfed the hot potatoes, too, amusing Rammy with their

excitement about a vegetable that had been under their feet the whole time: "I find out that they came from the city. And in the city, all you can see is lots of fruits, but no trees. So they don't know how they grow."

Starting with Decker, the medics poured peroxide and an antibacterial powder called sulfanilamide into his wounds and onto the gangrenous burns on his buttocks. The gash on Decker's head was spread too wide to stitch. Doc Bulatao—who took the lead on medical matters, with Rammy assisting—gently massaged the skin around the wound, pushing the two sides closer so they could eventually be knit together. Rammy worked on Decker's broken elbow. He fashioned a splint from tree bark and held it against Decker's arm as he wrapped it in bandages, immobilizing it. The medics decided not to set the break, fearing that without X rays they might do more harm than good.

They turned their attention to Margaret and spent the next two hours working on her legs. The bandages McCollom had applied were stuck fast to her burns. Doc Bulatao knew that removing them would be torture.

"He would try to work the bandages off without hurting me too much," Margaret wrote. "But he winced as much in the process as I did. 'You ought to see the way I rip them off!' McCollom encouraged him. 'But I'm afraid I'll hurt her,' Doc would reply."

SERGEANT KEN DECKER IN A MAKESHIFT LATRINE IN THE JUNGLE. (PHOTO COURTESY OF C. EARL WALTER JR.)

Margaret was more worried about losing her legs. "If I were back at Fee-Ask," she told Bulatao, "the G.I. medic would yank the bandages off and then scrub my legs with a brush. Go ahead, yank." So he did. "Not until long afterward did he tell me how shocked he was at the sight of me," Margaret wrote. "I was skin and bones. I doubt if I weighed ninety pounds at that time."

Bulatao knew there was little he could do that first night to treat the gangrene on Margaret or Decker. It would be a slow, painful fight. He and Rammy would cut away the rotten skin, wash what remained with peroxide, daub it with ointment, dress the wound, then repeat the process day after day. If it wasn't too late, eventually the gangrene would retreat and healing could begin. Otherwise, they'd have to consider more drastic steps, including amputation.

"Doc must have read the fear in my heart," Margaret wrote. "In the middle of bandaging up my sorry-looking gams, he smiled at me and said, 'You'll be jitter-bugging in three months.' But I knew he wasn't sure, and neither was I."

17

CUSTER AND COMPANY

AS MARGARET HASTINGS was enduring the removal of her bandages in the mountainous jungle, Earl Walter finally got a chance to experience danger serving his country. It wasn't a combat assignment or a spy patrol in the Philippines, but it was the next best thing: a rescue mission in Shangri-La.

Colonel Elsmore and the planners at Fee-Ask still weren't sure how they'd attempt to get everyone *out* of Shangri-La, but in the meantime they were certain they needed more soldiers *in* Shangri-La. They wanted Walter and five members of his paratrooper team to set up a base camp in the main valley, hike through the jungle to the survivors' clearing, collect them and the two medics, and return with everyone to the base camp to await pickup or further instructions. While Walter and his group were en route to the survivors' campsite, the other three paratroopers would stay in the main valley to maintain the base camp and to level and create a makeshift runway by clearing brush, trees, mud, quicksand, and other obstacles.

The runway idea emerged as planners continued to narrow their options for rescue. A helicopter had already been ruled out because of the inability to fly a whirlybird over the mountains. Elsmore's team also nixed a suggestion that they use an amphibious plane; unaware that Richard Archbold had landed on a lake near the valley with the *Guba* seven years earlier, they mistakenly believed such a plane was unsuitable for the mission. Marching the hundred and fifty miles to Hollandia was among the last resorts, along with the idea of piloting a U.S. Navy PT boat up a river from New Guinea's south coast to within fifty or so miles of the valley. Among a half dozen remaining options, some more outlandish than others, were landing a C-47 in the valley—a dubious prospect because of the conditions—and the equally implausible idea of dropping motorless gliders into the valley, loading them with passengers, and using low-flying planes to snatch them back into the sky.

In the meantime, at ten o'clock on the morning of Sunday, May 20, Walter and eight of his men, weighed down and clanking with parachute packs, guns, ammunition, bolo knives, and sundry supplies, climbed aboard a C-47 at the Sentani Airstrip destined for Shangri-La.

Walter told the pilot, Colonel Edward T. Imparato, to take the plane in low—a few hundred feet above the valley floor. Walter, about to make his forty-ninth jump, didn't want the swirling winds to turn their parachutes into kites and spread him and his men miles apart. He also hoped that a low jump might escape the natives' notice, as opposed to a long, slow descent that would be seen by every tribesman for miles.

For a drop zone, Walter and Imparato chose an area with no huts or sweet potato gardens in the immediate vicinity, a relatively flat stretch of land in the shadow of a soaring rock wall, with only a few trees and shrubs and small knolls between hundreds of otherwise uninterrupted acres of kunai grass. Shortly before noon, with Imparato flying only 350 feet above the valley floor, the paratroopers tumbled from the plane like dominoes off a table. Their parachutes deployed as designed, and all nine men reached the ground without incident.

They gathered in a defensive formation they'd planned beforehand—in close proximity to one another but not bunched together. Walter had heard radio reports from the survivors and the two medics that the natives near the crash site were welcoming, but his landing site was fifteen to twenty air miles away from that happy scene. The natives in the main valley of Shangri-La could be different altogether, and far less hospitable.

"When we first landed," Walter said, "everybody was spread around different places. Not far apart, but I wanted them to be spread out a little bit so we didn't all get speared or whatever to start with."

His wish for a stealth landing proved a pipe dream. Even before the parachutes reached the ground, scores of men with spears and bows and arrows came running from all directions into the landing field. Walter estimated that more than two hundred Stone Age warriors surrounded him and his men. Master Sergeant Santiago "Sandy" Abrenica put the number at three hundred.

Walter tensed. He grabbed his carbine. Abrenica was at his side, equally ready for combat.

"Captain," Abrenica said, "you know what this reminds me of?"

"No, not really, Sandy. What?"

"Custer's last stand."

Stifling laughter, Walter held the carbine under one arm, his hand near the trigger. In his other hand he held a .45-caliber pistol—a gift from his father. He sensed that the natives were hostile but hesitant to attack. Walter shouted to his men to stay ready but to hold their fire until he gave the command.

"For God's sake," Walter called, "don't get itchy fingers and pull the trigger just to scare someone. I don't want anything like that to happen. If we hurt any of them or kill any of them, then we'd really have a problem."

Abrenica didn't like the natives' trilling alarm cry, a "frightening, weird sound like the call of the Australian kookaburra." Abrenica mistakenly thought the sound came from natives rubbing their spears together, but, in fact, it arose from their throats.

Although they were outnumbered more than twenty to one, Walter believed the superiority of their firepower put them squarely in control. "Of course we had a lot of weapons," he said. "No mortars or anything like that, but we had machine guns and submachine guns and our own carbines."

Said Abrenica: "We had jumped fully equipped for a combat mission, so we hastily erected a barricade and set up our machine guns behind it. We thought we'd have to shoot our way out."

In the middle of Shangri-La, the modern and prehistoric warriors stood their ground, locked in a standoff.

WALTER AND HIS men had landed in the northwest part of the valley, in an area known to the natives as Wosi. Specifically, they were in the part of Wosi called Abumpuk, not far from a village called Koloima. No huts were nearby because the paratroopers' drop zone was smack in the middle of a no-man's-land—a designated battlefield—that separated the neighborhoods of two warring groups of Dani tribesmen, the Logo-Mabel clans on one side and the Kurelu on the other.

The Dani people in this part of Shangri-La were separated by distance, heritage, and politics from the Yali people of Uwambo and the clans that lived near the survivors' clearing in the jungle. They hadn't seen or heard anything about the *Gremlin Special* crash. With enemies all around them, an event that took place twenty miles away might as well have happened in China. That is, if they knew China existed.

Like the Yali people near the crash site, the Dani people around Wosi had grown accustomed to seeing planes, which they called *anekuku*. But they hadn't made a connection between the noisemakers that flew over their valley and the nine strange-looking creatures in their battlefield. Instead, like the people of Uwambo, at least some of them thought the strangers were embodiments of an ancient legend.

"When we saw them, we thought they were coming down on a vine from the sky," said Lisaniak Mabel, who witnessed the paratroopers' arrival as a boy.

Although some natives thought the visitors were spirits, others believed that they were warriors like themselves who'd escaped a massacre of their people. The coverings on the strangers' bodies reinforced that impression. When Dani people mourn, they cover their shoulders or their entire bodies in light-colored mud. Surely, they believed, the strangers' khaki-colored coverings must be made of mud.

The men and boys surrounding the paratroopers were from the Logo-Mabel clans, and their leader was a powerful warrior with many kills in battle and a large collection of "dead birds" captured from fallen enemies. He was a Dani, but his name was Yali, and he was from the Logo clan.

As Yali Logo and his clansmen studied Walter and his men, they felt certain of one thing: the strangers weren't their Kurelu enemies, so they had no immediate need to kill them.

WALTER HAD NO idea what thoughts passed through the minds of the spear-carrying, penis-gourd-clad men surrounding him and his troops. But he sensed that the eyes upon him were filled more with curiosity than with hostility. None of the local people moved to throw a spear or notch an arrow. In turn, none of the soldiers used a firearm. This museum-like diorama of first contact continued for three hours.

Before the jump, Walter and his men had been told by the rescue planners that a universal sign of friendship among New Guinea natives was to wave leaves over one's head. As the face-off lingered on, Walter tried it.

"I waved those damned leaves for hours," Walter said, "and then when I got no response I began to realize how foolish I must look, and I quit."

Finally, after what Walter described as energetic "motioning and beckoning," both sides relaxed and lowered their weapons. The paratroopers made a fire to gather around, and the natives followed suit nearby.

"When we first started to get acquainted with them, I think they realized almost as soon as we did that they had nothing to fear from us," Walter said. "And we realized we had nothing to fear from them because they were definitely not cannibalistic, at least not to us. As far as we could figure out, they only ate people from other tribes that they were fighting. That's where the cannibalism came in."

Writing that night in the journal he updated daily throughout the mission, Walter recorded his first impression of the locals: "Natives wear nothing but hollow gourds over the penis and tie their testicles up with string, suspending the whole works from a string which goes around their midsection. Seem very healthy, teeth are in excellent shape, feet are badly misshapen from constant barefoot walking. Some have long, matted hair and look like French poodles, some short and are all kinky. So far no malformity of the body. Believe each family has different markings and hairdos. Some, doglike features; others, slightly anthropoid in appearance, and still others are as finely featured as the average white race. We are the first in this valley from the outside world." Walter noted that the natives, redolent of pig grease and sweat, seemed to be people who "never bathed."

When both sides were at ease, the natives studied the soldiers' appearance, too. In a journal entry, Walter described a particularly flamboyant inspection by the men and boys of the Logo-Mabel clans that bloomed into a classic cultural misunderstanding.

As the two groups came close for a good look at one another, the natives gently stroked the soldiers' arms and legs, backs and chests. They also engaged in what Walter described as "a lot of hugging. It drove my men wild, because they couldn't figure out

EARL WALTER SPEAKING BY WALKIE-TALKIE WITH A SUPPLY PLANE AFTER PARA-
CHUTING INTO THE VALLEY. (PHOTO COURTESY OF C. EARL WALTER JR.)

what the hell." The natives murmured as they massaged Walter
and his men up and down.

Uncomfortable with the apparent shows of affection, Walter
and his men concluded that the natives had somehow arrived at
the mistaken conclusion that the paratroopers were women. What
other explanation could there be for nearly naked men to rub their
hands over the bodies of other men?

This touching scene went on awhile, until Walter and his paratroopers had had enough. The six-foot-four captain, towering over
the natives as well as his own men, tried to forcefully communicate
that they were male. No luck. The rubbing resumed. It reached a
point that Walter described as "making love."

When the tribesmen showed no sign of ending their laying on
of hands, Walter devised a strategy of decidedly unconventional
warfare, unknown to any military handbook. First, he unbuckled
his belt and pulled down his pants to show that he had the necessary equipment to wear a gourd of his own, if he so chose. After

revealing himself several times, Walter realized it wasn't working. He ordered his entire detachment of the 1st Recon to join him in World War II's most unusual show of force.

"God damn it, let's take our pants down," Walter told his men, "and show them that we're men, not women. I'm tired of this."

Walter stripped off his shirt, pants, and underwear. His men followed suit. They walked around nude for the next several hours while the natives wandered among them, more modestly attired in penis gourds.

"First time I ever had to do that to prove I was a man," Walter said.

Bringing out the heavy artillery, Walter pulled from his wallet a photo of his wife, "and they went wild with interest."

As far as Walter was concerned, this two-pronged display of his manhood and his mate did the trick. No longer did the natives "make love" to the paratroopers.

IN FACT, THE Dani people of the valley weren't at all confused about the soldiers' gender. If they were confused about anything, it was about the paratroopers' sudden nakedness.

When the men of the Logo-Mabel clans came in close after the standoff, they learned to their surprise that the strangers weren't covered in mud for mourning, after all. Narekesok Logo, who witnessed the scene as a boy, explained that he and the other men and boys were intrigued by the coverings on the men's bodies. Having never before seen clothes—he said the Archbold expedition didn't pass through their neighborhood—they were fascinated by this soft, apparently removable second skin.

Another witness, Ai Baga, said: "We came close and felt the clothes and said, 'That's not mud!'"

Equally perplexing to the Dani people was the soldiers' response. From the time a male Dani is about four years old, he never fully exposes himself in public. Even if the gourd doesn't fit, he wears it. What seemed like near-nudity to outsiders like Walter and his men was quite the opposite to the Dani men who surrounded them. Penis gourds, or *horim*, are worn at work, at play, at war, and even while sleeping. They only come off in private: for urination or sex, or when a man inside his hut exchanges one *horim* for another. A man wearing a *horim* is modestly attired in Dani culture. A man without a *horim* is caught in an embarrassing state of undress.

To the native men and boys in the battlefield that day, Walter and his men were making spectacles of themselves.

Word spread quickly about the soldiers' "show," said Lisaniak Mabel. More people flowed into the area from distant villages the next day. But after that first display Walter and his men kept their clothes on, and the latecomers returned home disappointed. Those natives who did see the naked soldiers told the story, laughing, for the rest of their lives.

AFTER DRESSING, THE paratroopers set up camp, scouted the area, and collected the equipment and supplies dropped from Colonel Imparato's plane, which he called *The Queen*. They also searched for a source of fresh water. By gulping from their canteens and pouring out a few drops, the soldiers expressed their need to the locals, who led them to a freshwater spring nearby. Walter and Sergeant Don Ruiz hiked near one of the villages, but the Dani people shooed them away, making it clear that the strangers weren't welcome inside the fence that ringed the huts and courtyard.

After dinner and a few Lucky Strike cigarettes around the campfire, Walter fended off swarms of dive-bombing mosquitoes. He organized his men into guard shifts that rotated every two hours. "No evidence of any hostility, but still do not want to take any chances," he wrote in his journal. Feeling better than he had in months, Walter could have stood the nightlong watch himself. "Too excited," he wrote. "Having a hell of a time getting to sleep."

THAT SAME DAY at the survivors' camp, Doc Bulatao followed breakfast by getting back to work on Decker's wounds. Margaret described the scene in her diary: "For six hours, he peeled the encrusted gangrene from the sergeant's infected burns. It was a very tedious and painful process. All of Doc's gentleness could not lessen Decker's ordeal. The sergeant lay rigid on his pallet. Decker was a very sick man, but never by a flinch or a whimper did he reveal the torment he was enduring. . . . There wasn't any anesthetic nor even a stiff drink of whisky available to ease Decker's pain." Margaret noted with surprise, and perhaps a little disappointment, that they found no evidence the natives had learned how to distill their crops into alcoholic drinks.

Decker's agony was difficult for McCollom to bear. Only half-joking, he suggested they "hit him in the head and put him out of his misery for a few hours." Margaret noticed that the lieutenant was as drenched in sweat as Decker and Doc, just from witnessing the excruciating procedure.

Also interested was Wimayuk Wandik, Pete to the survivors, who watched in rapt attention from nearby along with "his mob of natives," as Margaret described them.

The people of Uwambo were growing ever more relaxed about the survivors and the medics in their midst. With each passing day, they also became less afraid of the low-altitude supply drops that initially sent them running into the jungle for cover. They scoured the jungle for crates and parachutes, then hauled the supplies back to the survivors' camp.

One young man became entirely too comfortable with what he'd seen.

"A native came running into our camp," Margaret told her diary. "He was terribly excited and upset. He motioned for the men to follow him with such urgency that we knew some crisis had arisen. Our men hurried after him to the edge of the jungle. The native, in great distress, pointed up to the top of a fifty-foot tree. There was another native, with an open parachute preparing to make a free jump!"

The fall might have killed him, and the survivors and the medics feared that the people of Uwambo would blame them. Only after a great deal of yelling and pantomime negotiation would the young man relent. He gave up his dreams of flight and climbed down from the tree.

WHEN THE SUPPLY plane passed over that day, the radio operator informed the survivors and medics that Walter and eight enlisted paratroopers had landed in the main valley. The pilot underestimated their distance, saying they were about ten miles away. McCollom later estimated that the base camp was more like thirty air miles away, while Walter put it at twenty miles. The pilot told them that Walter and five of the paratroopers would soon start their hike to the jungle camp.

"They will be with you by nightfall," the radioman said.

Margaret, McCollom, and Decker dismissed the promise as cockeyed military optimism.

Margaret felt more energized by another message relayed by the radioman, this one about Walter "Wally" Fleming, the sergeant with whom she'd planned a swimming date the day of her trip to Shangri-La. She told her diary: "My beau, Wally . . . had been too frantic to talk coherently about the accident, even after he learned that I had survived by a miracle. Up to that moment, I had worried constantly for fear Wally would be terribly upset by first, the accident, and then my present predicament." The radioman's message changed her tune. "As soon as I knew he was worried half to death, I was pleased as punch!"

MENSTRUAL CYCLES WERE notoriously out of whack among WACs in Hollandia, a byproduct of tropical climate, weight loss, stress, and any number of other factors. Sometimes WACs would have their periods twice or more in a single month, and other times they'd skip several months. When WAC officers at the base learned that one of the survivors was a woman, they ordered the supply plane to have McCollom ask Margaret the dates of her last period. When she reported that it had been a couple of months, McCollom told the supply plane to drop a box of sanitary napkins, just in case. An act worthy of Abbott and Costello ensued.

When he returned to the base, radio operator Jack Gutzeit went to the WAC commander's office like a husband sent to the drugstore on an awkward mission.

"Maggie wants a couple boxes of Kotex," he told the top WAC.

She brushed him off, telling Gutzeit that medical supplies for the rescue were the responsibility of the hospital commander. He trudged to the base hospital, where the hospital commander said, "Go see the WAC commander. They're supposed to take care of all the women's stuff."

After more back-and-forth, Gutzeit got fed up with the pass-the-napkin game. He returned to the Sentani Airstrip and asked a telephone operator to place calls to the WAC commander and the hospital commander. With all the moxie of his native Brooklyn, the sergeant told them both:

"This plane is leaving in one hour, and if I don't have Kotex from you folks, I'm calling General Clement at Far East Air Service Command Headquarters!"

That day, the cargo drop included a half dozen boxes of sanitary napkins. In the days that followed, the supplies doubled, then tripled.

"I bet we had twenty boxes of Kotex down there every day!" McCollom said.

CARE FOR THE survivors' spiritual needs also came with that morning's supply drop. Major Cornelius Waldo, the Catholic chaplain from Indianapolis who'd been on the B-17 search plane that spotted the survivors, assembled a package with a Bible, prayer books, and Margaret's rosary beads. The religious supplies came in handy when Doc and Rammy went to work on Margaret.

"It was the same peeling process, and after five minutes I

A PAGE FROM MARGARET HASTINGS'S DIARY, WRITTEN IN SHORTHAND. IT READS IN PART: "DOC IS THE MOST GENTLE PERSON I HAVE EVER SEEN, ESPECIALLY FOR A DOCTOR. THE DAY HE ARRIVED HE DIDN'T GET AROUND TO DRESSING MY LEGS UNTIL LATE IN THE EVENING, AFTER HE HAD DONE DECKER. HE THEN STARTED TO REMOVE THE BANDAGES FROM MY LEGS, AND WHAT A MESS THEY WERE. THEY HAD BLED CONSIDERABLY AND THE BANDAGES HAD STUCK SO THAT YOU COULDN'T TELL WHAT WAS BURNED SKIN AND WHAT WAS BANDAGE. HE WAS PULLING VERY GENTLY AND KEPT SAYING, 'I AM SO AFRAID I WILL HURT YOU.' "

clutched my rosary and gritted my teeth," she wrote. "My pride was involved! I was determined to be as good a soldier as Decker. For four endless hours, Doc peeled my legs, my feet, and worked on my hand. I didn't cry or make a sound. But I was yelling bloody murder inside all the time."

Rammy remembered her reaction differently. "We had to slice, little by little, slice, slice, until it bleeds. . . . She always cried. Cry, cry, cry. It was painful when I cut, but I think she tried to hide it. It was painful. To me it was very painful."

The treatments left the medics exhausted and Decker and Margaret bedridden. Margaret was in such pain she had to lie on her back with her knees bent, to keep her clothes from chafing against her leg wounds. Despite her agony, she began to believe that Doc would save her legs.

As she settled in for the night, she called out to the four men nearby: "It's wonderful to go to bed and know you're on the road to recovery instead of ruin."

18

BATHTIME FOR YUGWE

MARGARET AWOKE THE next morning, eager to rid herself of
a hard week of sweat, blood, gangrenous shavings, and jungle
grime.

She gratefully accepted a toothbrush Doc Bulatao had tucked
in his pocket before the jump. Then she asked Rammy Ramirez
to help her with a bath. He was happy to oblige, but the question
was where. McCollom and the medics bathed in the cold creek,
about a hundred yards from the knoll where Rammy and Doc
had set up a little village: a cook tent and a shelter for supplies
made from draped parachutes, and pup tents for them to sleep in.
They dug a latrine and tented that, too. But the idea of Margaret
bathing alone at the creek worried them, and they didn't want to
intrude on her privacy by hovering close by.

Rammy solved the problem with the universal soldier's bath-
tub: his helmet. Hobbling on crutches he had made from branches
to ease his sore ankle, he found a semiprivate area on the far side of
the knoll and filled the helmet with fire-warmed water. He gathered soap, towels, a washcloth, and a small khaki uniform ear-
marked for Margaret in one of the cargo drops.

With McCollom's help, the medics carried Margaret to her
makeshift bath area and left her to wash in what they expected
would be complete privacy. She stripped off her soiled shirt and

FROM LEFT, CORPORAL CAMILO "RAMMY" RAMIREZ, CORPORAL MARGARET HAST-
INGS, AND SERGEANT BENJAMIN "DOC" BULATAO. (PHOTO COURTESY OF C. EARL
WALTER JR.)

tattered pants. Naked, she lathered the washcloth and began to
scrub. Almost immediately, she felt eyes upon her.

"I looked around and there on a neighboring knoll were the
natives," she told her diary. "I never could figure out whether they
were goggle-eyed at the queer rite I was performing, or at a skin so
different from their own."

McCollom spotted them, too: "Big smiles on their faces."

When she couldn't shoo them away, Margaret gamely finished
her bath. She dried off, pulled on her new clothes, and called for
her bearers to return her to her tent. The bath routine became a
daily event for Margaret, and a highlight for the men and boys of
Uwambo.

WHEN THEY FIRST met the visitors, the natives had been fascinated by McCollom's straight blond hair. Margaret's bath had
that beat. One of the smiling regulars at the show was young
Helenma Wandik.

"We saw she had breasts, so we knew she was a woman," he said. "She would wave us away, but we thought it was interesting so we stayed until she finished."

Once they were certain that Margaret was a woman, the tribespeople jumped to a conclusion. Although they still believed them to be spirits, they assumed that the three survivors were "a man, a woman, and the woman's husband," Helenma Wandik said. The "husband" was the man the natives called "Meakale," their attempted pronunciation of McCollom.

Although the survivors and medics didn't learn the names of the natives, the people of Uwambo tried to make sense of what to call their visitors. They'd heard McCollom calling Margaret "Maggie," but to their ears it sounded like "Yugwe," so that's what they called her. In her diary, Margaret wrote that she "always heartily detested" the nickname Maggie, "but I loved it the way the natives pronounced it." She said they softly slurred the syllables. She heard the result not as Yugwe, but as "Mah-gy."

The natives never witnessed sexual relations or intimate affection between "Meakale" and "Yugwe/Mah-gy." The basis for assuming the two were married, Helenma Wandik said, was their own culture. In male-dominated Yali and Dani society, a healthy woman who reached sexual maturity wasn't single long. The people of Uwambo didn't know that Margaret was thirty, but one look at her naked body told them she was past thirteen. They identified Meakale/McCollom as the group's leader, so they thought she must be his wife.

ON THEIR FIRST full day in the valley, Earl Walter and the eight enlisted paratroopers of the 1st Recon enjoyed ten-in-one rations for breakfast. Afterward, Walter took Master Sergeant Sandy Abrenica and two sergeants, Hermenegildo Caoili and Juan "Johnny" Javonillo, on what he described in his journal as "a short recon" of eight miles round-trip through the valley. Along with native tracks and a deserted village, they came upon "one skeleton near [the] trail, with rotten flesh" and a broken spear nearby. Walter wrote in his journal that the "cause of death [was] undetermined." But he suspected the body was evidence of the native battles and enemy raids.

During the hike, Walter got his first look at a native woman. Writing in his journal, he judged her looks with a harsh Western eye: "Very unattractive hairdo, not fancy hair, and . . . much less hair than the men. She wore a loose cloth draped around the crotch and private parts (very skimpy). No other clothing. Looked like she was pregnant."

Upon their return to camp, Walter found that the men who'd stayed behind had rigged a parachute as a tent to cover their equipment from the rains. As he put it, "The circus has come to Hidden Valley." In mid-afternoon, a C-47 dropped water, supplies, and, best of all, a stack of letters from home. Walter remained excited by the adventure, writing in his journal: "Everyone is in fine spirits. . . . This promises to be one of the most interesting parts of our lives."

As the paratroopers arranged their camp, people from the Wosi area crowded around to watch. Walter's men grew edgy from the proximity, the incessant touching, and the body odor. Walter pointed a carbine in the air.

"Fired a few shots to see effect on natives and most of them didn't stop running till they were out of sight," he wrote. His men followed suit, including one who fired a burst from a Thompson submachine gun, the famous "Tommy Gun." As the natives fled, "ass over tea kettle," as Walter put it, the men trampled the smaller boys. Some of his paratroopers got a kick out of it, but Walter ordered a cease-fire. "The men were doing it just for the hell of it, to make the natives run and yell and whatnot," he said.

The guns' noise frightened the natives, but Walter wrote in his journal that "they do not understand the killing power of the modern firearm." They seemed more afraid when the soldiers held up sticks or branches to resemble spears.

Later that day, Alfred Baylon, a stocky, cigar-smoking sergeant who was qualified as a medic, hiked to the Baliem River, followed by a group of natives. When a flock of ducks flew overhead, he used his carbine to shoot one. The natives retrieved it, and Baylon brought it back to camp. In his journal that night, Walter praised the "excellent dinner with barbecued duck." Of the natives, he wrote: "Imagine they now know our weapons can kill."

MORE THAN SIX decades later, the warning shots fired by the paratroopers and the duck hunt by Baylon—whom the natives called "Weylon"—still reverberated in the minds of old men who were boys when they witnessed the displays.

"One man, named Mageam, came in to the white men's camp," said Lisaniak Mabel. "He was getting too close, and the white people got irritated and fired shots to keep him away. We didn't know the sound, and we ran. . . . Then Weylon shot the duck. We understood he did it with the gun."

Several also remembered the hikes Walter took through the Wosi area. On one of his treks, Walter stopped at an area called Pika, near the edge of the no-man's-land, almost in enemy territory. Tribespeople believed that he was purposely standing guard at Pika. They viewed this as an act of bravery and a warning to their enemies. They called Walter "Pika," as a tribute to his apparent courage.

"Pika was shooting the gun a lot, to show the enemies not to come," said Ai Baga. "We liked when Pika went there. We told Pika to stay there, so our enemies wouldn't attack."

Narekesok Logo, his wiry body marked with long-healed arrow scars, remembered the paratroopers' visit as a time of peace: "Pika and Weylon were standing there with their guns, so our enemies didn't come."

Equally memorable to the tribespeople was the soldiers' practice

of digging a single hole covered by a tent where all of them went to
defecate. Native practice called for bodily waste to pass in private, in
the jungle or the high grasses. However revolting the soldiers found
the natives' hygiene, it couldn't exceed the natives' disgust at the
soldiers' use of a house for *inalugu*—a pile of feces.

THE NEXT DAY, Tuesday, May 22, 1945, Walter fueled up with
a breakfast of ham and eggs, biscuits, and marmalade, washed
down with hot chocolate. He and five men—Corporal Custodio
Alerta and sergeants Hermenegildo Caoili, Fernando Dongallo,
Juan "Johnny" Javonillo, and Don Ruiz—were ready to begin
the trek to the survivors' campsite. That left his first sergeant,
Sandy Abrenica, in charge of the base camp along with two sergeants, Alfred Baylon and Roque Velasco.

Walter enlisted a group of Dani men as carriers and "native
guides." After convincing himself that they understood his intended destination, they marched boldly out of base camp.

After three hours of steady uphill climbing, they broke for
lunch. Walter pulled out his journal. "God only knows why mountains are this high," he wrote. "Now we are going down again.
Passed by a few native villages and had to stop near each one so
that the people could gather around and satisfy their curiosity."
Along the way, the six soldiers gained and lost several groups of
guides, "as they do not seem to go far beyond their own villages."

With no maps, Walter and his men estimated that they traveled seven miles before stopping to pitch camp for the night. His
gut told him that the natives were no threat—he made a casual
reference in his journal to their spears and arrows, and wrote that
their "only means of cutting are stone axes." The paratroopers
needed rest for the next day's march, so Walter told his relieved
men that they wouldn't post guards that night.

———————

WALTER'S DECISION TO skip guard duty proved uneventful, but not solely because his judgment proved correct that the natives "seem very friendly," as he wrote in his journal. Unknown to Walter, tribal leaders along the route from the Wosi area base camp toward the Ogi ridge where the plane crashed had set aside their traditional enmities. They granted the strangers safe passage.

"A declaration, called a *maga*, was made that no one would attack them," said Yunggukwe Wandik, daughter of the Uwambo leader Yaralok Wandik. "It was said, 'Do not kill them. These are spirits. Don't kill them. They are not human.'" If not for the *maga*, the six sleeping soldiers might have been ambushed and slaughtered by hundreds of spear-carrying warriors whom a regional big man could have summoned on short notice.

Not everyone agreed with the *maga*. Clearly defined territorial boundaries were deeply ingrained in the people of the valley, and the idea of strangers traipsing through their neighborhoods didn't sit right with some. "There were people who thought killing them was a good idea," Yunggukwe Wandik said. If not for the soldiers' skin color—Walter's whiteness more than the Filipino-Americans' toffee coloring—the *maga* might not have held. "Do you think we had ever seen white skin before?" she said. "That made people afraid."

Despite the *maga*, more than once en route to the survivors' camp Walter and his men were met by antagonism when they came close to villages. "In a couple of cases they actually came out on a path and stopped us," he said. "They didn't want us going into their village." Walter attributed the defensiveness to a shortage of available wives. "Sandy Abrenica and I figured out later that they were afraid that we would steal their women. This happened over there. There was some thievery of women between tribes."

Walter's description of natives blocking his path echoed the confrontation that led to the shooting death of a native during Richard Archbold's expedition seven years earlier. It's not clear whether Walter and his men passed the same villages, but the paratroopers never found it necessary to use—in Archbold's euphemistic phrase for the shooting—"more than a show of force." At the same time, the natives the paratroopers encountered either were unaware of the shooting or chose not to avenge it for reasons lost to time.

Walter didn't know anything about the Archbold expedition or the Uluayek legend about the sky spirits and their rope to the valley, so he was unaware that the native men had good reason to suspect them of violence, pig theft, and wife stealing.

For his part, Walter said he wanted to avoid violence if at all possible. As for pigs, they had no time for a roast. And the last thing they wanted were native women. "Well, they didn't ever mingle," he said later. "And I told the men, absolutely not. I don't think any of them were good-looking enough for the men, anyway."

SPENT FROM HIS exertions, Walter fell into a deep sleep. The next morning, he and his men ate breakfast and waited for the supply plane, as much to get a fix on their location as to collect fresh provisions. Believing that they were on their last lap to the survivors' camp, they began the day in high spirits. But the plane never came and the latest group of native bearers proved unhelpful. "So far the natives are more bother than good," he wrote, "as they will not carry."

They broke camp and started out, believing that they had communicated to their latest guides where they were headed. But after an arduous twelve-mile hike, Walter and his men found themselves right back where they'd started. The previously buoyant tone in Walter's journal disappeared: "Did not understand that we want to go up to the wreck, not back to our camp. We are

slightly discouraged to say the least. Hiked too long before setting up camp and were caught in the rain, thus getting everything
soaking wet. Made camp and ate supper. What a rotten life."

On the third morning of their trek, they awoke chilled, water-
logged, and tired. Having planned a one- to two-day hike, Walter
and his men were out of food. Still unsure of their location, they
moved on, guided by Walter's innate sense of where they were going and "dead reckoning"—navigating in a fixed direction based
on a previous known location, in this case their base camp. They
headed toward a dip between two ridges that Walter called "the
saddle."

"Things look bad," he wrote. "Our last rations are gone and
we are still a long way from our objective. Broke camp and kept
on going up and up toward the saddle, which is somewhere at
the top of this canyon." Late in the morning he finally made contact with the supply plane to request rations. In the meantime,
they continued hiking without lunch. Much of the way they cut a
fresh trail as they went, slogging through brush and high grass. A
quick bath in a cold creek refreshed them, but the feeling didn't
last long. Soon they were exhausted, yet they "just kept going on
and on and up and up."

In late afternoon the rains came. Soaked, hungry, and cold, the
would-be rescuers made camp around five o'clock in the afternoon.
They laid out their bedrolls and went to sleep without dinner.

"God only knows where that last ridge is," Walter wrote that
night in his journal. "We can last for a few more days at this rate,
but sure as hell would like to know about where we are. Don't like
this fooling around without maps."

19

"SHOO, SHOO BABY"

THEIR STOMACHS EMPTY and growling, Walter and his team awoke early to a breakfast of hot water and hope. His top priority was receiving a drop of ten-in-one rations. He tried hailing the C-47 supply plane by walkie-talkie as it flew somewhere in the vicinity overhead, even as he worried that his campsite at the edge of the jungle might not be visible from the air. Trekking farther toward the survivors' campsite would only put them deeper under the canopy. So they stayed put, talked, and waited.

"Finally they are over us and have us spotted," he wrote in his journal on Friday, May 25, his first upbeat entry in two days. "Rations dropped. Best things I have seen in a long time. Men recovered the rations and I learned that we are two miles by air due west of the wreck."

Ravenous, Walter stuffed himself. He paid the price when they broke camp: "The first hour was terrible. Too much food." But eager to reach their destination, they pressed on, slower than usual and taking more frequent breaks. After several hours, they reached the crest of a ridge and began to hike on a downward slope. Walter hoped they were close.

AT THE SURVIVORS' camp, the radioman in the 311 supply plane passed on the news that the paratroopers were close by: "Earl will get down there pretty soon, and you'll hear him."

In late afternoon, Margaret heard what she called "that yapping noise peculiar to the natives." As the noise grew closer, it was replaced by an unmistakably American sound:

"Shoo, shoo my baby, Shoooo.
Goodbye baby, don't you cry no more.
Your big tall papa's off to the seven seas."

Walter marched buoyantly toward the campsite, swinging his bolo knife to clear the trail and singing the Andrew Sisters' recent hit, "Shoo, Shoo Baby."

Writing about the paratroopers' arrival in her diary, Margaret's first impression of Walter bordered on starry-eyed: "He looked like a giant as he came down the trail at the head of his Filipino boys and the ubiquitous escort of natives. The captain's arrival was like a strong, fresh breeze. He was not only a capable and efficient officer, but a one-man floor show. Two minutes after he arrived the camp started jumpin'."

Doc and Rammy rushed from their tents to greet their comrades. Walter was happy to see the survivors, but he was overjoyed to see the two medics. "I knew they were all right," he said, "but I wanted to see them and congratulate them again, first of all on the jump, and secondly on the good job they had done. And just to get back together with them. The rest of the men felt the same way. We were all quite concerned about them."

Margaret watched as Walter and the medics exchanged embraces, handshakes, and hearty pats on the back. She wrote in her diary: "His men worshipped Walter, and the affection was patently mutual."

Walter, meanwhile, couldn't help but notice that Margaret, despite her jungle haircut, her weight loss, and her injuries, "was a pretty good-looking gal."

WITH THE SURVIVORS' camp now expanded to ten men and one woman, Walter set his troops to work putting up more pup tents as sleeping quarters. They also erected a large pyramidal tent with a peaked roof and walls about sixteen feet long on each side, to serve as a combination headquarters, mess hall, and jungle social club for the two officers, Walter and McCollom; one WAC; and eight enlisted men.

Soon an American flag waved from a makeshift flagpole outside the big tent, making the camp a quasi-official U.S. Army base. In one journal entry, Walter called it "The Lost Outpost of Shangri-La." He wrote: "The Stars and Stripes now fly over the Oranje Mountain Range. Being the first white people here, we can claim this territory for Uncle Sam, but doubt if the Aussies would appreciate it."

After a bath in the creek and dinner served up by McCollom, Walter pulled out a deck of cards and organized the first of what became daily games of poker and gin rummy. Margaret was no

THE AMERICAN FLAG WAVING OVER "THE LOST OUTPOST OF SHANGRI-LA." (PHOTO COURTESY OF B. B. MCCOLLOM.)

poker player, preferring bridge, but she kept herself amused as they "won and lost thousands of dollars" in every session. Lacking chips, they bet with Raleigh and Chelsea brand cigarettes, along with wooden matches to light their winnings. She modeled her gambling style on the freewheeling ways of Sergeant Caoili, who'd bluff like mad on a pair of threes. Caoili was relentless in everything he did; when he wasn't winning and losing matchsticks, he earned the nicknames "Superman" and "Iron Man" for his powerful build and tireless work habits.

Sitting around their improvised card table in the big tent, Walter smoldered at Margaret's card-playing style. He stewed over what he viewed as her stubborn refusal to learn the rules of the game.

"There ought to be a law against women playing poker!" he shouted.

Neither was he impressed when she invented a pokerlike game she called "Deuces wild, roll your own, and fiery cross." Incomprehensible to everyone but Margaret, the game involved a muddle of wild cards and an opportunity for players to form the best possible hand using fifteen cards.

Walter declared: "Maggie, you don't know how to play cards."

"I do, too!" Margaret answered.

"Well, you probably know how to play bridge, but I don't know how to play bridge. This is poker we're playing, and there are a pair, three of a kind, a straight, a flush, and so on."

In Walter's view, Margaret could never remember the ranking of the best-to-worst poker hands. "We'd always get into an argument because I knew what I was drawing to, and she didn't," he said.

Margaret thought Walter's anger could be traced to another source: his machismo. "The captain played just as earnestly as if it were for real money," she told her diary, "and when I would bluff him out of a big pot he would be livid."

After cards, the paratroopers, the survivors, and the some of the natives passed the evening hours by entertaining each other.

Margaret, feeling better by the day, sang WAC tunes, and several paratroopers showed off their vocal stylings with Visayan love songs from the Philippines. The natives played the only musical instrument the survivors and paratroopers ever heard in Shangri-La: a simple mouth harp whose tune sounded to the outsiders like a monotonic funeral dirge. But there was only one star: Camp Shangri-La's commanding officer.

"Walter was a personality kid," Margaret wrote. "Often, after supper, he would put on a one-man floor show. He could give a wonderful imitation of a nightclub singer or a radio crooner. Then he would truck and shag, singing popular songs while not only we, but the natives, sat around entranced. 'Shoo, Shoo Baby' was always his favorite. Walter was wonderful for morale. No one could be downhearted for long in his presence."

As Margaret's health returned, so did her appetites. Soon Walter got the strong impression that Margaret found him sexually attractive. He picked up signals that she expected him to make a pass at her, and she looked for opportunities to spend time with him. Walter may have been tempted, but he insisted that he never made a move. Walter took seriously his marriage and his role as the mission's commanding officer. He never explained his behavior to Margaret, but she apparently got the message.

When Walter didn't rise to the bait, he said, Margaret turned her attentions to one of his men, Sergeant Don Ruiz.

Walter was no prude—only a few years earlier, he'd cut high school classes to visit L.A. strip clubs—and he didn't care what enlisted personnel did in private, on their own time. But he felt responsible for everything that happened on his watch in Shangri-La. He knew there was no birth control in the valley, and he didn't want unexpected consequences.

Not certain how best to proceed, Walter approached McCollom for help.

"I wanted him to tell Maggie to leave the men alone," Walter said. "I had one noncom that was the best-looking guy in the unit, Don Ruiz. He was one of my best noncoms, and also one of the handsomest men around. Maggie sort of had her eyes on him and tried to seduce him a couple of times."

Torn between interest in Margaret and respect for his captain, Ruiz found a private moment to speak with Walter.

"Captain," he said, "what am I going to do?"

"Just leave her the hell alone," Walter answered. "Walk away, just walk away."

A flirtation between the two continued, but as far as Walter knew, it remained unconsummated.

After speaking with Ruiz, Walter gathered his troops and laid down the law to the entire squad: "If anybody lays a hand on her, so help me God, you're busted to private the next minute."

Walter explained: "I had to remind my men a couple of times that I sure as hell didn't want a pregnant WAC flying out of there. . . . That would have given me a pretty bad reputation. So I had to be adamant about that."

THE DAY AFTER arriving at the survivors' camp, Walter watched Doc and Rammy slice and peel the gangrenous skin from Margaret's and Decker's wounds. He took admiring note of the medics' work in his journal, writing that "both men deserved all the credit in the world." But one look at the injuries convinced Walter that his hope of a quick return to the base camp in the big valley had been overly optimistic. He wrote in his journal they'd be stuck at the jungle campsite for at least a week, maybe longer. Even then, he thought that he and his men would have to carry Margaret and Decker at least partway through the jungle and down the slippery mountain slope.

That day, just before lunchtime, the supply plane dropped its usual load of provisions, as well as books and magazines to help pass the time. When they gathered the cargo, the paratroopers found supplies for their difficult next task: burial duty. The 311 dropped twenty-one freshly pressed silver dog tags, along with twenty wooden crosses and one wooden Star of David. The military believed that the crash victims included sixteen Protestants, four Catholics, and one Jewish WAC, Sergeant Belle Naimer of the Bronx. Only much later would the military learn that a second Star of David should have been dropped, for Private Mary Landau of Brooklyn.

Aboard the plane that day, helping to toss the funerary supplies out the cargo door, was Sergeant Ruth Coster, whose workload had kept her from flying aboard the *Gremlin Special*, but whose best friend, Sergeant Helen Kent, had died in the crash. Other than keeping Helen's memory alive, it was the last thing Ruth could do for her.

On Sunday, May 27, two weeks after the crash, Walter awoke at seven in the morning, ate a hearty breakfast, and set out for the wreck with five sergeants: Bulatao, Caoili, Dongallo, Javonillo, and Ruiz. Following detailed directions from McCollom, they tried to retrace the survivors' trail in reverse, using the stream to guide them up the mountain. But they became confused about which of its tributaries to follow. The paratroopers left their equipment and the grave markers at an easy-to-find spot and split up—Walter and Ruiz went one way, and the other four men went another. Trekking through the jungle proved impossible, especially since they weren't sure where they were headed. After several hours, both groups returned to the campsite, exhausted. To make matters worse, Walter had strained his groin on the hike.

The following day, Walter sent Caoili and Javonillo on another search mission for the crash site, but they had no better luck. Walter knew what he needed: someone who'd been there before. Finally, McCollom led a group back up the mountain toward the wreck, navigating by the river and a few landmarks he remembered. McCollom knew they were close when he spotted wispy strands of light-brown hair tangled in vines and shrubs. He recalled how Margaret's long hair had snagged in the brush when they'd left the crash site for the clearing, and how he'd used his pocketknife to give her a jungle cut. McCollom and the paratroopers followed the trail of Margaret's hair directly to the burned, broken remains of the *Gremlin Special*.

As they entered the area where the plane had mowed down trees and carved a hole through the canopy, McCollom hung back. "There it is," he told the paratroopers, pointing the way. He'd already seen enough. He didn't need to see the remains of his brother; his commander, Colonel Peter Prossen; and his friends, colleagues, and fellow passengers.

Later that night, McCollom relied on reports from the paratroopers who'd hiked with him to describe the situation to Walter. "Lieutenant Mac's report on the wreck is very disheartening," Walter wrote that night in his journal. "Only three bodies are identifiable—Captain Good, Sergeant Besley and Private Hanna. The last two are both WACs. The rest of the bodies are in a cremated jumble. Still not decided on disposition." Several days later, Walter received his orders via walkie-talkie: return to the crash site with the grave markers and shovels.

They started out just after dawn and reached what was left of the *Gremlin Special* in late morning. Joining Walter were the five paratroopers who'd accompanied him from the big valley. McCollom wouldn't join the burial patrol, and Margaret and Decker were too hurt to help. Even with McCollom's instructions, the jungle was so thick that at one point they came within twenty yards of the *Gremlin Special* without knowing it.

When the paratroopers reached the wreck, they buried Laura Besley and Eleanor Hanna side by side in an area they called the cemetery. "After that," Walter wrote in his journal, "we buried Captain Good and made a common grave for the eighteen unidentifiable persons."

As he recounted the day's events, the tone of Walter's journal shifted. He and his men had jumped into the valley for the adventure of a rescue mission. Now they were on grave duty, and the tragic reality hit home:

> Those eighteen were all mixed up, and most of the bodies had been completely cremated by the intense heat of the fire. It was the best burial we could give them under the circumstances. All of us had to use gas masks, as the odor was terrific. I don't mind dead women, but dead women in the nude is something different. Also the bodies were almost a month old. After the burials were completed, I took some camera shots of the wreck and the graves. God only knows how anyone got out of the plane alive. It is without a doubt the most thoroughly destroyed aircraft I have ever seen."

ONE OF THE CROSSES ERECTED BY THE BURIAL CREW NEAR THE WRECKAGE OF THE *GREMLIN SPECIAL*. (PHOTO COURTESY OF C. EARL WALTER JR.)

After covering the graves, Walter and his men pounded the crosses and the Star of David into the damp earth, draping each one with a dog tag. Their labors took until late afternoon, and by then the sun was setting, its last rays reflecting off mountain walls. The nightly mist slithered into the jungle.

As Walter and his men worked, circling overhead was a U.S. Army plane with two chaplains. One, Colonel August Gearhard, a Catholic priest from Milwaukee, was a hero in his own right, having received the Distinguished Service Cross, second only to the Medal of Honor, for bravery in World War I. The other was Lieutenant Colonel Carl Mellberg of Dayton, Ohio, who conducted the Protestant service. One of the chaplains also spoke Jewish prayers for Belle Naimer and, unknowingly, Mary Landau.

"Out of the depth I have cried unto thee, O Lord," prayed Father Gearhard, as the service was broadcast over the walkie-talkie to the cemetery area and the survivors' campsite. Chaplain Cornelius Waldo, who'd earlier dropped Bibles and prayer books to the survivors, later told a reporter that the scene "seemed to whisper a peace more living and beautiful than any spot I've ever seen."

Margaret wrote in her diary: "From that plane, over the radio, came the saddest and most impressive funeral service I have ever heard. We sat around the camp radio, silent and very humble as a Catholic, a Protestant and a Jewish chaplain in the plane read burial services for the dead on the mountaintop. We were very humble because we have been saved where so many had perished. Lieutenant McCollom sat with his head bowed, his usual controlled self. But Sergeant Decker's and my hearts ached for him. On one of those white crosses up that cruel mountain hung the dog tag of his twin brother, Lieutenant Robert E. McCollom, from whom only death could separate him."

The burial team hiked back toward the campsite, stopping along the way to bathe in the creek. They cleansed themselves, but without heavy-duty soap and hot water, they couldn't wash the stench of death out of their uniforms. Later, Walter would ask the supply plane for replacements, so they could throw away the clothes they'd worn for the burials. After their baths, the enlisted men had a late lunch, but Walter settled into a contemplative mood and skipped the meal.

That night at the campsite, McCollom kept to himself. Walter, Margaret, and Decker fell into what Walter called "a long discussion on the world at war." Decker gave up after a while and went to his tent, but Walter and Margaret kept arguing deep into the night about politics and the military. "She seems to have it in for the Army, will not listen to any logical reasoning," Walter wrote. "Man, but she is really stubborn."

Still, he respected her. "Margaret was a true blue gal," Walter said later. "She had a lot of gumption and a lot of guts. It might have been that she was the only woman surrounded by a lot of men, and she had to hold her own. But she would never listen to anyone trying to tell her anything!"

The bickering kept the camp from sleep. Rammy called to them that it was past midnight, and the debate ended. Walter wrote: "Off to bed we went with nothing at all settled."

THE PEOPLE OF Uwambo watched as the creatures they thought were spirits made repeated trips to the top of the Ogi ridge. The natives, who cremated their dead, didn't comprehend the burial rites. With no religious symbols of their own, they also didn't understand the meaning of the crosses and the Star of David.

"When they climbed the mountain," said Yunggukwe Wandik, "we all thought they wanted to know if they could see their homes from there."

BY THE TIME the funeral was complete, the U.S. War Department had sent two dozen telegrams to the next-of-kin of the crew and passengers of the *Gremlin Special*. All but three began with some variation of the standard military death notice: "The Secretary of War deeply regrets to inform you . . ." Upon receipt of those formal condolences, twenty-one hopeful blue-star families became twenty-one grieving gold-star families.

Margaret Nicholson of Medford, Massachusetts, the mother of Major George Nicholson, received condolence letters from three of America's top generals: Douglas MacArthur, Clements McMullen, and H. H. "Hap" Arnold. Although pilot error might have been suspected, Nicholson's full role in the crash wasn't known; even after it emerged that he was alone at the controls, the Army Air Forces never fixed blame for the wreck of the *Gremlin Special*. Talk of an investigation fizzled, and vague suppositions about sudden downdrafts remained the presumptive cause in the official record.

Hap Arnold, commanding general of the Army Air Forces, described Nicholson to his mother as having died "while he was flying in the service of his Country." McMullen, Fee-Ask's commanding general, wrote: "You may well be proud of the important part which your son took in forwarding the mission of this command." MacArthur wrote: "Your consolation for his loss may be that he died in the service of our country in a just cause which, with Victory, will give freedom from oppression to all peoples."

For the McCollom family, the official notices highlighted the twins' permanent separation. A condolence telegram went to the young wife of Robert McCollom. Her in-laws, who were listed as John McCollom's next-of-kin, received a different letter altogether. Theirs was the embodiment of answered prayers. It echoed the letters received by the parents of Ken Decker in Kelso, Washington, and Margaret Hastings's widowed father, Patrick Hastings, in Owego, New York.

On May 27, 1945, three long days after he received the initial "missing" telegram, Patrick Hastings opened a letter from the

U.S. Army saying that "a corrected report has now been received which indicates that your daughter was injured in a plane crash . . . and that she is safe instead of missing in action as you were previously advised." The letter promised updates on rescue operations and Margaret's condition.

A follow-up came twelve days later, in more human terms, from the Hollandia chaplain, Cornelius Waldo: "Notice has reached you by now that your dear daughter Margaret has had a very miraculous escape in a plane crash. Due to the fact that the survivors are in a rather inaccessible spot, it will be some time before she will be back at the base to write you herself. I talked to her on the radio the day we dropped supplies and paratroopers. She is quite all right in spite of her harrowing experience."

Waldo didn't mention her burns, her gangrene, or her other wounds, or the fact that the military still didn't know how to get Margaret, her fellow survivors, and their rescuers back to Hollandia.

20

"HEY, MARTHA!"

AFTER THE BURIALS, the jungle recuperation camp fell into a routine of medical treatments, meals, reading, card games, and bull sessions, punctuated by near-daily supply drops and encounters with the natives. Eager to get moving, Walter radioed Major George Gardner, who oversaw the supply runs from aboard the 311, to request a helicopter transport from the jungle campsite to the valley. That way, Walter figured, they wouldn't need to carry Margaret and Decker or wait until they were well enough to travel by foot.

Walter's request for a helicopter could be chalked up to wishful thinking, lack of aviation expertise, fatigue, or all three. If a helicopter could have flown over the surrounding mountains to ferry them from the jungle campsite, it presumably could have flown them out of the valley altogether, even if only one or two at a time. And if a helicopter had been a viable alternative, Colonel Elsmore and the other rescue planners in Hollandia might not have needed Walter, the medics, and the other paratroopers in the first place.

The most likely explanation for Walter's wish for a helicopter—expressed several times in his daily journal entries—was his desire to hasten his return to Hollandia. He thought he could parlay success in Shangri-La into a combat posting, and he was keen to play that card with the military brass.

While Walter waited for answers from Gardner on a helicopter,

THE "HEADQUARTERS" TENT AT THE JUNGLE CLEARING, WITH (FROM LEFT) JOHN MCCOLLOM, KEN DECKER, BEN BULATAO, AND CAMILO RAMIREZ. (PHOTO COURTESY OF C. EARL WALTER JR.)

and from the medics on the survivors' ability to move out, the young captain's growing impatience seeped into his journal:

> May 29, 1945: Decided to straighten up our kitchen, so Don [Ruiz] and I went to work on it, then waited around for the plane. Finally it came, a new plane and new crew. . . . They dropped one bundle two miles from us and it fell apart. They must think this is a tea party we are on. I blew my top and the plane took off for Hollandia. . . . All clothes for Hastings. She has enough now for a trousseau. No medical supplies. What a snafu bunch is running this show. . . . Here's hoping on the helicopter.

> May 30, 1945: Waited for the plane but it did not come. We have plenty of food but our medical supplies are very low. . . . Spent the afternoon in the sack reading and shooting the breeze. What a life. Certainly wish the answer on the helicopter would come through. Or at least that the patients would get well enough to travel. . . . Rain came early so we are all in

the sack and most of the boys are reading. Spirits are fine and we are only wishing for some excitement. . . . God only knows what is going on in the outside world.

May 31, 1945: Up a little later this morning as there was nothing in particular to do. After breakfast I sent Caoili and Alerta out on a recon for a shorter route to the valley. . . . The plane came over early this morning . . . and the helicopter is out, so that is that and we hike out. I certainly hope the three survivors can take it.

June 1, 1945: This is really going to be hell, just sitting around, waiting to get out of here. . . . Patients' recovery is all I am waiting for.

June 2, 1945: The plane came over at ten-thirty with our supplies and mail. We certainly needed the medical supplies and I received eight letters, which certainly helped the old morale. They gave us a brief resumé of the world news, and it is certainly encouraging. After lunch I read *Bedside Esquire* and then we got ready for dinner. . . . Certainly hope the recovery of the patients speeds up a bit.

June 3, 1945: What a morning. Slept till eleven-thirty. First time that has ever happened to me without a hangover involved, at least on Sunday anyway. Had some cereal and then waited for lunch. . . . This is quite a life and getting damn tiresome, but can't do anything till I am sure that the trip to my base camp will not hurt the patients. Oh well—it's a good rest.

June 4, 1945: In the morning, I fired a few rounds with the carbine. That is an excellent way to waste time. After you are through, you have to clean the weapon so it takes up a little time. Dinner tonight was really something. Prepared by Dongallo and Bulatao. Casserole of bacon, corned beef, sweet potatoes and peas, with rice on the side. Last but not least peaches for dessert. Weather still bad and no plane today. Morale is excellent.

June 7, 1945: . . . Sat around and talked about home.

June 8, 1945: Well, one year ago today I said goodbye to my wife Sal. It certainly seems a hell of a lot longer than that. I miss her more than ever up in this place, and that is going some. Don [Ruiz] woke me up this morning telling me that the plane was overhead. . . . Two war correspondents were in the plane, so I imagine this damn show is getting plenty of publicity back in the States. I hope so, as the men have worked plenty hard on this show, and maybe it will open a few people's eyes to the possibilities of my future plans. The two were Mr. Simmons of the *Chicago Tribune* and Mr. Morton of AP.

THE "SHOW"—THE CRASH, the survivors, the natives, and the rescue mission in Shangri-La—had indeed reached the United States and beyond. After a nearly three-week news blackout, Colonel Elsmore let out word to the press that something remarkable was happening in the heart of New Guinea. Several reporters took the bait, but none more avidly than the two reporters Walter mentioned in his journal.

Walter Simmons of the *Chicago Tribune* was thirty-seven, a native of Fargo, North Dakota, whose father sold patent medicine. After two years of college, Simmons signed on as reporter for the *Daily Argus-Leader* in Sioux Falls, South Dakota. Ten years later, in 1942, he moved to the big time with a job covering the war in the South Pacific for the *Tribune*. Beneath the gruff exterior of a grizzled war correspondent, Simmons showed a flair for rich images and tight, well-turned phrases. "The dawn comes up like thunder every morning and this is how it goes," he began a story about the daily life of American troops on Leyte Island. "Suddenly there is a sound like a giant hand beating a carpet. 'Whomp, whomp,

whomp' it goes. It is a 40 mm gun battery signaling a raid alert. Soldiers and civilians leave their beds."

In the weeks before Simmons hopped aboard the supply plane over Shangri-La, he'd kept busy feeding red meat to *Tribune* readers. Reporting in May 1945 from the Philippines while traveling with a division of the Illinois National Guard, Simmons wrote stories whose persistent theme was reflected in their headlines: "Midwest Yanks Fight Way Out of Jap Ambush," "Chicago Yank's Penknife Ends Fight with Jap," "Yanks Harvest Crop of 19 Japs in Rice Garden," and "Midwest Yanks' 'Banzai' Charge Wins a Jap Hill." In addition to appearing in the *Tribune*, Simmons's stories were distributed by the Chicago Tribune News Service, which had more than sixty newspapers as subscribers, and also by Reuters, the British news service.

Simmons's colleague and competitor, Ralph Morton of The Associated Press, reached an even wider audience. Like Simmons, Morton was thirty-seven and a reporter who'd reached the big leagues after years in the minors. A native of Nova Scotia, Morton had worked as a reporter for the *Halifax Herald*, the Canadian Press news service, and the *Protestant Digest*. He joined the AP in 1943 in New York, and early in 1945 was promoted to war correspondent and the wire service's Australia bureau chief. The AP served more than fourteen hundred newspapers during World War II, and the wire service also provided news to radio stations across the country. With the wire service's enormous reach, Morton's voice was amplified many thousand times over.

After flying over the survivors' campsite, Simmons and Morton filed stories that lit up newsrooms around the world. Every editor worth his or her salt recognized that the two war correspondents had found a humdinger of a story, known in the trade as a "Hey, Martha!" The phrase took its name from an imagined exchange between a mythical couple, long married and not necessarily happy about it. The husband, call him Harold, would be relaxing in his easy chair, his nose buried in a newspaper. Upon reading an especially surprising and interesting story, Harold would break his customary silence and loudly proclaim to his long-suffering wife, "Hey, Martha, wait 'til you hear this!"

The guts of the stories written by Walter Simmons and Ralph Morton were basically the same: A U.S. Army plane crashed near a lost valley in Dutch New Guinea inhabited by a tribe of Stone Age cannibals. Three of the twenty-four people aboard survived. One was a beautiful WAC. Another survivor had lost his twin brother in the crash. The third had suffered a terrible head injury. A crack squad of paratroopers jumped into treacherous terrain to help and protect them. Tense confrontations with tribe members evolved into cross-cultural understanding. Friendship, even. No rescue plan was yet in place.

Simmons's story began: "In a hidden valley, one-hundred-thirty miles southwest of Hollandia, a WAC and two airmen are awaiting rescue following one of the most fantastic tragedies of the war. No white man had ever set foot in this isolated paradise before a C-47 transport plane circled over it at 3:15 p.m., May 13." In the next paragraph, Simmons disclosed that the flight's purpose was for the passengers and crew "to see the queer, unclad people who threw spears at planes."

Simmons's story created suspense by focusing on the military's uncertainty about how the outsiders might exit the secluded valley: "For three weeks the tiny WAC secretary and the two men have been cheerfully awaiting rescue, but no plan has been definitely worked out. Several ideas have been suggested—an auto-giro [forerunner to the helicopter], a seaplane which might land on a lake thirty miles away, a glider snatch, and tiny liaison planes which could bring out one passenger each trip." Simmons pointed out obstacles to each approach, and that "an overland trek is possible but it would require weeks."

An Associated Press story, relying on Morton's dispatches, focused more squarely on the natives: "The crash of an Army transport plane in the wilds of Dutch New Guinea has unlocked the secrets of a mountain-bound 'Shangri-La' where six-foot tribesmen live in a state of barbaric feudalism inside walled towns." Ratcheting up the height of the mountains, and presumably the drama, the AP story claimed that the plane crashed into a seventeen-thousand-foot peak. That would have made it two thousand feet higher than New Guinea's tallest mountain.

Newspaper editors across the country, including those at *The New York Times*, ran the stories on page one. News of the war still occupied the hearts and minds of Americans—the savage, two-month Battle of Okinawa remained under way, with many thousands of dead on both sides. But a dramatic story about a military plane crash in a "real" Shangri-La, with a WAC and two male survivors, living among Stone Age tribesmen and a team of brave paratroopers, with no certain rescue plan, was war news with a new and exciting twist.

The widespread, enthusiastic response to the initial stories confirmed what Simmons, Morton, and their bosses no doubt suspected: the story of Shangri-La was hot. Even better, the *Gremlin Special* crash had what reporters call "legs"—a developing plotline, certain to yield more page-one stories and more urgent calls to Martha.

A FLOOD OF interest followed the dispatches from Simmons and Morton. Other war correspondents clamored for seats in the supply plane, all eager to write their own version of a story that, in journalistic shorthand, became known as "a WAC in Shangri-La." Colonel Elsmore, always enamored of press coverage, happily obliged. He even arranged for a WAC stenographer, Corporal Marie Gallagher, to fly aboard the 311 to transcribe walkie-talkie conversations between the plane and the survivors' camp.

In one transcript, one of Margaret's tentmates, Private Esther "Ack Ack" Aquilio, relayed a message through the radio operator. The message described Esther's fears for Margaret's safety and inquired about how Margaret was feeling. Margaret shot back: "Tell her to stop worrying and start praying!" The reporters ate it up.

In another transcript, Walter described Margaret as "the queen of the valley." He told the reporters how he and his men had limited success trading with the locals, but Margaret had collected woven rattan bracelets and "just about anything she wants from the natives." Again the reporters pounced. Their stories called her "the queen of Shangri-La." Major Gardner got in on the act on his daily talks with Walter via walkie-talkie, asking: "How's the queen this morning?" The major tried to goad Margaret into speaking directly to him and the reporters. She declined.

Walter and McCollom alternated on the ground end of the conversations, with Gardner, radio operator Sergeant Jack Gutzeit, and the AP's Ralph Morton taking turns manning the radio on the plane. Morton couldn't have been happier with his participation in the story. He even began taking supply orders from the ground crew. In one story—headlined "Shangri-La Gets Latest News from Associated Press"—Morton breathlessly described how he read a summary of the world and the war to the survivors.

To avoid being left behind, Walter Simmons started to file his stories with the dateline "Aboard Transport Plane over Hidden Valley." Within days, the *Tribune* offered Margaret, McCollom, and Decker $1,000 each for their "exclusive" stories upon their return. While the survivors considered the offer, Walter admitted to his journal that he suffered a pang of jealousy.

On one flight, Decker's cousin, WAC private Thelma Decker, came along to offer encouragement. But when she stood from her seat to approach the radio compartment, she was overcome with airsickness and felt too ill to speak.

Another time, radioman Jack Gutzeit brought a phonograph

to play Benny Goodman and Harry James records. Walter joked about jitterbugging in Shangri-La, but the music came through garbled.

Meanwhile, Gutzeit developed an air-to-ground crush on Margaret. On his day off, he hitched a flight to Brisbane, Australia, where he bought a box of chocolates and dropped them to her by parachute. A few days later, Gutzeit got cheeky when Walter relayed a request from Margaret for "one complete outfit—shirt, t-shirt, trousers and a bra."

"Tell her she doesn't need that down there," Gutzeit said. "She can go native."

The drops became so routine that the supply plane began treating them like milk runs. But one flight through the valley nearly ended with the deaths of two supply crew members. When the crew chief, Sergeant Peter Dobransky, and the cargo supervisor, Sergeant James Kirchanski, opened the rear cargo bay, the wind caught hold of a door and ripped it off its hinges. Dobransky and Kirchanski were sucked toward the opening. As Walter Simmons reported in the *Tribune*, the two men "clawed at the aluminum door frame and managed to keep each other from falling out of the plane." The wayward door slammed against the plane's tail section, but the 311 remained airworthy. The two sergeants suffered only scratches and bruises, and were back aboard the next flight.

During one supply run, the AP's Ralph Morton wondered if Shangri-La might contain hidden riches. He asked Walter if the paratroopers had tried panning for gold in the Baliem River. Walter delivered the disappointing news: not only were there no fish in the river, there were no precious metals, either.

Much of the radio conversation was devoted to Walter and McCollom making small talk with the reporters, Major Gardner, Jack Gutzeit, and a new pilot, Captain Hugh Arthur. Now and then they placed orders for supplies and seashells, for trading with the natives. As days passed, those orders included cases of beer, which meant that alcohol had entered Shangri-La for the first time in recorded history.

The flights also brought regular mail from home. For Margaret that meant letters from her two sisters, "who said my father was too overcome to write." McCollom and Decker heard from their parents, Walter from his wife, and the paratroopers from friends, sweethearts, and family. The mail drops gave editors at the *Chicago Tribune* an idea: they offered to have Walter Simmons deliver personal messages from the survivors' families. Although the families could just as easily have done so themselves in letters, they took up the newspaper's offer.

"We are all fine at home and will be looking for you just as soon as you can get here," said the message from Patrick Hastings. "Hope and pray you are well and unhurt. Your sisters want to say hello. It really is something to have a famous daughter. Wait till you see the papers. Thank the *Chicago Tribune* for getting this message thru to you. It is a real thrill to send it. We will be seeing you soon, we hope. Love, Dad."

Bert Decker's message to his son read: "We hope you are recovering satisfactorily and will soon be back at your post. Mother and I are fine, but anxious. Dad."

Rolla and Eva McCollom sent a message tinged with controlled midwestern sadness: "We are happy that you survived. Anxiously awaiting direct word from you. So sorry about Robert. Our love to you. Dad and Mom." Later, McCollom responded privately in a letter in which he tried to allay his parents' and sister-in-law's fears that Robert had suffered or had wandered, hurt and alone, into the jungle. He wrote: "Robert was killed instantly and the body was burned completely. I was up to the wreck fifteen days after the accident and could find none of his personal belongings. Even if I could have identified him it would be impossible to get his body out."

Morton and Simmons filed daily stories, and soon they began straining for news. Simmons seemed to get a kick out of reporting Margaret's one persistent supply request: "How about dropping me some panties? Any kind will do." But when other reporters repeated the story, the request got mangled.

"A few days later," Margaret wrote in her diary, "Major Gardner told me with great glee that a story had been published saying I was begging for a pair of pants. That was one of the few incidents that ever worried me. I knew if my father read the story and thought I was running around in the jungle without enough clothing, he'd have a fit." No matter how many times Margaret asked, no panties ever arrived.

Other times, the walkie-talkie transcripts read like letters home from summer camp:

Lieutenant John McCollom: We're listening to the beautiful morning breakfast club. Over.

Major George Gardner: So this is the breakfast club. What are you guys eating this morning? How about a little chatter?

McCollom: We had a pretty good breakfast. Rice pudding, ham and eggs, bacon, coffee, cocoa, pineapple—anything you want to eat. Drop in and see us some morning, boys. The best mess hall in the Southwest Pacific.

AS MARGARET AND Decker healed, Doc Bulatao found himself with hours of free time. Every morning, after checking on his American patients, Bulatao visited with the people of Uwambo. "Tropic skin diseases and festering sores yielded to Doc and to modern drugs like magic," Margaret wrote. The native wars remained on hiatus while the survivors and paratroopers were at the area the natives called Mundima, but the natives enjoyed demonstrating their bow-and-arrow skills nonetheless. Once, however, a native man became the victim of friendly fire, and Doc patched an arrow wound in the man's side.

The medical care provided by Bulatao and Ramirez endeared them to the natives, who called them "Mumu" and "Mua." Walter and the other paratroopers also received local names from the people of Uwambo, including Pingkong and Babikama, but which name belonged to which man was lost to time.

While waiting to move out, Walter recorded lengthy thoughts about the natives in his journal. He was generally respectful, and some of his conclusions showed anthropological insight. He admired their gardens as "excellent examples of hard work and common sense," and credited their homes as "well constructed and weatherproof."

Other observations, however, relied on incomplete data and mistaken assumptions. Because few women joined the men who visited the campsite, Walter believed there was a shortage of native women. And because he didn't see the natives eat pig, he assumed they were strict vegetarians. Elsewhere in his journal, Walter repeated cultural stereotypes of the natives as "childish in everything they do or say." A few of Walter's observations might best be classified as fraternity house humor:

Today we showed one of the natives some pictures of pinup girls. Immediately he seemed to understand that they were women and he tapped the gourd around his private parts in a knowing manner. Some of the boys goaded him on a bit, and soon the gourd could no longer contain his excitement. It appears that sexual pleasure is an uncommon occurrence amongst these natives due to the shortage of the female sex. He finally beat a hasty retreat when he found that the gourd could no longer contain or act as a covering for his state of mind. It appeared as though he was thoroughly embarrassed, to say the least.

Walter also enjoyed a laugh at the sight of a little boy, perhaps six years old, who couldn't quite fill his gourd. The dried shell hung to one side, exposing the boy's not-yet-proud manhood.

As part of his curiosity about the tribe, Walter conducted an experiment in which he drew simple pencil drawings on blank paper. He showed them to the same man involved in the pinup incident, then gave him paper and a pencil. "He then proceeded to draw many curving lines on the paper much like a baby would do when first meeting crayon and paper. He was very proud of his achievement and showed his efforts to me with a big smile." Walter concluded: "It seems to me that these natives could be educated easily with the proper methods."

Interviewed over walkie-talkie by the *Tribune*'s Walter Simmons, Walter described the natives' physical features, the "excellent condition" of their teeth, and their villages in great detail. Despite his impression of them as "an agile and strong race," Walter expressed surprise that they didn't make better bearers. He

TWO NATIVE TRIBESMEN PHOTOGRAPHED IN 1945. (PHOTO COURTESY OF C. EARL WALTER JR.)

chalked it up to "the fact that they are so used to going around naked and carrying nothing." In another interview, he said the natives "treat us like white gods dropped out of the sky." Then he gushed: "These are possibly the happiest people I've ever seen. They are always enjoying themselves."

Later, he elaborated: "They lived well, had all they needed to eat, they had a place to stay, and they were a happy bunch," he said. "It was a garden paradise all by itself, and nobody bothered them. They had clashes amongst themselves, but no trouble with the outside world. . . . The whole outside world was at war and here we had complete peace and happiness in this little valley. The outside world hadn't gotten to it."

In one important respect, the natives didn't acquiesce to the outsiders. Walter wrote in his journal that "they still don't want us in their villages and this feeling persisted during our entire stay. . . . Also, we are warned constantly about being around in the same area as their women and also they try to keep us away from their camote [sweet potato] patches as much as they can." When he happened upon a young woman, Walter appraised her more generously than he had the first woman he described: "This one was lighter than the others and quite attractive for a native girl. Her busts were large and well formed, but not out of proportion. She was without a doubt the best-looking girl we saw during our stay in the valley."

WALTER'S JOURNAL OBSERVATIONS reflected what he thought and experienced. But they were limited by a lack of knowledge of the tribe's language or perspective. He had no idea that the people of Uwambo regarded him and his companions as spirits from the sky, or that their appearance had fulfilled the prophecy of the Uluayek legend.

Their return having been foretold, the survivors and paratroopers were welcomed by the otherwise warlike natives. But there were limits. In the long-ago times recounted by the legend, the spirits climbed down the rope from the sky and stole women and pigs.

Had he known about Uluayek, Walter might have been less surprised by how the native men behaved when he came within range of the native women.

21

PROMISED LAND

AS DAYS PASSED, Walter encouraged the reporters' attention, viewing it as a potential steppingstone for his own interests. "Both W.C. [war correspondent] men were along again today, and it appears that this little job is making headlines all over the world," he wrote in his journal. "All I hope is that out of this possibility we might get a combat mission." Another day he wrote: "If this deal is getting all the publicity it appears to be, I am sure that my prayers on the future will be answered."

Within days of writing those words, Walter learned that his prayers had indeed come true, up to a point. It's unclear whether the press coverage played any role, but Walter learned via walkie-talkie that he and his men had received orders to ship out for the Philippines, if and when they returned to Hollandia. The Japanese had almost given up the fight in the islands—resistance on Mindanao was nearing an end, and General MacArthur was on the verge of declaring the Philippines "secure." Still, Walter was as eager as ever to join his guerrilla leader father in action. "My last news of Dad said that he was okay, but still out on patrol," he wrote after learning about his orders.

When the excitement faded, Walter despaired that the survivors' slow recuperation seemed to be conspiring against him. Twice Walter pushed back his target date for the return hike to the valley base camp, after Doc Bulatao declared that Margaret and Decker were much improved but still weren't ready for the arduous trek. In his journal, Walter described the conflict he felt between responsibility and desire: "I will not risk any further infections of the patients' wounds, possibly resulting in amputation." Immediately afterward, he added: "The whole party is a little discouraged by this delay, especially my boys and myself, who are on orders to leave for the P.I. [Philippine Islands]. There is a war going on, and we are tired of being left behind."

ON FRIDAY, JUNE 15, thirty-three days after the crash, Doc Bulatao gave Margaret and Decker a thorough going-over to be sure their wounds had sufficiently healed. After the exams, he pronounced his two patients fit enough to travel. They'd need more medical treatment—Decker, in particular—but he believed that they were out of immediate danger and capable of a hike, with help, to the big valley.

Walter couldn't wait to strike camp and hit the trail, but he delayed their departure until noon, so the supply plane could drop extra flares and a spare walkie-talkie, in case of problems en route to the base camp.

With the AP's Ralph Morton doing double duty as reporter and radio operator, the supply plane made the cargo drop and checked in with the jungle campsite. After exchanging small talk and details about Walter's planned route to the valley, it became clear that Margaret was the reporters' primary interest. No matter how hard John McCollom tried to distract him, Morton kept after his journalistic prey:

Ralph Morton: How's Corporal Hastings this morning?

Lieutenant McCollom: She's feeling pretty good. In fact, everybody is feeling good. We're pretty anxious to get out of here. The three of us have been sitting here for better than a month, and we're kind of anxious to get back to work in Hollandia. And the paratroopers have been here for three weeks or so.

Ralph Morton: Is Margaret able to carry anything for you?

Lieutenant McCollom: Corporal Hastings is carrying a small pack—probably weighs about fifteen pounds. The rest of us have packs weighing from fifty pounds to seventy-five pounds. It will be rough going until we pick up some natives [as bearers].

Ralph Morton: That sounds like a pretty good load for a ninety-eight-pound girl to carry. . . .

EVEN WHEN FAR back from enemy lines, standard practice among reporters in war zones was to painstakingly record, and then publish, the names and hometowns of servicemen and -women. That way, their families and friends back home could enjoy the acknowledgment of their loved ones' courage, as well as the reflected glory of knowing someone involved in the war effort. "Names are news," as the saying went. Publishers encouraged the practice for commercial reasons as much as journalistic ones: printing a local person's name in the newspaper generated loyalty among readers and encouraged the purchase of extra copies, for posterity.

With one glaring, categorical exception, the reporters covering the *Gremlin Special* crash faithfully followed this practice. They published the names and hometowns of the survivors and the crash victims, and also the chaplains who flew over the valley for the funeral rites, the planners in Hollandia, and the crew of the 311 supply plane. They included the names of not only the pilot, copilot, and radio operator but also the flight engineer, Sergeant Anson Macy of Jacksonville, Florida, and the cargo crew.

But as obvious as the reporters' obsession with Margaret was their tendency to overlook the 1st Recon paratroopers of Filipino descent. That oversight came despite the fact that all but Rammy Ramirez were natives or residents of the United States, and all were full-fledged members of the U.S. Army. When speaking with the reporters by walkie-talkie, Walter and McCollom repeatedly tried to draw attention to the enlisted paratroopers, particularly the heroic jump by Bulatao and Ramirez into death-defying terrain, and their life-and-limb-saving ministrations to Margaret and Decker.

Yet in one story after another, the medics and paratroopers received little or no credit. Sometimes they appeared anonymously, as in one typical mention: "Two Filipino medics laden with supplies also were dropped by parachute."

To his credit, Ralph Morton of The Associated Press eventually devoted some ink to the enlisted men of the 1st Recon, as did the *Tribune*'s Walter Simmons, who focused most on Sergeant Alfred Baylon. Simmons's interest in "the stocky, cigar-smoking" Baylon was piqued by the fact that the sergeant hailed from Chicago and had previously worked as an orderly in the city's Garfield Park Community Hospital.

When the supply plane dropped news clippings about the events in Shangri-La, Walter reacted angrily in his journal to how little acclaim his men received: "So few reporters have given my men the credit due them and are always bringing in outsiders for credit. I certainly hope that when I get out of here I can give the credit to those who deserve it and [to] my enlisted men, who made possible the rescue of these people. It has definitely been no cake party jumping into unexplored country and climbing mountains over the damnest trails ever seen. No complaining, but just slugging along, doing their job."

As the paratroopers' leader, Walter received glowing mentions in the press reports. Reporters gave him the title of "rescue chief," as Ralph Morton put it, presumably to distinguish him from the

native chiefs. But throughout the mission reporters used his un-
loved given name, "Cecil." And they routinely added an "s" to his
last name, calling him "Walters."

BEFORE SETTING OFF to the valley base camp, the survivors
and paratroopers picked through their supplies to decide what
to carry and what to leave behind. As he stuffed provisions in
his backpack, McCollom noticed the unused boxes of Kotex
that had been dropped for Margaret. Ever the engineer, an idea
crossed his mind.

"Maggie," he asked, "you gonna use any of this?"

When she scoffed, McCollom tore open the boxes. He handed
out the white sanitary napkins to each of the men, who tucked
them under the shoulder straps of their heavy backpacks. Reflecting later on his innovation in infantry padding technology, Mc-
Collom said: "Man, those are good for that sort of thing."

As she collected her belongings, Margaret focused on the natives. "We tried to say our farewells to Pete and his men," she
wrote in her diary. "The term 'savages' hardly applied to such
kind, friendly and hospitable men as these natives. We could never
understand each other's language. But we could always understand
each other's hearts and intentions. The greatest miracle that befell
McCollom, Decker and me, aside from our escape from death in
the crash, was the fact the natives were good and gentle people."

Eager to return to the base camp, Walter wrote in his journal that he didn't see the natives as he left camp. But before she
started down the trail, Margaret searched for Wimayuk Wandik,
the man she called Pete. She found him weeping at their departure along with his men.

"Some of us could have wept, too," she wrote in her diary.

Unknown to Margaret and the other outsiders, the natives had
given them a parting gift. When Wimayuk and his clansmen
understood that the visiting spirits intended to walk out of the

jungle toward the valley, the people of Uwambo communicated with their allies. They bestowed another *maga*—a declaration of safe passage—along the intended route.

As she fell into line for the march, Margaret glanced back over her shoulder at the campsite. She took one last look at the sweet potato garden that had been her salvation after the crash; the place where she, McCollom, and Decker were spotted by Captain Baker in his B-17; the jungle "hospital" where her gangrene was treated and her legs were saved by Bulatao and Ramirez. Her final vision of the place: the pyramidal tent they left behind, with the American flag flying above it.

DURING THE MONTH they spent in the little camp near the Mundi River, the survivors and paratroopers had repeatedly offered extra food to the natives. They found no takers, not even for a taste. McCollom tried everything: rice, canned beef, a chocolate bar. "We'd break off a bite and eat it," he said. "They wouldn't touch it."

When the visitors broke camp, the natives gathered the food left behind and placed it in a cave. "Nobody knew what the food was," said Tomas Wandik. "The people were afraid of it, so they put it all in one place and it became sacred objects. Pigs were killed and their blood was sprinkled on it in a purification ceremony." The natives planted a bamboolike tree near the entrance to the cave, to mark it as a place of magic. They also conducted a blood-sprinkling ceremony along the path the spirits followed down the mountain.

Although he wouldn't eat their food, Wimayuk Wandik accepted McCollom's offer of a machete with a rope tied through a hole in the handle. Chopping wood was daily, time-consuming work, and the blade—by all indications the natives' first exposure to a metal tool—was prized for slicing through trees faster than any stone ax or adze. At first, Wimayuk returned the gift every morning, only to be reassured on a daily basis that the ax was his to keep. When McCollom left, Wimayuk kept the machete for good.

Although Wimayuk, Yaralok, and others were sorry to see the spirits leave, not everyone in Uwambo was unhappy. "Some people were getting mad at Wimayuk because he was going in with the spirits too much," said his son Helenma. "They said, 'Take that machete back!' " Some of the objectors' anger might have stemmed from the paratroopers erecting their tents in the middle of the community garden. "They destroyed the sweet potato and taro," he said.

Throughout the spirits' stay, a consistent pacification effort involved cigarettes. "They loved them," Margaret wrote, "but they were always terrified by matches or cigarette lighters. So we used to light cigarettes from our own and hand them over to Pete and his men." She noted that "Pete" became a Raleigh man.

After the spirits left, Wimayuk climbed to the top of the Ogi ridge. He used the machete McCollom gave him to chop up pieces of the *Gremlin Special* wreck for tools and building supplies. One piece became part of a village fence. It remained in use for more than six decades after the crash.

In the months that followed the spirits' departure, the people of Uwambo returned to the rhythms and routines they'd followed for untold centuries. They raised their pigs and sweet potatoes, they tended to their villages and their families, and they resumed their wars with their enemies. One difference was that when they told their children the Uluayek legend, now it included the tale of Yugwe, Meakale, Mumu, Mua, Pingkong, Babikama, and the other spirits who came from the sky.

It would take a few years, but just as the legend had prophesied, the spirits' return indeed marked the beginning of the end of the lives they'd always known.

WITH OVERLOADED PACKS on their backs, Kotex pads on their shoulders, and no clear route to follow, the survivors and the paratroopers began the treacherous trek from the jungle campsite toward the base camp.

"It was up and down and crevice to crevice," Walter recalled. "We had to go across the creek that went down the mountainside for a long ways. We had to crisscross that a half-dozen times because it was the only way that we knew exactly how to keep our bearings as to where the hell we were going."

Margaret set out feeling strong and brimming with confidence. As they walked single-file through the rain-slicked jungle, she felt like one of the troops. She kept up as they crawled over fallen logs, edged along a precipice "that fell away into a bottomless gorge," and hopped from one tree stump to another. But a half hour into the hike, Margaret found herself struggling to catch her breath. Her thoughts flashed back to the nightmare journey after the crash, crawling and inching her way down the mountainside and through the stream.

"I thought I was well and strong, much stronger than Sergeant Decker, who still looked gaunt and ill," she wrote in her diary. She discovered otherwise. "The steady, rhythmic infantry pace set by the paratroopers was too much for me."

"Please, stop!" she called to Walter. "I've got to rest."

"Me, too," Decker said, much to Margaret's relief. She felt certain that if she hadn't called a halt, Decker would have continued silently and stoically until he dropped.

Walter noted in his journal that the lack of native bearers and the needs of the "two patients" slowed his intended pace. But he added: "Hats off to Sergeant Decker and Corporal Hastings. They are both showing great spirit."

Three hours into the first day of their trek, they stopped to pitch camp for the night. The early hiatus gave the medics time to re-dress Margaret's and Decker's wounds. It also spared them from being caught in the nightly rains. Quickly a little camp emerged: Margaret got a pup tent of her own, McCollom and Decker shared another, a few paratroopers crammed into a third, and the rest hung jungle hammocks from trees.

The next morning, they were up early and back on the trail shortly after eight o'clock. Walter described the day's route as "plenty rugged, straight up and down." Margaret's right thigh ached terribly from muscle cramps—"Corporal Hastings was really hurting today, but she is game," Walter wrote—so they slowed again.

When the supply plane passed overhead and they established a radio connection, Walter told Major Gardner about the absence of natives who could be put to work as bearers. He speculated that the natives didn't like the outsiders passing close to their villages.

"Are they hostile?" Gardner asked.

"I doubt it very much," Walter answered. "But we're all set on that score. Don't worry. We have plenty of ammunition, but we're not expecting anything. They are very peaceful and very friendly. As long as we stay away from their women and their camote patches, we'll be all right."

Later that day, several natives from a village along the way proved willing to lug the trekkers' bedding and bedrolls. By the time the hikers made camp in the mid-afternoon, Walter had achieved his goal of a ten-mile day. "Our main trouble is water," he wrote in his journal. "There is plenty around, but God only knows where in this jungle."

Walter didn't want anyone to know it, but he'd wrenched his left ankle while hopscotching from rock to rock. "My main concern was Maggie and the other two survivors, Ken Decker and Mac," Walter recalled. "So I wasn't paying attention and I stepped on this rock, which was covered with moss. I slipped badly and got a pretty bad sprain out of it, which lasted a long time." It swelled to nearly twice its normal size, so he asked Doc Bulatao

THE SURVIVORS, PARATROOPERS, AND TRIBESMEN REST DURING THEIR TREK FROM THE JUNGLE TO THE VALLEY CAMPSITE. (PHOTO COURTESY OF C. EARL WALTER JR.)

to apply a tight wrapping. The pain continued, but at least Walter could stay on it. "We are rolling too well to hold up the progress for me," he wrote in his journal. "So 'Bahala Na.' I'll go with it."

Margaret's throbbing leg eased, and she grew stronger each day. By Sunday, June 17, their third day on the trail, Walter proclaimed that she had the makings of a first-rate infantry soldier. He wrote in his journal: "My hat's off to Corporal Hastings, Sergeant Decker and Lieutenant McCollom. Lots of spirit and great people. Corporal Hastings deserves plenty of credit and I don't mean maybe."

Margaret noted the change in her diary, writing that she felt "like a million dollars." But now that her strength had returned, she had a new concern: unwanted suitors.

"One of the natives we instantly named 'Bob Hope,'" she wrote. "He had a ski nose just like his namesake. Unfortunately, our Bob developed a terrific crush on me. His idea of courtship was to hang around and leer at me hour after hour." Margaret's discomfort at the attention deepened into frustration when the paratroopers teased her about her new love interest. It only got worse.

"Suddenly Bob had a rival," she wrote. "A young native who must have been in his teens was smitten, too. His idea of wooing a girl was to pick up a stick and throw it at her. Obviously, I was expected to throw it back. He was like a pup." Eventually the amorous natives backed off, and the march continued.

On the morning of Monday, June 18, the ragged little band cleared the gap between two mountains that Walter called "the saddle." They followed a winding path alongside the muddy Pae River and broke for lunch. After two more hours of marching, the three paratroopers who'd remained at the base camp—Sergeants Sandy Abrenica, Roque Velasco, and Alfred Baylon—spotted them and came running up the trail. Walter beamed at the sight of men he called "the best damn field soldiers in the world."

As the supply plane flew overhead to herald their arrival in the valley, the three survivors jumped up and down and waved. At the controls was the chief planner himself, Colonel Elsmore, with the AP's Ralph Morton sitting beside him in the cockpit.

Five weeks after they left Hollandia, Margaret, McCollom, and Decker finally got a firsthand look at Shangri-La.

"Surely the followers of Moses when they came upon the Promised Land saw a sight no more fair," Margaret wrote in her diary. "It was a beautiful, fertile land, ringed by the giant peaks of the Oranje Mountains. A copper-colored river wound through the valley's green length. It was *our* Promised Land, too."

When the survivors settled down, they learned that Elsmore had a surprise in store.

22

HOLLYWOOD

WHEN MARGARET HEARD that the supply plane carried a surprise, she was certain her admirers onboard would drop a few cases of beer for a base camp arrival party. She was right, in a way. The beer had, in fact, been dropped—back at the jungle campsite, after they'd left. "And there it lies today," she wrote in her diary. "Two fine cases of American beer to greet the lucky Robinson Crusoe or Trader Horn who stumbles on them. The natives will never touch it."

The surprise did, however, have something to do with alcohol.

AFTER BRIEFLY SURVEYING the base camp, Walter heard one of his men calling him to the walkie-talkie. The radioman on the 311 told him the supply plane carried a filmmaker who planned to make a documentary about life, death, the natives, and the rescue effort. The filmmaker had slipped into a parachute harness and was preparing to jump when Walter made contact with the plane.

"This guy ever make a jump before?" Walter asked.

"No."

Worried, Walter learned that a fellow 1st Recon paratrooper back in Hollandia had given the filmmaker a half-hour verbal lesson on the basics of avoiding certain death.

"For Christ's sake," Walter said, "tie a rope on his ripcord!" At least then, if the man froze in fear in midair, the chute would open and he'd have a fighting chance.

The survivors and paratroopers watched as the plane swooped through the valley with an open jump door, but no sign of the promised filmmaker. Another pass, and still no movement to the door. Finally, on a third pass over the base camp, a large figure appeared unsteadily in the opening, camera equipment strapped to his body. He lurched through the jump door, out into thin air. A puffy white canopy blossomed above him as he floated toward the valley floor.

As they watched, the paratroopers sensed a problem. The chutist was oddly limp.

By her own admission, Margaret knew next to nothing about parachuting. Still, she knew enough to brand the jumper "a rank amateur."

"He swung in a vast arc from one edge of the chute to the other," she told her diary. "We were terrified that he would swing all the way over, spill the air out of his chute and plummet to earth."

Walter and his men yelled frantically to the human metronome dangling above them.

"Pull your legs together!"

"Check your oscillation!"

"Pull on your risers!"

No response.

Margaret joined the chorus, repeating the paratroopers' expert shouted advice, all of which went unheeded by the falling, swinging, apparently lifeless man.

Somehow, the parachute held its air. The parachutist landed, spread-eagled on his back, in a clump of tall briar bushes some distance from the base camp. Fearing that he was dead or seriously wounded, several paratroopers raced through the high valley grasses to his aid. First to reach him was Sergeant Javonillo.

After a momentary inspection, Javonillo popped up from the bushes—"looking as if he'd seen a ghost," Margaret wrote. He called to Walter.

"Captain, sir?" Javonillo said. "This man is drunk!"

McCollom arrived in the bushes moments after Javonillo and confirmed the diagnosis: "Drunker than a hoot owl."

When they pulled the man out of the thicket, Walter took stock of the filmmaker in his midst. After confirming the diagnosis of alcohol-impaired descent, Walter radioed a wry message to the departing supply plane: "The valley is going Hollywood—and fast."

Walter had no idea how right he was.

THE PRONE, BESOTTED man in the shrubbery was Alexander Cann, a dashing forty-two-year-old adventurer who'd taken an unlikely path from respectability to Shangri-La.

Born in Nova Scotia, Alex Cann was the eldest child of a prominent banker named H. V. Cann and his wife, Mabel Ross Cann, whose father was a member of the Canadian House of Commons. Mabel Cann died when Alex was young. When the boy was seven, H. V. Cann moved the family from Canada to

ALEXANDER CANN. (PHOTO COURTESY OF B. B. MCCOLLOM.)

Manhattan, where in 1914 he helped to launch the Federal Reserve Bank of New York. The family spent seven years in the United States before returning to Canada, when H. V. Cann became a top executive with the Bank of Ottawa.

Alex Cann attended the Royal Naval College of Canada, then returned to New York to study structural engineering at Columbia University. His timing couldn't have been worse: when the Great Depression struck, new building stopped, which made structural engineers as unnecessary as stockbrokers.

Adding to his misfortune, he proceeded to gamble away his sizable inheritance on poker. "He was very roguish, my father, and hopeless about money," said his daughter and namesake, Alexandra Cann, a London literary agent.

But being broke didn't mean he didn't have assets. Tall, dark, and hazel-eyed, deep-voiced, handsome, and powerfully built, funny, cultured, and charming, the well-bred young Alex Cann drifted west to Hollywood, where those qualities retained great value despite the Great Depression. Worried about sullying his family's good name, he took the stage name Alexander Cross—literally a cross between his surname and his mother's maiden name, Ross.

In no time, Alexander Cann/Cross found his way into small movie roles. In 1936 he won parts in half a dozen studio movies, including roles as a watchman in *Fury*, a Spencer Tracy film directed by Fritz Lang; as a detective in *Smart Blonde* with Glenda Farrell; and as a crew member in *China Clipper*, starring his drinking buddy Humphrey Bogart. His acting run stretched into 1937, including a part playing a prison guard in the movie *San Quentin*, again starring Bogart. He moved up the Hollywood food chain by landing roles with more lines, playing characters with actual names, such as Bull Clanton in the 1937 western *Law for Tombstone*. His star kept rising, as he won the role of bad guy Black Jack Carson in the Hopalong Cassidy series of films starring William Boyd and Gabby Hayes.

But just when the actor Alexander Cross began to hit his stride, his real-life alter ego Alexander Cann disproved the old Hollywood adage, "Any publicity is good publicity."

On March 28, 1937, the *Los Angeles Times* featured a can't-miss "Hey, Martha!" story on page one, headlined "Actor Confesses Theft of Gems at Palm Springs." The story explained that a "film character actor" whom police identified as Alexander Howard Cross Cann had confessed to stealing a diamond bracelet and a bejeweled ring from Alma Walker Hearst, the beautiful ex-wife of newspaper magnate William Randolph Hearst Jr. The story went on to describe possibly the worst-planned jewel heist in history.

Cann, a ladies' man who'd met the former Mrs. Hearst a month earlier in Sun Valley, Idaho, attended a small gathering at her Palm Springs home ten days before the *Times* story ran. Late in the evening, the party moved to downtown Palm Springs. Somewhere around one in the morning, Cann doubled back to Alma Hearst's home and pocketed her jewels. Later that day, Cann walked into a Hollywood pawnshop and sold the gems, which were valued at more than $6,000. He negotiated a terrible deal, collecting just $350.

"In his confession," the *Times* story said, "Cann . . . told the officers he had been losing heavily in horse race-betting, and was hard pressed financially when he took the jewelry. He also said he had been drinking at the time of the theft."

When Alma Hearst noticed her jewelry missing, she provided police with a list of her servants and guests. Investigators focused quickly on Cann, and a deputy sheriff called his home. Cann admitted the crime over the phone and told the officer where to find the jewels, which were recovered from the pawnshop and returned to their owner. At the officer's insistence, Cann went to Palm Springs and turned himself in. He was charged with burglary and hauled off to jail.

With her jewels in hand, Alma Hearst decided that she'd

had enough of the attention and of Alex Cann. The following day, the *Times* ran a second story reporting that charges against Cann would be dropped if he made restitution. Netting only $350 turned out to be a small bit of good luck; it was relatively easy for Cann to repay.

An officer quoted Alma Hearst as saying: "Nobody likes to prosecute a friend. But when people do such things, they must expect to pay."

Before the story—and Cann—disappeared, the wire services had a field day. Newspapers far from Hollywood ran headlines such as "Host's Jewels Are Stolen by Thespian." Even *The New York Times* couldn't resist a story about a Hearst and a heist.

As Alexander Cross, in 1939, Cann appeared in one more Depression-era film, *The Human Bomb.* He played the title character—an unnamed bomber. The role was a fitting coda to Alex Cann's Hollywood years; his arrest blew his movie career to smithereens.

Cann shrugged it off as best he could and kept moving. By the end of 1941, he'd been married and divorced three times, though he hadn't yet fathered any children. With no spouse, no dependents, and no immediate prospects, he returned to his roots and joined the Royal Canadian Navy. But his fortunes didn't change.

En route to the South Pacific, Cann's troop ship was struck by a Japanese torpedo that blew him into the water. He survived, but with a broken back that would pain him the rest of his life. In 1943, while recuperating in Australia, Cann washed up regularly in local nightclubs. A convivial drinker and gifted storyteller, he'd tell tales of his Hollywood days. "He managed to convince several people that he knew a great deal more about filmmaking than he did," said his daughter.

Through his nightclub connections, Cann learned that the Dutch government-in-exile in London needed correspondents and filmmakers for its newly created Netherlands Indies Government

Information Service, an agency whose aim was to counter Nazi propaganda and keep Dutch concerns on the world stage.

Based on Cann's exaggerated claims of filmmaking expertise, and also, presumably, on the limited military use for a forty-year-old sailor with a broken back, the Canadian Navy "loaned" Cann to the Melbourne-based Australia section of the Netherlands Information Service, as the agency was known. He gained the title "War Correspondent and Cinematographer," acquired a 35mm camera, and used his charm and Canadian accent to cadge hard-to-get film from the U.S. Army Signal Corps.

Cann threw himself into his new role, fearlessly covering combat throughout the Philippines and the Borneo campaign. During the Allies' October 1944 invasion of Leyte, in the Philippines, Cann found himself aboard the heavy cruiser HMAS *Australia* when it came under fire from a Japanese dive-bomber. The Japanese plane, a model known to the Allies as a "Betty," slammed full-speed into the *Australia,* mortally wounding the captain and the navigator and killing or mortally wounding twenty-eight others. Numerous accounts declared it the first successful kamikaze attack of the war. But as an eyewitness and a survivor, Cann challenged that claim. A week after the attack, he told a reporter for The Associated Press that the pilot was already dead when the plane struck the ship. "The Jap Betty came through a terrific barrage, out of control and with smoke already pouring out," Cann told the reporter.

By that point in his life, Cann had survived gambling away his inheritance, three divorces, an arrest as an actor turned jewel thief, a torpedo attack that broke his back, and a Japanese plane crashing into his ship. In that light, an uncontrolled, drunken skydive into Shangri-La seemed an almost predictable next step.

When the news stories by Walter Simmons, Ralph Morton, and other reporters spread word about the survivors, the paratroopers, and the Stone Age tribe in Shangri-La, Alex Cann decided to try his luck once more. He flew from Melbourne to Hollandia on June 17. The next morning he hitched a plane ride over the crash site before returning to the Sentani Airstrip to request a parachute. He received a few pointers from a captain in the 1st Recon named Isaac Unciano, but Cann apparently spent his brief lesson joking around. Unciano best remembered Cann for promising "six quarts of whisky and a party" if he returned safely.

"He knew it was obviously dangerous," said his daughter. "But he wanted to go in, so my father volunteered. He'd never parachuted in his life. They offered to train him but he said, 'No thanks, I'll only do this once. If I don't jump, push me.'"

CANN NEVER PERSONALLY confirmed the drunken jump story, but he came close. In an account distributed by The Associated Press, he wrote: "I don't know whether I jumped or was pushed at the 'go' signal, but I was busy shooting pictures on the descent after the chute opened. Then I landed unhurt, flat on my back in some bushes."

After Javonillo and the others untangled him, Cann put a dent in the camp's aspirin supply, then found himself propped up at a dinner of Filipino-style chow mein and fried potatoes. When Cann sobered up enough to talk, Walter inquired how he ended up in the valley anaesthetized.

"I drank a full fifth of Dutch gin before I jumped," Cann said, according to Walter.

"Why'd you do that?" Walter asked.

"I didn't want to hesitate."

Walter considered that explanation and rendered a verdict: "You ought to be a paratrooper."

Later, Major Gardner asked Walter via walkie-talkie whether Cann was hungover. Walter answered: "He says he'll never do that again—at least not until another story comes along."

When Cann regained the ability to focus, he got his first good look at Margaret Hastings. His eye for a beautiful woman was unaffected by his crash landing. Cann asked Walter to relay a message to the AP's Ralph Morton: "Corporal Hastings is the most magnificent survivor that I have ever seen."

He added: "To the boys in the rescue party, she is known as the Queen of Shangri-La." Asked about the royal title, Margaret finally responded: "I am ready to go, and will give up my crown at any time."

Walter and Cann became fast friends. The captain soaked up the wisdom and the lessons that Cann had learned from what Walter called "experience and hard knocks." They spent hours talking, playing poker, swimming in the river, hiking around the valley, and arguing about sports figures and military policies. Cann believed that the military shouldn't censor reporters' stories from war zones. Walter disagreed, vehemently. "I like to get a man like that riled up," Walter wrote in his journal, "as I can then really learn something." Walter paid his highest compliment to Cann, declaring him "one hell of a swell egg."

With Cann's arrival, the camp that Walter renamed "United

ALEXANDER CANN FILMING IN "SHANGRI-LA."
(PHOTOS COURTESY OF B. B. MCCOLLOM.)

States Army Outpost at Shangri-La, D.N.G. [Dutch New Guinea]"—"Camp Shangri-La" for short—reached its full and final complement of fifteen people: commanding officer Captain C. Earl Walter Jr.; ten enlisted paratroopers; three crash survivors; and one Canadian-born engineer-turned-actor-turned-jewel-thief-turned-sailor-turned-war-correspondent.

They settled into a "pretty little city," in Walter's phrase, spread out in the shadow of the mountain wall, on a mostly flat area of the valley floor. The three sergeants who'd stayed behind organized the camp as a cluster of canopies and tents, including a red one for supplies and a pink one for a mess hall.

The camp also featured an improvised pigpen made of rough-cut branches, filled with seven pigs that Abrenica, Baylon, and Velasco had "purchased" from the natives with cowrie shells dropped by the supply plane. One pig was a runt, "cute as a button," Margaret wrote. The sergeants named it "Peggy" in her honor.

"Peggy must have thought she was a dog," Margaret wrote. "She followed everyone around, and the moment any of us sat down, climbed on our laps. The paratroopers scrubbed Peggy every day until she shone."

The most elaborate structure was a pyramidal tent outfitted as VIP and officers' quarters. One section, partitioned off for Margaret's privacy, had a deep bed made from dried, golden valley grass, over which hung a canopy made from a yellow cargo parachute. Artfully arranged mosquito netting completed the fit-for-a-queen decor. Lest her feet touch ground without shoes, empty parachute bags became a bedside rug.

"I was so touched I wanted to cry," Margaret wrote in her diary. "Everything about the camp was deluxe, including a bathroom! The three sergeants had even made a tub of empty, waterproof ration cartons. They had dug a well nearby, and filling the tub was very easy work."

YOUNG WARRIORS FROM DIFFERENT WORLDS. THE FILIPINO-AMERICAN SOLDIERS ARE (FROM LEFT) CAMILO RAMIREZ, CUSTODIO ALERTA, DON RUIZ, AND JUAN "JOHNNY" JAVONILLO. (PHOTOS COURTESY OF C. EARL WALTER JR.)

As officers, McCollom and Walter were assigned bunks on the men's side of the pyramidal tent. But Walter insisted that his bed go to Decker, to speed the sergeant's ongoing recovery. Walter and his men strung up jungle hammocks, amusing Margaret with the sight of the oversize captain pretzeling his frame into the hanging sack.

On the first full day that all fifteen of them were together at the base camp, the paratroopers celebrated by roasting two suckling pigs in a Filipino *lechon* feast, slowly turning them on spits until they were golden brown. Margaret made sure that "Peggy" was spared that honor. The meal reminded Walter of his boyhood; almost a decade had passed since his last *lechon*. "After making a pig of myself (on pig), I staggered over to the supply tent and laid down in agony," Walter wrote in his journal. "The boys are really great cooks."

The following day, the survivors and paratroopers indulged Alex Cann in his role as filmmaking auteur. Although he was supposed to be making a fact-based documentary, Cann wasn't above a bit of Hollywood staging. He'd missed the survivors' entrance into base camp, yet he wanted the arrival as a plot point in his film. He persuaded everyone to re-create the last leg of the journey. No one wanted to lug a seventy-five-pound backpack up and down the mountain, so they filled their bags with empty ration boxes that gave the appearance of bulk without the weight.

This time they skipped the Kotex pads.

23

GLIDERS?

AFTER THE INITIAL exhilaration about the discovery of the survivors wore off, Colonel Elsmore and his staff at Fee-Ask struggled to devise the best way to empty Shangri-La of U.S. Army personnel and, now, a filmmaker for the Dutch government.

Throughout their deliberations, the planners' top priority was safety. Fifteen lives depended on their judgment. More, really, taking into account the risk to pilots, crew, and anyone else who took part in the operation. Yet the planners also must have known that success or failure would affect their own lives as well, personally and professionally. They cared about the survivors and the paratroopers not just as soldiers but as individuals, and they were responsible for Alex Cann. Also, they knew how the military worked: there'd be hell to pay if the widely publicized story of Shangri-La ended tragically because of a poorly planned or executed rescue effort.

Elsmore and his team debated numerous possibilities, rejecting one after another as impractical, illogical, impossible, or just plain doomed to fail. After crossing off rescue by blimp, helicopter, amphibious plane, PT boat, and overland hike back to Hollandia, they briefly debated dropping into the valley members of a U.S. Navy construction battalion—the Seabees—with small bulldozers to create a temporary landing strip. That plan foundered when Elsmore decided that landing a C-47 at high altitude on a short, improvised airstrip, then trying to take off again over the surrounding mountains, carried too great a risk of becoming a *Gremlin Special* sequel.

Next they discussed using a small, versatile plane called the L-5 Sentinel, affectionately known as the Flying Jeep. Used throughout the war for reconnaissance missions and as frontline airborne ambulances, Sentinels had what the army called "short field landing and takeoff capability." That meant they might be useful on the bumpy ground of the valley floor, without the need for a Seabee-built runway. But Sentinels had drawbacks, too.

One concern was that a flight from Hollandia to the valley would take a Sentinel approximately three hours and consume all its fuel. Cans of fuel would have to be parachuted to the valley floor for each return trip. Also, each Sentinel could carry only a pilot and one passenger, which meant that fifteen round trips would be needed, with each flight carrying the same risk. Still, the planners kept the L-5 Sentinel under consideration.

As Elsmore weighed the Sentinel's pros and cons, he sought advice from an expert: Henry E. Palmer, a thirty-one-year-old lieutenant from Baton Rouge, Louisiana. Palmer, a lanky country boy nicknamed "Red," had extensive experience with Sentinels and other light aircraft. He was stationed nearby, at an airstrip on the tropical island of Biak, off the northern coast of New Guinea.

Elsmore arranged for Palmer to fly low over Shangri-La in a B-25 bomber to assess the situation. One pass convinced Palmer that the Sentinel was wrong for the job. He had another idea, involving another type of aircraft altogether. Like the Sentinel, it was designed to land in tight spaces, on rough terrain. But Palmer thought this other type of aircraft had a better chance of safely clearing the mountains with passengers aboard. Plus, it wouldn't require a drop of fuel.

When Palmer returned to Hollandia, he walked into the planners' headquarters and headed for a blackboard. With chalk dust flying, Palmer drew what must have looked like a child's illustration of a mother plane and a baby plane, connected by an umbilical cord.

The sketch, he explained, depicted a motorless aircraft being pulled through the sky by a twin-engine tow plane. Lieutenant Henry E. Palmer had just made a case for the highest-altitude and downright strangest mission in the history of military gliders.

THE FIRST MOTORLESS flight is credited to Icarus, whose mythical journey ended with melted wings and a fatal plummet into the sea. Military glider pilots, an especially wry bunch, considered Icarus a fitting mascot. Their aircraft seemed to have been designed for crash landings, too. In the words of General William Westmoreland, "They were the only aviators during World War II who had no motors, no parachutes, and no second chances."

The Wright brothers and other aircraft pioneers experimented with gliders on the path to motorized flight. But after the Wrights' triumph at Kitty Hawk, gliders became almost-forgotten second cousins to airplanes. During the early decades of the twentieth century, gliders were used primarily for sport, by enthusiasts who competed for distance records and bragging rights. Still, glider aficionados built larger and more elaborate craft, capable of carrying multiple passengers and soaring long distances once in flight with help from motorized airplanes.

In the 1930s Germany became a leader in glider technology, largely because after its defeat in World War I the country was banned from having a motorized air force. Hitler overturned that ban in 1935, but he didn't forget about German glider pilots. His generals began plotting possible uses for them in war. German engineers designed gliders that resembled small airplanes without motors, able to carry a pilot and nine soldiers or a ton of equipment. They could land on rough fields in the heart of combat zones, as opposed to the manicured runways needed by planes.

Equally appealing to the Nazis, manned gliders could be released from tow planes many miles from their destinations; once freed from their tethers, they were silent in flight.

The Germans saw an opportunity to test their quiet war machines in May 1940, nineteen months before the United States entered the fight. Poland had already fallen, and Hitler wanted to sweep through Belgium into France. Standing between him and Paris was Belgium's massive Fort Eben Emael, on the German-Belgian border. Dug deep into the ground, reinforced by several feet of concrete, the newly built fort was considered impregnable. A traditional assault might have taken weeks, and success was hardly assured. Even if the Belgian fort fell, a long, costly battle would have spoiled the Germans' hope for a blitzkrieg, a surprise lightning invasion. Helicopters might have speeded the effort, but the incessant *thwomp-thwomp* of their rotors would have alerted the fort's defenders long before the German troops' arrival. The same disadvantages applied for planes delivering paratroopers, who would have been sitting ducks as they floated under their parachutes to earth.

Gliders provided a stealth answer for the Germans' invasion plans. On May 10, 1940, tow planes from the Luftwaffe pulled a small fleet of gliders aloft into the skies approaching Belgium. Once released from their tow planes, the gliders, each carrying nine heavily armed German infantrymen, soared silently through the predawn darkness. Ten gliders landed on the "roof" of the dug-in fort—a grassy plain the length of ten football fields. German soldiers poured out of the gliders in full attack mode. Though badly outnumbered, they overwhelmed the stunned Belgians, deployed heavy explosives to destroy Fort Eben Emael's big guns, and captured the fort within the day. Columns of German tanks rolled past on their way to northern France.

Though the United States still wasn't at war, the Belgian disaster at Fort Eben Emael was a wake-up call. It suggested that gliders might play a significant role in future combat. An American military glider program began in earnest immediately after Pearl Harbor, with a sudden call to train one thousand qualified glider pilots, a number that within months rose to six thousand. Design work on military-grade gliders got under way at Wright Field in Ohio, where two young flight engineers, Lieutenants John and Robert McCollom, were soon stationed. The McCollom twins weren't directly involved in the glider program, but they watched with interest as it took shape.

The American aircraft industry was already at full capacity, trying to build enough planes to meet the military's growing demand. Consequently, the glider program took a more entrepreneurial approach, and government contracts for motorless flying combat and cargo aircraft went to a mix of unlikely bidders, including a refrigerator manufacturer, a furniture company, and a coffin maker. Eventually, the military settled on the fourth version of a cargo glider made by the Waco Aircraft Company of Ohio, called the Waco CG-4A, or the Waco (pronounced "*Wah*-coh"), for short.

A WACO CG-4A GLIDER IN FLIGHT. (PHOTO COURTESY OF U.S. AIR FORCE.)

Waco gliders were more fowl than falcon—clumsy, unarmored flying boxcars made from plywood and metal tubing covered with canvas. Wacos had a wingspan of eighty-three feet, eight inches, stood more than twelve feet high, and stretched more than forty-eight feet in length. Each glider weighed 3,700 pounds empty but could carry a payload greater than its own weight in cargo and troops. Guided by a pilot and copilot, a Waco glider could transport up to thirteen fully equipped soldiers, or a quarter-ton truck, or a serious piece of rolling thunder such as a 75mm howitzer, complete with ammunition and two artillerymen. Most were towed into the air by thick 350-foot-long nylon ropes attached to C-47s, though some were pulled aloft by C-46s.

Before the war was over, the U.S. military would take delivery of nearly 14,000 Wacos. Ironically, for a motorless aircraft, a major supplier was the Ford Motor Company, which built the gliders for about $15,000 each. For the same price as one glider, the government could have bought seventeen deluxe, eight-cylinder Ford sedans.

Wacos got their first taste of combat during the July 1943 invasion of Sicily. A year later, gliders delivered troops in the Normandy landing on D-Day, though scores fell prey to ten-foot-high wooden spikes that German field marshal Erwin Rommel had ordered placed in French fields where he thought Wacos might land. Gliders also participated in Operation Dragoon in southern France and Operation Varsity in Germany. They delivered supplies during the Battle of the Bulge and were used in a variety of other combat missions in Europe. They also served in the China-Burma-India theater of operations, and in Luzon, in the Philippines.

A major advantage of Waco gliders as troop-delivery aircraft was that, if the pilot braked hard enough on landing, he could stop quickly—within two hundred yards of touchdown—on uneven ground. Not infrequently, however, the glider came to rest with its nose buried in the dirt and its tail in the air. More than a few flipped over completely. Yet those landings were relative successes. Many others missed their intended landing zones entirely, as a result of weather, broken tow cables, pilot error, and other mishaps. Even when everything worked perfectly, Waco gliders made slow, fat targets for enemy antiaircraft guns.

In short order, Wacos earned the nicknames "flak bait," "bamboo bombers," and "flying coffins." Glider pilots were known as "suicide jockeys" who made oxymoronic "controlled crash landings." When they gathered to drink, glider pilots saluted each other with a mordant toast: "To the Glider Pilots—conceived in error, suffering a long and painful period of gestation, and finally delivered at the wrong place at the wrong time."

In September 1944, a young London-based reporter for the United Press named Walter Cronkite was assigned to fly in a Waco glider during Operation Market Garden in Holland. Years later Cronkite admitted, "I came close to disgracing myself" by refusing the mission. He ultimately agreed only to save face with his fellow reporters. "I had seen what had happened to the gliders in Normandy. The wreckage of hundreds of them was scattered across the countryside." Cronkite landed safely, but he never forgot the experience: "I'll tell you straight out: If you've got to go into combat, don't go by glider. Walk, crawl, parachute, swim, float—anything. But don't go by glider!"

During the early phase of the war, Waco gliders were regarded as almost disposable—once they landed and discharged their troops or supplies, they were abandoned. But as costs mounted, efforts were made to retrieve Wacos that hadn't been reduced to kindling. However, because most touched down in areas far from conventional airstrips, their tow planes couldn't simply land, reconnect their tethers, and pull the gliders aloft. As a solution, engineers developed a retrieval system in which low-flying aircraft—low, as in twenty feet off the ground—could zoom past and "snatch" a Waco glider back into the air.

Nearly five hundred glider retrievals were executed from battlefields in France, Burma, Holland, and Germany, with nearly all the gliders empty except for the pilots. But in March 1945, two Wacos retrofitted as medevac aircraft landed in a clearing near Remagen, Germany. Twenty-five wounded American and German soldiers were loaded aboard the two gliders. C-47s snatched the Wacos off the ground, and soon afterward they landed safely at a military hospital in France.

Now, three months after those successful snatches, Lieutenant Henry Palmer wanted to borrow a page from that mission, albeit with a much higher degree of difficulty.

PALMER'S SCHEME WAS a plan only the military or Hollywood could love. Fortunately for Palmer, it just so happened that both had representatives in Shangri-La.

As Palmer envisioned it, the operation would begin in Hollandia. A C-46 would pull a Waco airborne and tow it a hundred and fifty miles, into the skies over the valley. Once safely through the mountain pass, the glider pilot would disengage from the tow plane and guide the Waco down to the valley floor, where passengers would board. At such a high altitude, at least a mile above sea level, the glider couldn't carry its usual load. Only five people would clamber aboard for each trip, with priority going to the survivors. Then the glider and its passengers would brace for the snatch.

The basic premise was that a C-47 would fly over the glider and, using a hook extending from the fuselage, pull the glider back into the air. Tethered together, the tow plane and the trailing glider would fly up and over the surrounding mountains and soar toward Hollandia. After separating, both pilots would make smooth landings and enjoy a celebratory welcome home, ticker tape optional.

That's how it worked on Palmer's blackboard. In practice, several dozen potential malfunctions or miscalculations could turn the gliders into free-falling kites, the tow planes into fireballs, and their passengers into casualties. Beyond the usual dangers that came with gliders, an attempted snatch in Shangri-La carried a host of added perils.

No previous military snatch had occurred a mile above sea level. The thinner air at higher altitude meant that, even if the snatch was successful, chances were increased that the C-47 would be slowed by the glider's weight to the point where the plane might stall. Depending on the C-47's altitude at that point, the glider might become the oversize equivalent of a paper airplane on a full-speed collision course with the valley floor. The same fate might befall the C-47.

Even if the plane didn't stall, no one knew whether a C-47, pulling a loaded glider in thin air, had the horsepower to climb to roughly ten thousand feet quickly enough to make it through the pass that led out of the valley. In addition, the pilots of both aircraft would have to contend with the low clouds and the shifting winds that made getting in and out of the valley a challenge. Although the daily supply flights to Shangri-La made the trip seem routine, no pilot involved in the mission would forget that mistakes had cost twenty-one lives aboard the *Gremlin Special*.

To top it off, if the first snatch succeeded, the rescuers would have to repeat the feat twice more, each time with the same dangers.

As Colonel Elsmore considered the idea, three factors played into its favor. First, Elsmore knew of no better or safer rescue option. Second, Palmer boosted confidence in the plan by volunteering to pilot the first glider himself. Third, Elsmore was a sky cowboy with a flair for the dramatic.

If it worked, they could count on hugs from Margaret, backslaps from the men, page-one publicity, featured roles in Alex Cann's movie, and possibly medals. Maybe Elsmore could even repeat the glide-and-snatch routine to make his own long-awaited visit to the valley. On the other hand, if it failed, Palmer likely wouldn't be alive to take responsibility, so Elsmore would shoulder all the blame.

After consulting with his fellow planners, balancing the risks and rewards, Colonel Ray T. Elsmore announced that Waco CG-4A gliders would be used to extract the fifteen temporary residents from Shangri-La.

ELSMORE'S DECISION SET in motion a scramble to find pilots and qualified crew members for the tow plane. He also needed several other glider pilots to work with Palmer, assorted maintenance personnel, and hard-to-find glider pickup equipment. Gliders were used less extensively in the Pacific than in Europe, so the specialized gear was scattered all over the region, from Melbourne, Australia, to Clark Field in the Philippines.

The mission struck a piece of good luck when news of the planned glider pickup reached Major William J. Samuels, commander of the 33rd Troop Carrier Squadron based at Nichols Field, in Manila. At twenty-nine, a former Eagle Scout from Decatur, Illinois, Samuels had been a pilot with United Airlines before the war. More important, he'd been a glider snatch instructor at Bergstrom Field, in Austin, Texas. As far as Samuels knew, he was the most experienced glider pickup pilot in the entire Southwest Pacific. When Samuels volunteered to oversee equipment collection and crew training, as well as to pilot the snatch plane, Elsmore was so pleased that he turned over his own quarters to the major.

If everything went as hoped, Samuels would execute the first glider snatch from the cockpit of a C-47 known as *Louise.* The plane, an "old bird" in Samuels's phrase, was borrowed from a unit that seemed glad to be rid of it. The engine nearly quit on the flight from Manila to New Guinea, and Samuels had to make an emergency landing en route for repairs. He renamed it *Leaking Louise* for its tendency to spray engine oil all over its wings.

The headquarters Elsmore chose for glider snatch training was tiny Wakde Island, a two-by-three-mile speck of land a hundred miles off the coast of Hollandia. Wakde's most notable feature was a runway that ran almost its entire length. Another advantage was its isolation. If a glider fell on a deserted airstrip and no one was there to witness it, chances were excellent that it wouldn't make a sound.

Days passed with little progress. The effort seemed snakebit by delays caused by torrential rains, missing equipment, and a three-day case of dysentery suffered by Samuels. The delays gave glider pilot Henry Palmer plenty of time to think about what he'd gotten himself into. Eventually, he dubbed his Waco glider the *Fanless Faggot*, not as a slur but for its missing motor and its resemblance to a rough bundle of sticks.

To get a better idea of what they'd volunteered for, Samuels and his copilot, Captain William G. McKenzie of La Crosse, Wisconsin, flew over the valley to pick a spot for a glider landing and pickup strip. Neither liked the looks of Shangri-La.

"What do you think, Mac?" Samuels asked.

"Well, Bill, we'll never know 'til we try," McKenzie replied.

Samuels looked back to their crew, staring dubiously out the windows, assessing their chances of success, not to mention survival.

WHILE THE GLIDER work crawled along, the three sergeants who organized the valley base camp, Abrenica, Baylon, and Velasco, laid out a landing area to Samuels's specifications. They cut and burned brush—leaving it no more than one to two feet high—in a relatively flat area some four hundred yards long and one hundred yards wide. They outlined the field with red cargo parachutes and used white paratrooper parachutes to make a center line for the landing strip. Appropriately for a make-do operation, they laid out toilet paper in the shape of giant arrows that pointed the pilots toward the airfield.

On Wakde Island, much of the preparation was devoted to the most treacherous part of the operation: the snatch. When all the gear reached the island, crews installed equipment in the *Leaking Louise* that looked and functioned like a giant fishing reel, complete with line and hook. The reel, bolted to the cabin floor, was a huge winch, an eight-hundred-pound mechanical device the size of a washing machine. A crew member would use the winch to let out or pull in the line attached to the glider. The line, wrapped around the winch's drum, was one thousand feet of half-inch steel cable. The hook, attached to the end of the cable, was just that: a six-inch-long steel hook.

When the time came to attempt a snatch, crewmembers on the *Leaking Louise* would unspool the cable. They'd feed it hook-first down a wooden pickup arm, sometimes called a boom, that extended below the C-47's fuselage. The hook would be set at the end of the pickup arm, to hold it steady.

Meanwhile, the glider would be towed to the valley by another plane. After releasing their Waco from the tow plane and landing in Shangri-La, the glider's crew would erect two twelve-foot-high poles, set some twenty feet apart. From the top of one pole to the top of the other, they'd string a section of an eighty-foot-long loop made from inch-thick nylon rope. The result would resemble a pole-vault setup, with a section of the nylon loop as the crossbar. The remainder of the loop would hang down from the poles and be laid out neatly on the ground. Another nylon rope, about 225 feet long, would be attached to the ground end of the loop. Its far end would be fastened to the nose of the glider, parked fifty to one hundred feet back from the poles. When the setup was complete, the loop of nylon rope hanging from the two poles would be attached to the nylon tow rope, which would be attached to the glider.

In a successful snatch, the C-47 would swoop low over the pickup site. The steel hook at the end of the pickup arm would catch the nylon loop at the top of the poles. The C-47 would fly onward, with the pilot leaning hard on the throttles to gain altitude with the added drag of the glider. The winch operator inside the C-47 would consider speed, glider weight, and other factors to judge how many feet of steel cable to pay out from the reel to prevent the nylon rope from snapping. If he misjudged, the cable would rip off the glider's nose, snap its wings, or worse. Glider pilots described the sensation at the moment of the snatch as comparable to being shot out of a giant slingshot.

As the C-47 climbed, the glider would be jerked into the air from its parking spot within three seconds. It would be airborne within sixty feet, and its speed would go from zero to more than one hundred miles per hour within seven seconds of the snatch. When the glider was airborne, the winch operator on the C-47 would reel in cable to draw it closer to the tow plane, so it trailed the C-47 by about 350 feet. The two aircraft would fly in graceful tandem, connected by the nylon-and-steel tether. In sight of Hollandia, the glider pilot would release his craft from the tow plane, and the Waco and the C-47 would make safe, separate landings.

That's how the planners envisioned it. In practice, the first trial runs of the *Leaking Louise* and the *Fanless Faggot* on Wakde Island were plagued by injuries, ruined equipment, and growing doubts about the wisdom of using gliders to escape from Shangri-La.

24

TWO QUEENS

AS JUNE 1945 wound down, so did the war.

After the bloodiest battle of the Pacific, the Allies took Okinawa. Its capture on June 21—after the deaths of twelve thousand Americans and more than one hundred thousand Japanese—provided a staging area for an air and land attack on the main islands of Japan. That is, unless Emperor Hirohito could be persuaded to surrender. Secretly, America's leaders thought a new weapon, a bomb of unimaginable power, might accomplish that goal without sending troops to Tokyo. The bomb would be tested within weeks; if it worked, President Truman would decide whether to use it. Already, though, much of the world seemed eager to look beyond war. While the outsiders in Shangri-La awaited rescue, envoys from forty-four countries landed in San Francisco to sign a charter creating the United Nations.

WHILE THE GLIDER crews worked, Camp Shangri-La played. Before an audience of natives, Decker shaved off six weeks' growth of beard. McCollom got a haircut from Ben Bulatao, but he and Walter kept their nonregulation whiskers. Walter told the crew of the 311, "We want to look like we've been someplace after we get out of here." They ate communal meals; explored the valley; posed for Alex Cann's camera; talked about their families; and read books, magazines, and letters dropped by the supply plane.

One supply drop included a book on jungle survival techniques; it arrived so late the survivors were certain it was someone's idea of a joke.

A native man whom the paratroopers called "Joe" oversaw daily swap meets between the natives and the outsiders. When the market was up and running, five cowrie shells could be exchanged for a stone adze, the most sought-after souvenir. Walter established a going rate for other native weaponry, exchanging eighteen shells for sixty-two arrows and three bows. At first, a pig could be had for as little as two to four shells, but inflation crept in, and the price rose to fifteen shells. This proved costly when the pigpen built by the paratroopers collapsed and eight plump, fifteen-shell swine headed for the hills. So many shells changed hands that McCollom worried that the survivors and paratroopers were ruining the local economy.

IN FACT, THE outsiders' use of cowrie shells as a kind of coin represented the natives' first tentative step toward a money-based

A DANI TRIBESMAN TRIES ON A UNIFORM. (PHOTO COURTESY OF C. EARL WALTER JR.)

economy. Although they had long traded shells with people from outside their villages to obtain twine, feathers, or other goods that weren't readily available, the natives didn't treat shells as a universal currency among themselves. In their communal villages, there was nothing to buy from each other. They used shells and shell necklaces primarily to cement social bonds. At a funeral, for instance, mourners would briefly drape the dead body with gifts of shell necklaces. As a highlight of the ceremony, a village leader would redistribute those necklaces, creating obligations to him and shared remembrances of their previous owner.

McCollom's worry about the local economy was only the half of it. By tossing around shells as though their only value was as a means of trade, the outsiders risked undermining the glue that kept the community together.

Although most natives were willing to provide pigs, adzes, bows, and arrows in exchange for shells, some felt trepidation about the deals. "We'd never seen so many shells. Our parents were telling us to be careful, don't take the shells," said Lisaniak Mabel. He and his friends heeded the warning. "The white guys got frustrated that we were rejecting the shells they were offering."

ONE DAY, THE native trader the paratroopers called Joe brought three women to the camp. Confused at first, Alex Cann and the paratroopers concluded that they were being offered the women in exchange for shells.

"Walt, you've got to be careful," Cann told Walter, "because he wants to sell you the women."

"Hell, I've got enough trouble," Walter replied. "I don't want a bunch of women running around!" Walter's men cracked up when they heard that.

Walter wrote in his journal: "He [Joe] is quite a money monger, and by the looks on the women's faces, they were little impressed by us." The feeling was mutual. Walter wrote that it would take him "a few years, plus the realization that we would never get out of here, plus a ton of soap, before they would be even presentable as far as I am concerned." Walter waved off the deal.

THE MAN THE outsiders called "Joe" was Gerlagam Logo, a son of the chief named Yali Logo and a warrior with a fierce reputation. Many years later, tribe members remembered Gerlagam as having been friendly with the outsiders. But they doubted that he ever tried to sell them women. Gerlagam had a wife and two daughters. Perhaps, they said, he wanted his new acquaintances to meet his family.

EACH DAY WHEN the supply plane flew overhead, Walter and Mc-Collom placed orders for food and provisions. Sergeant Ozzie St. George, a reporter for the U.S. Army magazine *Yank* who covered the mission alongside civilian journalists, made a sport of tracking the cargo drops. Among the items he recorded were: twenty pairs of shoes; three hundred pounds of medical supplies; fourteen .45-caliber pistols with three thousand rounds of ammunition; six Thompson submachine guns; knives; machetes; tents; cots; clothes for the survivors; seventy-five blankets; camp stoves; gasoline; canteens; water; seventy-five cases of ten-in-one rations; rice; salt; coffee; bacon; tomato and pineapple juice; and "eggs that landed unscrambled." St. George claimed that Margaret received "scanties," but she insisted that the underwear never arrived.

Walter continued his amateur anthropology. He searched for signs of religion, with no luck. "They're believers in mankind and that's about all the religion they seem to have," Walter told Major Gardner by walkie-talkie.

While hiking with his men and some natives near the Baliem River, Walter arranged a footrace on the riverbank to test their speed. Earlier he'd recorded his disappointment with their potential as porters, complaining in his journal that they tired more quickly than the Filipino bearers he recalled from his boyhood. The race did nothing to improve his view. "Natives not very fast," he wrote, "as we outran them with equipment on." He didn't record whether the Dani men might have been amused, confused, or both by the notion of running full speed when they weren't chasing a lost pig or escaping a deadly enemy.

During one hike, Walter and the survivors found corpses from recent warfare. "One warrior had been shot through the heart with an arrow," Margaret wrote. "Another had died from a spear driven through his head." Separately, Walter and McCollom found the skeleton of a man they thought must have stood more than six feet tall and weighed more than two hundred pounds. It was the closest they ever came to seeing one of the "giants" they'd heard so much about.

CAPTAIN C. EARL WALTER JR. AND LIEUTENANT JOHN MCCOLLOM EXAMINE A NATIVE JAWBONE THEY FOUND ON A HIKE. (PHOTO COURTESY OF C. EARL WALTER JR.)

After a walk with Alex Cann, Walter estimated the valley's population at five thousand and concluded that the natives belonged to "a dying race." He based that assumption on his observations of few children and some overgrown sweet potato fields. In fact, Walter's population estimate was about one-tenth to one-twentieth the actual number, and he didn't know that the Dani people left old fields fallow to regain their nutrients. However, Walter was onto something about children. Because Dani women abstained from sex for up to five years after childbirth, the birthrate wasn't as high as in some other native populations.

The natives reached mistaken conclusions about their guests, as well, beyond their belief that the visitors were spirits. Decades later, several old men who were boys and teenagers in June 1945 swore that they'd witnessed a strange miracle. As they described it, after the paratroopers ate pig meat, the animals emerged whole and alive when the men defecated. Narekesok Logo said: "You could see where the cuts were on the pig" after its rebirth.

DURING HIS WEEKS at the base camp, Alfred Baylon—"Weylon" to the natives—made regular medical calls in the nearby hamlets. The sergeant earned the natives' trust by treating minor wounds, pig bites, and a variety of skin ailments, including a form of athlete's foot. He treated their dandruff, too. "In the Army, they say to make the most of what you have," Baylon told a reporter. "So I smeared their heads with mosquito repellant. It seemed to work surprisingly well." When a woman with an infection on her breast began to heal within days of treatment, Baylon became the tribespeople's favorite outsider. The feeling was mutual. "They are a wonderfully carefree people," he said. "Living in a land of perpetual summer, they never worry about their next meal."

Walter encouraged the sergeant, to a degree. When a local woman went into labor, the natives came running for Baylon.

"But the captain forbade it," Margaret wrote in her diary, "fearing that if anything happened to the woman or the baby, the natives might turn on all of us."

Before the others reached the valley, Baylon usually visited the village alone or with Sergeant Velasco, who became relatively adept at the native language. Now, Alex Cann, Walter, and the three survivors joined the sergeants on their rounds. But as they headed toward the nearest village, an old man blocked their way.

"He was a man of dignity and authority," Margaret wrote. "He knew and liked Sergeants Velasco and Baylon, and there was no ill will and nothing threatening in the chief's attitude. But he made it abundantly clear that he didn't want his village invaded all the time."

When a pantomime negotiation went nowhere, Margaret tried a charm offensive: "I pouted as prettily as I knew how and I batted what few stubby little eyelashes had begun to grow back after the originals were singed off in the plane crash."

"Aw, Chief, don't be mean," she told the native leader.

Margaret laughed about it in her diary: "Walter, McCollom, Decker and the sergeants stared at me as if I had lost my mind. But it worked. Right before our eyes, the old chief melted."

Still, the native leader had limits. He allowed the two sergeants, Margaret, and Alex Cann into the village, but he turned away Walter, McCollom, and Decker. Rather than risk an incident, Walter and the two male survivors returned to camp.

That day, Margaret met a woman in the village whom she described as "regal in manner." Based on her belief that the woman was a village leader's wife, or at least one of his wives, Margaret called her "the queen."

THE MEETING AND its aftermath revealed a profound change in Margaret since the crash. She'd flown aboard the *Gremlin Special* hoping to see strange creatures she believed were "primitive."

During her time in the jungle clearing, she came to see them as people. Since reaching the base camp, her views had evolved further. No longer did she describe natives in her diary as savages or childlike, for instance. Upon getting to know "the queen," Margaret's outlook took an evolutionary leap. Any remaining hint of superiority vanished. In its place came respect.

"The queen and I liked each other immediately," she wrote. They spent long stretches together: "All we lacked, from the American point of view, was a front porch and a couple of rocking chairs." Margaret described their ability to communicate as "a case of understanding the heart, for neither of us was ever able to understand a word of the other's language."

The native woman invited Margaret into the long hut the village women used as a communal cookhouse. She fed Margaret hot sweet potatoes, declining the butter that Margaret brought with her from the base camp. Margaret, too, hesitated to abandon her traditional ways. The native woman tried to persuade her to strip

THE NATIVE WOMAN MARGARET CALLED "THE QUEEN" GREETS HER OUTSIDE A HUT. (PHOTO COURTESY OF B. B. MCCOLLOM.)

down to what Margaret called a "G-string of woven twigs worn by herself and her ladies in waiting." Margaret demurred: "I just clutched my khaki tighter around me." The queen didn't seem to mind.

After a few days, the native woman was so eager for Margaret's visit that she met her halfway between the camp and the village. "Occasionally the trail was rough or we would have to cross small streams with precarious log bridges," Margaret wrote. When Margaret feared she'd fall, she'd appeal to the nimble-footed woman for help: "She always knew what I meant. The queen would take my hand in hers and give me an assist along the way."

When the sergeants teased Margaret for slowing their pace en route to the village, the queen sensed that the men were making sport of her friend. "She turned on them, and there was no mistaking the fact that they were getting a royal dressing down, for such unseemly behavior toward a royal guest." The same tongue-lashing befell a group of native girls and young women working in the sweet potato gardens who giggled when the two women walked past.

Walter noticed Margaret's growing connection. With a combination of envy and admiration, he told the men in the supply plane: "The natives will take stuff from her, but they won't take anything from the rest of us."

The more Margaret came to appreciate the locals, the more she admired them for refusing the paratroopers' goods. "The natives of Shangri-La are a wise people," she wrote. "They are happy. They know when they're well off. They are too smart to permit a few chance visitors from Mars to change the rhythm of centuries."

Walter, meanwhile, tried repeatedly to trade machetes, knives, and other modern conveniences for an ornate necklace of small shells arranged in vertical rows on a strip of rawhide that hung from the wearer's throat to his breastbone. Each time he failed.

The necklace belonged to a man named Keaugi Walela. In

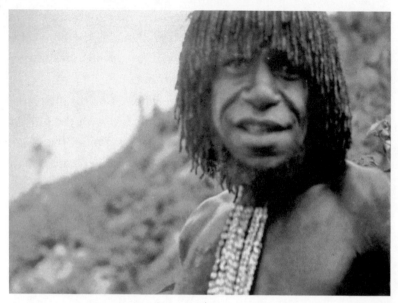

KEAUGI WALELA WEARING THE NECKLACE THAT EARL WALTER TRIED UNSUCCESS-
FULLY TO OBTAIN. (PHOTO COURTESY OF C. EARL WALTER JR.)

later years, Keaugi became a chief with ten wives. When Keaugi
died, his son Dagadigik inherited the necklace. One day in battle
it fell from his neck. An enemy warrior retrieved it, and the necklace became a spoil of war, in Dani terms a "dead bird."

SOON WALTER HAD bigger worries than souvenirs. Reports on
the glider snatch tests, delivered via walkie-talkie, sounded
grim.

After the pickup equipment was installed in the *Leaking Louise*, snatch pilot Major William Samuels, copilot Captain William
McKenzie, glider pilot Lieutenant Henry Palmer, and a second
glider pilot, Captain G. Reynolds Allen, agreed on what sounded
like a straightforward plan. First, they'd make a few practice runs
on Wakde Island to test the gear, get in sync with each other, and
hone the glider and pickup crews. Then the *Leaking Louise* would
tow the *Fanless Faggot* halfway across New Guinea to Mount Ha-

gen, a large, accessible valley at the same mile-high altitude as Shangri-La. If they tested it there, they thought, the first high-altitude Waco glider pickup snatch wouldn't involve crash survivors as guinea pigs and reporters as witnesses.

The plan unraveled almost immediately. On the first trial run on Wakde Island, Samuels came in too low with the *Leaking Louise*. No one was hurt, but the snatch failed. Worse, the C-47's propellers severed the nylon tow rope, and the radio compass mast was knocked off the underside of the plane. After repairs, Samuels tried again. On the second effort, the steel tow cable broke, destroying the winch. No one was hurt, but replacing it caused more delays. Then calamity struck.

The *Tribune*'s Walter Simmons had flown to Wakde Island to witness the tests. Despite the danger, Simmons volunteered to be one of eight passengers aboard the *Fanless Faggot* for the third trial run. Just after the snatch, the steel cable inside the *Leaking Louise* again snapped as the crew tried to reel in the glider. "The winch just blew up," said McKenzie, the copilot.

The broken cable whipped around the C-47's cabin like an angry snake, tearing through the wall of the navigator's compartment. The slashing cable struck the winch operator, Master Sergeant Winston Howell, in the head. Only days earlier, Howell had told the AP's Ralph Morton he was certain they'd have no trouble. The cable slashed the radio operator, Sergeant Harry Baron, across the back.

"A shower of aluminum, wood, glass and smoke inundated the cockpit," Samuels wrote in a self-published memoir. "I looked back to ask if the boom was retracted so we could land. All I could see was everyone lying down and much blood." The injuries to Howell and Baron weren't life-threatening, but both were hospitalized.

Before the other half of the broken steel cable could slice through the *Fanless Faggot,* glider pilots Palmer and Allen detached the Waco and made an emergency landing. Walter Simmons and the other glider passengers and crew emerged shaken but unhurt. Later, Allen blamed the accident on the hastily scavenged snatch equipment, saying it "was unused for several years and was badly rusted."

Alarmed, Colonel Elsmore put out a call for another replacement winch and flew to Wakde Island to supervise. He told Walter Simmons that if they encountered more problems, he might cancel the glider snatch altogether. In the meantime, Elsmore quietly revived the idea of inviting the Seabees to build a runway in Shangri-La; it would take longer than a glider snatch and pose its own problems, but he wouldn't have to worry about exploding winches, snapping cables, and the other perils inherent with "flying coffins."

Even before the snapped cable, Walter and his men had been unsettled by the idea of a glider ride. They were blasé about jumping out of airplanes. But gliders were something else entirely, and the Waco's reputation preceded it. In his daily radio conversations with the supply plane, he told the planners not to rush: "We wouldn't want any haphazard attempt made to get us out of here. . . . We are perfectly willing to wait until everything is set. . . . We don't want to take any chances by pushing the thing to get out of here before the pickup and glider pilots are ready." After learning of the accident and injuries, Walter repeated those messages with more urgency.

Adding to his anxiety was the need for multiple pickups to get all fifteen people out of the valley. "Each trip increased the possibility of a bad accident, trouble, whatever," Walter said. He spoke privately with his top sergeant, Sandy Abrenica, about trying to hike out, or "whether we had to come up with other ways to get out of there, if the glider pickup didn't work." Without telling Elsmore, Walter and Abrenica made rough calculations of how many more men they'd need to mount a trek during which they might face headhunters, hiding Japanese troops, or both.

Margaret turned to prayer. The night she learned about the

broken glider cable, she huddled in her private corner of the big tent: "I said my Rosary over and over, asking God that no one be hurt in trying to save us." Major Samuels, the snatch pilot, had the same idea. He later told Margaret that he'd gone to Sunday services and asked a chaplain to pray for their mission.

THE FIRST THREAT to Margaret's friendship with the native woman came one day in the village when she pulled out a comb and absentmindedly ran it through her hair. The queen was mesmerized: "She had never seen a comb before or anyone doing such queer things to their hair. The other natives were equally delighted with this toy. Half the village gathered 'round and I combed my hair until my arm was tired."

Margaret handed the comb to her friend. Rather than use it on herself, the woman "carefully combed my hair down over my face." Margaret smiled as the woman completed the styling. Then Margaret combed her hair back off her forehead to its usual swept-back arrangement. The queen took the comb and again plastered Margaret's hair over her face. Alex Cann captured the comic back-and-forth scene on film. But the woman's husband became involved, and it stopped being funny.

"Sergeant Velasco was about to put a stop to this beauty business when the chief decided to join the game," Margaret wrote. "He started to run his hands through my hair. This was a good-will gesture from which I shrank inwardly. But I didn't want to offend him and his followers. So I sat still a moment and said, 'Unh, unh, unh' at what I deemed were appropriate intervals in the conversation."

Velasco kept an eye on Margaret's friend. The native woman began speaking in what sounded like an agitated tone, and he sensed that she was growing jealous.

"Scram," Velasco told Margaret, and they ran together from the village.

MARGARET BRUSHES BACK HER HAIR AFTER A NATIVE SALON TREATMENT. (PHOTO
COURTESY OF B. B. MCCOLLOM.)

On their way back to base camp, he said: "I guess you might
have been queen. But I also suspect you might have been dead."

Margaret worried the friendship was ruined. But on her next
visit to the village, the woman was her usual gracious self. From
the woman's improvised sign language, it appeared that she
wanted Margaret to move from the base camp into the women's
hut. "Velasco and Baylon told me they were certain she wanted to
adopt me. But I didn't think my father back in Owego would like
that very much," Margaret wrote. She politely declined.

On another visit, with Decker and McCollom in tow, several
women approached Margaret and motioned for her to hold out her
right hand. "As I did so, one of the women raised a stone ax," Margaret wrote. "I was so amazed by this first sign of violence in the
natives that I could scarcely move."

Realizing what was happening, McCollom shoved Margaret
out of the way.

Afterward, McCollom tried to explain what he believed was

afoot: "When a girl is of marriageable age, they chop off the tips of all the fingers on her right hand. I guess this is a hint to you to nab off one of us handsome guys."

McCollom had added one and one but got three. Having noticed that nearly all the women in the village who'd reached sexual maturity had lost several fingers, he assumed there was a relationship between the two.

IN FACT, THE Dani people of Koloima were trying to help Margaret mourn.

Unlike the natives near the jungle campsite, the villagers in the valley didn't know about the plane crash; news of an event so many miles away would have had to pass through the territory of enemies with whom communication usually occurred at spearpoint. Instead, the natives in the valley assumed that Margaret and the other visitors had escaped from some terrible event in their world. The people of Koloima were so sure of this, their name for Margaret was Nuarauke, which meant "fleeing."

By their logic and experience, whatever tragedy had caused Margaret to seek refuge in the valley must have involved death. To honor and appease the dead, they assumed that Margaret would want to sacrifice her fingers. When she declined, the natives weren't insulted; any reprisal against Margaret would come not from them, but from the spirit world.

Margaret also apparently misunderstood when she thought that the native leader wanted to take her as his bride. To the contrary, the natives thought that the male survivors and paratroopers wanted to give Margaret in marriage to a native leader named Sikman Piri. "The white men said to him, 'Sleep with this woman,' " said Hugiampot, who was a teenager at the time. "She said, 'Sleep with me.' But Sikman Piri said, 'No, I am afraid.' So he didn't take her as a wife."

Margaret/Nuarauke wasn't the only outsider given a native

name. Sergeant Caoili was called Kelabi—a rough pronunciation of his surname that had no meaning in the Dani language. Other names included Bpik, Pisek, Araum, Mamage, and Suarem, though the passage of time blurred which name belonged to whom. Some natives knew Alex Cann as Onggaliok, but others remembered him as Elabut Muluk, a Dani phrase that means "big belly."

WHEN WALTER FIRST arrived at the base camp with the survivors, he was happy to see the people of Koloima. The captain wrote in his journal: "All of the natives appreciate our help, as we do theirs." But three days later, Walter sensed tension bordering on hostility. The change was subtle; fewer smiles, fewer visitors hanging around the base camp.

That night, he heard angry shouts coming from the village. He put the base camp on alert and for the first time in weeks posted guards throughout the night. "It is good to be prepared," he wrote in his journal. "The natives have been less friendly the last few days. However, with our weapons we can stand here easily. And so we prepare for our first uneasy night since we got here."

Morning arrived without incident, but Walter ordered his men to remain vigilant. He kept closer tabs on the survivors' movements, ordering them to stay close to base camp.

Walter tended to be cautious, but in this case he wasn't imagining things. As much as the natives appreciated the medical care and liked Margaret, the outsiders' presence had disturbed their routines, their wars in particular.

The base camp was in the middle of the no-man's-land the natives regularly used as a battlefield. As long as the outsiders were there, the Dani people of Koloima couldn't satisfy their desire to confront their enemies in open combat. In addition, some local leaders didn't like how Walter and his men handed out fistfuls of shells, fired their frightening guns, and wandered wherever they

REGIONAL "BIG MAN" YALI LOGO (CENTER).
(PHOTO COURTESY OF C. EARL WALTER JR.)

pleased. For many years, the native leader named Yali Logo had been the regional big man. Now the outsiders behaved as big men, and Yali didn't like it.

Unaware that the outsiders were preparing to leave the valley, Yali began plotting their departure on his own terms. He visited the base camp by day, where Walter photographed him standing calmly, though unsmiling, with his tribesmen. But according to his tribesmen, at night Yali sent a messenger to his sworn enemy and frequent battlefield opponent, a legendary big man named Kurelu from the neighboring territory.

"At night the enemies talked," said Ai Baga, a teenager at the time. "Yali wanted to drive them out, and he wanted Kurelu to help. But Kurelu said no."

It's possible, said several Dani men who witnessed the events, that Kurelu was pleased to see Yali's authority undermined by the outsiders; as a result, Kurelu had no incentive to join a conspiracy.

As days passed with no sign of gliders, Yali kept plotting and Walter kept posting guards.

25

SNATCH

UPON ARRIVING AT Wakde Island, Colonel Elsmore canceled the original plan to practice a mile-high glider snatch at Mount Hagen. Instead, they'd focus on fixing the problems and getting it right at sea level on Wakde. To compensate for the higher altitude in Shangri-La, they'd overload the glider during the trial runs, filling it with nine passengers and three hundred pounds of sandbags.

Elsmore believed the maxim that a leader shouldn't ask his troops to do anything he wouldn't do himself. He sat in the glider's copilot seat for the last three snatch tests. It's not clear whether Elsmore's hands-on approach reflected confidence that nothing would go wrong or lingering doubts that something might. Either way, those runs went off without a hitch. Satisfied, Elsmore declared that the snatch was on.

The plan called for three glider drops into Shangri-La, and three subsequent snatches, to get all fifteen people out of the valley. Bad weather added several more days of delays, so the glider and tow crews cooled their heels in Hollandia. In the valley, the temporary inhabitants waited in nervous anticipation, only to be told to stand down until the cloud cover cleared.

THE BIG DAY came on June 28, 1945. All fifteen members of Camp Shangri-La awoke at 6:00 a.m. to mostly clear skies with wisps of clouds that the *Tribune*'s Walter Simmons compared to "puffs of cigar smoke."

The first plane into the valley was the supply plane.

"Does the queen think she wants to pull out of there today?" Major Gardner asked via walkie-talkie.

"She's been wanting to get out of here for a week," Walter replied.

"I suppose that goes for everybody," Gardner said.

The major told Walter that Colonel Elsmore would supervise the mission from the cockpit of his own plane, a B-25 bomber he'd named for his seventeen-year-old son, Ray Jr. Instead of bombs, Elsmore loaded the plane with enough reporters for a media circus, with him as ringmaster. After telling Walter about the colonel and the correspondents, Gardner relayed a message to Walter that almost certainly came directly from the press-conscious Elsmore: "We should like it very much if on the first trip out, you, Mac, Maggie, and Decker could be on that glider."

Walter knew that he'd get enormous attention as a hero if he stepped out of the first glider as the rescue leader alongside the three survivors. Only weeks earlier, he'd repeatedly noted in his journal how much he valued such exposure: "If this deal is getting all the publicity it appears to be, I am sure that my prayers on the future will be answered." Worldwide page-one coverage of him with Margaret, McCollom, and Decker—perhaps with Colonel Elsmore pinning a medal on his chest—might have made it impossible for the brass to ignore Walter's combat requests. Just as important, after the war he could show the stories and photos to his hero father. Walter also knew that he might have only one chance to bask in the acclaim; days might pass before the second and third glider pickups, and by then the media train might have rolled on.

None of that mattered as much as it once did. Walter wasn't the same man who parachuted into the valley six weeks earlier, hungry for a mission and focused on his own career. He was no less gung-ho, but he was more mature; for the first time since he was drafted, he felt he had proved his mettle. Not only to the U.S. Army brass; not only to his men; not only to the imagined eyes of his father; but to himself. Walter understood what it meant to be a leader, and rushing to the front of the line wouldn't do.

"I will not be on the first glider," Walter answered, according to a transcript of the ground-to-air exchange. "I will send the three survivors and one or two of my men on the first glider. I will be the last man to leave here with my master sergeant and a couple of tech sergeants."

Major Gardner could have ordered him aboard the first glider, but he let it drop. Gardner turned the conversation to wind speed on the valley floor. Walter assured him that it was minimal. That was the last discussion about when Walter would leave the valley.

A FEW MINUTES later, the radio in the supply plane crackled with word that the *Fanless Faggot* was en route to Shangri-La, gliding at the end of a tow cable pulled by a C-46. Elsmore joined the conversation, reporting from his B-25 cockpit that the glider was making good time. He corrected the tow plane's course, and within minutes the C-46 cleared the last ridge and entered the valley with the glider trailing a few hundred feet behind on its nylon leash.

When he saw Shangri-La spread out below him, Lieutenant Henry Palmer grabbed an overhead lever in the glider cockpit. He pulled down, releasing the Fearless Faggot from the tow cable.

Within seconds, the glider slowed from more than one hundred miles per hour to less than eighty. As the C-46 flew off, engine noise faded away. Glider pilots Palmer and G. Reynolds Allen could hear the wind rushing past as they gently banked the engineless aircraft to further reduce speed. They lined up the glider's

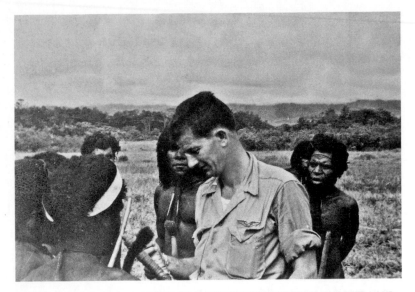

GLIDER PILOT LIEUTENANT HENRY E. PALMER INSPECTS A NATIVE AX AFTER LAND-
ING THE *FANLESS FAGGOT* IN THE VALLEY. (PHOTO COURTESY OF B. B. MCCOLLOM.)

nose between the red parachutes that outlined the makeshift landing strip and touched down. As they slowed to a stop, the glider's
tail rose like a whale's fluke, then eased back down for a perfect
landing. Alex Cann captured the moment for posterity.

"We were all out on the field, jumping up and down with happiness," Margaret wrote in her diary. Dozens of natives gathered
around, whooping and hollering at the sight. "This was their first
chance to see, close up, one of those monsters of the air that had
been so terrifying to them at first. Now they gazed at it with no
more fear than we did."

Henry Palmer knew that Major Samuels had only enough fuel
in the *Leaking Louise* to circle a few times before attempting the
snatch. Samuels also worried about a new cloud bank settling over
the mountains surrounding the valley. Over the radio, he warned:
"We haven't too much gas or time." Samuels was serious about his
concern. Before leaving Hollandia, he and his men had tossed out
their heavy boots, their .45-caliber sidearms, the plane's Thomp-

son submachine guns, and every other nonessential item to lighten the load.

As the clouds thickened, Samuels expressed doubts that a snatch attempt would be possible that day. The glider crew might have to sleep in the base camp overnight, and they'd try again the following morning, weather permitting.

Colonel Elsmore wouldn't hear of it: "It looks like a damn good day to me," he said.

Samuels relented, and the *Leaking Louise* began to prepare for a pickup. He announced over the radio that he wanted to try a couple of "dry runs"—swooping low over the field without grabbing the glider. Again Elsmore objected.

"You better not try a dry run," the colonel commanded. "If you're short on gas, don't take the time. You can make it OK without a dry run."

While Samuels and Elsmore sparred overhead, Lieutenant Palmer jumped down from the glider and called to the survivors: "You ready to go? This express takes off here on schedule in thirty minutes."

"Thirty minutes?" Margaret said. "Why, I'm not even packed." Neither were McCollom, Decker, and the two paratroopers Walter had chosen for the flight: Sergeants Fernando Dongallo and Ben Bulatao. By putting "Doc" on the first glider, Walter wanted to focus attention on the medics who'd risked their lives by jumping into the jungle.

As the survivors and the sergeants hurriedly gathered their belongings and souvenirs, the glider pilots went to work setting up the snatch poles. With the camp bustling, Alex Cann aimed his camera at a remarkable scene: twenty or more tribesmen pitched in to help Walter and the paratroopers roll the *Fanless Faggot* into position for the snatch. Leaning forward, their hands pressed against the glider's canvas skin, the modern soldiers and the Stone Age warriors worked together, shoulder to shoulder, to muscle

NATIVE TRIBESMEN HELP PUSH THE *FANLESS FAGGOT* INTO POSITION FOR A
SNATCH ATTEMPT. (PHOTO COURTESY OF C. EARL WALTER JR.)

the Waco into place on the no-man's-land-cum-battlefield-cum-
improvised-glider-landing-strip.

With the clock ticking and the snatch plane's fuel tanks emp-
tying, Palmer hustled the five passengers onto the glider. Margaret
realized she hadn't said good-bye to the natives. "But they understood that we were going," she wrote. Margaret was especially
sorry to leave without a final visit with "the queen."

The native leader Yali Logo wasn't sorry to see them leave, but
Margaret felt certain that some of the tribesmen were distraught:
"Tears streamed down their black faces. They felt they were losing friends, and I knew I was losing some of the best and kindest
friends I would ever have. I blew my nose rather noisily, and discovered that McCollom and Decker were doing the same thing."

IT'S POSSIBLE THAT the weeping natives were sad to see Margaret climb aboard the glider. It's also possible that their tears
reflected complex emotions among the people of Koloima.

The glider fascinated them, but according to several witnesses, they wouldn't understand until later that their new acquaintances intended to fly away forever. They thought the glider's arrival was the last sign of the Uluayek legend. Frightened, they appealed to their ancestors.

"We had a crying ceremony," said Binalok, a son of Yali Logo. "It was to say, 'Oh, we feel this deeply.' As we cried, we named our dead ancestors. We thought we would be going back to the ways of our ancestors."

Almost nothing had changed for generations in the valley, where the people lived and farmed and fought as their forefathers had. One exception involved styles of penis gourds and women's wrapped skirts. After the crying ceremony, the men of Koloima stopped storing tobacco in the tips of their penis gourds, reverting to the practice of their elders. Native women changed how they wrapped their grass skirts, adopting a more traditional style. The changes might have seemed inconsequential to an outsider, but not to a Dani. Unable to envision what a new age would look like or how dramatically it would affect their lives, the people of Koloima made the most drastic change they could imagine—a return to older styles of gourds and skirts.

In the end, the natives were right about Uluayek but wrong about its effects. In a relatively short time, the world would come to Shangri-La, and the valley would change in ways they could never imagine.

INSIDE THE GLIDER, Palmer snapped Margaret out of her thoughts about the natives with a sharp warning: "Don't be surprised if the tow rope breaks on the first try."

"What happens if it does?" McCollom asked.

Palmer laid on a Louisiana accent: "Well, suh, the Army's got me insured for ten thousand dollars."

Margaret wasn't laughing. She gripped her rosary and looked around the glider cabin, so flimsy when compared to the plane that had brought her to the valley nearly seven weeks earlier. She told her diary: "I wondered if we had survived a hideous plane crash and so much hardship, illness and pain, only to be killed when rescue was so near."

Palmer helped to fasten their seat belts and showed them where to hold on, to avoid whiplash when the snatch came. They held tight as the *Leaking Louise* grew closer.

Major Samuels circled the C-47 at fifteen hundred feet above the valley floor. His crew made sure the pickup arm was in place, hanging below the plane's belly, to grab the nylon loop. Peering through the windshield, he looked to the horizon and saw clouds closing in on the valley.

"I don't think I can pick up today," he radioed to Elsmore in the *Ray Jr.* and also to the crew in the supply plane.

Relying on his rank and his expertise, gained from a year of flying into and out of Shangri-La, Elsmore commanded otherwise: "This is the best weather I've seen in the valley in many a day.

THE *LEAKING LOUISE*, PILOTED BY MAJOR WILLIAM J. SAMUELS, APPROACHES THE *FAN-LESS FAGGOT* FOR A SNATCH ATTEMPT. (PHOTO COURTESY OF C. EARL WALTER JR.)

You can do it. Go right down there and pick up the glider. You'll never get much better weather here." Samuels knew better than to argue.

At one point during the conversation, Samuels turned away from the radio and asked his copilot, Captain William McKenzie: "Are you nervous, Mac?"

"Hell, yes," McKenzie said. "Are you?"

"I guess you could say that."

Samuels wrenched his neck to look into the cabin. "You guys all ready back there?" he asked the crew. They responded with thumbs up.

"OK, here we go. Lower the boom."

Samuels pulled back on the throttles, slowing the C-47 to just over 135 miles per hour. He pushed forward on the control wheel, guiding the plane down to twenty feet above the valley floor and headed toward the spindly posts with the nylon loop draped across them.

At 9:47 a.m., the steel hook caught hold of the loop. Samuels slammed the throttles forward to gain power as he pulled back on the control wheel to gain altitude.

Inside the glider, the passengers and crew felt a neck-snapping jolt.

Watching from his B-25 at six thousand feet, Colonel Elsmore spat a machine-gun litany into his radio: "Oh boy. Oh boy. Ohboy, Ohboy, OHBOY!"

The drag from the glider slowed the *Leaking Louise* to a dangerous 105 miles per hour. The snatch plane was flying barely above the speed at which a C-47 was doomed to stall, a failure almost certain to be fatal.

Making matters worse, just before becoming airborne, the left wheel of the *Fanless Faggot* had snagged one of the parachutes laid down the center of the field. The white cloth billowed and thrashed against the glider's underbelly as it struggled to gain al-

AS THE *FANLESS FAGGOT* MOVED
FORWARD AT THE END OF
THE NYLON CABLE AFTER THE
SNATCH, A PARACHUTE USED
AS A FIELD MARKER CAUGHT ON
THE GLIDER'S WHEEL. (PHOTOS
COURTESY OF C. EARL WALTER
JR. AND THE U.S. ARMY.)

titude at the end of the tow rope. Lieutenant Palmer's black humor
about government life insurance now seemed more relevant and
even less funny. If it were even possible, an emergency landing in
the *Fanless Faggot* would likely be a twisting, uncontrolled affair.

Margaret prayed harder as the glider swept treacherously low
toward the jungle-covered mountains. Seven hundred feet of
steel cable had spun out from the winch inside the *Leaking Louise*. Added to the three hundred feet of nylon rope from the loop
and the towline, the *Fanless Faggot* trailed the C-47 by about one
thousand feet, or several hundred feet farther than ideal. With
Samuels struggling to gain altitude, the longer distance between
the two aircraft meant that the glider was being tugged too low

toward the mountains. Samuels pulled back harder on the control wheel and applied full power. It wasn't enough. Still the tow rope dragged through the trees—pulling the glider and the seven people on board through the upper branches.

When the glider grazed a treetop, Margaret clenched in fear. Her mind raced back to the sickening sound of branches scraping against the metal skin of the *Gremlin Special* just before it crashed.

The *Leaking Louise* clawed for altitude, climbed, and hauled the damaged *Fanless Faggot* into the clear. "When the glider swayed into our line of vision," Samuels reported, "we could see pieces of fabric fluttering off in the wind."

The trees were only the first obstacles. His hands sweating, Samuels fought to bring the C-47 up to ten thousand feet, the altitude he knew would be needed to clear the surrounding ridges. As Samuels overheated, the twin engines of the *Leaking Louise* did so, too. The plane began losing altitude.

"I've pushed her as far as she can go," he radioed. Samuels announced that he wanted to cut the glider loose to avoid killing the C-47's engines—along with everyone aboard both aircraft.

Elsmore demanded that the major do no such thing. Watching from a higher altitude in his B-25, he believed the *Leaking Louise* had climbed high enough to clear the pass. He radioed back: "Let 'em heat up. Keep goin'!"

Clouds shrouded the highest ridges, blocking Samuels's vision.

INSIDE THE *FANLESS FAGGOT,* the five passengers were exhaling with relief over the tow rope's refusal to break in the trees. But while congratulating each other on their apparent survival, they heard a persistent *slap-slap* noise from underneath the glider. The sound came from the parachute that had snagged on the wheel during takeoff. As it whipped against the glider's belly, the chute tore through the canvas-covered floor, adding to the damage caused by the sweep through the branches. Strapped in their seats, the passengers looked through ragged gashes to the jungle several thousand feet below. The chute kept thwacking, the canvas kept shedding, and the holes kept growing.

Nearing panic, Margaret tried not to look, but she couldn't stop herself. It reminded her of a ride on a glass-bottomed boat, only with no bottom.

John McCollom, who'd twice reentered the burning *Gremlin Special*, who'd swallowed the grief over his dead twin to lead Margaret and Decker down the mountain, who'd walked across a log to confront the ax-wielding natives, had one more task thrust upon him.

McCollom unbuckled his seat belt and dropped to his knees. He crawled toward the tail of the glider, wind pounding against his face. Hanging on to keep from plummeting to his death, McCollom reached through the hole and grabbed a handful of parachute cloth. He pulled it inside, then grabbed another handful, then another, until the chute was safely stowed away.

IN THE COCKPIT of the snatch plane, Samuels's struggles continued. He obeyed Elsmore's order not to cut loose the glider, even as he watched a temperature gauge on the dashboard show that the cylinder heads of both engines were overheating.

With help from copilot William McKenzie, Samuels flew the equivalent of a high-altitude tightrope, with a dozen lives in two aircraft hanging in the balance. He throttled back just enough to keep the engines from seizing while maintaining enough altitude for both his C-47 and the trailing Waco glider to narrowly clear the valley walls.

"We dropped her down to eight thousand feet," Samuels said, "and . . . we were practically brushing the mountain tops." But the plane didn't quit. The C-47 remained aloft, and so did the glider.

As they flew through the final mountain pass out of the valley, the overheating *Leaking Louise* and the damaged *Fanless Faggot* passed over the charred wreckage of the *Gremlin Special*.

Even with a two-foot-wide hole in the glider floor, Margaret, McCollom, and Decker couldn't spot the crash site. But they knew that under the jungle canopy, pressed into the moist soil, there stood twenty white wooden crosses and one Star of David, silently marking the loss of friends, comrades, and family, left behind in Shangri-La.

THE VIEW FROM THE *FANLESS FAGGOT* AS THE *LEAKING LOUISE* PULLED THE GLIDER OUT OF SHANGRI-LA, EN ROUTE TO HOLLANDIA. (PHOTO COURTESY OF B. B. MCCOLLOM.)

EPILOGUE:

AFTER SHANGRI-LA

AS COLONEL ELSMORE predicted, the remainder of the ninety-minute trip was uneventful, with one small glitch. A pack of generals, VIPs, and reporters gathered at Hollandia's Cyclops Airstrip for the survivors' arrival, but the *Fanless Faggot* landed a quarter mile away on the Sentani Airstrip, completing a round-trip begun seven weeks earlier with the *Gremlin Special*. The greeting party raced to Sentani, where the survivors posed for photos with the crews of the glider and tow planes. Later they gave a press conference that made the front pages of newspapers around the world. Asked what they wanted to do next, the trio played it cute:

"Get a haircut and shave, and then go up to Manila," McCollom said.

"A haircut and a shower will do me," Decker said.

"I'd like a shower and a permanent," Margaret said.

The *Fanless Faggot* was too damaged to fly again, so a new glider was used the following day in a snatch that brought out Alex Cann and five paratroopers: Corporal Custodio Alerta and Sergeants Alfred Baylon, Juan Javonillo, Camilo Ramirez, and Don Ruiz. Two days later, on July 1, 1945, out came the third and final group—Walter called them "The Four Musketeers"—sergeants Santiago Abrenica, Hermenegildo Caoili, and Roque Velasco, and Walter himself. Along with souvenirs of bows, arrows, and axes, they decorated their caps with pig tusks and feathers to make a grand entrance. They left behind the tents and most of their supplies, but took their weapons.

The paratroopers tried to convince several native boys to board the glider, without success. "We were excited to go," said Lisaniak Mabel. "We said, 'Let's go!' but our parents said, 'We don't want to lose you.'"

THE THREE SURVIVORS OF THE *GREMLIN SPECIAL* CRASH UPON THEIR RETURN TO HOLLANDIA. (PHOTOS COURTESY OF B. B. MCCOLLOM.)

The paratroopers had better luck with the little pig named Peggy. Squealing and wriggling, it left Shangri-La on the last glider flight to Hollandia. Peggy's subsequent fate is unknown.

FOUR MONTHS AFTER the rescue, Shangri-La and the "Grand Valley" discovered in 1938 by Richard Archbold were formally acknowledged to be one and the same. As the journal *Science* reported: "The identity of the valley came about through a comparison of photographs taken by the Army just before the survivors were rescued with airplane photographs taken by the Archbold expedition. The identity is acknowledged by the Army, and particularly by Colonel Ray T. Elsmore, who directed the recent rescue operations."

Archbold never returned to New Guinea, never married, and never engaged in further exotic expeditions. He devoted the remainder of his life, and his considerable fortune, to the Archbold Biological Station, a five-thousand-acre preserve near Lake Placid, Florida, dedicated to ecological research and conservation. He died in 1976 at sixty-nine.

JUST AS THE Uluayek legend foretold, a new age dawned after the return of the sky spirits. Changes in the valley during the ensuing decades have been dramatic, but whether for better or worse is a matter of debate.

Spurred in part by news stories about the natives during coverage of the *Gremlin Special* rescue, Christian missionaries established camps in the valley in the decade after the war. They flew in aboard new amphibious planes that could land and take off from a straight stretch of the Baliem River. After initially reacting with hostility, in time a majority of native families accepted Christianity. Today, more than a dozen large churches dot the valley's one town of any size, Wamena, a dusty former Dutch government post with trash-strewn streets and a population of ten thousand and rising. Wamena is also now the site of a small airport; aircraft remain the only way in and out, but the valley's former isolation has surrendered to regularly scheduled flights.

After the missionaries came Indonesian troops, who arrived in force in the 1960s and '70s, after the Netherlands ended colonial control over the western half of New Guinea. Dutch New Guinea is now an Indonesian province called Papua. (The eastern half of the island of New Guinea is a separate country, called, confusingly, Papua New Guinea.) Hollandia has been renamed Jayapura. Shangri-La is now the Baliem Valley.

Tribal affiliations remain intact among valley people, but natives throughout the province are collectively called Papuans. A low-intensity independence movement has sputtered along seeking a "Free Papua." But hundreds of miles from the Baliem Valley, mining companies are extracting major gold and copper deposits. The Indonesian government has no intention of ceding control over Papua or its resources.

Years of persuasion by missionaries and force by Indonesian authorities put an end to the perpetual wars that formerly defined native life in the Baliem Valley. But an absence of war has also meant an absence of strong leaders, and peace hasn't meant prosperity. The province has the highest rates of poverty and AIDS in Indonesia. Health care is woeful, and aid workers say school is a sometimes thing for valley children. The Indonesian government provides financial support, but much of the money ends up in the hands of nonnative migrants who run virtually all the businesses of Wamena.

Elderly native men in penis gourds walk through Wamena begging for change and cigarettes. Some charge a small fee to pose for photos, inserting boar tusks through passages in their nasal septums to look fierce. More often, they look lost.

One village near Wamena earns money by displaying a mummified ancestor to the few tourists who obtain special government

A DANI TRIBESMAN PHOTOGRAPHED IN THE
BALIEM VALLEY CITY OF WAMENA IN 2010.
(PHOTO COURTESY OF MITCHELL ZUCKOFF.)

permits to visit the valley. Younger men and women have largely abandoned penis gourds and twine skirts. Instead they wear Western castoff shorts and T-shirts with unfamiliar logos and images. In February 2010, a young man walked toward his remote village wearing a T-shirt that displayed a portrait of Barack Obama. Asked if he knew the identity of the man on his shirt, he smiled shyly and said no.

Robert Gardner, a documentary filmmaker who first visited the valley in 1961 to film the Dani people in their original state, despairs at the changes during the past half century. "They were warriors and independent people," he said. "Now they're serfs in their own country." Others, however, say the transition to modern ways, though difficult, will eventually lead to improved opportunities and standards of living.

Outside Wamena, large parts of the landscape remain unchanged from scenes depicted in photographs taken by Earl Walter and the movie made by Alex Cann. Families still live in thatch-roofed huts and grow sweet potatoes and other root crops, and they still count their wealth in pigs.

Logging companies have stripped some nearby mountainsides of trees, but the Ogi ridge where the *Gremlin Special* crashed remains pristine. Large pieces of wreckage can still be found there by anyone willing to make an arduous hike up the mountain, using moss-covered logs as bridges over small ravines, cutting through thick vines, and avoiding missteps that could send them over cliffs. Buttons, belt buckles, and pieces of human bones can be found in the muddy tomb where the wreck sits. Not long ago, a boy digging with friends turned up a silver dog tag. It was stamped with the name, address, and serial number of WAC Sergeant Marion McMonagle, a widow from Philadelphia who had no children and whose parents died before her.

The tale of the plane crash and the sky spirits is still told by those who remember it, though their numbers are dwindling. When the author of this book visited in early 2010, Yunggukwe Wandik, whose pig was killed by falling cargo, refused to talk about the episode for nearly an hour. She only relented when the author offered an apology on behalf of his countrymen. She never asked for money, but after she shared her memories, she accepted a few dollars as long-belated compensation for her first pig.

Throughout the author's visit, natives crowded around to view copies of Earl Walter's photos. When Helenma Wandik saw a photo of Wimayuk Wandik, known to the survivors as Pete, his eyes welled with tears. He held the photo close to his face, then stroked it with his long, bony fingers. "This is my father," he said in Dani, drawing it to his chest. He accepted a copy of the photo and offered a polished stone in exchange.

AFTER THE WAR, the U.S. Army tried to send troops to Shangri-La to recover the crash victims' remains. That plan was scuttled in 1947 when two amphibious planes that were supposed to be used in the mission were destroyed in a typhoon. No one was hurt. In letters to the victims' families, the military declared that "the many extreme hazards involved in this plan posed serious threats to the lives of the members of this proposed expedition." The bodies from the *Gremlin Special* were declared "non-recoverable" and their common gravesite received an official name: "USAF Cemetery, Hidden Valley, No. 1," at longitude 139° 1' east, and latitude 3° 51' south.

However, a decade later, a Dutch team searching the jungle for the wreck of a missionary plane stumbled upon the *Gremlin Special*. The finding was reported by The Associated Press, prompting a search and recovery mission by the U.S. Army. Using detailed directions from John McCollom and Earl Walter, the team located the crash site in December 1958. The bodies of Sergeant Laura Besley, Captain Herbert Good, and Private Eleanor Hanna were identified and recovered. As for the eighteen others, in the words of an officer who notified the next of kin, "segregation was not possible." The team collected as many bones and personal effects as possible and hiked out.

Herbert Good was buried at Arlington National Cemetery. Eleanor Hanna was buried in a private cemetery in Pennsylvania. Her Chinese coin bracelet, and the two others she'd left behind in her tent, were returned to her family.

Laura Besley was buried at the National Memorial Cemetery of the Pacific, in Hawaii. Her second funeral was May 13, 1959, the fourteenth anniversary of the crash. Every WAC then stationed in Hawaii served as an honorary pallbearer. A few weeks later, one WAC who attended the funeral returned to be sure a proper grave marker had been installed. To her surprise, a lei of vanda orchids rested on Laura Besley's grave. She never learned who left them.

The eighteen others were buried together on June 29, 1959, at the Jefferson Barracks National Cemetery in St. Louis. Their remains rest under a large granite headstone inscribed with their names, ranks, birth dates, and home states. Among the mourners were Colonel Peter Prossen's two sons, Peter Jr. and David. John McCollom attended the ceremony with his brother's widow, Adele, and her fourteen-year-old daughter, Dennie.

Robert McCollom's wedding ring, found among the remains,

was returned to his widow. She never remarried. After her death the ring passed to their daughter, who wore it to feel connected to her parents. It was stolen from her home in 1991, but she still hopes it will turn up.

JAMES LUTGRING, WHOSE place on the *Gremlin Special* crew was taken by Melvin "Molly" Mollberg, never forgot his best friend. Lutgring knew that, months before his death, Mollberg had tried unsuccessfully to join a unit that flew P-47 Thunderbolts. As a tribute, Lutgring and some friends arranged to nickname a P-47 "Molly." They took pictures of themselves gathered around the fighter's nose, its name painted in flowing script. Lutgring also named his son after his lost pal, though Melvyn Lutgring never learned why his parents substituted a "y" for the "i." Melvyn Lutgring served in Vietnam as a U.S. Army helicopter mechanic.

LIEUTENANT HENRY E. PALMER received an Air Medal for Meritorious Achievement for piloting the *Fanless Faggot*. He returned to Louisiana after the war, married, had four daughters, and became registrar of voters in East Feliciana, Louisiana. In that role, he played a small part in a much larger historical event: the investigation into the assassination of President John F. Kennedy. In 1967 New Orleans district attorney Jim Garrison charged a businessman named Clay Shaw with conspiring with Lee Harvey Oswald to kill the president. Henry Palmer was called to testify during Shaw's trial, as part of the prosecution's effort to establish a connection between Shaw and Oswald. Witnesses said Oswald tried to register to vote in Palmer's office on a day when Shaw was nearby. Shaw was found innocent, but Henry Palmer continued to field questions about the case from conspiracy theorists until he died in 1991 at seventy-seven.

For piloting the *Leaking Louise*, Major William J. Samuels

received a Distinguished Flying Cross, given for "heroism or extraordinary achievement while participating in aerial flight."
Shortly afterward, he was offered a choice: go to Okinawa and be
promoted to lieutenant colonel or go home. He chose the latter and
spent the next thirty-three years as a pilot for United Airlines. He
died in 2006 at ninety-one.

AFTER THE WAR, Colonel Ray T. Elsmore cofounded Transocean
Air Lines, an upstart company created by aviation mavericks to
fly unscheduled routes that other carriers couldn't or wouldn't.
He served as a Transocean director and executive vice president
from 1946 to 1952. Elsmore later became president of Western
Sky Industries in Hayward, California. His military honors included the Legion of Merit, the Distinguished Service Medal,
the Commendation Award, and six Presidential Unit Citations.

An obituary published in *The New York Times* recalled how
Elsmore arranged General MacArthur's flight from the Philippines and "directed the dramatic rescue of a Women's Army
Corps member and two service men from the wilds of the 'Valley
of Shangri-La' in Netherlands New Guinea." He died in 1957 at
sixty-six. There's no evidence he ever set foot in the valley.

A year later, the *Times* published the obituary of George Lait,
one of the reporters who flew with Elsmore in 1944 and named
the valley Shangri-La. Fittingly, Lait went to Hollywood after the
war and became a top publicist in the movie business. He died at
fifty-one.

Ralph Morton remained Australia bureau chief for The Associated Press until 1948, after which he worked on the AP's foreign
desk in New York and taught at the Columbia University School
of Journalism. In 1954, he and his wife founded the weekly *Dartmouth Free Press* in Nova Scotia. He died in 1988 at eighty.

Walter Simmons of the *Chicago Tribune* stayed in the Far East
for a decade after the rescue. He wrote one of the first accounts of

North Korean soldiers crossing the thirty-eighth parallel at the start of the Korean War. He returned to Chicago in 1955 and became the newspaper's features editor, Sunday editor, and Sunday magazine editor before his retirement in 1973. He died in 2006 at ninety-eight.

Alexander Cann edited his film into an eleven-minute quasi-documentary called *Rescue from Shangri-La*. It opens with images of forbidding mountains shrouded by clouds, then Cann begins the narration: "High in the mountains of Dutch New Guinea, beneath these clouds, an American Army plane crashed some time ago." The film climaxes with the glider snatch.

After the war, Cann married for a fourth and final time, had two sons and a daughter, and continued making documentaries in Australia. His wife, theatrical agent June (Dunlop) Cann, told a reporter that he "stopped off to be an alcoholic for twelve years," so she left the film industry to raise their children. Late in life, he sobered up and returned to acting, winning roles on the television series *Skippy*, about a heroic kangaroo, and in the 1970 movie *Ned Kelly*, starring Mick Jagger. Cann died in 1977 at seventy-four.

AT THE URGING of Earl Walter, medals were awarded to all ten enlisted paratroopers from the 1st Recon—Santiago Abrenica, Custodio Alerta, Alfred Baylon, Ben "Doc" Bulatao, Hermenegildo "Superman" Caoili, Fernando Dongallo, Juan "Johnny" Javonillo, Camilo "Rammy" Ramirez, Don Ruiz, and Roque Velasco. All but Bulatao and Ramirez received the Bronze Star. The two medics received the Soldier's Medal, the U.S. Army's highest noncombat award, for risking their lives to save the three survivors. Bulatao and Ramirez left few public traces after the war. In September 1945 Ramirez traveled to Kelso, Washington, to see Ken Decker. During the visit, Decker's parents hosted a wedding reception for Ramirez and a Texas woman named Lucille Moseley with whom he'd been exchanging letters for several years. A brief news story about the wedding described her as "a twenty-eight-year-old night club entertainer." The marriage didn't last. Ramirez died in 2005 at eighty-seven. Ben Bulatao got married in Reno, Nevada, in 1968, and divorced in California in 1984. He died in 1985 at seventy-one.

AFTER THE RESCUE, Earl Walter and the men of the 1st Recon finally shipped out to the Philippines. By then the islands were secure. On August 15, 1945, six days after an atomic bomb was dropped on Nagasaki, the Japanese announced their surrender. The same day, General MacArthur dissolved the 1st Recon in a letter expressing gratitude for battalion members' service.

Walter completed his bachelor's degree at the University of Oregon. He rose through the sales department at the Mail-Well Envelope Company, where he worked for thirty-seven years. He became a major in the U.S. Army Reserves and raised three daughters and two sons with his wife Sally, whom he lost to a heart attack in

FROM LEFT, JOHN MCCOLLOM, KEN DECKER, AND EARL WALTER IN 1995. (PHOTOGRAPH COURTESY OF C. EARL WALTER JR.)

1989. Walter regained his passion for swimming and became a U.S. Masters champion, winning medals into his eighties.

Like the two medics, Walter received a Soldier's Medal. In 2009, a few weeks after his eighty-eighth birthday, Walter showed it to a visitor in his apartment in an assisted-living complex near the Oregon coast. The octagonal medal, about the size of a Kennedy half-dollar, hung beneath a faded red, white, and blue ribbon. A framed citation that hung on the wall credited Walter with "exceptional courage and leadership." It described the mission, then concluded: "Captain Walter's heroism in personally leading the rescue party was directly responsible for the safe return of these survivors."

After the war, he showed the medal to his father. "He asked, 'Did you earn that?' " Without hesitating, C. Earl Walter Jr. told C. Earl Walter Sr., "Yes, Dad, I did."

In the last entry in his journal, dated July 3, 1945, Walter wrote: "And so temporarily we close the tale of The United States Army Outpost at Shangri-La, Dutch New Guinea, and hope that in the years to come we can still look back and say it was a job well done and let it go at that."

In early 2010, Walter learned from this book's author that some older natives in New Guinea still remembered him and his men. He choked up at the rush of memories. After a long pause, he cleared his throat and said: "It was the highlight of my life."

IN THE SPRING of 1995, Walter met John McCollom and Ken Decker in a Seattle restaurant to mark the fiftieth anniversary of the crash. They posed with photos taken of their younger selves in Shangri-La. They laughed and reminisced, filling gaps in each other's stories. Decker, at eighty-four, flirted with a waitress. They raised a glass to each other, to the paratroopers of the 1st Recon, and to the "Queen of Shangri-La," who couldn't be with them.

AFTER THE SNATCH, Ken Decker spent several months in the hospital recovering from his injuries. Once healed, he enrolled in the University of Washington, where he received a degree in engineering. He worked for the Army Corps of Engineers, then joined the Boeing Company, where he remained until his retirement in 1974.

Decker married late in life and had no children. He seldom spoke publicly about the crash, in part because he never regained any memory of what happened between the time the *Gremlin Special* took off and when he stumbled out of the wrecked plane.

Before he died in 2000 at age eighty-eight, Decker received a telephone call every year on May 13, his birthday and the anniversary of the crash. On the other end of the line was his old friend John McCollom.

FOR AS LONG as McCollom lived, the memory of Captain Baker wagging the wings of his B-17 brought tears to his eyes.

McCollom left the military in 1946, but was called back to active duty during the Korean War. He spent thirty-eight years as a civilian executive at the Wright-Patterson Air Force Base in Ohio. After retiring, McCollom became an aerospace consultant and vice president of the Piper Aircraft Company.

He married, had a son and a daughter, divorced, then remarried and had four stepchildren. At the wedding of his twin brother's daughter, Dennie, he stood in for Robert and gave her away. He became a surrogate grandfather to her two sons.

McCollom rarely spoke publicly of his twin, lest the enormity of the loss overwhelm him. When he acknowledged feeling survivor's guilt, he spread it among all the people who died aboard the *Gremlin Special*: "Why wasn't I killed instead of them?" he'd say. Most often, when asked about what happened, he'd answer, "I was lucky."

JOHN MCCOLLOM AND HIS NIECE, DEN-
NIE MCCOLLOM SCOTT, IN 1998. (PHOTO
COURTESY OF B. B. MCCOLLOM.)

Yet pain has a way of finding an outlet, and the deepest pain for McCollom was reserved for thoughts about his twin. On rare occasions, he'd admit that a sorrowful thought wormed its way into his mind: "Maybe it should have been me instead of my brother, who was married and had a baby daughter he had never seen."

For a long time after the crash, he regularly dreamed that he, Decker, and Margaret hiked back through the jungle to the wreckage. And there was Robert, alive, waiting for them to return.

Visitors to McCollom's home couldn't miss a wall of photos of John and Robert, young, nearly indistinguishable, and completely inseparable, at least in memory.

In August 2001, near the end of his life, McCollom's legs were too weak to carry him upstairs to an office over his garage. One day, his wife, Betty, came home from the grocery store to an empty house. Worried, she called to him. He replied: "I'm upstairs."

She went to the office and asked: "How'd you get up here?"

"One step at a time, on my back end. I was looking for something," he said.

John McCollom died several days later. He was eighty-two. When Betty McCollom went to the office, she discovered that he'd assembled all his insurance, deeds, titles, and other important documents. Among his papers was the certificate from Colonel Elsmore inducting him into the "Shangri-La Society." McCollom also authored his own obituary, at one point writing simply: "In May of 1945, his airplane crashed in New Guinea. He was rescued in June 1945 but his twin brother was killed in the accident."

After her husband's death, Betty McCollom created a scholarship for aerospace engineering students at the University of Minnesota. She knew he wouldn't have wanted the tribute alone. She called it the John and Robert McCollom Memorial Scholarship.

"Mac was determined," she said. "A number of tough things happened in his life. He just gritted his teeth and took it, and then he'd go forward. He was amazing."

THREE WEEKS AFTER the snatch, Margaret returned to the United States a star. Describing her reception, a *Los Angeles Times* correspondent pronounced her "the most celebrated young woman of the war." Not to be outdone, the *Boston Sunday Advertiser* declared: "She's blonde. She's cute. She's the No. 1 adventure girl in World War II."

Photographers tracked her stops from Hollandia to Manila to California to New York City; radio shows jockeyed to interview her; a newspaper syndicate purchased her diary; her hometown paper announced that she was fielding offers from "promoters, exhibitionists, theatrical agents, circus booking agents, publicity experts, columnists, commentators and just plain reporters." A national magazine, *Calling All Girls*, won the U.S. Army's permission to publish a "true comic" about her experiences in Shangri-La. As a publicity stunt, a newspaper arranged for Margaret to make her long-overdue date with Sergeant Walter "Wally" Fleming. Instead of swimming in the surf off Hollandia, they dined at Toots Shor's, the landmark New York restaurant. They saw each other once or twice afterward, then called it quits.

A crowd estimated at three thousand people—the entire village, really—stood in sweltering heat to greet Margaret's train when it pulled into the Owego station. The Owego Free Academy

MARGARET HASTINGS FLANKED BY HER SISTERS, CATHERINE AND RITA, DURING
THE PARADE UPON HER ARRIVAL HOME IN OWEGO, NEW YORK. (PHOTO COURTESY
OF B. B. MCCOLLOM.)

band struck up a rousing march as she stepped from the train into
her father's arms. The president of the Chamber of Commerce proclaimed her "Owego's Number One Citizen." No detail was too
small for reporters to capture: "Tanned and with a fresh wave in
her feather-cut bob, Margaret wore a smart WAC summer silk
uniform and alligator pumps." A representative from a New York
talent agency let slip that Margaret was choosing among several
movie offers. A gossip columnist wrote that Hollywood beauty
Loretta Young wanted the role, but others expected Margaret to
star as herself. Neighbors pushed through a police line seeking au-
tographs and cheered as she rode to her home on McMaster Street
with her father and sisters in a convertible. Margaret's most lasting
memory of her parade was two old women sitting on a porch, waving their handkerchiefs and crying.

At the end of a thirty-day furlough, the military decided not
to ship Margaret back to New Guinea. Instead, the brass sent her
on a nationwide tour hawking Victory Bonds. During one six-

week stretch, she spoke in fourteen different states. Over time, she gave more than two hundred speeches. At each stop, she repeated a brief version of her ordeal and posed with celebrities and generals, including Dwight Eisenhower. Her mailbox swelled with thousands of fan letters, poems, autograph requests, and proposals from unknown suitors, including a young man who boasted that he was his town's champion spitter. One letter came from Sergeant Don Ruiz, the paratrooper whom Walter believed Margaret tried to seduce. The letter is chaste, catching her up on news of the paratroopers and describing the photos Walter took in the valley. "You look swell standing by your golden grass mattress bed and also in the little pup tent back in the potato field," he wrote. The closest Ruiz came to flirting was to write about the beautiful women he danced with at a party. He signed off: "Long live the Queen of Shangri-La."

Not everyone appreciated the attention lavished on Margaret. The mother of the *Gremlin Special* copilot, Major George Nicholson, lodged a complaint with the U.S. Army. "She developed a lot of resentment toward Margaret Hastings," said John McCarthy, George Nicholson's first cousin, once removed. Margaret Nicholson apparently feared that her son would be blamed for the crash. In response to one of her letters, a colonel in the War Department's Public Relations office wrote: "I have the deepest sympathy for your bereavement, and I can well understand your concern that nothing be published that would tend to minimize the sacrifice made by your gallant son. You can be sure that anything which would be of this nature would be disapproved for publication." Nicholson's wife, Alice Nicholson, asked to speak directly with Margaret, but Margaret declined. John McCarthy explained: "My great aunt Alice said, 'Do you refuse to see your commander's wife?' Margaret Hastings replied, 'I refuse to see my commander's widow.' "

The criticism added to Margaret's growing disenchantment

with fame. She didn't consider herself a hero, just a fortunate survivor, and she longed for her old routines. Her wish came true when movie plans fizzled. "The war ended and they were overwhelmed with war stories," said Margaret's sister, Rita Callahan. "Once they wanted to make a B movie and she wouldn't sign up for it."

A year after the snatch, a reporter for the *Los Angeles Times* found Margaret living contentedly on McMaster Street. "Almost any morning, she can be seen in faded GI pants and shirt, sweeping and dusting inside the green frame house that she shares with her father," he wrote. "Margaret is not writing a book about her experiences. She has no movie ambitions. She signs no testimonials for canned goods, cigarettes or camping equipment. The biggest thing in her life right now is a plan—to go to Syracuse University for a degree."

Margaret spent more than two years at Syracuse, but left without graduating. She married Robert Atkinson, whom her sister

THE SURVIVORS, PILOTS, PARATROOPERS, AND, IN MARGARET'S LAP, PEGGY THE PIG, AFTER THE RESCUE FROM SHANGRI-LA. (MISSING: KEN DECKER, WHO WAS BEING TREATED FOR HIS INJURIES WHEN THE PHOTO WAS TAKEN.) (PHOTO COURTESY OF C. EARL WALTER JR.)

Rita described as a former Olympic bobsledder turned insurance salesman. They had a son, but separated when Margaret was pregnant a second time, with a daughter. They divorced and Margaret raised her children on her own, in Rome, New York, where she worked an administrative job on the Griffiss Air Force Base. Now and then, reporters sought her out, most often on anniversaries of the crash. They also called when Michael Rockefeller, the son of New York's governor and scion of the storied family, disappeared in New Guinea. "He'd have an excellent chance of surviving, if he didn't drown," she told them.

Margaret's last public appearance as the "Queen of Shangri-La" came in 1974, when she, McCollom, and Decker became honorary members of the National World War II Glider Pilots Association. Three decades after their ordeal, the three survivors embraced, laughed, and reminisced during a reunion at the glider pilots' convention that year. During brief remarks, Margaret described a lesson she carried with her from the valley. "Fear is something I don't think you experience unless you have a choice. If you have a choice, then you're liable to be afraid. But without a choice, what is there to be afraid of? You just go along doing what has to be done."

Someone asked Margaret if she'd like to return to New Guinea. Without hesitating, she answered, "You bet!"

She never made it. Four years later, Margaret was diagnosed with uterine cancer. "She put up a good fight," her sister said. "She never felt sorry for herself. When she knew she was going to lose, she took herself off treatments and came home."

Margaret Hastings died in November 1978 at sixty-four. She is buried next to her parents, in a pretty little cemetery dotted with American flags, a short walk from McMaster Street.

CAST OF CHARACTERS

(In Alphabetical Order)

SANTIAGO "SANDY" ABRENICA—Master sergeant in U.S. Army 1st Reconnaissance Battalion (Special). Right-hand man to Captain C. Earl Walter Jr.

CUSTODIO ALERTA—Corporal in the 1st Reconnaissance Battalion (Special). Volunteered for rescue mission following *Gremlin Special* crash.

G. REYNOLDS ALLEN—Captain in the U.S. Army Air Forces and a pilot of the Waco glider dubbed the *Fanless Faggot*.

RICHARD ARCHBOLD—Biological researcher and sponsor/organizer of the 1938 expedition that "discovered" the New Guinea valley later nicknamed "Shangri-La."

WILLIAM D. BAKER—Captain in Army Air Forces and pilot of B-17 search plane that spotted the survivors in the jungle clearing.

ALFRED BAYLON—Sergeant in the 1st Reconnaissance Battalion (Special). Volunteered for rescue mission following *Gremlin Special* crash.

LAURA BESLEY—Sergeant in the Women's Army Corps from Shippenville, Pennsylvania. Passenger aboard the *Gremlin Special*. Close friend of Margaret Hastings.

BENJAMIN "DOC" BULATAO—Sergeant in 1st Reconnaissance Battalion (Special). Lead medic in volunteer rescue mission following *Gremlin Special* crash.

ALEXANDER CANN—Canadian-born filmmaker for the Netherlands Indies Government Information Service. Former Hollywood actor and failed jewel thief.

HERMENEGILDO CAOILI—Sergeant in the 1st Reconnaissance Battalion (Special). Volunteered for rescue mission following *Gremlin Special* crash.

KENNETH DECKER—Tech sergeant from Kelso, Washington, who worked as a draftsman in the engineering department of the Far East Air Service Command. Passenger aboard the *Gremlin Special.*

FERNANDO DONGALLO—Sergeant in the 1st Reconnaissance Battalion (Special). Volunteered for rescue mission following *Gremlin Special* crash.

RAY T. ELSMORE—Colonel and commander of the 322nd Troop Carrier Wing of the U.S. Army Air Forces. Confirmed Major Myron Grimes's report of a large valley in central New Guinea and subsequently became the U.S. military's leading authority on the region. Directed rescue operations following *Gremlin Special* crash.

WALTER "WALLY" FLEMING—Army sergeant based in Hollandia, New Guinea, and sometime boyfriend of Margaret Hastings.

GEORGE GARDNER—Major in the U.S. Army Air Forces who supervised supply runs to the *Gremlin Special* survivors.

HERBERT F. GOOD—Army captain from Dayton, Ohio. Passenger aboard the *Gremlin Special.*

MYRON GRIMES—Major in the Army Air Forces who was the first U.S. military pilot to "discover" the New Guinea valley later nicknamed "Shangri-La."

JACK GUTZEIT—Sergeant and radioman on C-47 search and supply plane known as the 311, following the *Gremlin Special* crash.

ELEANOR HANNA—Private from Montoursville, Pennsylvania, in the Women's Army Corps. Passenger aboard the *Gremlin Special.*

MARGARET HASTINGS—Corporal from Owego, New York, in the Women's Army Corps. Secretary to Colonel Peter Prossen, close friend of Laura Besley. Passenger aboard the *Gremlin Special.*

PATRICK HASTINGS—Widowed father of Margaret Hastings. Foreman in shoe factory in Owego, New York.

EDWARD T. IMPARATO—Colonel in the U.S. Army Air Forces and pilot of plane that dropped C. Earl Walter Jr.'s paratrooper team into Shangri-La.

JUAN "JOHNNY" JAVONILLO—Sergeant in the 1st Reconnaissance Battalion (Special). Volunteered for rescue mission following *Gremlin Special* crash.

HELEN KENT—Sergeant from Taft, California, in Women's Army Corps. Passenger aboard the *Gremlin Special.*

GEORGE LAIT AND HARRY E. PATTERSON—War correspondents who flew over the New Guinea valley with Colonel Ray T. Elsmore and coined the nickname "Shangri-La."

YALI LOGO—Leader of the Logo-Mabel clan who plotted to murder the *Gremlin Special* survivors.

JOHN AND ROBERT MCCOLLOM—Twin brothers from Trenton, Missouri, both lieutenants in the maintenance section of the Far East Air Service Command. Passengers aboard the *Gremlin Special.*

WILLIAM G. MCKENZIE—Captain in the U.S. Army Air Forces, from La Crosse, Wisconsin. Copilot to Major William J. Samuels in glider snatch plane.

HERBERT O. MENGEL—Captain in the U.S. Army Air Forces, from St. Petersburg, Florida, and pilot of the 311 supply plane.

MELVIN MOLLBERG—Private in the Army Air Forces, from Baudette, Minnesota. Assistant engineer on the *Gremlin Special.* Joined the crew as a favor to his best friend, Corporal James "Jimmy" Lutgring, who didn't want to fly with Colonel Peter Prossen.

RALPH MORTON—War correspondent for The Associated Press who led coverage of the *Gremlin Special* crash, along with Walter Simmons of the *Chicago Tribune*.

GEORGE H. NICHOLSON JR.—Major in the Army Air Forces, from Medford, Massachusetts. Copilot on the *Gremlin Special*.

HENRY E. PALMER—Lieutenant in the U.S. Army Air Forces, from Baton Rouge, Louisiana. A glider pilot aboard the *Fanless Faggot*.

PETER J. PROSSEN—Colonel in the Army Air Forces, from San Antonio, Texas. Chief of the maintenance section of the Far East Air Service Command in Hollandia, Dutch New Guinea. Pilot of the *Gremlin Special*.

CAMILO "RAMMY" RAMIREZ—Corporal in the U.S. Army's 1st Reconnaissance Battalion (Special). Volunteer medic in rescue mission following *Gremlin Special* crash.

DON RUIZ—Sergeant in the 1st Reconnaissance Battalion (Special). Volunteered for rescue mission following *Gremlin Special* crash.

WILLIAM J. SAMUELS—Major in the U.S. Army Air Forces and commander of the 33rd Troop Carrier Squadron, from Decatur, Illinois. The most experienced U.S. pilot in the Southwest Pacific in "snatching" gliders from the ground into the air.

WALTER SIMMONS—War correspondent for the *Chicago Tribune* who led coverage of the *Gremlin Special* crash, along with Associated Press reporter Ralph Morton.

ROQUE VELASCO—Sergeant in the 1st Reconnaissance Battalion (Special). Volunteered for rescue mission following *Gremlin Special* crash.

C. EARL WALTER JR.—Captain in the U.S. Army's 1st Reconnaissance Battalion (Special), from Portland, Oregon. Was awaiting a combat posting with his Filipino-American paratroopers when he volunteered to lead the rescue mission into Shangri-La.

WIMAYUK WANDIK—Known to the *Gremlin Special* survivors as "Pete," a leader of the native village of Uwambo.

Additional Passengers and Crew Killed in the May 13, 1945,
Crash of the Gremlin Special:

Major Herman F. Antonini of Danville, Illinois; Major Phillip J. Dattilo of Louisville, Kentucky; Private Alethia M. Fair of Hollywood, California; Captain Louis E. Freyman of Hammond, Indiana; Private Marian Gillis of Los Angeles; First Lieutenant Lawrence F. Holding of Raleigh, North Carolina; Private Mary M. Landau of Brooklyn, New York; Sergeant Marion W. McMonagle of Philadelphia; Corporal Charles R. Miller of Saint Joseph, Michigan; Sergeant Belle Naimer of the Bronx, New York; Private George R. Newcomer of Middletown, New York; Sergeant Hilliard Norris of Waynesville, North Carolina; and Corporal Melvyn Weber of Compton, California.

ACKNOWLEDGMENTS

THIS STORY WAITED a long time to be told, but it didn't wait untended. A remarkable collection of people lovingly preserved documents, letters, scrapbooks, maps, photographs, movies, and, most of all, memories.

I am indebted above all to C. Earl Walter Jr., without whom I would never have attempted to write this book. Earl welcomed me into his home; shared his scrapbooks, photos, and journals; and poured out stories of Shangri-La. Thanks also to his daughter Lisa Walter-Sedlacek.

Buzz Maxey provided indispensable help during my trip to the Baliem Valley, aka Shangri-La. He guided me to the surviving witnesses, translated their accounts, and interpreted the cultural meaning of their responses. I admire his dedication to the welfare of the people of Papua, and I encourage others to follow his path. Thanks also to Myrna, Ben, and Dani Maxey. Tomas Wandik skillfully guided me up the mountain and through the jungle to the crash site. His daughter Nande Mina Wandik made an ideal hiking companion. I'm deeply grateful to Helenma Wandik, Yunggukwe Wandik, Ai Baga, Lisaniak Mabel, Hugiampot, Narekesok Logo, and Dagadigik Walela for their eyewitness accounts.

Emma Sedore, historian of Tioga County, New York, provided priceless assistance and suggestions. Without her, much of Margaret Hastings's story might have been lost. Thanks also to Roger Sharpe and Kevin Sives at the Tioga County Historical Society.

The lovely Betty "B.B." McCollom gave me rich insight into her late husband, John, and graciously shared his scrapbooks and photographs. Dennie McCollom Scott provided invaluable information and suggestions. Rita Callahan told me stories about her sister Margaret Hastings and their father, Patrick Hastings. She directed me to Margaret's childhood friend Mary Scanlon, whose memories enriched me and this book.

Peter J. Prossen Jr. helped me to understand his father, and I admire his candor. Maryrose Condon, John McCarthy, and Michael McCarthy helped me to know their cousin, Major George H. Nicholson Jr. Roberta Koons kindly shared memories of her sister, Eleanor Hanna. Gerta Anderson helped me to know Laura Besley. My new friend Melvyn Lutgring generously told the story of his father's guilt over giving his job on the flight crew to his best friend, Melvin "Molly" Mollberg. Alexandra Cann delighted me with yarns about her larger-than-life father, for whom she was named.

Documentary filmmaker Robert Gardner spent time in the 1990s researching this story as a possible follow-up to *Dead Birds*, his brilliant film about the Dani people. He gave me rare files that would have been impossible to replicate. His unaired interviews with John McCollom enabled me to see and hear Mac from beyond the grave. Thanks also to Michael Hutcherson for reproducing the interview tapes.

My understanding of the Dani was greatly enriched by Dr. Myron Bromley, whose close reading of this manuscript and thought-provoking suggestions are sincerely appreciated. I also thank James Sunda, who along with Myron was among the first missionaries to enter the valley. Professor Karl Heider's impressive research on the Dani, amplified by his e-mail correspondence, was enlightening.

Dona Cruse learned of the crash through her mother, Ruth Coster, who was supposed to be aboard the flight. Dona shared her voluminous knowledge and research of these events. Colonel Pat Jernigan (retired) was a remarkable, indefatigable resource who answered my questions and provided valuable insight.

Major Myron Grimes (retired) never got much credit for being the first U.S. Army Air Forces pilot to spot the valley from the air. He made me feel as though I was in the cockpit with him, and I'm thankful for the ride. George Theis of the National Association of World War II Glider Pilots saved me from gliding into a fusillade of errors.

At the end of World War II, Gene Hoops was an army corporal sent to the base in Hollandia as part of a cleanup patrol. His job was to destroy all military files, but when he opened a metal drawer and found photos from the crash site, he knew they were worth saving. For the next six decades he did just that, and I'm thankful that he did.

In his excellent film, *An Untold Triumph*, documentary filmmaker Noel "Sonny" Izon brought to light the contributions of Filipino-American soldiers during World War II. He generously shared information about the Filipino paratroopers who bravely jumped into the valley.

The late Colonel Edward T. Imparato, who played an important role in the supply and rescue effort, published verbatim documents, transcripts, Walter's journal, news stories, and his own reflections in his book, *Rescue From Shangri-La* (Paducah, Kentucky: Turner Publishing, 1997). Colonel Imparato died before I had a chance to meet him, but I salute him for his work in the valley and on his book.

Justin Taylan, director of PacificWrecks.org, was an enormous help throughout. Thanks to professors Alex Fabros and Dan Gonzales for teaching me about Filipino-American soldiers;

Jette Flipse for her helpful suggestions; Robert Knox for sharing his great-uncle's stirring account of a C-47 crash; James W. Zobel at the MacArthur Memorial Archives; Ed Christine and Tom Wilbur at the *Binghamton Press & Sun*; Norm Landis at the *Rome Daily Sentinel*; Sissy Burge at *The Watchman* of Clinton, Louisiana; Lynn Gamma at the Air Force Historical Research Agency; David Freece at the Cowlitz County Historical Museum; Heidi Reutter of the University of Central Arkansas; Mary Jane Vinella of the Bellevue, Washington, Regional Library; Lisa Rickey of the Dayton, Ohio, Metro Library; telegraphy historian Thomas C. Jepsen; transcriptionist Steve Wylie; intrepid traveler Jan Versluis; and my graduate assistant, Roxanne Palmer.

My colleagues and students at Boston University indulged and encouraged me throughout this project. Special thanks to Dean Tom Fiedler and Professor Lou Ureneck for their support and for the sabbatical that enabled me to complete this book, and to Bob Zelnick and Isabel Wilkerson for setting such inspiring examples.

At a crucial moment, Helene Atwan of Beacon Press convinced me to trust my instincts. She made me an author a decade ago, and I'm forever grateful. Richard Abate is the best friend and agent any author could ask for. He stuck with me as I searched for the right idea, and then he found the ideal home for this book.

My editor Claire Wachtel embraced me and this story from start to finish. She improved this book with her ideas, her insights, and her confidence. Thanks also to Jonathan Burnham, for everything. I'm grateful to Melissa Kahn of 3Arts, who believed, and to the entire team at HarperCollins, including Elizabeth Perrella, Diane Aronson, and Miranda Ottewell.

Deep thanks to my own tribe: Brian McGrory; Ruth, Emily, and Bill (Air William) Weinstein, whose generosity sent me to New Guinea in comfort; Colleen Granahan, Dan Field, and Isabelle and Eliza Granahan-Field; Jeff Feigelson, who should have been an editor; Kathryn Altman; Dick Lehr; Chris Callahan; Nancy and Jim Bildner; Naftali Bendavid; the late Wilbur Doctor; Allan Zuckoff; and the extended Kreiter and Zuckoff clans.

Special thanks to my parents, first teachers, and first readers: Sid and Gerry Zuckoff.

I was struggling with a much different writing project when my beloved daughters informed me that I was lost in the wrong jungle. "That's not the kind of story you like," Isabel said. Eve agreed. "Write about Margaret and Shangri-La," she said. Smart girls.

My wife, Suzanne (aka Rose, aka Trixie) Kreiter, makes life the closest thing I'll find to Shangri-La.

NOTES ON SOURCES AND METHODS

This is a work of nonfiction. No liberties have been taken with facts, dialogue, characters, or chronology. All quoted material comes from interviews, reports, diaries, letters, flight logs, declassified military documents, news stories, books, or some other source cited in the notes below. Descriptions of people and places are based on site visits, interviews, written materials, photographs, and newsreel images. Unless noted, the author conducted all interviews, either in person or by phone. Interviews with natives of the Baliem Valley, or Shangri-La, were translated by Buzz Maxey, an American missionary relief and development manager who has lived there most of his life.

Abbreviations of key source materials:

IDPF—Individual Deceased Personnel File, an official U.S. Army document generally running more than one hundred pages, detailing the circumstances of death, recovery and identification of remains, dispersal of belongings, and burial. IDPFs for nineteen of the *Gremlin Special* victims were obtained using the Freedom of Information Act. Army officials said they could not locate files for Laura Besley and Louis Freyman.

CEW—C. Earl Walter Jr.'s daily journal, which he wrote during his weeks in Shangri-La. Walter granted permission for its use here. Much of the journal was reproduced by Colonel Edward T. Imparato in *Rescue from Shangri-La* (Paducah, Ky.: Turner Publishing, 1997).

MACR—Missing Air Crash Report No. 14697, the declassified U.S. Army Air Forces account of the incident, including survivors' sworn statements taken upon their return to Hollandia; the names, ranks, and home addresses of the victims; a map showing the crash location; and an official account of the flight, the crash, and the search and rescue.

SLD—"Shangri-La Diary" is an account of the crash and rescue written by Margaret Hastings in secretarial shorthand while in the valley. Inez Robb of the International News Service helped to expand it into a serial distributed to newspapers in the summer of 1945. *Reader's Digest* published a condensed version in December 1945. Tioga County historian Emma Sedore transcribed the version of the diary used here. In an unaired interview with documentary filmmaker Robert Gardner, John McCollom vouched for its accuracy. C. Earl Walter Jr. agreed, with one exception: he denied singing "Shoo, Shoo Baby" as he entered the survivors' camp. However, in a joint interview in 1998, McCollom insisted that it was true, and Walter relented. Walter acknowledged as much to the author. Walter's initial denial might be traced to the ribbing he took from friends and family about singing in the jungle.

TCHS—Tioga County Historical Society, in Owego, N.Y., which preserved Margaret Hastings's personal scrapbook, letters, telegrams, photographs, and other materials.

NOTES

1. MISSING

1   On a rainy day: National Severe Storms Laboratory Historical Weather Data
Archives, Norman, Oklahoma, http://data.nssl.noaa.gov (retrieved October
17, 2009).

1   a green, farm-style house: Description comes from author's interviews with
Margaret Hastings's sister Rita Hastings Callahan, August 1, 2009, and
childhood friend Mary Scanlon, August 2, 2009, and also from the author's
visits to Owego, N.Y.

1   in a front window: Callahan, interview.

1   grew up a farm boy: Ibid.

2   visible signs of her absence: Ibid.

2   walked into a recruiting station: Margaret Hastings's enlistment records at
NARA.

3   the combat death toll: U.S. Department of Veteran Affairs Fact Sheet, dated
November 2008, www1.va.gov/opa/fact/amwars.asp (retrieved January 27,
2010).

3   messengers fanned out across the country: Hometowns of crash victims'
families were contained in the declassified Army Air Force account of the
crash, MACR.

3   THE SECRETARY OF WAR DESIRES: Telegram located in archives at TCHS.
The original had no punctuation, which was added here for readability, and
abbreviated the word *corporal*.

3   most recent letter home: "Owego WAC, Reported Missing, Is Safe," news
clipping in Margaret Hastings's personal scrapbook, TCHS. Story described
Margaret Hastings's most recent letter and her family's hope that she would
be found alive.

4   Margaret is missing: Callahan, interview.

2. HOLLANDIA

5   "fit me like sacks": Margaret Hastings to Verna Smith, published as "Owego
WAC Writes of Her Life in New Guinea," *Owego Gazette*, March 8, 1945.

6   usual 5:30 a.m. reveille: Details of Margaret Hastings's daily routine in
New Guinea are contained in SLD, part 2. See also Hastings, "Owego WAC
Writes."

6   just under five-foot-two: Margaret Hastings, SLD, part 11. Margaret notes
      her height in comparison with the native women, pleasantly surprised that
      they are shorter than her "five-feet, one-and-one-half inches."

6   teenage nickname: *Owego Free Academy Tom-Tom Yearbook*, 1932, p. 18,
      TCHS.

6   hitchhiked when she wanted: Scanlon, interview.

6   "drank liquor," "liked the boys": Margaret Hastings, "A Tribute to Mother,"
      undated college paper in correspondence file, TCHS.

6   average marrying age for women: U.S. Census Bureau, "America's Family
      and Living Arrangements," in *Current Population Survey: Annual Social and
      Economic Supplement*, 2003, table MS-2, "Estimated Median Age at First
      Marriage, by Sex, 1890–Present," Current Population Report ser. P20-553
      (Washington, D.C.: U.S. Bureau of the Census, 2003).

7   "To tell the truth": James R. Miller, "Reconversion of a Heroine," *Los Ange-
      les Times Magazine*, July 7, 1946, p. 5.

7   more exciting than Atlantic City: Hastings, SLD, part 1.

7   "blood, toil, tears and sweat": John Lukacs, *Blood, Toil, Tears and Sweat:
      The Dire Warning; Churchill's First Speech as Prime Minister* (New York: Basic
      Books, 2008), p. 11.

7   "The western world has been freed": Harry S. Truman, transcript of speech
      announcing the surrender of Germany, found at Miller Center of Public Af-
      fairs, University of Virginia, http://millercenter.org/scripps/archive/speeches/
      detail/3340 (retrieved January 3, 2010).

8   House Speaker Sam Rayburn: C. P. Trussell, "Blackout Lifted on Capitol
      Dome," *New York Times*, May 9, 1945.

8   "It will be a busy summer": Hanson W. Baldwin, "A New Phase Now
      Opens in the Pacific War," *New York Times*, May 13, 1945.

8   Between sunrise and sunset: Day-by-day chronology of World War II Pa-
      cific history, compiled by U.S. Air Forces and provided by Justin Taylan
      of PacificWrecks.org, http://www.pacificwrecks.com/60th/1945/5-45.html
      (retrieved October 11, 2009). See also chronology at http://www.onwar.com/
      chrono/index.htm (retrieved October 11, 2009).

10   named it for an African country: Karl Heider, *Grand Valley Dani: Peaceful
      Warriors*, 3d ed. (Belmont, Calif.: Wadsworth Group, 1997), p. 1.

10   Sri Lankan potentates: Tim Flannery, *Throwim Way Leg: Tree-Kangaroos, Pos-
      sums and Penis Gourds* (New York: Grove Press, 1998), 3.

10   Captain Cook visited in 1770: Hobart M. Van Deusen, "The Seventh Arch-
      bold Expedition," *BioScience* 16 (July 1966): 450.

11   a daring strike called "Operation Reckless": Samuel Eliot Morison, *History
      of U.S. Naval Operations in World War II*, vol. 8, *New Guinea and the Mari-
      anas, March 1944-August 1944* (Champaign: University of Illinois Press,
      2002), pp. 68–90. See also Stanley Sandler, *World War II in the Pacific: An
      Encyclopedia* (New York: Garland, 2001), pp. 400–403.

11   "Release a Man for Combat": Ibid., p. 184.

11   "my best soldiers": Sandler, *World War II in the Pacific*, p. 1050.

12   a sidearm to keep under her pillow: Dona Cruse, interview by author, August 11, 2009. Dona is the daughter of WAC Ruth Coster, who passed up a chance to fly over Shangri-La on May 13, 1945. See also Steven Mayer, "Taft Veteran Killed in Crash Only Woman Listed on Wall," *Bakersfield Californian*, Nov. 12, 2007, www.bakersfield.com/102/story/283703.html, included in the Ruth Coster Collection at the University of Central Arkansas.

12   "Hey Joe—hubba, hubba": Colonel Ray T. Elsmore, "New Guinea's Mountain and Swampland Dwellers," *National Geographic Magazine* 88, no. 6 (December 1945): 676.

12   the safety precautions' real aim: Judith A. Bellafaire, *The Women's Army Corps: A Commemoration of World War II Service*, U.S. Army Center of Military History pub. 72-15 (Washington, D.C.: Government Printing Office, 1990). See also p. 422 in the definitive history of the WACs, Mattie E. Treadwell, *The Women's Army Corps* (Washington, D.C.: Government Printing Office, 1954); and Selene H. C. Weise, *The Good Soldier: The Story of a Southwest Pacific Signal Corps WAC* (Shippensburg, Pa.: Burd Street Press, 1999).

12   "blanket parties": Margaret Hastings to Kitty Dugan, February 2, 1945, archives, TCHS.

13   The letter didn't give away: A notation on the envelope indicates that the letter was "censored by Lt. Margaret V. Bogle," the same officer who informed Margaret Hastings about the trip to Shangri-La.

13   enlisting . . . in August 1942: Background information on Laura Besley from U.S. World War II army enlistment records at www.ancestry.com (retrieved September 11, 2009), and *Harrisburg, Pa., City Directory* (Detroit: R. L. Polk, 1936–37), p. 62. See also 1930 U.S. federal census records.

13   a "sassy" young woman: Gerta Anderson, interview by author, April 26, 2010. Laura Besley's mother and Gerta Anderson's maternal grandmother were sisters. Laura was named Earline, after her father, Earl, but took the name Laura from her grandmother.

13   tables made from boxes and burlap: Hastings, "Owego WAC Writes."

14   parachute cloth hung as decoration: Hastings to Dugan, February 2, 1945. Details of WAC tents in Hollandia also from Mary L. Eck, *Saga of a Sad Sack*, self-published pamphlet recounting military life in New Guinea and elsewhere, 1979.

14   double electric socket: Hastings, SLD, part 2.

14   "Get skinny in Guinea": Ibid., p. 16.

15   showered at least twice a day: Hastings, "Owego WAC Writes."

15   "in order to keep respectable": Ibid.

15   "There was 'jungle rot' ": Lieutenant Colonel Anne O'Sullivan (retired), "Recollections of New Guinea," *Women's Army Corps Journal* 5, no. 5 (October–December 1974): 14.

15   almost enough to make her feel cool: Hastings, SLD, part 2.

16   the health of military women: Treadwell, *Women's Army Corps*, p. 446.

16   several hundred WACs: Ibid., p. 427.

16   a letter to his family: All quotes from Colonel Peter J. Prossen come from
      his letters to his wife on May 12 and 13, 1945, copies of which were pro-
      vided by his son, Peter J. Prossen Jr.

16   his elder son . . . knew him: Peter J. Prossen Jr., interview by author, July 28,
      2009.

18   hundred or so men and the twenty-plus WACs: John McCollom, unaired
      interview with filmmaker Robert Gardner, Dayton, Ohio, October 1997.

18   Coca-Cola syrup and fresh fruit: Eck, *Saga of a Sad Sack*, p. 29.

18   sightseeing flights up the coastline: John McCollom, interview, October 1997.

3. SHANGRI-LA

19   a more direct, low-altitude pass: Elsmore, "Mountain and Swampland
      Dwellers," p. 671. See also John McCollom, interview, October 1997.

19   "Colonel, if we slip": Elsmore, "Mountain and Swampland Dwellers," p. 671.

19   late for a hot date in Australia: C. Earl Walter Jr., interview by Patrick
      O'Donnell, 1988, http://www.thedropzone.org/pacific/walters.htm (retrieved
      October 10, 2009).

20   a mostly flat, verdant valley: Major Myron J. Grimes (retired), interview by
      author, August 31, 2009.

20   stamped the area "unknown" or "unexplored": Ozzie St. George, "Rescue
      from Shangri-La," *Yank: The Army Weekly*, August 17, 1945, p. 6. See also
      Gordon L. Rottman, *World War II Pacific Island Guide: A Geo-Military Study*
      (Westport, Conn.: Greenwood Press, 2001), p. 148.

20   "estimated 14,000-foot peak": St. George, "Rescue from Shangri-La," p. 6.

20   a mountain might be hiding inside: Elsmore, "Mountain and Swampland
      Dwellers," p. 671. (At one point Elsmore writes of a cloud bank, "We could
      see the occasional rift, but we knew that peaks lurked in its innocent white
      walls.")

20   a flying instructor during World War I: "Ray Elsmore, 66, Helped
      M'Arthur," *New York Times*, February 19, 1957, p. 31.

20   deputy county prosecutor: William H. Carleton, "History of the Director-
      ate of Air Transport, Allied Air Force South West Pacific Area and the 322
      Troop Carrier Wing," at http://home.st.net.au/~dunn/usaaf/dat.htm (re-
      trieved September 1, 2009).

21   MacArthur's evacuation flight: "Ray Elsmore, 66," p. 31.

21   the Southwest Pacific: Rottman, *Pacific Island Guide*, pp. 146–52.

21   prepared to veer up and away: Grimes, interview.

21   "Push on through": Elsmore, "Mountain and Swampland Dwellers," p. 673.

22   "a riot of dazzling color": Ibid., p. 674.

22 "Crops were in full growth": Elsmore, "Mountain and Swampland Dwellers," p. 674.

22 "diving into the drainage ditches": Ibid.

23 "one of the most impressive sights": Ibid., p. 676.

24 "a pilot unfamiliar with this canyon.": Colonel Ray T. Elsmore to General George C. Kenney, secret letter (since unclassified) titled "Route Survey," May 29, 1944, MacArthur Memorial Archives, Norfolk, Va.

24 "anxious to avoid incidents and bloodshed": Elsmore, "Mountain and Swampland Dwellers," p. 677.

25 "pygmy type": Ibid., p. 689.

25 models of sinewy manhood standing seven feet tall: "The Hidden Valley," *Pulse: A 27 General Hospital Publication*, Vol. 3, No. 46, July 8, 1945, Supplement, p. 1. The publication was a hospital bulletin saved by Capt. Earl Walter. Also, Eck, *Saga of a Sad Sack*.

25 the size of ponies: Lieutenant William Jeff Gatling Jr. to his family, published as "Shangri-La," *Arkansas Gazette*, May 20, 1945, n.p.; in the Ruth Coster Collection at the University of Central Arkansas.

25 "Dorothy Lamours in blackface": Hastings, SLD, part 2.

26 ever set foot in the valley: Elsmore, "Mountain and Swampland Dwellers," p. 677.

26 "I suppose I would have regretted it": Gatling, "Shangri-La."

27 suspending their battle: St. George, "Rescue from Shangri-La," p. 6. Also, Colonel Edward T. Imparato, *Rescue from Shangri-La* (Paducah, Ky.: Turner, 1997), p. 8.

27 His father: "George Lait Weds; War Correspondent Takes Jane Peck Harrington as Bride," *New York Times*, September 8, 1945. See also "Jack Lait, 71, Dies; Editor of Mirror," *New York Times*, April 2, 1954; and "The Press: Blue Bloomers and Burning Bodies," *Time*, July 26, 1948.

27 correspondent for the International News Service: Ibid.

27 knocked out cold: International News Service, "Newsman Kayoed in London Raid," *St. Petersburg Times*, April 20, 1941.

27 blown out of a car seat: Ernie Pyle, "Rambling Reporter," *Pittsburgh Press*, March 27, 1941.

27 "As a war correspondent": Inez Robb, "Robb's Corner," *Reading (Pa.) Eagle*, January 29, 1958. It's fitting that Robb wrote this tribute to George Lait, who helped to name the valley Shangri-La. When Margaret Hastings turned her diary into an eighteen-part newspaper series in 1945, Robb was brought on as a professional writer to help.

28 a dispatch rich in description: Donald Collier, "U.S. Fliers in New Guinea Discover a Shangri-La," *Chicago Natural History Museum Bulletin*, nos. 3–4 (March–April 1945), quoting a story by George Lait "published in a New Guinea news sheet of the Army," www.archive.org/stream/bulletin16chic/ bulletin16chic_djvu.txt (retrieved August 30, 2009).

28   Patterson's story: Harry E. Patterson, "Real Shangri-La in New Guinea,"
      Milwaukee Journal, March 11, 1945.

29   disappointed by the name Hidden Valley: Elsmore, "Mountain and Swamp-
      land Dwellers," p. 680.

29   "matched a whole army": James Hilton, *Lost Horizon* (New York: Pocket
      Books, 1933), p. 157.

29   "He foresaw a time": Hilton, *Lost Horizon*, p. 158.

30   a 1937 speech: President Franklin D. Roosevelt, "Quarantine the Aggressors
      Speech," delivered in Chicago on October 5, 1937. Roosevelt paraphrased
      slightly, changing the tense from "would" to "will." The result was to make
      the prediction even more ominous. Text located at http://fletcher.tufts.edu/
      multi/texts/historical/quarantine.txt (retrieved September 1, 2009).

4. GREMLIN SPECIAL

31   comically ornate certificate: Membership in the "Shangri-La Society" was
      extended to survivors of the May 13, 1945, crash and their rescuers. Mar-
      garet Hastings's certificate can be found at TCHS; those of John McCollom
      and C. Earl Walter, in their personal scrapbooks. Ken Decker's could not be
      located.

31   "leading authority on the valley": Walter Simmons, "Glider Takes Six More
      Out of Shangri-La," *Chicago Tribune*, July 1, 1945.

31   "a case of 'head you lose' ": Ray Zeman, "Pilot Finds Shangri-La," *Los Angeles
      Times*, October 16, 1944.

32   "fully equipped with bargaining trinkets": Harold Streeter, "Pacific Re-
      porter: Shangri-La," *Hartford Courant*, May 13, 1945.

32   "navigational training": MACR, p. 1.

32   Prossen's first trip to Shangri-La: John McCollom, interview, October 1997.

32   a date after work: Hastings, SLD, part 1. In her published diary, Margaret
      says she had been informed of the flight a day earlier by Colonel Prossen,
      but in her sworn statement after the crash, dated June 29, 1945, MACR, she
      said she was invited that morning.

32   desperate to visit Shangri-La: Hastings, SLD, part 2.

32   she leaped at Prossen's offer: Prossen issued the invitation through the chain
      of command, so it was delivered by Lieutenant Margaret V. Bogle, accord-
      ing to Hastings's sworn statement, MACR.

32   prizes at local dog shows: Hastings, SLD, part 2.

33   savoring each cold spoonful: Ibid.

34   leather and hydraulic fluid: Details of the C-47 from www.boeing.com/his-
      tory/mdc/skytrain.htm (retrieved September 5, 2009). See also www.war-
      birdalley.com/c47.htm.

34   at a cost to the military of $269,276: Copy of Aircraft Record Card #41-
      23952, from U.S. Air Force Historical Division, Research Studies Institute,
      Maxwell Air Force Base, Montgomery, Ala.

34   *Gremlin Special*: The MACR lists "Merle" as the nickname, but *"Gremlin Special"* is cited in an account of the crash in Michael John Clarinbould, *The Forgotten Fifth: A Photographic Chronology of the U.S. Fifth Air Force in World War II* (Hyde Park, N.Y.: Balus Design, 2007), pp. 103–4.

34   *The Gremlins*: Roald Dahl, *The Gremlins* (1943; reprint, Milwaukie, Ore.: Dark Horse, 2006).

34   "Let the girls in first": Hastings, SLD, part 2.

35   "showing partiality": Ibid.

35   caught Laura's eye and winked: Hastings, SLD, part 2.

35   spent time in a German prisoner-of-war camp: Background information on Eleanor Hanna from her sister, Roberta (Hanna) Koons, interview by author, September 11, 2009.

35   singing wherever she went: Hastings, SLD, parts 2 and 4.

35   "Isn't this fun!": Ibid., part 2.

36   bracelet made from Chinese coins: Eleanor Hanna's U.S. Army individual deceased personnel file (IDPF) contains a Xerox image of part of the bracelet, which was found in the grave she shared with Laura Besley. At first it wasn't clear to whom it belonged, but a May 14, 1959, letter in the file from her father to the army quartermaster general makes a claim on the bracelet and refers to the two others she owned just like it.

36   daughter of a newspaper publisher: "Pfc. Gillis from East Orange," *New York Times*, June 9, 1945. Although the *Times* said she was from New Jersey, MACR lists her hometown as Los Angeles.

36   fleeing from Spain with her mother: Ibid.

36   grieving the death of her fiancé: Associated Press, "Airfield Is Built to Rescue a Wac and 2 Men in New Guinea," *New York Times*, June 9, 1945.

36   relieve her loneliness: Information about WACs Helen Kent and Ruth Coster from Dona Cruse, interviews by author, August 11, 2009, and September 4, 2009. Dona is the daughter of Ruth, who died in 2005.

36   tell her what it was like: Ibid.

36   Three more WACs: World War II enlistment records, www.ancestry.com (retrieved November 1–3, 2009).

37   trailed by his copilot: Background on George H. Nicholson from MACR. Also, 1920 and 1930 U.S. Federal Census at www.ancestry.com (retrieved September 11, 2009). Also, interviews by author with Maryrose Condon, a first cousin of Major Nicholson, and John and Michael McCarthy, first cousins once removed, on September 13, 2009.

37   graduated from Boston College, then received master's degrees: Interviews with Maryrose Condon and John McCarthy, September 13, 2009. See also "Major Geo H. Nicholson Killed in Plane Crash," *Malden (Mass.) Evening News*, May 31, 1945, p. 1; and "Maj. George H. Nicholson, Killed in Pacific Plane Crash," undated newspaper clipping saved by Nicholson's family.

37 served under Lord Mountbatten: "Major Geo H. Nicholson Killed," *Malden Evening News.*

37 skipped a "Victory in Europe" party: Alice K. Nicholson Cadley to friends and family, "Mother's Day 1995," in which she marked the fiftieth anniversary of the crash by distributing copies of Nicholson's letter.

37 a vivid fifteen-page narrative: George H. Nicholson to his wife, Alice K. Nicholson (later Cadley), May 9, 1945, provided by his cousin Maryrose Condon.

39 three other crew members: Crew list, MACR, p. 3.

39 a month earlier: "Melvin Mollberg Killed In Plane Crash in the Pacific," undated newspaper clipping provided by Melvyn Lutgring.

39 Corporal James "Jimmy" Lutgring: Melvyn Lutgring, interview by author, January 5, 2010. Lutgring was named for Melvin Mollberg, despite the different spelling of their first names.

40 asked her on a date: Hastings, SLD, part 2.

40 an oil salesman and a leader in his Presbyterian church: "Daytonian, Two Valley Men Reported Killed in Action," *Dayton Journal*, May 30, 1945, p. 2. See also *Williams' Dayton (Montgomery County, Ohio) City Directory 1944* (Cincinnati: Williams Directory, 1944), p. 484.

41 "The Inseparables": Betty McCollom, widow of John McCollom, interview by author, August 1, 2009. See also information about John and Robert McCollom from Marjorie Lundberg, "Baby Girl's Father Killed, but Uncle Is Dad's Replica," *St. Paul Dispatch*, June 8, 1945, n.p., from John McCollom's personal scrapbook.

41 Eagle Scouts together: John S. McCollom's obituary, *Dayton Daily News,* August 21, 2001, provided by Betty McCollom.

42 a wedding photo: "Tragic Shangri-La Figures and Kin," *St. Paul Dispatch*, undated story and photographs in McCollom's scrapbook.

43 "Mind if I share this window": Hastings, SLD, part 2. McCollom's location is confirmed in his sworn statement, dated June 29, 1945, MACR.

5. EUREKA!

44 twisted in their seats for a look: Hastings, SLD, part 3.

44 "Oh, what is so rare": Ibid.

44 *The Vision of Sir Launfal*: The famous line from Lowell's 1848 poem is, "And what is so rare as a day in June?"

45 as soft as green feathers: Hastings, SLD, part 3.

45 a heading of 224 degrees: McCollom, sworn statement, MACR, p. 1.

46 standing in the narrow radio compartment: Ibid.

46 alone at the controls: Ibid.

46 an altitude of about one thousand feet: Ibid.

46 four hundred feet: Hastings, SLD, part 3.

46 "Eureka!": Ibid.

47   "I want to come again!": Ibid.

47   "Give her the gun and let's get out of here": Ibid.

47   thought he was joking: Ibid. Margaret wrote, "I thought he was joking. So did everyone else."

47   applying full power to climb: McCollom, sworn statement, MACR, p. 1.

48   learned to fly only three years earlier: "Maj. George H. Nicholson Killed In Pacific Plane Crash," undated newspaper clipping saved by Nicholson's family.

48   Turbulent air was common: MACR does not make an official determination whether the cause of the crash was pilot error, a sudden downdraft, or a combination of factors.

48   especially treacherous: Imparato, *Rescue from Shangri-La*, p. 170. Imparato knew the terrain from flying over it.

49   "a sudden down-draft of air current": *Historical Data Regarding the Loss of a FEASC C-47 and the Rescue of Survivors of the Crash*, declassified document prepared by the U.S. Air Force Historical Division, Research Studies Institute, Maxwell Air Force Base, Montgomery, Ala., November 17, 1952.

49   "flat on the deck": Hastings, SLD, part 3.

49   "This is going to be darn close": McCollom, sworn statement, MACR, p. 1.

50   The cabin crumpled forward: This account of the crash is taken from the sworn MACR statements of John McCollom and Margaret Hastings, as well as photographs of the wreckage provided to the author by Eugene M. Hoops. At the end of World War II, Hoops was part of an American military unit sent from the Philippines to New Guinea to clean up the base at Hollandia and to destroy remaining files. Upon opening a metal file drawer, he discovered a set of photographs from the May 13, 1945, crash and its aftermath. Despite orders to destroy the material, Hoops believed the photos might be significant and decided to preserve them for posterity.

50   turning somersaults as he fell: McCollom, sworn statement, MACR, p. 1.

50   momentarily blacked out: John McCollom, interview, October 1997.

50   flattened down like a stepped-on tin can: Ibid.

51   "all by myself on a Sunday afternoon": Ibid.

51   spoiled by a plane crash: Hastings, SLD, part 3. She writes that she was "indignant because this thing had happened to me!"

51   thick arms around her: Ibid.

52   "My God! Hastings!": Ibid.

52   McCollom doubted it would explode: John McCollom, interview, October 1997.

52   "Give me your hand!": Hastings, SLD, part 3.

52   Her hair still crackled with burning embers: McCollom, sworn statement, MACR, p. 2.

53   a bloody . . . gash on the right side of Decker's forehead: Decker details his injuries in his sworn statement, MACR, p. 2. See also Hastings, SLD, part 4; McCollom, sworn statement, MACR, p. 2.

53   "My God, Decker, where did you come from?": Hastings, SLD, part 4.

53   his deliverance into the jungle: Decker, sworn statement, MACR, p. 1.

53   catapulted through the cockpit and out through the windshield: John McCollom, interview, October 1997.

53   "Helluva way to spend your birthday": Ibid.

53   "Hastings, can't you do something for these girls?": Hastings, SLD, part 4.

54   seared off all her clothes: John McCollom, interview, October 1997.

54   "Let's sing": Hastings, SLD, part 4.

54   only superficial burns: Ibid.

54   McCollom invited him to join in the fun: John McCollom, interview, October 1997.

54   tangled in the roots of a tree: McCollom, sworn statement, MACR, p. 2.

55   They left Good's body where it fell: Photograph of the wreckage, courtesy of Eugene M. Hoops.

56   wedding ring with a white inlay: Lt. Col. Donald Wardle, chief of the Army Disposition Branch, Memorial Division, to Mrs. Cecelia A. McCollom, May 13, 1959. See also letter from Lt. Col. Donald L. Wardle to Louis Landau, father of Private Mary Landau, May 1, 1959, about the recovery of remains and personal items from the crash site. Contained in Mary Landau's IDPF, provided by the U.S. Army under a Freedom of Information Act request.

6: CHARMS

58   "surrounded by fire if we don't": Hastings, SLD, part 4.

58   "You're all right": Ibid.

59   "Everything in the jungle had tentacles": Ibid., part 6.

60   pulled off her khaki shirt: Ibid., part 4.

60   arms draped over his shoulders: John McCollom, interview, October 1997.

60   still dangled from her wrist: Eleanor Hanna's IDPF notes that the bracelet was found in the grave she shared with Laura Besley, which means it remained in her possession after the crash. She had no clothes, and therefore no pockets, so it stands to reason the bracelet remained on her wrist.

60   a broken rib: John McCollom, interview, October 1997.

61   help McCollom with Eleanor Hanna: Ibid.; see also sworn statements in MACR of Decker, p. 1, and McCollom, p. 2.

61   compounding their misery: Hastings, SLD, part 4. She writes: "Now the daily and eternal rain of New Guinea began to fall. Soaked clothing was added to our miseries."

61   .45-caliber pistol: McCollom, sworn statement, MACR, p. 2.

61   Cracker Jack–size boxes of K-rations: Jerold E. Brown, *Historical Dictionary of the U.S. Army* (Westport, Conn.: Greenwood Press, 2001), p. 270.

61   burn until the middle of the next day: McCollom, sworn statement, MACR, p. 3.

62   no one would have survived: John McCollom, interview, October 1997.

62   couldn't find any flares: The survivors gave separate accounts of the contents of the life rafts. Margaret Hastings, in SLD, part 4, said the kit contained flares, but in his sworn statement, MACR, John McCollom states: "I looked all over the life raft equipment, but I never could find any flares." He later writes about trying to use Margaret's mirror to signal planes, adding veracity to his account.

63   "Let's sing": Hastings, SLD, part 4.

63   the plane was still aflame: John McCollom, interview, October 1997.

63   might be lightning: Imparato, *Rescue from Shangri-La*, p. 184.

63   hike all 150-plus miles: Sergeant Ozzie St. George, "Hidden Valley," *Yank: The Army Weekly*, Far East ed., Aug. 10, 1945.

63   yaps and barks of wild dogs: John McCollom, interview, October 1997.

63   "Eleanor's dead": Margaret Hastings describes finding Eleanor Hanna dead in SLD, part 4, while in his sworn statement, MACR, John McCollom says only, "I guess that Private Hanna died about 8 o'clock that night," referring to the previous night.

64   "I can't stop shaking": Hastings, SLD, part 5.

64   seventeen cans of water: Ibid. McCollom's MACR statement mentions the cots, but the more complete inventory is in Margaret's diary.

64   black electrical tape and a pair of pliers: Decker, sworn statement, MACR, p. 1.

64   burned feet covered by cotton bandages: Hastings, SLD, part 5.

65   a five-pointed white star: Photos of the downed C-47, taken shortly after the crash, provided by Dona Cruse.

65   impossible to see except from a short distance: Photograph of the wreckage, courtesy of Eugene M. Hoops.

65   between the plane and ground controllers: MACR, p. 1.

66   worked it furiously to flash snatches of sunlight: McCollom, sworn statement, MACR, p. 3. See also Hastings, SLD, part 5, and John McCollom, interview, October 1997.

66   "Don't worry": John McCollom, unaired interview with Robert Gardner, Seattle, May 13, 1998.

66   at peace with her mother's death: Hastings, SLD, part 5.

66   Margaret's middle name: Callahan, interview.

66   In a school essay: Hastings, "Tribute to Mother," TCHS.

67   hugging tightly to keep from falling off: Hastings, SLD, part 5.

67   "Everyone else is dead and we're very lonely, aren't we?": Ibid.

67   "Laura has died!": Hastings, SLD, part 5.

67   "Don't be a dope, Hastings": Ibid.

68   " 'Now the shoes belong to me' ": Ibid.

69   hated the nickname: Hastings, SLD, part 15.

70   lit a cigarette and handed it to her: Ibid., part 5.

70   "No night will ever again be as long": Ibid.

7: TARZAN

71   McCollom climbed a tree: In his MACR statement, p. 3, McCollom says he
      saw the clearing from the tail of the plane. But in his October 1997 inter-
      view with Robert Gardner, McCollom explained that he had to climb a tree
      to see the clearing.

71   a course they could follow: McCollom, sworn statement, MACR, p. 3. See
      also John McCollom, interview, October 1997.

71   an officer wrote back: Susan Sheehan, *A Missing Plane: The Dramatic Tragedy
      and Triumph of a Lost and Forgotten World War II Bomber* (New York: Berke-
      ley Books, 1986), p. 210.

72   More than six hundred American planes: Justin Taylan, interview by au-
      thor, October 2, 2009. Taylan is an authority on World War II plane crashes
      and director of Pacific Wrecks Web site.

72   more missing airplanes than any country on earth: Sheehan, *Missing Plane*,
      p. 9. Sheehan focused her work on the eastern half of the island, but in the
      estimation of Taylan, this was true for all of New Guinea.

72   *Flying Dutchman*: This account of the November 10, 1942, crash and cargo
      door diary is based on Clarinbould, *Forgotten Fifth*, p. 39. See also "Agony of
      the Flying Dutchman," at www.aerothentic.com/historical/Unusual_Sto-
      ries/C47FlyingDutchman.htm (retrieved August 23 and September 14,
      2009), and "C-47A Flying Dutchman," at www.pacificwrecks.com (retrieved
      August 23, 2009).

73   "so light that he 'felt like a baby' ": "Agony of the Flying Dutchman."

74   two tins of water and a few cellophane-wrapped Charms: Hastings, SLD, part
      5. Margaret Hastings's account is the primary source of the trio of survivors'
      journey through the jungle to the clearing. McCollom corroborated signifi-
      cant parts and added important details in his October 1997 interview with
      Robert Gardner, and also in newspaper interviews he gave over the years.

75   Later, writing in her diary: Ibid.

76   "Let's go": Ibid.

76   crawling on their hands and knees: Jack Jones, "Survivor Recalls Crash, 47
      Days in Wild Jungle," *Dayton Daily Camera*, June 10, 1959.

76   "three-inch 'feather' bob": Hastings, SLD, part 5.

76   never complained: John McCollom, interview, October 1997.

77   "It is foolish to think that we could have cut our way out": Hastings, SLD,
      part 6.

77   intended to fill their stomachs: Ibid.

78   returned with a new idea: Ibid.

78   "understudy Johnny Weissmuller": Ibid.

78   point of pride with her: Ibid.

79 "the old mother hen instinct": Remarks of Colonel Jerry Felmley at John McCollom's retirement dinner, September 23, 1980, Wright Patterson Air Force Base Officers' Club. Felmley interviewed Decker for the occasion.

79 a fresh human footprint: John McCollom, interview, October 1997.

79 strange barking sounds: St. George, "Rescue from Shangri-La," p. 6.

8: GENTLEMAN EXPLORER

80 never much of a traditional student: (Gainesville: University Press of Florida, 2000), p. 2.

80 brusque manner: Roger A. Morse, *Richard Archbold and the Archbold Biological Station* Ibid., p. 61.

81 "Why don't you collect mammals?": Ibid., p. 4.

81 learned from his many mistakes: Ibid., p. 4. Archbold's autobiographical notes indicate that, in Morse's words, he "botched the job."

81 his grandfather had been a major benefactor: Ibid., p. 9.

81 put his inheritance to work: Ibid., pp. 11–14.

82 "a comprehensive biological survey of the island": Richard Archbold, A. L. Rand, and L. J. Brass, "Results of the Archbold Expeditions, No. 41," *Bulletin of the American Museum of Natural History* 79, art. 3 (June 26, 1942): 201.

82 frustrated by the logistical challenges: Morse, *Richard Archbold*, p. 15.

82 largest privately owned airplane in the world: Ibid., p. 23. The plane is sometimes called the *Guba II*, because it was the successor to a similar flying boat that Archbold sold to the Soviet Union, with U.S. permission, to help the Russians search for a plane that crashed while trying to fly over the North Pole. Archbold called the second plane simply the *Guba* in his accounts in the *New York Times* and elsewhere.

82 a range exceeding four thousand miles: Richard Archbold, "Unknown New Guinea," *National Geographic Magazine* 79, no. 3 (March 1941): 315.

83 nearly two hundred people: Ibid.

83 "convict carriers": Morse, *Richard Archbold*, p. 25. See also Susan Meiselas, *Encounters with the Dani: Stories from the Baliem Valley* (New York: Steidl/International Center for Photography, 2003), p. 8.

83 collecting mammals, birds, plants, and insects: A. L. Rand, "The Snow Mountains—New Guinea Group in the American Museum of Natural History," *Scientific Monthly* 52, no. 4 (April 1941): 380–82. See also Richard Archbold, "Expedition Finds Rats 3 Feet Long and Kangaroos That Climb Trees," *New York Times*, January 1, 1939.

84 "a pleasant surprise": Archbold, Rand, and Brass, "Results of the Archbold Expeditions," p. 211.

84 called the area a *Groote Vallei*: L. J. Brass, "Stone Age Agriculture in New Guinea," *Geographical Review* 31, no. 4 (October 1941): 556.

84 stumbling upon Kansas City, Kansas: U.S. Census table, "Population of

100 Largest Urban Places, 1940," http://www.census.gov/population/www/documentation/twps0027/tab17.txt (retrieved September 26, 2009).

85   expeditions in 1907, the early 1920s, and 1926: H. Myron Bromley, *The Phonology of Lower Grand Valley Dani: A Comparative Structural Study of Skewed Phonemic Patterns* ('s-Gravenhage: Martinus Nijhoff, 1961), pp. 1–2.

85   the light-skinned men, who must really be ghosts: Denise O'Brien, "The Economics of Dani Marriage: An Analysis of Marriage Payments in a Highland New Guinea Society," Ph.D. diss., Yale University, pp. 7–8.

86   "the last time in the history of our planet": Flannery, *Throwim Way Leg*, p. 4.

86   "Forestation is so heavy": Editor's note attached to Archbold, "Unknown New Guinea," p. 318.

86   rough weather prevented him from changing course: Brass, "Stone Age Agriculture," p. 556.

86   L. J. Brass, described what they saw: Ibid., p. 557.

87   farm country . . . central Europe: Archbold, "Unknown New Guinea," p. 316.

87   "One was evidently a man of some importance": Ibid., p. 321.

88   started their treks at opposite ends of the valley: Ibid., p. 321.

88   the natives practiced cannibalism: Archbold, Rand, and Brass, "Results of the Archbold Expeditions," p. 253.

88   discourage the explorers from traveling to the next village: Archbold, "Unknown New Guinea," p. 324.

88   tribesmen "in large numbers": Meiselas, *Encounters with the Dani*, p. 12. The remainder of the Van Arcken reports from August 9 and 10, 1938, also come from Meiselas, *Encounters with the Dani*, pp. 12–15. In her translation, she uses "Papuan" rather than "native."

89   "Here the natives seemed to take our party for granted": Archbold, "Unknown New Guinea," p. 336.

90   the most awful moment: The details of this incident were explored vividly by Susan Meiselas in her insightful book *Encounters with the Dani*. Meiselas reprints original copies of Van Arcken's patrol reports and the map he drew of the valley, including his obfuscating label showing the location where "one Papuan died due to a lance attack." Meiselas declares, "The colonial government forbade Archbold from discussing the August 10 shooting in exchange for Archbold's continued access to the region." Credibility for that claim is enhanced knowledge that colonial rule was already under challenge, as well as by a brief item in the *New York Times* on March 8, 1940, reporting that Archbold had been appointed "Officer of the Order of Orange Nassau" by Dutch Queen Wilhelmina.

90   guaranteed that the significance would be overlooked: Archbold, Rand, and Brass, "Results of the Archbold Expeditions." Roughly six of the report's ninety-one pages are devoted to Teerink's and Van Arcken's journeys, based on their diaries.

90 "where more than a show of force was necessary": Ibid., p. 219.

90 "one native died due to a lance attack": Meiselas, *Encounters with the Dani*, p. 15.

90 "reception the natives will extend is unpredictable": Archbold, Rand, and Brass, "Results of the Archbold Expeditions," p. 205.

9: GUILT AND GANGRENE

92 "this aching, miserable night": Hastings, SLD, part 7.

92 "a sickening sight": Ibid.

92 "evil-smelling, running sores": Ibid., part 10.

93 She walked in agony: Ibid., part 7, in which she wrote, "I forced myself to walk back and forth . . . it was agony."

93 burns on the left side of her face: Ibid., part 9.

93 the only one left alive: Pat Pond, "Reunion: Thirty Years After," *Women's Army Corps Journal* 5, no. 5 (October–December 1974): 19.

94 "as much for myself as for them": John McCollom to Colonel Edward T. Imparato, n.d., reprinted in Imparato, *Rescue from Shangri-La*, p. 160.

94 walk all the way to the ocean: John McCollom and C. Earl Walter, unaired joint interview with Robert Gardner, Seattle, May 13, 1998. McCollom says, "I never even doubted that even if they didn't find me, that I was going to make it—if I had to walk to the ocean."

94 separated the candies by color: St. George, "Rescue from Shangri-La," p. 6.

94 "delicious battery acid": Hastings, SLD, part 7.

95 "we're going to starve to death": Ibid.

96 "I doubted him for a moment": Ibid.

96 Several hundred U.S. women had already died: Information on the deaths of women in World War II was provided by retired colonel Pat Jernigan, who has done notable work on the history of women in the military, and also by http://www.nooniefortin.com/earlierwars.htm (retrieved October 2, 2009).

97 six nurses were among twenty-eight crew members killed: Ibid.

97 "a handful of icicles": The story of the homemade WAC flag comes from Pat Jernigan and also from Eck, *Saga of a Sad Sack*, pp. 29–30. See also letter titled "I Am Proud," by WAC Margaret Durocher, in Margaret Hastings's correspondence file at TCHS.

98 calls were made to Allied landing strips: *Report of Circumstances Surrounding Flight and Search for C-47 Aircraft Number 41-23952*, U.S. Army document, MACR, contained in IDPFs of the crew and passengers who died.

98 "a forced landing": Ibid.

98 twenty-four planes took part: Ibid.

98 A volunteer crew member: Lutgring, interview, January 5, 2010.

98 "this is it": Hastings, SLD, part 7.

99 flew away without spotting them: John McCollom, sworn statement, MACR, p. 4. In her diary, Margaret Hastings does not record the first plane

they saw at the clearing. Decker's MACR statement is vague, but he seems to agree with McCollom by writing that they reached the clearing around 11:00 a.m. and "we were spotted by a plane that same noon."

99 "Get out the tarps!": Hastings, SLD, part 7.

99 brought along an unusual passenger: Ibid., part 13.

99 "They see us by now": Ibid., part 7. Hastings, SLD, is the source of the entire dialogue following their discovery by Captain Baker in the B-17.

100 "a limitless sea of green": Sheehan, *Missing Plane*, p. 214.

100 saved them in the middle of a jungle: "End of Adventure Is Only Beginning, McCollom Finds," undated clipping from Trenton, Missouri, newspaper, McCollom's scrapbook.

100 they weren't alone: Helenma Wandik, interview by author, February 1, 2010.

100 drop two life rafts as markers: Russell Brines, "Shangri-La On New Guinea," Associated Press story datelined Manila, June 8, 1945, Walter's scrapbook. See also St. George, "Rescue from Shangri-La," p. 6.

100 a message to the Sentani Airstrip: Ibid. See also MACR, p. 4.

101 "back in Hollandia by Sunday": Hastings, SLD, part 7.

101 "the damn hard candy": Ibid.

102 a faraway pack of dogs: John McCollom, interview, October 1997.

102 "Do you hear something funny?": Hastings, SLD, part 7.

102 the noise that native children made: Ibid.

102 "a tasty dinner was waiting in the camote patch": Ibid.

103 dozens of nearly naked black men: John McCollom, interview, October 1997. In his account, McCollom places the number of natives at "about forty." In SLD, part 8, Margaret Hastings writes there were "about a hundred men."

10: EARL WALTER, JUNIOR AND SENIOR

104 "enough equipment to stock a small country store": St. George, "Rescue from Shangri-La," p. 6.

104 lipstick and bobby pins: Ibid.

105 outfitting an overland trek: St. George, "Rescue from Shangri-La," p. 6. See also Gerard M. Devlin, *Silent Wings: The Saga of the U.S. Army and Marine Combat Glider Pilots During World War II* (New York: St. Martin's Press, 1985), p. 354.

106 the 503rd had recaptured the island of Corregidor: Rottman, *Pacific Island Guide*, p. 305.

106 the 511th had carried out a lightning raid: Larry Alexander, *Shadows in the Jungle: The Alamo Scouts behind Enemy Lines in World War II* (New York: NAL Caliber, 2009), p. 261.

107 taught biology and chaired the science department: "Col. Babcock Will Head Black-Foxe," *Los Angeles Times*, May 20, 1962.

107 C. Earl Walter Jr.'s boyhood: C. Earl Walter Jr., interviews by author, July 6, 7, and 8, 2009. Walter provided the account of his family and upbringing, as well as his military service, the details of which were confirmed by sources including Gordon L. Rottman, *U.S. Special Warfare Units in the Pacific Theater, 1941–45: Scouts, Raiders, Rangers and Reconnaissance Units* (New York: Osprey, 2005). Parts of Walter's account of his boyhood came from an undated interview he gave to filmmaker Sonny Izon for the documentary *An Untold Triumph.*

108 "We had been hiking all day": Walter, interview by author, July 7, 2009.

108 "old enough to wonder about women": Ibid.

108 "a machine gun over there": Walter, interview with Izon.

109 "that might straighten me out": Walter, interview by author, July 7, 2009.

109 Buster Keaton, Bing Crosby, Bette Davis, and Charlie Chaplin: Steven Mikulan, "Men of the Old School," *LA Weekly*, May 17, 2001.

109 "sleep-away school for the sons of Hollywood rich people": Valerie J. Nelson, "Sydney Chaplin Dies at 82; Stage Actor and Son of Charlie Chaplin," *Los Angeles Times*, March 6, 2009.

109 "more money than I knew what to do with": Walter, interview by author, July 7, 2009.

110 "no interest in anybody else": Ibid.

110 "most likely stay on in the islands": "Summary of Interview with Lt. Col. L.E. Parks, for Commander Vining, Per Cecil E. Walter Jr., 1. Lt., Inf., C-1314597," document dated 15 July 1944, MacArthur Memorial Archives, Norfolk, Va.

111 the rank of major . . . lieutenant colonel: Robert Ross Smith, "The Conquest of Eastern Mindanao," ch. 32 of *U.S. Army in World War II: The War in the Pacific, Triumph in the Philippines*, n. 43, http://www.ibiblio.org/hyperwar/ USA/USA-P-Triumph/USA-P-Triumph-32.html (retrieved September 4, 2009).

111 a fellow guerrilla leader: John Keats, *They Fought Alone* (New York: Pocket Books, 1965), pp. 170–71. The book focuses on Colonel Wendell Fertig and is based on his recollections, diaries, and reports. Forty years after its publication, in January 2003, the accuracy of the book, including the account involving C. Earl Walter Sr., was challenged by Clyde Childress, a retired army officer, in the *Bulletin of the American Historical Collection* 31, no. 1 (2003), http://ahcf.virtual-asia.com/html/pdf/123_Wendell_Fertig_s.pdf (retrieved October 25, 2009).

112 sent word to the younger Walter: "Summary of Interview with Lt. Col. L.E. Parks."

112 "make me proud of his work": Ibid.

112 "enough to make me envy": Ibid.

112 the 5217th Reconnaissance Battalion: Rottman, *U.S. Special Warfare Units*, p. 39.

113   "do my bit in their extermination": "Summary of Interview with Lt. Col.
L. E. Parks."

113   "my liking for combat": Ibid.

11: UWAMBO

115   Time never knew it existed: Except where noted, this summary of Dani
and Yali life, elaborated upon elsewhere, relies heavily on the work of Karl
Heider, primarily *Grand Valley Dani*. It also synthesizes elements of the
author's visit to the Baliem Valley in January and February 2010: Robert
Gardner's 1964 documentary film *Dead Birds*; interviews in October and
November 2009 with Myron Bromley and James Sunda, who in the 1950s
were among the first missionaries to establish outposts in the Baliem Valley;
Robert Gardner and Karl G. Heider, *Gardens of War: Life and Death in the
New Guinea Stone Age* (New York: Penguin Books, 1974); Peter Matthiessen,
Under the Mountain Wall: A Chronicle of Two Seasons in Stone Age New Guinea
(1962; reprint, New York: Penguin Books, 1990); and H. L. Peters, "Some
Observations of the Social and Religious Life of a Dani Group," *Irian: Bul-
letin of Irian Jaya Development* 4, no. 2 (June 1974).

Upon reading this summary of Dani ways, Dr. Myron Bromley objected to the notion that the Dani people created no works of art. He wrote:
"I think 'no art' is unfair. The carvings on arrowheads and water gourds
were certainly decorative, and the colorful, showy body paint patterns and
headdresses were eye catching both for local people and us. . . . And they
were conscious of appearance in their clothing, too. I still recall the man
who asked me, 'Do you think I look better in the straight gourd I have on
today, or the curled one I had on yesterday?' There was attention given to
tying the gourd as it grew to cause it to curl, if that was the desired 'style.' "
In deference to Dr. Bromley's objections, I changed the wording to read "no
lasting works of art." Ultimately, on this point I relied upon Professor Karl
Heider, who writes on page 62 of *Grand Valley Dani*: "There are countless
ways to define 'art,' but according to most of them, the Dani have little or
none." Heider acknowledges the ornamentation of certain items such as
arrow points and spears, but he says they lie "somewhat in the hazy area
between art and craftsmanship."

115   a single word to describe both place and time: Douglas Hayward, "Time
and Society in Dani Culture," *Irian: Bulletin of Irian Jaya Development* 11,
nos. 2–3 (June and October 1983): 31–32.

116   terms for only two: Eleanor R. Heider, "Probabilities, Sampling, and Eth-
nographic Method: The Case of Dani Colour Names," *Man*, n.s., 7, no. 3
(September 1972): 448–66.

116   ignored the stars: Hayward, "Time and Society," p. 35.

116   "Let me eat your feces": Heider, *Grand Valley Dani*, p. 9.

116   natives . . . organized themselves: Ibid., pp. 67–69.

117   Their enemies were *dili*: Ibid., pp. 94–95.

117   "We people of the Baliem": H. L. Peters, "Some Observations," p. 76.

118   a moral obligation: Douglas Hayward, "Dani of Irian Jaya Before and Af-
      ter Conversion" (Sentani, Indonesia: Regions Press, 1980), p. 102. See also
      Peters, "Some Observations," p. 77.

118   "If there is no war, we will die": Peters, "Some Observations," p. 76.

118   different parts of speech: Ibid., p. 77.

118   ghosts, called *mogat*: Heider, *Grand Valley Dani*, p. xi.

119   flesh of their enemies: Helenma Wandik, interview. See also Russell T. Hitt,
      *Cannibal Valley: The Heroic Struggle for Christ in Savage New Guinea—The
      Most Perilous Mission Frontier in the World* (New York: Harper & Row, 1962),
      pp. 120–29.

120   hoot of a cuckoo dove: Heider, *Grand Valley Dani*, p. 101.

120   hurled insults across the front lines: Ibid., p. 99.

120   gained social standing: Peters, "Some Observations," p. 78.

120   abstained from sex for up to five years: Heider, *Grand Valley Dani*, p. 22. See
      also Karl G. Heider, "Dani Sexuality: A Low Energy System," *Man*, n.s., 11,
      no. 2 (June 1976): 188–201.

120   a source of pleasure and recreation: Heider, *Grand Valley Dani*, p. 104.

120   one party would simply move away: Ibid., p. 93.

121   leaving them half-blind: Karl Heider noted this in the 1960s. Even after the
      end of native wars, boys still played with bows and grass arrows, and several
      boys with missing eyes were seen in early 2010.

121   all thumbs: Heider, *Grand Valley Dani*, p. 134.

121   An anthropologist: Ibid.

121   greasy orchid fibers: Ibid., p. 59.

122   "These are clearly human beings": Margaret Mead, from a review of *Dead
      Birds*, included in a "promotional flyer" for the film dated November 18,
      1963. Reprinted in Meiselas, *Encounters with the Dani*, p. 67.

122   driven inland by subsequent arrivals: Heider, *Grand Valley Dani*, p. 1.

122   "In the beginning": Meiselas, *Encounters with the Dani*, p. 2, quoting Peter
      Sutcliffe in "The Day the Dani People Become Civilized, the Sun Will No
      Longer Rise," *Papua New Guinea Post-Courier*, 1972.

123   called themselves *iniatek*, the originals: Peters, "Some Observations,"
      p. 10.

123   humans became separate: Heider, *Grand Valley Dani*, p. 127.

123   men, like birds, must die: Ibid., p. 126. See also Peters, "Some Observa-
      tions," p. 114.

123   "dead birds": This idea is explored most vividly by filmmaker Robert Gard-
      ner in his landmark 1964 documentary about the Dani, *Dead Birds*. Gard-
      ner understood that the gap between the Dani and westerners was not as
      large as it might seem. He once wrote: "In *Dead Birds* my fondest hope was
      that my camera be a mirror for its viewers to see themselves."

123 "Let us take revenge on our enemies together": Peters, "Some Observations," p. 76.
123 spirits that lived in the sky: Interviews by author with Tomas Wandik, February 1, 2010; Yunggukwe Wandik, February 3, 2010; and Helenma Wandik. See also Matthiessen, *Under the Mountain Wall*, p. 105.
124 village the natives called Uwambo: Tomas, Yunggukwe, and Helemna Wandik, interviews. This account of the natives' reaction to the plane also draws from interviews conducted by Buzz Maxey in 1999 with the same Yali tribespeople and several others in a group.
125 A village leader named Yaralok Wandik: This story was recounted by his son, Tomas Wandik, and also by his nephew, Helenma Wandik, in interviews on February 1, 2010. A separate version of these events that agreed with this account was given to Buzz Maxey in 1999 by Helenma and Tomas Wandik, and a group of other Yali men that included Miralek Walela, Yilu Wandik, Waragin Dekma, and two others whose first names were Yare and Wasue.

12: WIMAYUK WANDIK, AKA "CHIEF PETE"

128 The native men: Helenma and Tomas Wandik, interviews.
128 tasted human flesh: Helenma Wandik confirmed that his people ate the hands of enemies killed in battle in an interview with the author. Cannibalism among the valley people is discussed in numerous anthropological research papers, but perhaps the most vivid description is found in Hitt, *Cannibal Valley*, pp. 120–29.
128 themselves, their allies, and their enemies: Bob Connolly and Robin Anderson, *First Contact: New Guinea's Highlanders Encounter the Outside World* (New York: Viking Penguin, 1987), p. 36.
129 come into contact with the Archbold expedition: Helenma and Tomas Wandik, interviews.
130 "matched a whole army": Hilton, *Lost Horizon*, p. 157.
130 Albert Einstein: This famous quote has many forms. The one used here is commonly accepted, though another frequently cited version is: "I do not know how the Third World War will be fought, but I can tell you what they will use in the Fourth—rocks!" See Alice Calaprice, *The New Quotable Einstein* (Princeton, N.J.: Princeton University Press, 2005), p. 173.
130 a native stew: Hastings, SLD, part 8: "If I was going to end up in a jungle stew-pot, the natives would have to come and get me."
130 "We haven't any weapon": Hastings, SLD, part 7.
130 McCollom watched: John McCollom, interview, October 1997.
131 more like one hundred: Hastings, SLD, part 8. Except where otherwise noted, the account of the first meeting between the natives and the survivors, including dialogue, comes from this portion of the SLD.
131 "feed us before they kill us": Robert Pearman, "Three Who Lived to Tell About It," *Milwaukee Journal*, December 22, 1961, p. 16.

131 He was wiry and alert: Photograph of the native the survivors called "Pete," courtesy of Betty McCollom.

132 meet him halfway: In his interview with Robert Gardner, McCollom described the scene of the two of them on the log. In SLD, Margaret Hastings tells the story slightly differently, with the natives coming across the log to meet the survivors in the clearing. In other respects, their accounts agree.

132 McCollom reached out: John McCollom, interview, October 1997. In her SLD, Margaret Hastings credited the native leader with extending his hand, after which McCollom, "weak with relief, grabbed it and wrung it."

133 a college classmate: John McCollom, interviews, October 1997 and May 13, 1998.

133 Wimayuk Wandik: The native the survivors called "Pete" was identified as Wimayuk Wandik by his son, Helenma Wandik, on February 1, 2010, from a photograph taken by C. Earl Walter Jr. This identification was subsequently confirmed by Wimayuk Wandik's niece and nephew, Yunggukwe and Tomas Wandik.

134 He and his fellow villagers were traders: Helenma Wandik, interview.

135 "Pete and his boys": Hastings, SLD, part 9.

135 a terrible smell: Helenma and Tomas Wandik, interviews.

136 bit into the stalk: Ibid.

136 "The native who had the garden": John McCollom, interview, October 1997.

138 bright blue eyes: Helenma and Tomas Wandik, interviews.

138 "loved Pete and his followers": Hastings, SLD, part 9.

139 might dislodge . . . his *etai-eken*: This discussion of the "seeds of singing" and the treatment of wounds relies largely on Gardner and Heider, *Gardens of War*, pp. 88, 140–41. This treatment of wounds is also described in several places by Matthiessen, *Under the Mountain Wall*, p. 227.

140 "They took the chow": St. George, "Hidden Valley."

13: COME WHAT MAY

142 Newspapers had detailed the atrocities: Authoritative reports about the Bataan Death March became common fare in early 1944. One example among many was an editorial published in *The New York Times* on January 30, 1944: "Revenge! The Nation Demands It."

142 a daring escape: Camilo Ramirez, interview by filmmaker Sonny Izon, n.d.

142 leading grueling runs: Walter, interview by author, July 7, 2009.

142 "'As soon as I can get us there'": Ibid.

142 the son of General Courtney Whitney: Captain C. Earl Walter Jr., to Brigadier General Courtney Whitney, March 13, 1945, in Walter's personnel file at MacArthur Memorial Archives, Richmond, Va. It's worth noting that Whitney was not universally admired. MacArthur's biographer, William Manchester, wrote, "From the standpoint of the guerrillas, [Whitney] was a disastrous choice. Undiplomatic and belligerent, he was condescending

toward all Filipinos except those who, like himself, had substantial investments in the islands." See William Manchester, *American Caesar: Douglas MacArthur, 1880–1964* (New York: Little, Brown, 1978), p. 378.

142 a blunt letter: Ibid.

143 "a trait I inherited from my father.": Ibid.

143 responded two weeks later: Whitney to Walter, March 27, 1945, in Walter's personnel file at MacArthur Memorial Archives.

143 He wrote the general in response: Walter to Whitney, April 2, 1945, in Walter's personnel file at MacArthur Memorial Archives.

144 frustrated to the point of distraction: Walter, interview by author, July 7, 2009.

144 "I was an only son": Ibid.

144 Whether his father had such power: A personnel file for C. Earl Walter Sr. at the MacArthur Memorial Archives contains only a single sheet of paper, confirming his commissioning as an officer, according to archivist James Zobel.

145 "uplift and Christianize them": General James Rusling, "Interview with President William McKinley," *Christian Advocate,* January 22, 1903, p. 17, reprinted in Daniel Schirmer and Stephen Rosskamm Shalom, eds., *The Philippines Reader* (Boston: South End Press, 1987), pp. 22–23.

145 "a humane war": Stuart Creighton Miller, *Benevolent Assimilation: The American Conquest of the Philippines, 1899–1903* (New Haven, Conn.: Yale University Press, 1984), p. 253. See also Thomas Bender, *Rethinking American History in a Global Age* (Berkeley and Los Angeles: University of California Press, 2002), p. 282.

145 opportunities were limited: Alex S. Fabros, "California's Filipino Infantry: A Short History of the 1st and 2nd Filipino Infantry Regiments of the U.S. Army in World War II," California State Military Museum, www.military-museum.org/Filipino.html, p. 3 (retrieved November 21, 2009).

146 more than a hundred thousand transplanted Filipinos: Ibid., p. 1.

146 a strange limbo: Linda A. Revilla, " 'Pineapples,' 'Hawayanos,' and 'Loyal Americans': Local Boys in the First Filipino Infantry Regiment, US Army," *Social Process in Hawaii* 37 (1996): 61, www.efilarchives.org/pubications (retrieved November 29, 2009).

146 "Life is so small a property": Ibid., p. 62. The quote is from Sergeant Urbano Francisco.

147 more than seven thousand: Ibid.

147 several thousand took the oath: Fabros, "California's Filipino Infantry," p. 4.

147 An American reporter: James G. Wingo, "The First Filipino Regiment," *Asia* 42 (October 1942): 562–63. (A tagline with the story notes that Wingo "was, until the occupation of Manila, the Washington correspondent of the Philippines Free Press.")

147 one battle on Samar Island: Fabros, "California's Filipino Infantry," p. 5.

147 heavy combat against the Japanese on Leyte Island: Ibid.

148 " 'I've got just the people to go in there' ": Walter, interview by author, July 6, 2009.

150 a four-part warning: Ibid. See also Imparato, *Rescue from Shangri-La*, pp. 16–17.

151 each one took a step forward: Walter, interview by author, July 6, 2009.

14. FIVE-BY-FIVE

152 "We can clear enough space": Hastings, SLD, part 9.

152 a C-47: John McCollom, interviews, October 1997 and May 13, 1998.

153 the "walkie-talkie": The survivors didn't specify the model, but Margaret Hastings's description makes it likely that it was the Motorola SCR-300, a celebrated two-way radio used extensively in the Pacific during the war. See www.scr300.org and Harry Mark Petrakis, *The Founder's Touch: The Life of Paul Galvin of Motorola* (New York: McGraw-Hill, 1965), pp. 144–47.

153 "McCollom swiftly set it up": Hastings, SLD, part 9.

153 too choked up to speak: St. George, "Hidden Valley."

153 "This is Lieutenant McCollom": Hastings, SLD, part 9.

153 Sergeant Jack Gutzeit: The crew members of the 311 supply plane were identified in *Jungle Journal* (newsletter of the Far East Air Service Command) 1, no. 4 (June 20, 1945): 3.

154 "almost too weak to move": Hastings, SLD, part 9.

154 Captain Herbert O. Mengel: *Jungle Journal*, p. 3.

155 the natives had returned: The source of the scene and dialogue from the morning of Thursday, May 18, 1945, is SLD, parts 9 and 10.

156 New Guinea housing project: Hastings, SLD, part 10.

157 permanently embittered one resident: Yunggukwe Wandik, interview. After she reluctantly agreed to tell her story, the author paid her for the pig, on behalf of the people of the United States.

158 tomatoes and tomato juice: In SLD, Margaret Hastings only mentions tomatoes, but John McCollom, in his interview with Robert Gardner, said he and Decker found "about a half-dozen big cans of tomato juice and tomatoes."

158 "Come on, Maggie": Hastings, SLD, part 10.

158 tend more thoroughly to their wounds: Information and quotes about their first medical treatment, including quotes, come from Hastings, SLD, part 10.

15: NO THANKSGIVING

162 the best soldier he'd ever met: Walter, interview by author, July 6, 2009.

162 raced model airplanes: "Model Planes Continue Championship Flights," *Los Angeles Times*, September 6, 1938, p. 8. Background on Abrenica also comes

from his immigration and enlisted records, www.ancestry.com (retrieved November 29, 2009).

163 more perilous: Ramirez, interview. His enlistment records support Ramirez's account of his involvement with the Philippine Scouts; his tale of capture and escape is supported by contemporaneous newspaper accounts of his involvement in the rescue at Shangri-La, including an undated news story in Walter's scrapbook headlined "Shangri-La Hero Here; Filipino Visits Pal, Claims U.S. Bride."

163 "'I will get through there'": Ibid.

164 "his gung-ho attitude": Walter, interview with Izon.

165 spoke again with Colonel Elsmore: Walter, interview by author, July 7, 2009. Also Walter's personal diary, dated May 17, 1945.

166 "It's gonna be your operation": Walter, interview with Izon.

166 "That was a mess": Walter, interview by author, July 7, 2009.

166 "Do you really want to do this?": Walter, interview with Izon.

167 Walter noted in a journal: Walter, CEW.

167 "Don't let anyone jump": Hastings, SLD, part 11.

167 "I could no longer move": Ibid.

168 fleas in the blankets: Remarks of Colonel Jerry Felmley at John McCollom's retirement dinner, September 23, 1980, Wright Patterson Air Force Base Officers' Club. Felmley interviewed Decker for the occasion.

168 "Eureka! We eat!": Hastings, SLD, part 11.

169 "Honest, Maggie": Ibid.

169 "He was in great pain": Ibid.

169 "They would chatter like magpies": Ibid., part 9.

170 sized up the native woman: Ibid., part 11.

170 name was Gilelek: Helenma Wandik, interview.

170 "They held out a pig": Hastings, SLD, part 11.

171 "It is the remembrance of pigs": Heider, *Grand Valley Dani*, p. 39.

16: RAMMY AND DOC

173 Flying . . . over the survivors' clearing: Walter, interview by author, July 7, 2009. This account also relies on Walter's interview with Izon.

173 "The reason I dropped five": Walter, interview with Izon.

174 "it looked like hell": Ibid.

176 "It was patent to all of us": Hastings, SLD, part 12.

176 "God bless you": Kenneth Decker, interview by Sonny Izon, n.d.

176 "I said more 'Our Fathers' ": Hastings, SLD, part 12.

177 "a hundred feet above the jump zone": Ramirez, interview.

177 "The natives have spears": Ibid.

179 "they came from the city": Ibid.

179 more harm than good: Hastings, SLD, part 13.

179 "work the bandages off": Ibid., part 12.

180 "how shocked he was": Ibid.

180 "sorry-looking gams": Ibid.

17: CUSTER AND COMPANY

182 Colonel Edward T. Imparato: Imparato, *Rescue from Shangri-La*, p. 55.

182 take the plane in low: Walter, interview by author, July 7, 2009.

183 "When we first landed": Ibid. Except where otherwise noted, the dialogue throughout this scene of the paratroopers' landing in the valley comes from the author's July 7, 2009, interview with Walter.

183 three hundred: "The Hidden Valley," *Pulse* (suppl.), typewritten military newsletter, found in Walter's scrapbook, p. 4.

183 "Custer's last stand": Walter, interview by author, July 8, 2009.

183 "frightening, weird sound": " Hidden Valley," Walter's scrapbook, p. 4.

184 "fully equipped for a combat mission": Ibid.

184 an area known to the natives as Wosi: Lisaniak Mabel, interview by author, February 2, 2010.

185 "a vine from the sky": Ibid.

185 his name was Yali: The leader of the Logo-Mabel clans was identified in photographs taken by C. Earl Walter Jr. by four separate witnesses interviewed February 1 to 3, 2010, including Yali's grandson, Reverend Simon Logo.

185 "I waved those damn leaves": "Hidden Valley," Walter's scrapbook, p. 4.

186 "they had nothing to fear from us": Walter, interview by author, July 6, 2009.

186 Writing that night in the journal: Walter, CEW, May 20, 1945.

186 "never bathed": Walter, interview by author, July 6, 2009.

186 "a lot of hugging": Ibid.

188 "let's take our pants down": Walter, interview by author, July 7, 2009. See also Walter, CEW, May 21, 1945.

188 " 'That's not mud' ": Ai Baga, interview by author, February 2, 2010. The Dani reaction to the soldiers' nudity also relies on interviews the same day with Lisaniak Mabel and the following day with Narekesok Logo.

189 *The Queen:* Imparato, *Rescue from Shangri-La*, p. 105.

189 strangers weren't welcome inside the fence: Walter, CEW, May 20, 1945.

190 "For six hours": Hastings, SLD, part 13.

190 scoured the jungle: John McCollom, interview, October 1997.

190 "A native came running into our camp": Hastings, SLD, part 13.

191 "with you by nightfall": Ibid.

191 "My beau, Wally": Ibid.

192 returned to the base: John McCollom, interview, October 1997. McCollom is the source of the dialogue for this entire exchange.

194 "We had to slice": Ramirez, interview.

18: BATHTIME FOR YUGWE

195 Margaret awoke the next morning: Hastings, SLD, part 13. This account of Margaret's bath also came from McCollom, interview by Gardner, October 1997.

196 "I looked around": Hastings, SLD, part 13.

197 "We saw she had breasts": Helenma Wandik, interview.

197 "a man, a woman, and the woman's husband": Ibid.

197 "always heartily detested": Hastings, SLD, part 13.

197 "a short recon": Walter, CEW, May 21, 1945.

198 "one of the most interesting parts of our lives": Ibid.

198 "Fired a few shots": Ibid.

198 "just for the hell of it": Walter, interview by author, July 7, 2009.

199 "our weapons can kill": Walter, CEW, May 21, 1945.

199 "One man, named Mageam": Lisaniak Mabel, interview.

199 "Pika was shooting the gun": Ai Baga, interview.

199 "our enemies didn't come": Narekesok Logo, interview by author, February 3, 2010.

200 a house for *inalugu*: Ai Baga, interview.

200 fueled up with a breakfast: Walter, CEW, May 22, 1945.

200 "God only knows": Ibid.

201 "A declaration, called a *maga*": Yunggukwe Wandik, interview.

201 "came out on a path and stopped us": Walter, interview by author, July 6, 2009.

202 "more bother than good": Walter, CEW, May 23, 1945.

202 "Did not understand": Ibid.

203 "Things look bad": Ibid., May 24, 1945.

203 "God only knows": Ibid.

19. "SHOO, SHOO BABY"

204 "Finally they are over us": Walter, CEW, May 25, 1945.

204 "Earl will get down there": McCollom and Walter, joint interview, May 13, 1998.

205 "that yapping noise": Hastings, SLD, part 14.

205 "He looked like a giant": Ibid.

205 "I knew they were all right": Walter, interview with Izon.

205 "His men worshipped Walter": Hastings, SLD, part 14.

205 "a pretty good-looking gal": Walter, interview by author, July 6, 2009.

206 an American flag waved: Ibid., July 7, 2009.

206 "The Lost Outpost of Shangri-La": Walter, CEW, May 29, 1945.

206 "The Stars and Stripes now fly": Ibid., May 31, 1945.

207 "won and lost thousands of dollars": Hastings, SLD, part 14.

207 "Superman" and "Iron Man": In her diary, Hastings refers to Caoili as "Superman," but in captions on photos in his scrapbook, Walter uses the nickname "Iron Man."

207 "There ought to be a law": Hastings, SLD, part 14.
207 "Deuces wild, roll your own": "Here's a Soldier Who Refuses to Embrace a WAC," *Chicago Daily Tribune*, July 12, 1945.
207 "don't know how to play cards": Walter, interview by author, July 6, 2009.
207 "The captain played": Hastings, SLD, part 14.
208 "Walter was a personality kid": Ibid.
209 "leave the men alone": Walter, interview by author, July 6, 2009.
209 "just walk away": Ibid.
209 "all the credit in the world": Walter, CEW, May 25, 1945.
210 burial duty: Walter, CEW, May 27 to May 29, 1945.
210 a second Star of David: Document in the IDPF of Private Mary M. Landau, signed by her brother, Jack Landau, dated June 29, 1959.
210 helping to toss the funerary supplies: Oral history interview with Ruth Johnson Coster, University of North Carolina, Greensboro, Object ID WV0145.5.001.
211 the trail of Margaret's hair: Hastings, SLD, part 14.
211 "There it is": McCollom and Walter, joint interview, May 13, 1998.
211 "Lieutenant Mac's report": Walter, CEW, May 29, 1945.
212 "we buried Captain Good": Walter, CEW, June 6, 1945. News reports at the time said the burial service took place May 26, but Walter's journal puts the date at June 6. The credibility of his account is enhanced by previous entries in which he writes that he is waiting for orders about the disposition of remains.
213 a hero in his own right: Air Force Link, www.af.mil/bios/bio .asp?bioID=5510 (retrieved February 18, 2010).
213 "Out of the depth": Russell Brines, Associated Press staff writer, " 'Shangri-La' on New Guinea," June 9, 1945, found in Walter's scrapbook.
213 "seemed to whisper a peace": Ibid.
213 "the saddest and most impressive funeral": Hastings, SLD, part 14.
214 "a long discussion on the world at war": Walter, CEW, June 6, 1945.
214 "a true blue gal": Walter, interview by author, July 6, 2009.
214 "When they climbed the mountain": Yunggukwe Wandik, interview.
215 condolence letters: Copies of letters from General Douglas MacArthur, General Clements McMullen, and General H. H. Arnold provided by Major Nicholson's family.
216 "a corrected report": General Robert W. Dunlop to Patrick J. Hastings, May 27, 1945, Hastings's archive file at TCHS.
216 "a very miraculous escape": Chaplain Cornelius Waldo to Patrick J. Hastings, dated 8, 1945, Hastings's archive file at TCHS.

20. "HEY, MARTHA!"

218 seeped into his journal: Walter, CEW, excerpted entries from May 29 to June 8, 1945.

220   Walter Simmons . . . was thirty-seven: Trevor Jensen, "Walter Simmons, 1908–2006: Editor and War Reporter," *Chicago Tribune*, December 1, 2006.

221   Reporting in May 1945: Headlines are from stories published in the *Chicago Tribune* under Walter Simmons's byline on May 13, May 17, May 21, and May 31, 1945.

221   A native of Nova Scotia: "Ralph Morton, Former War Reporter," *Newsday*, October 20, 1988, p. 41.

221   more than fourteen hundred newspapers: *Encyclopædia Britannica*, www .britannica.com/EBchecked/topic/136280/Kent-Cooper (retrieved February 22, 2010). See also www.encyclopedia.com/doc/1G2-3445000019.html.

222   "In a hidden valley": Walter Simmons, "WAC, 2 Yanks Marooned in Hidden Valley," *Chicago Tribune*, June 8, 1945.

223   "The crash of an Army transport plane": Associated Press, "Chutists Land in Shangri-La to Rescue Fliers," *Deseret News*, June 9, 1945.

223   *The New York Times*: Associated Press, "Airfield Is Built to Rescue a Wac and 2 Men in New Guinea Crash," *New York Times*, June 9, 1945.

224   "stop worrying and start praying!": "Plane-to-Ground Conversations Reveal Details of Survivors' Life in Shangri-La Valley," *Trenton Republican-Times*, July 13, 1945.

224   "the queen of the valley": Ibid.

224   "Shangri-La Gets Latest News": Ralph Morton, "Shangri-La Gets Latest News from Associated Press," *St. Petersburg Evening Independent*, June 13, 1945.

224   $1,000 each: Walter, CEW, June 16–18, 1945.

224   a pang of jealousy: Ibid.

224   WAC private Thelma Decker: "Plane-to-Ground Conversations."

225   bought a box of chocolates: Associated Press, "Shangri-La Trio Hikes Out Today," *Salt Lake Tribune*, June 14, 1945.

225   "She can go native": U.S. Army air-to-ground transcript, June 24, 1945, reprinted in Imparato, *Rescue from Shangri-La*, p. 120.

225   "clawed at the aluminum door frame": Walter Simmons, "Crew Supplying Hidden Valley Averts Mishap," *Chicago Tribune*, June 21, 1945.

225   panning for gold: Ibid., p. 122.

226   cases of beer: Walter, CEW, June 9, 1945.

226   "too overcome to write": Ibid.

226   deliver personal messages: "Tribune Sending Kin's Notes to 'Hidden Valley,' " *Chicago Tribune*, June 15, 1945.

226   "Robert was killed instantly": John McCollom to Rolla and Eva McCollom, quoted to the author by Robert's daughter, Dennie McCollom Scott, May 30, 2010.

227   "dropping me some panties?": Simmons, "WAC, 2 Yanks."

227   "begging for a pair of pants": Hastings, SLD, part 15.

227   "Tropic skin diseases": Ibid.

228 "Mumu" and "Mua": Helenma Wandik, interview.

228 lengthy thoughts about the natives: C. Earl Walter Jr., "Miscellaneous Notes on the Natives," CEW.

228 "some pictures of pinup girls": Ibid.

229 couldn't quite fill his gourd: Ibid.

229 "many curving lines on the paper": Ibid.

230 "white gods dropped out of the sky": Associated Press, "Three in 'Shangri-La' May Quit Peak Today," *New York Times*, June 14, 1945.

230 "the happiest people I've ever seen": Walter Simmons, "Hidden Valley Dwellers Hide Nothing, but All Wear Smiles," *Chicago Tribune*, June 16, 1945.

230 "They lived well": Walter, interview by author, July 6, 2009.

230 "the best-looking girl": Walter, "Miscellaneous Notes."

21: PROMISED LAND

232 "headlines all over the world": Walter, CEW, June 11, 1945.

232 "my prayers on the future": Ibid., June 13, 1945.

232 "My last news of Dad": Ibid.

233 "I will not risk": Ibid., June 10, 1945.

233 delayed their departure: Ibid., June 15, 1945.

233 kept after his journalistic prey: U.S. Army air-to-ground transcript, June 15, 1945, in Imparato, *Rescue from Shangri-La*, pp. 79–80.

235 "Two Filipino medics": Simmons, "WAC, 2 Yanks."

235 hailed from Chicago: Walter Simmons, "Glider Takes Six More Out of Shangri-La," *Chicago Tribune*, July 1, 1945.

235 reacted angrily in his journal: Walter, CEW, June 22, 1945.

236 "you gonna use any of this?": John McCollom, interview, October 1997.

236 "farewells to Pete and his men": Hastings, SLD, part 15.

236 weeping at their departure: Ibid.

237 bestowed another *maga*: Yunggukwe Wandik, interview.

237 glanced back over her shoulder: Hastings, SLD, part 15.

237 "break off a bite and eat it": John McCollom, interview, October 1997.

237 "Nobody knew what the food was": Tomas Wandik, interview.

237 a place of magic: Yunggukwe Wandik, interview.

237 McCollom's offer of a machete: His son, Helenma Wandik, fondly remembered the machete sixty-five years later, as did his niece and nephew, Tomas and Yunggukwe Wandik.

238 "Some people were getting mad at Wimayuk": Helenma Wandik, interview.

238 "They loved them": Hastings, SLD, part 13.

238 It remained in use: Author's visit to a village near the site of Uwambo in February 2010. Yali and Dani villages tend to move over the years, and Uwambo was no longer a village site.

239 "up and down and crevice to crevice": Walter, interview by author, July 6, 2009.

239 "I thought I was well": Hastings, SLD, part 15.

239 "Hats off to Sergeant Decker": Walter, CEW, June 15, 1945.

240 "plenty rugged": Ibid., June 16–18, 1945.

240 "Are they hostile?": U.S. Army air-to-ground transcript, June 16, 1945, in Imparato, *Rescue from Shangri-La*, p. 82.

240 "Our main trouble is water": Ibid.

240 "My main concern": Walter, interview by author, July 7, 2009.

241 "We are rolling too well": Walter, CEW, June 16–18, 1945.

241 "like a million dollars": Hastings, SLD, part 15.

241 "we instantly named 'Bob Hope' ": Ibid.

242 running up the trail: Walter, CEW, June 16–18, 1945.

242 "the best damn field soldiers": Ibid.

242 jumped up and down: Far East Air Service Command Report, June 18, 1945, reprinted in Imparato, *Rescue from Shangri-La*, p. 87.

242 sitting beside him: Ralph Morton, "Survivor Trio of Shangri-La Safe in Valley," *Sarasota Herald-Tribune*, June 20, 1945.

242 "Surely the followers of Moses": Hastings, SLD, part 16.

22: HOLLYWOOD

243 "there it lies today": Hastings, SLD, part 16.

243 "ever make a jump before?": John McCollom, interview by Gardner, October 1997.

244 "a rank amateur": Hastings, SLD, part 16.

244 "Pull your legs together!": Ibid.

244 "Pull on your risers!": McCollom, interview by Gardner, October 1997.

245 "This man is drunk!": Walter, interview by author, July 6, 2009.

245 "Drunker than a hoot owl": McCollom, interview by Gardner, October 1997.

245 "The valley is going Hollywood": Associated Press, "Shangri-La Trio Eat Pork Chops, Await Rescue," *Sarasota Herald-Tribune*, June 21, 1945.

245 Canadian House of Commons: Ernest J. Chambers, *The Canadian Parliamentary Guide* (Ottawa, Canada: Mortimer, 1908), p. 143.

246 helped to launch the Federal Reserve Bank of New York: "H. V. Cann Returns to Canada," *New York Times*, March 3, 1917.

246 study structural engineering: Alexandra Cann, interview by author, August 15, 2009.

246 gamble away his sizable inheritance: Ibid.

246 small movie roles: resume of Alexander Cross, www.imdb.com (retrieved August 15, 2009). See also Cann, interview.

246 drinking buddy Humphrey Bogart: Cann, interview.

247 can't-miss "Hey, Martha!" story: "Actor Confesses Theft of Gems at Palm Springs," *Los Angeles Times*, March 28, 1937.

248 "Nobody likes to prosecute a friend": "Mrs. Hearst Not to Prosecute Cann in Gem Theft Case," *Los Angeles Times*, March 29, 1937.

248 "Host's Jewels Are Stolen by Thespian": Associated Press, "Host's Jewels Are Stolen by Thespian," *Brownsville (Texas) Herald*, March 29, 1937.

248 a Hearst and a heist: "Ex-Wife of Hearst Jr. Robbed," *New York Times*, March 28, 1937.

248 married and divorced three times: Cann, interview.

248 survived, but with a broken back: Playwright Keith Dewhurst, Alexander Cann's son-in-law, interview by author, September 15, 2009.

248 "a great deal more about filmmaking": Cann, interview.

248 Netherlands Indies Government Information Service: David J. Snyder, "The Netherlands Information Service Collection: An Introduction," *Historia Actual Online* 3, no. 8 (2005): 201–9.

249 "War Correspondent and Cinematographer": Correspondence between Robert Gardner and John Daniell, son of Fred Daniell of the Dutch East Indies Film Unit, December 17, 1997.

249 his charm and Canadian accent: Ibid.

249 slammed full-speed into the *Australia*: "The First Kamikaze Attack?" Australian War Memorial, www.awm.gov.au/wartime/28/article.asp (retrieved March 2, 2010).

249 "smoke already pouring out": Associated Press, "Jap Plane with Dead Pilot Rips Allied Cruiser," *Los Angeles Times*, November 2, 1944.

250 flew from Melbourne to Hollandia on June 17: Alexander Cann, "Chuting Photog Pictures Life in 'Shangri-La,' " *Chicago Tribune*, July 2, 1945.

250 "six quarts of whisky and a party": U.S. Army air-to-ground transcript, June 22, 1945, in Imparato, *Rescue from Shangri-La*, p. 117.

250 "obviously dangerous": Cann, interview.

250 "whether I jumped or was pushed": Cann, "Chuting Photog."

250 aspirin supply: Hastings, SLD, part 16.

250 chow mein and fried potatoes: Ibid.

250 "a full fifth of Dutch gin": Walter, interview by author, July 6, 2009.

250 "not until another story comes along": U.S. Army air-to-ground transcript, June 24, 1945, in Imparato, *Rescue from Shangri-La*, p. 122.

251 "the most magnificent survivor": "Hidden Valley," *Pulse*; *Pulse* was the newsletter of the USS *Barnstable*, which took Walter and his men to Manila. A slightly different version of this quote appears in "Modern Legend of Shangri-La," *Jungle Journal* (newsletter of the Far East Air Service Command) 1, no. 4 (June 20, 1945): 3.

251 "I . . . will give up my crown": U.S. Army air-to-ground transcript, June 24, 1945, in Imparato, *Rescue from Shangri-La*, p. 122.

251 became fast friends: Walter, interview by author, July 6, 2009.

251 "experience and hard knocks": Walter, CEW, June 21, 1945.

251 "really learn something": Ibid., June 23, 1945.

251   "a swell egg": Ibid., June 29, 1945.

252   "thought she was a dog": Hastings, SLD, part 16.

252   "I wanted to cry": Ibid.

253   insisted that his bed go to Decker: Ibid.

254   "laid down in agony": Walter, CEW, June 20, 1945.

254   re-create the last leg of the journey: Walter, CEW, June 21, 1945. See also
      Walter and McCollom, interview by Gardner, May 13, 1998.

                              23: GLIDERS?

255   navy construction battalion: Don Dwiggins, *On Silent Wings: Adventures in
      Motorless Flight* (New York: Grosset & Dunlap, 1970), p. 109.

256   L-5 Sentinel: Devlin, *Silent Wings*, p. 354. See also National Museum of
      the U.S. Air Force, www.nationalmuseum.af.mil/factsheets/factsheet.
      asp?id=519 (retrieved March 5, 2010).

256   consume all its fuel: Devlin, *Silent Wings*, p. 254.

256   lanky country boy: Margaret Palmer Harvey, daughter of Henry Palmer,
      interview by author, March 12, 2010.

256   headed for a blackboard: Devlin, *Silent Wings*, pp. 354–55.

257   "no second chances": Ibid., p. xi.

257   a leader in glider technology: Ibid., pp. 29–36.

258   quiet war machines: Ibid. See also David T. Zabecki, *World War II in Europe*,
      (New York: Routledge, 1999), pp. 1471–72.

259   one thousand qualified glider pilots: Major Michael H. Manion, "Gliders of
      World War II: 'The Bastards No One Wanted,' " master's thesis, School of
      Advanced Air and Space Studies, Air University, Maxwell Air Force Base,
      Montgomery, Ala., June 2008, p. 56.

259   watched with interest: McCollom, interview, October 1997.

259   furniture company, and a coffin maker: Manion, "Gliders of World War II,"
      p. 53. See also Dwiggins, *On Silent Wings*, p. 78.

260   wingspan of eighty-three feet, eight inches: Waco CG-4A specs come from
      the National Museum of the U.S. Air Force, www.nationalmuseum.af.mil/
      factsheets/factsheet.asp?id=504 (retrieved March 7, 2010).

260   14,000 Wacos: Turner Publishing, *World War II Glider Pilots* (Paducah, Ky.:
      Turner, 1991), p. 16.

260   about $15,000 each: Ibid.

260   seventeen deluxe, eight-cylinder Ford sedans: Marvin L. Arrowsmith, "OPA
      Set New Car Price Ceilings near 1942 Averages," *St. Petersburg Evening Inde-
      pendent*, November 19, 1945.

260   within two hundred yards: Turner Publishing, *World War II Glider Pilots*,
      p. 16.

261   "suicide jockeys": Lloyd Clark, *Crossing the Rhine: Breaking into Nazi Ger-
      many, 1944 and 1945* (New York: Grove Atlantic, 2008), p. 87.

261   a mordant toast: National World War II Glider Pilots Association Web site,

www.pointvista.com/WW2GliderPilots/GliderPilotHumor.htm (retrieved
March 7, 2010).

261 "don't go by glider!": Walter Cronkite, foreword to John L. Lowden, *Silent
Wings at War: Combat Gliders in World War II* (Washington, D.C.: Smithsonian Institution Press, 2003), p. ix.

262 Nearly five hundred glider retrievals: Keith H. Thoms et al., "Austere
Recovery of Cargo Gliders," www.ndu.edu/inss/Press/jfq_pages/editions/
i48/29.pdf (retrieved March 9, 2010).

262 retrofitted as medevac aircraft: Leon B. Spencer, former World War II glider
pilot, and Charles L. Day, "WW II U.S. Army Air Forces Glider Aerial
Retrieval System," www.silentwingsmuseum.com/images/Web%20Con-
tent/WWII%20USAAF%20Glider%20Aerial%20Retrieval%20System.pdf
(retrieved October 20, 2009).

264 scattered all over: Imparato, *Rescue from Shangri-La*, p. 59.

264 a pilot with United Airlines: William Samuels, *Reflections of an Airline Pilot*
(San Francisco, Calif.: Monterey Pacific, 1999), p. 46.

264 most experienced glider pickup pilot: Ibid., p. 72.

264 turned over his own quarters: Ibid., p. 73.

265 *Leaking Louise*: Ibid., p. 72.

265 a three-day case of dysentery: Ibid., p. 74.

265 *Fanless Faggot*: St. George, "Rescue from Shangri-La," p. 6.

265 "What do you think, Mac?": Samuels, *Reflections of an Airline Pilot*, p. 73.

265 one to two feet high: U.S. Army air-to-ground transcript, June 19, 1945, in
Imparato, *Rescue from Shangri-La*, p. 110.

266 toilet paper: "Reynolds Allen Clears Up Several Hidden Valley Facts Re-
lated in Prior Articles," *Silent Wings* (newsletter of the National World War
II Glider Pilots Association) 1, no. 4 (September 1974): 16.

266 a huge winch: Ibid. Details on glider snatch technique and equipment also
came from Spencer and Day, "Glider Aerial Retrieval System"; Imparato,
Rescue from Shangri-La; Lowden, *Silent Wings at War*; Thoms et al., "Austere
Recovery of Cargo Gliders"; Devlin, *Silent Wings*; and Roy Gibbons, "Brake
and Reel Device Used in Glider Snatch," *Chicago Tribune*, July 1, 1945.

267 within three seconds: Lowden, *Silent Wings at War*, p. 17. See also Leon B.
Spencer and Day, "Glider Aerial Retrieval System," p. 5.

24: TWO QUEENS

268 "after we get out of here": Frank Kelley, "Weather Delays Rescue of
Shangri-La Shutins," *New York Tribune*, June 23, 1945, in Walter's scrapbook.

269 five cowrie shells: Hastings, SLD, part 16.

269 sixty-two arrows and three bows: Walter, CEW, June 23, 1945.

269 four shells: Kelley, "Weather Delays Rescue."

269 pigpen . . . collapsed: John McCollom, interview, October 1997.

269 ruining the local economy: Ibid.

270 At a funeral: Heider, *Grand Valley Dani*, pp. 132–33.

270 "don't take the shells": Lisaniak Mabel, interview.

270 "be careful": Walter, interview by author, July 6, 2009.

270 "quite a money monger": Walter, CEW, June 30, 1945.

271 Gerlagam Logo: Narekesok Logo and Dagadigik Walela, interviews by author, February 3, 2010.

271 "eggs that landed unscrambled": St. George, "Rescue from Shangri-La," p. 6.

271 "believers in mankind": U.S. Army air-to-ground transcript, June 21, 1945, in Imparato, *Rescue from Shangri-La*, p. 117.

272 "Natives not very fast": Walter, CEW, June 24, 1945.

272 "shot through the heart": Hastings, SLD, part 17.

272 found the skeleton: Walter, CEW, June 27, 1945.

273 "a dying race": Walter, CEW, June 22, 1945.

273 "You could see where the cuts were": Narekesok Logo, interview. The story of the pig was confirmed in interviews with Dagadigik Walela on the same day, and with Ai Baga and Lisaniak Mabel on February 2, 2010.

273 "smeared their heads with mosquito repellant": Simmons, "Glider Takes Six More."

273 infection on her breast: U.S. Army air-to-ground transcript, June 21, 1945, in Imparato, *Rescue from Shangri-La*, p. 114.

273 "a wonderfully carefree people": Simmons, "Glider Takes Six More."

274 "the captain forbade it": Hastings, SLD, part 17.

274 "a man of dignity and authority": Ibid., part 16.

275 "a word of the other's language": Ibid., part 17.

276 "a royal guest": Ibid.

276 "the rest of us": U.S. Army air-to-ground transcript, June 21, 1945, in Imparato, *Rescue from Shangri-La*, p. 114.

276 "a wise people": Hastings, SLD, part 17.

276 an ornate necklace: Walter, CEW, June 20 and 21, 1945.

277 a chief with ten wives: Interview with Dagadigik Walela, February 3, 2010.

278 severed the nylon tow rope: Samuels, *Reflections of an Airline Pilot*, p. 74. See also Hastings, SLD, part 18.

278 compass mast was knocked off: St. George, "Rescue from Shangri-La," p. 6.

278 the steel cable: Devlin, *Silent Wings*, p. 357.

278 "The winch just blew up": Walter Simmons, "Glider Rescue Test Again Fails," *Chicago Tribune*, June 26, 1945.

278 Winston Howell: A dispute exists over the first name and rank of the winch operator. Some accounts call him Private James Howell. However, stories by Sergeant Ozzie St. George of *Yank* and Walter Simmons of the *Chicago Tribune*, both of whom covered the mission, identify him as "Master Sergeant Winston Howell." In his memoir, *Reflections of an Airline Pilot*, William J. Samuels identifies him as "Frank" Howell.

278   certain they'd have no trouble: Ralph Morton, "Survivor Trio of Shangri-La
        Safe in Valley," *Sarasota Herald-Tribune*, June 20, 1945.

278   "A shower of aluminum": Samuels, *Reflections of an Airline Pilot*, p. 74.

279   "badly rusted": "Reynolds Allen," *Silent Wings*, p. 16.

279   cancel the glider snatch: Simmons, "Glider Rescue Test."

279   inviting the Seabees: Associated Press, "Five More Rescued At Shangri-La,"
        Miami News, June 30, 1945.

279   "any haphazard attempt": U.S. Army air-to-ground transcript, June 19,
        1945, in Imparato, *Rescue from Shangri-La*, p. 111.

279   "possibility of a bad accident": Ibid.

279   "if the glider pickup didn't work": Walter, interview by Izon.

280   "I said my Rosary": Hastings, SLD, part 18.

280   asked a chaplain to pray: Ibid. See also Samuels, *Reflections of an Airline Pilot*,
        p. 74.

281   "might have been dead": Hastings, SLD, part 17.

282   "one of us handsome guys": Ibid.

282   their name for Margaret was Nuarauke: Ai Baga, interview.

282   " 'Sleep with this woman' ": Interview with Hugiampot, February 2, 2010.

283   Caoili was called Kelabi: Ibid. The names were confirmed by others in the
        valley, including Lisaniak Mabel, Narekesok Logo, and Dagadigik Walela.

283   "appreciate our help": Walter, CEW, June 19, 1945.

283   "our first uneasy night": Ibid., dated June 22, 1945.

284   on his own terms: Ai Baga, Lisaniak Mabel, and Hugiampot, interviews.

284   "the enemies talked": Ai Baga, interview.

25: SNATCH

285   overload the glider: U.S. Army air-to-ground transcript, June 22, 1945, in
        Imparato, *Rescue from Shangri-La*, p. 116. See also Walter Simmons, "Clouds
        Defeat Hidden Valley Rescue Effort," *Chicago Tribune*, June 29, 1945, p. 2

285   sat in the glider's copilot seat: Simmons, "Clouds Defeat." See also Impar-
        ato, *Rescue from Shangri-La*, p. 72.

285   reflected confidence: Pilot William J. Samuels was certain Elsmore's act was
        a mark of confidence in the C-47 crew. See Samuels, *Reflections of an Airline
        Pilot*, p. 74.

285   awoke at 6:00 a.m.: U.S. Army air-to-ground transcript, June 28, 1945, in
        Imparato, *Rescue from Shangri-La*, p. 139.

286   "puffs of cigar smoke": Walter Simmons, "Glider Saves Yanks Marooned in
        Shangri-La Valley," *Chicago Tribune*, June 30, 1945.

286   "Does the queen": U.S. Army air-to-ground transcript, June 28, 1945, in
        Imparato, *Rescue from Shangri-La*, p. 139.

286   a B-25 bomber: Don Caswell, "It's Not Exactly Shangri-La," United Press
        story datelined July 1, 1945, in Walter's scrapbook.

286   "my prayers on the future": Walter, CEW, June 13, 1945.

287 "I will not be on the first glider": U.S. Army air-to-ground transcript, June 28, 1945, in Imparato, *Rescue from Shangri-La*, p. 139.

288 glider's tail rose: Alexander Cann's film *Rescue from Shangri-La*, copy provided by Robert Gardner.

288 "jumping up and down": Hastings, SLD, part 18.

288 whooping and hollering: Transcript of June 29, 1945, press conference, reprinted in Imparato, *Rescue from Shangri-La*, p. 189.

288 "gas or time": U.S. Army air-to-ground transcript, June 28, 1945, in Imparato, *Rescue from Shangri-La*, p. 141.

289 lighten the load: Report of Major William Samuels, reprinted in Imparato, *Rescue from Shangri-La*, p. 143.

289 "a damn good day": Ibid.

289 "better not try a dry run": Ibid., p. 142.

289 "ready to go?": Hastings, SLD, part 18.

290 "they understood that we were going": Hastings, SLD, part 18.

291 "We had a crying ceremony": Transcript of interview with Binalok conducted by Buzz Maxey, 1997, no month given. Binalok had since died when the author visited the Baliem Valley, but his explanations were confirmed during discussions with other witnesses quoted throughout the book.

291 a more traditional style: Ibid. A man named Lolkwa joined Binalok during this part of the discussion.

291 "insured for ten thousand dollars": Hastings, SLD, part 18.

292 "survived a hideous plane crash": Ibid.

292 "I don't think I can pick up": "Corporal Margaret Hastings and Two Companions Are Rescued by Glider," news clipping in Hastings's scrapbook, TCHS.

292 "This is the best weather": Ibid.

293 "Are you nervous": Report of Samuels, reprinted in Imparato, *Rescue from Shangri-La*, p. 143.

293 135 miles per hour: United Press, "Glider Rescue Almost Ends in Second Tragedy," *Schenectady (N.Y.) Gazette*, July 2, 1945.

293 "Oh boy. Oh boy": Ozzie St. George, "Rescue From Shangri-La," *Yank: The Army Weekly*, August 17, 1945, p. 6.

293 slowed the *Leaking Louise*: Ibid.

294 about one thousand feet: United Press, "Glider Rescue Almost Ends in Second Tragedy," *Schenectady (N.Y.) Gazette*, July 2, 1945, p. 7.

295 through the upper branches: Ibid.

295 grazed a treetop: Hastings, SLD, part 18.

295 "into our line of vision": Ibid.

295 hands sweating: Ibid.

295 "as far as she can go": Associated Press story, unbylined but written by Ralph Morton, "Trio, Snatched Out of Valley, Arrive Safely," Walter's scrapbook.

295 cut the glider loose: John McCollom, interview, October 1997.

295 "Let 'em heat up": Ibid.

295 a persistent *slap-slap* noise: Hastings, SLD, part 18.

296 tried not to look: Ibid.

296 one more task: McCollom and Walter, joint interview, May 13, 1998.

296 cylinder heads . . . overheating: Report of Samuels, reprinted in Imparato, *Rescue from Shangri-La*, p. 144.

296 "brushing the mountain tops": United Press, "Glider Rescue Almost Ends in Second Tragedy," *Schenectady (N.Y.) Gazette*, July 2, 1945.

EPILOGUE: AFTER SHANGRI-LA

298 landed a quarter mile away: St. George, "Rescue from Shangri-La," p. 6.

298 "Get a haircut and shave": Transcript of press conference, reprinted in Imparato, *Rescue from Shangri-La*, pp. 184–89.

298 "The Four Musketeers": Walter, CEW, June 30, 1945.

299 "We were excited to go." Lisaniak Mabel, interview. This account is supported by a passage in a story printed in the *Jungle Journal* 1, no. 5 (July 4, 1945): "One boy the Filipinos were reluctant to leave behind was a chap whom they named Smiley. . . . For a few minutes, they thought they had him talked into a new future, but in the end he backed out."

300 "The identity of the valley": *Science*, n.s., 102, no. 2652 (October 26, 1945): 14.

303 letters to the victims' families: Lt. Col. Donald Wardle, chief of the Army Disposition Branch, Memorial Division, to Mr. Rolla McCollom, father of Robert and John McCollom, May 1, 1959, in McCollom's IDPF.

304 "segregation was not possible": Ibid.

304 honorary pallbearer: Lieutenant Colonel Anne O'Sullivan, "Plane Down, WACs Aboard," *Women's Army Corps Journal* 5, no. 5 (October–December 1974): 16.

304 a lei of vanda orchids: Ibid.

304 Robert McCollom's wedding ring: Wardle to Mrs. Cecelia A. McCollom, the widow of Robert McCollom, May 13, 1959. (Coincidentally, fourteen years to the date after the crash.)

305 his best friend: Melvyn Lutgring, interview by author, January 9, 2010.

305 larger historical event: Inteview with Margaret Harvey, Henry Palmer's daughter, on March 12, 2010. See also obituary of Henry Earl Palmer, *Watchman* (Clinton, La.), October 28, 1991.

306 offered a choice: Samuels, *Reflections of an Airline Pilot*, p. 76.

306 military honors: "Ray Elsmore, 66."

306 An obituary: Ibid.

306 obituary of George Lait: "George Lait, Coast Publicist, Dies at 51," *New York Times*, January 13, 1958.

306 Ralph Morton: Associated Press obituary, "Ralph Morton, Former War Reporter," *Newsday*, October 20, 1988, p. 41.

306 Walter Simmons: Jensen, "Walter Simmons, 1908–2006."

307 "stopped off to be an alcoholic": Tony Stephens, "Talented Agent Loved His Actors," obituary of John Cann, *Sydney Morning Herald*, September 25, 2008, www.smh.com.au/news/obituaries/talented-agent-loved-his-actors/2008/09/24/1222217327095.html (retrieved August 14, 2009).

307 returned to acting: Reuters obituary, "Canadian Actor Dies," *Ottawa Citizen*, December 22, 1977. See also Cann, interview, and follow-up e-mails.

307 Lucille Moseley: "Filipino Scout Weds U.S. Girl," undated news clipping in Walter's scrapbook. Accompanied by a second unbylined, undated clipping headlined "Shangri-La Hero Here."

308 dissolved the 1st Recon: Commendation letter signed by Douglas MacArthur, dated August 15, 1945, found in Margaret Hastings's correspondence file at TCHS.

309 " 'Did you earn that?' ": Walter, interview by author, March 1, 2010.

309 last entry in his journal: Walter, CEW, July 3, 1945.

309 "highlight of my life": Walter, interview by author, March 1, 2010.

310 married late in life: Betty McCollom, interview.

310 a telephone call every year: John McCollom, interview, October 1997.

310 tears to his eyes: John S. McCollom to retired Colonel Edward T. Imparato. See Imparato, *Rescue from Shangri-La*, p. 160.

310 left the military in 1946: John S. McCollom's obituary, *Dayton Daily News*, August 21, 2001, p. 10, provided by Betty McCollom.

310 "Why wasn't I killed instead of them?": Ibid.

311 "a baby daughter he had never seen": McCollom to Imparato, printed in *Rescue from Shangri-La*, p. 160.

311 Robert, alive, waiting for them: Pond, "Reunion," pp. 18–19. During his unaired interview with John McCollom, Robert Gardner tried sensitively to raise the subject of Robert McCollom's death, but each time John McCollom changed the subject or said something along the lines of, "I was lucky."

311 too weak to carry him: Betty McCollom, interview.

312 his own obituary: McCollom's obituary.

312 "most celebrated young woman": Miller, "Reconversion of a Heroine," p. 5.

312 "She's blonde": "Read Shangri-La Diary," *Boston Sunday Advertiser*, July 15, 1945, n.p., Margaret Hastings's scrapbook, TCHS.

312 fielding offers: "The Price of Fame," editorial, apparently from the *Owego Gazette*, July 14, 1945, in Margaret Hastings's scrapbook, TCHS.

312 "true comic": Frances Ullman, editor of *Calling All Girls* magazine, to Margaret Hastings, July 19, 1945, in Margaret Hastings's correspondence file, TCHS.

312 dined at Toots Shor's: Miller, "Reconversion of a Heroine," p. 5.

312 three thousand people: Stuart A. Dunham, "Shangri-La WAC Home, Finds Every Girl's Dream Come True," *Binghamton Press*, July 20, 1945.

313 "alligator pumps": "Owego Welcomes WAC Home," *Owego Gazette*, July 20, 1945.

313 movie offers: Ibid.

313 Loretta Young: Sidney Skolsky, "Hollywood Is My Beat," undated gossip column clipping in Margaret Hastings's scrapbook, TCHS.

313 waving their handkerchiefs and crying: Miller, "Reconversion of a Heroine,", p. 5.

314 fourteen different states: Tour schedule contained in Margaret Hastings's correspondence file, TCHS.

314 letter is chaste: Letter from Don Ruiz to Margaret Hastings, dated October 10, 1945, in Margaret Hastings's correspondence file, TCHS.

314 "I have the deepest sympathy": Colonel Luther Hill to Margaret G. Nicholson, July 21, 1945, provided by Major Nicholson's family.

314 " 'my commander's widow' ": Interview with John McCarthy, September 13, 2009.

315 "overwhelmed with war stories": Callahan, interview.

316 "if he didn't drown": Associated Press, "Former WAC Recalls 47-Day Jungle Ordeal," *Los Angeles Times*, November 26, 1961.

316 honorary members: "Hidden Valley Survivors to be Honored," *Silent Wings* 1, no. 4 (September 1974): 1.

316 "doing what has to be done": Pond, "Reunion."

316 "You bet!": Ibid., p. 18.

316 "a good fight": Callahan, interview.

SELECT BIBLIOGRAPHY

Alexander, Larry. *Shadows in the Jungle: The Alamo Scouts Behind Enemy Lines in World War II.* New York: NAL Caliber, 2009.

Bender, Thomas. *Rethinking American History in a Global Age.* Berkeley and Los Angeles: University of California Press, 2002.

Brown, Jerold E. *Historical Dictionary of the U.S. Army.* Westport, Conn.: Greenwood Press, 2001.

Clarinbould, Michael John. *The Forgotten Fifth: A Photographic Chronology of the U.S. Fifth Air Force in World War II.* Hyde Park, N.Y.: Balus Design, 2007.

Connolly, Bob, and Robin Anderson. *First Contact: New Guinea's Highlanders Encounter the Outside World.* New York: Viking, 1987.

Devlin, Gerard M. *Silent Wings: The Saga of the U.S. Army and Marine Combat Glider Pilots during World War II.* New York: St. Martin's Press, 1985.

Diamond, Jared. *Collapse: How Societies Choose to Fail or Succeed.* New York: Viking, 2005.

———. *Guns, Germs, and Steel: The Fates of Human Societies.* New York: W. W. Norton, 1997.

Dwiggins, Don. *On Silent Wings: Adventures in Motorless Flight.* New York: Grosset & Dunlap, 1970.

Flannery, Tim. *Throwim Way Leg: Tree-Kangaroos, Possums and Penis Gourds.* New York: Grove Press, 1998.

Gardner, Robert. *Making Dead Birds: Chronicle of a Film.* Cambridge, Mass.: Peabody Museum Press, 2007.

Gardner, Robert, and Karl G. Heider. *Gardens of War: Life and Death in the New Guinea Stone Age.* New York: Random House, 1968.

Hampton, O. W. "Bud." *Culture of Stone: Sacred and Profane Uses of Stone among the Dani.* College Station: Texas A&M University Press, 1999.

Harrer, Heinrich. *I Come from the Stone Age.* London: Companion Book Club, 1964.

Hayward, Douglas. *The Dani of Irian Jaya Before and After Conversion*. Sentani, Indonesia: Regions Press, 1980.

Heider, Karl G. *The Dugum Dani: A Papuan Culture in the Highlands of West New Guinea*. Chicago: Aldine, 1970.

————. *Grand Valley Dani: Peaceful Warriors*. 3rd ed. Belmont, Calif.: Wadsworth Group, 1997.

Hilton, James. *Lost Horizon*. New York: Pocket Books, 1960.

Hitt, Russell T. *Cannibal Valley: The Heroic Struggle for Christ in Savage New Guinea—The Most Perilous Mission Frontier in the World*. New York: Harper & Row, 1962

Imparato, Edward T. *Rescue from Shangri-La*. Paducah, Ky.: Turner, 1997.

Keats, John. *They Fought Alone*. New York: Pocket Books, 1965.

Lowden, John L. *Silent Wings at War: Combat Gliders in World War II*. Washington, Smithsonian Institution Press, 1992.

Manchester, William. *American Caesar: Douglas MacArthur, 1880–1964*. New York: Little, Brown, 1978.

Matthiessen, Peter. *Under the Mountain Wall: A Chronicle of Two Seasons in Stone Age New Guinea*. New York: Viking, 1962.

Meiselas, Susan. *Encounters with the Dani: Stories from the Baliem Valley*. New York: Steidl/International Center for Photography, 2003.

Miller, Stuart Creighton. *Benevolent Assimilation: The American Conquest of the Philippines, 1899–1903*. New Haven, Conn.: Yale University Press, 1984.

Morison, Samuel Eliot. *History of U.S. Naval Operations in World War II*. Vol. 8, *New Guinea and the Marianas, March 1944–August 1944*. Champaign: University of Illinois Press, 2002.

Morse, Roger A. *Richard Archbold and the Archbold Biological Station*. Gainesville: University Press of Florida, 2000.

Rottman, Gordon L. *U.S. Special Warfare Units in the Pacific Theater, 1941–45: Scouts, Raiders, Rangers and Reconnaissance Units*. New York: Osprey, 2005.

————. *World War II Pacific Island Guide: A Geo-Military Study*. Westport, Conn.: Greenwood Press, 2001.

Samuels, William. *Reflections of an Airline Pilot*. San Francisco, Calif.: Monterey Pacific, 1999.

Sandler, Stanley. *World War II in the Pacific: An Encyclopedia*. New York: Garland, 2001.

Sargent, Wyn. *People of the Valley: Life with a Cannibal Tribe in New Guinea*. New York: Random House, 1974.

Schieffelin, Edward L., and Robert Crittenden. *Like People You See in a Dream: First Contact in Six Papuan Societies*. Stanford, Calif.: Stanford University Press, 1991.

Schneebaum, Tobias. *Where the Spirits Dwell: Odyssey in the Jungle of New Guinea*. New York: Grove Press, 1988.

Sheehan, Susan. *A Missing Plane: The Dramatic Tragedy and Triumph of a Lost and Forgotten World War II Bomber.* New York: Berkeley Books, 1986.

Souter, Gavin. *New Guinea: The Last Unknown.* Sydney, Australia: Angus & Robertson, 1964.

Treadwell, Mattie E. *The Women's Army Corps.* Washington, D.C.: Office of the Chief of Military History, Dept. of the Army, 1954.

Weise, Selene H. C. *The Good Soldier: The Story of a Southwest Pacific Signal Corps WAC.* Shippensburg, Pa.: Burd Street Press, 1999.

Yellin, Emily. *Our Mothers' War: American Women at Home and at the Front During World War II.* New York: Free Press, 2004.

INDEX

Page numbers in italics refer to illustrations. Page numbers 329 and higher refer to notes.

Abrenica, Santiago "Sandy," 162–63, 183–84, 197–98, 200, 201, 242, 252, 265, 279, 298, 307, 317
Abumpuk, 184
ahkuni (people), 117
AIDS, 301
Air Medal for Meritorious Achievement, 305
airplanes:
  and Native New Guineans, 25, 27, 38, 86, 124–26, 288, 290, 291
  see also gliders; *specific airplanes*
alcohol, 190, 226, 243
Alerta, Custodio, 165, 200, 219, 253, 298, 307, 317
Allen, G. Reynolds, 277–79, 287, 317
alliances, 117
American flag, 206, *206*, 237
Amundsen, Roald, 80
ane (noise), 124
anekuku (planes), 124, 184
anewoo (planes), 124–26
Antonini, Herman F., 56
Aquilio, Esther "Ack Ack," 224
Archbold, John D., 80–81
Archbold, Richard:
  discovery of Shangri-La by, 79, 80–91, *83*, 181, 300, 317
  later years and death of, 300
  and Native New Guinean shooting death, 89, 90–91, 129, 202, 342
Archbold Biological Station, 300
Arlington National Cemetery, 304

Arnold, H. H. "Hap," 215
Arthur, Hugh, 225
Atkinson, Robert, 315
atom bomb, 29, 129–30, 268, 308
Australia, HMAS, 249

B-17 Flying Fortress bombers, 98, 99, 100–101, 104, 130, 310
B-24 Liberator bombers, 8, 98
B-25 Mitchell bombers, 8, 98, 256, 287, 293
Babcock, John, 106–7, 109, 147–48
Baga, Ai, 199, 284
Bahala na! (Come what may!) motto, 141, 151, 166, 241
Baker, William D., 99–101, 104, 152, 237, 310, 317
Baliem River, 88, 105, 199, 225, 271, 300
Baliem Valley, 24–25, 116, 122, 134, 301, *302*
  see also Shangri-La
"bamboo bombers," 261
Baron, Harry, 278
Barron, Theodore "Ted," 73, 74
Bataan Death March, 142, 146, 163
Baylon, Alfred "Weylon," 165, 199, 200, 235, 242, 252, 265, 273–74, 298, 307, 317
Besley, Laura, 13, *14*, 211, 304, 317, 331, 334, 338
  aboard *Gremlin Special*, 35
  death of, 67–68, 69, 74–75

(Cont.) Besley, Laura
  in *Gremlin Special* crash, 52–54, 60,
    63–64
  shoes of, 64–65, 68
"Betty" (dive-bomber), 249
big man (tribal leader), 117, 201, 284
biological research, 81–91
blue-star families, 1–3, 154, 215
Boston Sunday Advertiser, 312
Brass, L. J., 86–87
Bronze Star, 307
Bulatao, Benjamin "Doc" "Mumu,"
    162–65, *165*, 166–67, 173–80, 190,
    193–94, *193*, 195, *196*, 208, 210,
    219, 227–28, 232–33, 235, 237,
    240, 268, 307–8, 317
*Bulletin of the American Museum of
  Natural History*, 90
burial mission, 210–14, *212*

C-46, 260
C-47 Skytrain, 33–34, *33*, 72, 98, 152,
    156, *159*, 173, 182, 198, 255–56,
    260
  as tow plane in glider snatch mission,
    262–63, 267, 293, 295; *see also*
    Leaking Louise
  see also Gremlin Special
C-60 transport plane, 19–20, 23, 98
Callahan, Rita Hastings, 2, 4, 226,
    313, 315, 316
Calling All Girls, 312
"Camp Shangri-La," 242–45, 252–54,
    268–84
  glider snatch of survivors from, *see*
    glider snatch mission
Camp X, 112
Cann, Alexander (Alexander Cross),
    243–51, *245*, 246, 255, 271, 274,
    283, 298, 318
  alcoholism of, 245, 247, 248
  back injury of, 248–49
  charm of, 246, 247, 248

  drunken parachute jump of, 243–45,
    250
  as filmmaker, 248–49, 251, 254, 268,
    280, 288, 289, 307
  Hollywood acting career of, 246–48
  jewel heist scandal of, 247–48
  later life and death of, 307
  in military, 248–49
  recklessness of, 243–45, 250
  Shangri-La documentary of, 243,
    251, 254, 263, 280, 288, 289,
    302, 307
Cann, Alexandra, 246, 250
Cann, H. V., 245–46
Cann, June Dunlop, 307
Cann, Mabel Ross, 245
cannibals, cannibalism, 25, 28, 30, 88,
    119, 129, 130, 132, 150, 186, 222,
    348
Caoili, Hermenegildo "Superman"
    "Iron Man," 165, 197–98, 200, 207,
    210, 219, 298, 307, 318
Challenger Bay, *83*
Chicago Tribune, 220–21, 224, 225, 226,
    306
clans, 117
Clement, General, 192
Comfort, USS, 97
Commendation Award, 306
confederations, 117
Cook, Captain, 10
Copernicus, 116
Corregidor island, 21, 106, 141, 146
Coster, Earl, 56
Coster, Ruth, 36, *36*, 56, 154, 219
cowrie shells, 87, 88, 134, 252,269–70
Cronkite, Walter, 261
Cross, Alexander, *see* Cann, Alexander
crying ceremony, 291
cultural misunderstandings, 125–26,
    134–35, 186–89, 196–97, 214,
    270–71, 272, 273, 280–83, 285,
    291

Dahl, Roald, 34
Daily Argus Leader, 220
Dani tribe, 117, *117, 119,* 122, 134,
    135, *171,* 184, 197, 200, 269,
    272, 273, 277, 284, *302,* 346,
    357
  base camp near, 268–91
Dartmouth Free Press, 306
Dattilo, Phillip J., 56
D-Day, 28, 260, 261
"dead birds," 123, 185, 277
Dead Birds (film), 347–48
"dead reckoning," 203
Decker, Bert, 226
Decker, Kenneth, 40, *179,* 215, 281,
    299, 316, 318, 334
  aboard *Gremlin Special,* 40
  in aftermath of crash, 58, 60–65,
    67–70, 69, 126
  at "Camp Shangri-La," 268, 290
  death of, 310
  helpfulness of, 61
  humor of, 78, 94, 101, 131
  injuries of, 52–54, 74, 76, 93–94, 95,
    135, 138–39, 154, 156, 159–61,
    167, 168–69, 176, 239, 310
  and life after Shangri-La, 307, *308,*
    309
  medics' treatment of, 179–80, 190,
    194, 209, 233
  stoicism of, 76, 93, 156, 158, 160–61,
    169, 190, 239
  see also Gremlin Special *survivors*
Decker, Thelma, 224
defecation, 200
dengue fever, 163–64
dili (enemies), 117
Distinguished Flying Cross, 306
Distinguished Service Medal, 306
Dobransky, Peter, 225
Dongallo, Fernando, 165, 200, 210,
    219, 308, 318
Douglas DC-3, 33

Dyak tribe, 83–84, 88
dysentery, 85, 163, 265

Eagle Scouts, 41, 52, 61
Earhart, Amelia, 85
education, 301
Eisenhower, Dwight D., 314
Elizalde, Joachin Miguel "Mike,"
    110–12
Elsmore, Ray T., 20–21, *21, 24,* 27, 28,
    30, 46, 86, 124, 146, 318
  cultural bias of, 28, 31–32
  expertise of, 292–93, 295
  and first view of Shangri-La, 19–25
  as head of search and rescue mission,
    96, 98, 104–5, 149, 165, 181, 217,
    242, 255–56, 263–64, 279, 285–
    86, 287, 289, 292–93, 300
  later life and death of, 305
  press attention to, 28–29, 31–32,
    220, 223, 263, 286
  self-promotion of, 31–32, 80, 105,
    220, 223, 263
  as self-styled discoverer of Shangri-
    La, 26, 80, 91
End of Days, 124, 126
etai-eken (soul), 139–40

Fair, Alethia M., 36–37, 56
Fanless Faggot, 265, 267, 277–78, 287,
    288, 290, 292, 294–97, *294, 297,*
    298, 305
Far East Air Service Command (Fee-
    Ask), 16, 32, 96, 107, 165, 192
Filipino-Americans:
  discrimination against, 145–46, 350
  immigration of, 145
  as paratroopers under Walter, 112–
    13, 141–42, 144, 148, 162–65,
    253
  in World War II, 144–47, 164
  see also 1st Reconnaissance Battalion;
    5217th Reconnaissance Battalion

fingers, amputation of, 116, 121, 281–82

1st Reconnaissance Battalion (Special), 141, 143–44, *149*, 162–65, 197–98, *241*, 309, *315*
  medals awarded to, 307
  scant press coverage of, 234–35

5217th Reconnaissance Battalion, 112, 141, 164, 308

"flak bait," 261

Flannery, Tim, 86

Fleming, Walter "Wally," 32, 101, 191, 312, 318

"flying boats," 82–83

"flying coffins," 261, 279

Flying Dutchman, crash of, 72–74, 104

Freyman, Louis E., 56

funeral services, for crash victims, 213, 304–5

Gallagher, Marie, 223

gangrene, 92–94, 135, 154, 158, 160, 168–69, 179–80, 190, 209, 237

Gardner, George, 217, 224, 225, 226, 227, 250, 271, 286–87, 318

Gardner, Robert, 302, 343, 347–48

Garrison, Jim, 305

Gatling, William J., Jr., 26

Gearhard, August, 213

Germany, Nazi, 7, 30, 249, 257–58

Gillis, Marian, 36, 56

gliders:
  American military use of, 258–62
  German use of, 257–58
  history of, 257
  in rescue mission, *see* glider snatch mission
  in World War II, 257–62
  see also Waco CG-4A

glider snatch mission, 262–67, 277–80, 285–97, 292
  cooperation of natives in, 289–90, 290

impediments to, 294–97
second and third retrievals in, 298
see also Waco CG-4A

gold-star families, 1, 215

Good, Herbert F., 40–41, 54–55, *55*, 58, 211–12, 304, 318

"Gooney Birds," 34

Grand Valley, 84, 91, *300*
  see also Shangri-La

Gremlins, The (Dahl), 34

Gremlin Special, 34–43, *36*, *39*, 298, 302
  aftermath of crash of, 58–70, 75
  camouflage of, 34
  casualties of, 55–57, 63, 67–68, 154, 297
  crash of, 50–57, 65, 72, 124, 125, 154, 238–39, 295, 296
  fiftieth anniversary of crash of, 309
  name of, 34
  passengers and crew seating on, 34–43, 68
  possible causes for crash of, 48–49, 337
  recovery and reburial of bodies from, 304–5
  remains at crash site of, 303–4
  salvage from, 61–62, 64, 71
  sighting of Shangri-La from, 44–47
  specs of, 33–34
  survivors of, *see* Decker, Kenneth; *Gremlin Special* survivors; Hastings, Margaret; McCollom, John "Mac"
  Walter's burial mission at site of, 210–14, *212*

Gremlin Special survivors, 68–70, *241*, 299, *315*
  bond of respect and affection among, 93
  at "Cape Shangri-La" base camp, 243–45, 252–54, 268–91
  in first encounter with Native New Guineans, 128–40

on first glider, 286–87, 289–97
hopefulness of, 65–66, 78, 99, 101
humor of, 160, 172, 190, 298
hunger of, 168
jungle trek of, 74–79, 92–99
media frenzy over, 220–24
medical care for, 106
return trek of, 239–42
sighting by Baker of, 100–101
at Uwambo survivors' camp, 124–40,
    155–57, 167–72, 176–80, 190–
    203
Grimes, Myron, discovery of Shangri-
    La by, 19–24, 26, 30, 31, 45, 80,
    318
Guba, 82–83, *83*, 84, 86, 87, 181, 341
guerrilla fighters, 111–12, 142, 144,
    147
Gutzeit, Jack, 153–55, 193, 224, 225,
    318

Halifax Herald, 221
Hal-loak-nak, 116
Hanna, Eleanor, 35–36, 211, 304, 318,
    339
   in *Gremlin Special* crash, 52–54,
    60–64, 68
   souvenir bracelets of, 36, 60, 304,
    334, 338
Hastings, Catherine, 2, 4, 226, *313*
Hastings, Julia Hickey, 2, 66–67
Hastings, Margaret, 2, *136*, *196*, 263,
    275, 299, *315*, 316, 319, 337
   aboard *Gremlin Special*, 35, 42, 45,
    47, 49
   adventurous nature of, 2, 7, 13, 68,
    316
   and affection for medics, 178, *193*
   in aftermath of crash, 58–70, *68*
   allowed into native village, 274–76
   and attraction to Ruiz, 208–9, 314
   and attraction to Walter, 208
   basic training and promotion of, 9, 60

beauty of, 6, 205, 312
bond between "Chief Pete" and, 136,
    138, 172, 236–37
childhood and early life of, 6–7,
    66–67
children of, 316
cultural bias of, 134–35, 137
death of, 316
and death of mother, 66–67
in departure from base camp, 236–
    37, 238–40
diary of, 59, 64–65, 66, 68, 70, 75,
    77, 92, 95, 131, 132, 133, 134–35,
    137, 138, 140, 154, 155, 156, 159,
    160, 161, 167, 176, 178, 179, 180,
    190–91, *193*, 205, 213, 226, 236,
    238, 241–42, 288, 292, 333
disappearance of, 1–4, 9
and disenchantment with fame,
    314–15
enlistment of, 2–3
and evolving view of natives, 274–76
and fear, 295–96, 316
feisty nature of, 8, 159
in first encounter with Native New
    Guineans, 130–33
flirtatious nature of, 6, 208
and friendship with "the queen,"
    274–76, 275, 280–82, 290
gangrene and amputation fears of,
    92–94, 159, 161, 169, 176, 180
in *Gremlin Special* crash, 51–54
hair cut of, 76, 138, 205, 221, 280,
    281, 313
homecoming parade for, 131, 312–13,
    313
independence of, 6–7
injuries of, 59–60, 64–65, 74, 76,
    92–94, 95, 135, 154, 158–59, 161,
    167, 168–69, 176, 237, 239
and life after Shangri-La, 312–16
"Maggie" nickname of, 69, 93, 197
marriage and divorce of, 315–16

(Cont.) Hastings, Margaret,
  in media frenzy, 222, 223, 224, 227,
    235, 312
  medics' treatment of, 179–80, 193–
    94, *193*, 209, 233–34
  movie offers for, 312, 315
  as petite, 6, 330
  and prayer, 51, 75, 161, 176, 193–94,
    279–81, 291, 294
  and preparations for sightseeing trip,
    32–33
  pride of, 194
  as Queen of Shangri-La, 224, 241,
    286, 309, 314, 316
  resentment against, 314
  resourcefulness of, 51, 60, 75
  and respect and affection for Native
    New Guineans, 138, 140, 155,
    274–76, 290
  return to Owego of, 312–13
  social life of, 12–13, 32, 101, 191
  as spokesperson for Victory Bonds,
    313
  stoicism of, 78, 93
  stubbornness of, 214
  unselfishness of, 167
  unwanted suitors of, 241–42
  vanity of, 5–6
  wartime job of, 6, 15
  see also Gremlin Special *survivors*
Hastings, Patrick, 1–4, 226, 313, 315,
    319
  and news of Margaret's disappear-
    ance, 3–4, 215–16
headhunters, 24, 25, 28, 30, 31, 94,
    150, 166
health care, 301
Hearst, Alma Walker, 247–48
Hearst, William Randolph, Jr.,
    247
helicopters, 105, 181, 217, 255, 258
"Hey, Martha!" news stories, 221–22,
    223, 247

Hidden Valley, 19–20, 24–25, 26, 91,
    197
  see also Shangri-La
Hilton, James, 29
Hitler, Adolf, 7, 257–58
Holding, Lawrence F., 56
Hole, The, 122–23
Hollandia, Dutch New Guinea, 5, *10*,
    11, 301
  Archbold's camp in, 83
  Walter's team in, 141–44, *149*
Hollandia military base, 5–18, *5*, 20,
    54, 63, 74, 94, 96–98
  WAC living conditions at, 5, 12,
    13–16
  WAC swimming death at, 97–98
Hollywood:
  Cann in, 246–48
  offers to Margaret from, 312, 315
homecoming parade, 312–13, *313*
Hoops, Eugene, M., 337
Howell, Winston, 278, 362
Hugiampot, 282
Human Bomb, The (film), 248
"human wind dummies," 174
huts, 23, 47, 116–17, 156, 275, 302

Imparato, Edward T., 182, 319
inalugu (pile of feces), 200
iniatek (originals), 123
"Inseparables, The," 41

Japan, Japanese, in World War II,
    8, 11–12, 105, 111, 142, 146–47,
    150–51, 163, 166, 232, 249, 268,
    308
Javonillo, Juan "Johnny," 165, 197–98,
    200, 210, 245, 250, 253, 308, 319
Jayapura, 301
Jefferson Barracks National Cemetery,
    304
John and Robert McCollom Memorial
    Scholarship, 312

kain (big man), 117, 201, 284
kamikazes, 30, 97, 249
Kelabi, 283
Kennedy, John F., 305
Kenney, George C., 24
Kent, Helen, 36, 36, 46–47, 49, 56, 154, 210, 319
Kirchanski, James, 225
Koloima, 184, 282, 268–91
Korean War, 307, 310
Kremer expedition, 85
Kurelu (big man), 284
Kurelu clan, 184, 185

L-5 Sentinel "Flying Jeep," 156
Lait, George, 27–30, 31, 319, 333
    later life and death of, 306
    press credentials of, 27–28
    Shangri-La described by, 28, 122
Lait, Jack, 27
Landau, Mary M., 37, 56, 210, 213
Landikma, 128
Leaking Louise, 3–5, 264–65, 266, 267, 277–78, 288–89, 292–95, 292, 297, 297
    hazards aboard, 278–79
lechon feast, 254
Legion of Merit, 306
Leyte Island, 97, 141, 147, 163, 220, 249
Lindbergh, Charles, 41
logging, 302
Logo, Gerlagam "Joe," 269–71
Logo, Narekesok, 199, 273
Logo, Yali, 185, 271, 284, 290, 319
Logo-Mabel clans, 184–85
Los Angeles Times, 247, 312, 315
Los Banos Internment Camp, 106
Lost Horizon (film), 29–30, 122
Lost Horizon (Hilton), 29–30, 130
"Lost Outpost of Shangri-La, The," 206, 206

Louise, see Leaking Louise
Lowell, James Russell, 44
Lutgring, James "Jimmy," 39–40, 39, 98, 154, 305
Lutgring, Melvyn, 305
Lutz, Aleda, 96
Luzon Island, 9, 106, 141, 146, 162
Lynch, T. R., 165–66

Mabel, Inggimarlek, 125
Mabel, Lisaniak, 185, 189, 199, 270, 298, 365
MacArthur, Douglas, 11–12, 21, 36, 54, 106, 114, 142, 146, 215, 232, 306, 308
McCarthy, John, 314
McCollom, Betty, 311–12
McCollom, Cecelia Connolly "Adele," 42, 56, 215, 226, 304–5
McCollom, Eva Ratliff, 41, 226
McCollom, John "Mac," 134, 227, 233–34, 259, 272, 281–82, 298, 316, 319, 334, 337
    aboard *Gremlin Special*, 46–50
    in aftermath of crash, 58–70, 69
    bravery of, 132, 296
    in burial mission, 210–11
    at "Camp Shangri-La," 268–70, 290
    compassion of, 169, 190
    competence of, 47–48, 69, 71, 100
    death and obituary of, 311–12
    determination of, 94, 311, 343
    as emotional, 153–54, 310
    fear of, 94
    in *Gremlin Special* crash, 50–54, 56–57
    in handshake with "Pete," 132–33
    as identical twin, 14, 41–43, 41, 42, 51, 52, 53, 57, 61, 68, 75, 94, 95–96, 153, 211, 213, 215, 296, 310, 311, 343
    injuries of, 51, 52, 60
    kindness of, 14

(Cont.) McCollom, John "Mac,"
  leadership qualities of, 14, 52–53, 58,
    69, 74–76, 79, 93, 95, 130, 156
  and life after Shangri-La, 304, *308*,
    309, 310–11, *311*
  in media, 224–25
  resourcefulness of, 61, 74–75, 78
  and respect and affection for fellow
    survivors, 93
  survivor's guilt of, 310
  see also Gremlin Special *survivors*
McCollom, Mary Dennise "Dennie,"
    42, 304–5, 310, *311*
McCollom, Robert Emert, 41–43,
    41, 42, 51, 52, 56–57, 68, 75, 94,
    95, 211, 213, 215, 226, 259, 296,
    304–5, 310, 311, 319, 343
McCollom, Rolla, 41, 226
machete, 237
McKenzie, William G., 265, 277, 278,
    319
McKinley, William, 144–45
McMonagle, Marion W., 36, 56, 303
McMullen, Clements, 215
Macy, Anson, 234
maga (declaration of safe passage), 201,
    236–37
Mageam, 199
malaria, 14, 163–64
Mayr, Ernst, 81–82
Mead, Margaret, 122
medics, *see* Bulatao, Benjamin "Doc"
    "Mumu"; Ramirez, Camilo
    "Rammy" "Mua"
Mellberg, Carl, 213
Mengel, Herbert O., 154, 319
mep mili (dark blood), 135
Merle, 34
Miller (Walter Jr.'s friend), 110
Miller, Charles R., 56
mining, 301
missionaries, 300–301, 304
mogat (spirits, ghosts), 118, 137

Mollberg, Melvin "Molly," 37, *37*, 56,
    98, 154, 305, 319
Molly, 305
Morton, Ralph, 220–27, 233–34, 235,
    242, 249, 278, 306, 320
Moseley, Lucille, 307–8
Mother's Day (1945), 7, 17, 32
mourning:
    finger amputation in, 116, 121, 282
    mud ritual for, 188
mouth harp, 208
Mundima, 134, 177, 227
Mundi River, 125, 134, 177

Nagasaki, 308
Naimer, Belle, 36, 56, 210, 213
Nakmatugi, 123
National Geographic, 86, 89
National Memorial Cemetery of the
    Pacific, 304
National World War II Glider Pilots
    Association, 316
Native New Guineans, 9–10, 12,
    72–73, 79, *241*, *253*
    agriculture of, 22, 86, 87, 102
    and airplanes, 25, 27, 28, 86, 124–26,
        288, *290*, *291*
    anthropological inaccuracies about,
        25, 28–29, 31–32, 102–3, 134–35,
        228, 273, 281–82
    appearance and dress of, 22, 87, 103,
        115–16, 134–35, 170, 188–89,
        229–30, *291*, *302*, *330*, *346*
    art of, 115, *346*
    attempts at communication with,
        169–70, 177, 185–86, 273, 275
    beginning of the end for, 238
    and belief in spirits and ghosts, 85,
        116, 118–19, 123–24, 126–27,
        137, 197, 201, 214, 230–31, 238
    children, 116, 121, *136*, 273
    contemporary cultural decline of,
        301–2

cooperation of, 289–90, 290
corpses of, 272
creation myths of, 122–24
cultural bias against, 28, 198, 200, 202, 222, 228, 230
and cultural changes after western contact, 291, 300–303
cultural misunderstandings about, 186–89, 270–71, 280–83
curiosity of, 200
defensiveness of, 201–2
economy of, 269–70
and fear of westerners, 85, 126, 201
and festival, 119
first metal tool of, 237
healing arts of, 139–40
and increasing comfort with westerners, 190–91
isolation of, 115
languages of, 9–10, 115–18, 273, 275
lifestyle and mores of, 115–22, 188–89, 270, 282
and Margaret's baths, 195–97
medical treatments for, 273–74
misconceptions about westerners by, 85, 125–26, 134–35, 196–97, 214, 272, 273
regard for survivors of, 139–40, 155
sexual practices of, 120, 197, 228, 273, 282
social structure of, 117
Stone Age culture of, 22, 26–27, 129, 183, 222
survivors' first encounter with, 103, 115, 128–40
survivors sighted by, 100
temporary suspension of warfare by, 201, 227
and viewing of Gremlin Special crash, 125–27
villages of, 22–24, 23, 47, 86–87, 189; see also Uwambo
violence against, 79, 89, 90–91

warfare and, see warfare, as basis of Native New Guinean society
as wary of survivors, 136–37
weapons of, see weapons, Native New Guinean
westerners' early encounters with, 87–89
women, see women, Native New Guinean
see also Dani tribe; Yali tribe
neighborhoods, 117, 184
Newcomer, George R., 39, 56
New Guinea:
contemporary, 300–303
downed and missing planes in, 71–74
flora and fauna of, 14, 58–59, 74, 84
geography and topography of, 9–11, 10
inhospitable jungle habitat of, 58–59, 61, 63, 76–79, 150, 166, 174
isolation of, 10–11, 301
maladies and illnesses in, 15
maps of, 10, 20, 90, 98
native inhabitants of, see Dani tribe; Native New Guineans; Yali tribe
natural beauty of, 15, 58–59
as part of Indonesia, 301
trading with, 11
western exploration of, 10–11, 84–85
in World War II, 11; see also Hollandia military base
New York Mirror, 27
New York Times, 8, 89, 223, 247–48, 306
Nicholson, Alice, 314
George Nicholson's letter to, 37–39, 55
Nicholson, George H., Jr., 38, 215, 314, 320
as co-pilot on Gremlin Special, 37, 45–50, 65, 98
death of, 55

(Cont.) Nicholson, George H., Jr.,
  educational and military background
    of, 37–39
  exoneration of, 215
  limited piloting experience of,
    45–50, 65
  personal misgivings of, 38–39
Nicholson, Margaret, 215, 314
nicknames, bestowed by natives, 228,
  273, 282–83
no-man's land, 184, 199, 283
Norris, Hilliard, 39, 56
Nuarauke, 282

Obama, Barack, 302
O'Brien, Denise, 85
Ogi ridge, 125, 201, 214, 238, 302
Okinawa, battle of, 8, 223, 268
Oranje mountain range, 19, 44, 105,
  206, 242
Oswald, Lee Harvey, 305
Owego, New York, 1, 3, 6–7, 12, 13,
  312–13
Owego Free Academy, 312

P-38 Lightning fighters, 8
P-47 Thunderbolts, 305
Pallas Athena, 97–98
Palmer, Henry E. "Red," 256–57, *288*,
  305, 320
  and gilder snatch mission, 262–63,
    265, 277, 287–94
Papua New Guinea, 301
Papuans, 301
Papua province, Indonesia, 301
Parachute Infantry Regiments, 105
parachutes, 166–67, 243–45, 250,
  295–96
  and dangers of jungle jumps, 173–77,
    182–83
paratroopers, 106–7, 141
  Filipino-American, 112–13, 141–42,
    144

see also 1st Reconnaissance Battalion
  (Special); 5217th Reconnaissance
  Battalion
Patterson, Harry E., 27–30, 31, 122,
  319
Pattisina, Corporal, 89
PBY bombers, 82–83
Pearl Harbor, 7, 21, 30, 108, 110, 146,
  163, 259
Peggy (pig), 252, 254, 300
penis gourds (*horim*), 86, 129, 131, 135,
  185, 188, 189, 228, 229, 291, 301,
  346
Philippine-American War (1898–
  1902), 145
Philippines, 107, 110–11, 145–46
  World War II in, 8–9, 11, 21, 36,
    106, 111, 113, 142, 146–47, 163,
    249, 306, 308
Philippine Scouts, 163
pig feasts, 171–72, 202
pigs, 22, 25, 85, 86, 118, 122, 134, 170,
  237, 238, 252, 269, 302
  rebirth of, 273
"Pika," 199
Piri, Sikman, 282
poverty, 301
Pratt & Whitney engines, 14
Presidential Unit Citations, 306
press, media, 27, 220–27, 232, 233–34,
  271, 286, 298, 300
  attention to Margaret in, 223, 224,
    225, 227, 235, 312
  Morton-Simmons journalistic rivalry
    in, 222–24, 249
  scant coverage of 1st Recon in, 234–35
  sensational tone of, 222–23
Prossen, David, 16, *17*, 304
Prossen, Evelyn, 16–17, 32
Prossen, Lyneve, 16
Prossen, Peter, Jr., 16, 17, *17*, 304
Prossen, Peter J., *17*, 37, 45, 211, 220,
  304

as caring commander, 18, 32, 45
death of, 55
as devoted family man, 16–17
as pilot on *Gremlin Special*, 39–40,
    44–50, 98, 104
Protestant Digest, 221
Pyle, Ernie, 27

queen, the (native woman), 274–76,
    275, 280–81, 290
husband of, 280
Queen, The (airplane), 189

Ramirez, Camilo "Rammy" "Mua,"
    142, 162–65, *165*, 166–67, 173–80,
    193–94, 195, *196*, 208, 227–28,
    235, 237, 253, 298, 307–8, 320
Ray Jr., 292
Rescue from Shangri-La (film), 307
Reuters, 221
Riley, Frank, 154
Robb, Inez, 333
Rockefeller, John D., 80
Rockefeller, Michael, 316
Roosevelt, Franklin D., 1, 8, 30,
    145–47
Roosevelt, Theodore, 145
Ruiz, Don, 165, 200, 210, 220, 253,
    298, 307, 314

St. George, Ozzie, 271
Sambom, Maruk, 137
Sambom, Pugulik "Trouble Maker,"
    125, 136–37
Samuels, William J., 264–65, 277–78,
    280, 288–89, 292–95, *292*, 305–6,
    320
sanitary napkins, 192, 236, 254
Science, 300
Scott, Dennie McCollom, *see* McCol-
    lom, Mary Dennise "Dennie"
Scott, Robert Falcon, 80
Seabees, 255, 279

seaplanes, amphibious aircraft, 105,
    181 255, 300, 303
see also Guba
search and rescue mission:
    base camp for, 181–89, 243–45,
        252–54, 268–91
    burial duty of, 210–14
    departure from base camp of, 232–38
    evacuation plans for, 255–57, 262–67
    glider snatch mission of, *see* glider
        snatch mission
    Hollandia plans for, 96, 98, 181
    impediments to, 105–6, 150, 165,
        173–75, 256
    rescue options for, 105–6, 181–82
    supply drops of, 152–53, 155–57, *159*,
        167–68, 192, 193, 198, 209–10,
        268–69, 271
    survivors' hope for, 65–66, 78, 99
    Walter's personnel choices for,
        162–65
Sentani Airstrip, 32, 34, 44, 53, 65,
    96, 101, 173, 182, 192, 250, 298
sepsis, 93
Shangri-La, 19–30, 301
    Archbold's discovery of, 79, 80–91,
        300
    base camp at, *see* Camp Shangri-La
    beauty of, 21–22
    Elsmore's first view of, 19–25
    Grimes's discovery of, 19–24
    isolation of, 26–27, 115
    native inhabitants of, *see* Native New
        Guineans
    origin of name, 29–30, 31, 333
    population estimates of, 84, 85–86,
        116, 273
    potential dangers of, 24
    press coverage of, *see* press, media
    as undiscovered, 84–86
"Shangri-La Society," 31, 36, 311, 334
Shaw, Clay, 305
shell necklace, 276–77

shooting death, of Native New
Guinean, 79, 89
misleading reports of, 90–91
sightseeing flights, 19, 26, 32–43
see also Gremlin Special
Simmons, Walter, 220–27, 229, 235,
249, 278–79, 320
later life and death of, 306–7
sky spirits, 123–24, 126–27, 133–34,
184–85, 197, 201, 202, 214, 230–
31, 236, 238, 300, 303
western appearance of, 124, 126
see also Uluayek legend
smiles, 130–32
Smiley (native boy), 365
snatches, 261–64
mechanics of, 266–67
Waco mission, *see* glider snatch mission
Soldier's Medal, 307, 309
Spanish-American War (1898), 144–45
Stars of David, 210, 213, 214, 297
"streamers," 175
swap meets, 269
Swart Valley, 85
sweet potatoes (*camote; hiperi*), 47, 87,
102, 122, 129, 135, 140, 170, 178–
79, 230, 238, 275, 302

Teerink, C. G. J., 88, 89
Thanksgiving feast, 171
33rd Troop Carrier Squadron, 264
311 supply plane, 205, 234, 268, 271,
286, 287, 292
tobacco, smoking, 88, 116, 134, 155,
238, 291, 301
tomatoes, 155–56, 158
"Tommy Gun," 198
Toots Shor's, 312
tourism, 301–2
tow planes, 257, 258, 260, 264–65,
266–67
tribes, 117

Truman, Harry S., 1
and atom bomb, 268
Mother's Day declaration of, 7–8
"turbulence testers," 174

Ulio, James A., 3
Uluayek legend, 123–24, 126, 230–31,
291, 300
survivors included in, 238
Unciano, Isaac, 250
unh, 138, 169, 280
United Nations charter, 268
"United States Army Outpost at
Shangri-La," 252, 309
USAF Cemetery, Hidden Valley,
No. I, 304
Uwambo, 124–40, 155–57, 165–72,
176–80, 184, 190–203, 214, 216–
20, 224–31, 240–42, 357

Van Arcken, J. E. M., 88–89, 90, 342
V-E Day, 7–8
Velasco, Roque, 165, 200, 242, 252,
265, 274, 280–81, 298, 307, 320
Verne, Jules, 105
Victory Bonds, 313
Vietnam War, 305
Vision of Sir Launfal (Lowell), 44

Waco CG-4A, 259–62, 259
as dangerous, 260–61, 263
in glider snatch mission, 262–67,
277–80, 285–97
impediments to evacuation by, 263,
277–80
snatches of, 261–62
in World War II, 261–62
Wakde Island, 265, 266, 277–78, 285
Waldo, Cornelius, 99, 193, 213, 215
Walela, Dagadigik, 277
Walela, Keaugi, 276–77, 277
walkie talkies, 153, 167, 187, 204, 213,
227

Walter, C. Earl, Jr., *107*, *111*, *117*, 119,
  149, *165*, *187*, 272, 273–74, 298,
  302, 303, 320, 334
 admiration of survivors for, 239–41
 as amateur anthropologist, 228–31,
  271
 ankle injury of, 240–41
 at "Camp Shangri-La," 268, 271–73
 cultural bias of, 186–89, 198, 202,
  228, 230, 270–71
 description of Native New Guineans
  by, 229–30
 determination of, 148
 as eager for combat, 113–14, 141–44,
  148, 217, 232–33, 286, 308
 and encounter with Dani tribe,
  184–89
 father's approval sought by, 148, 151,
  232, 309
 in friendship with Cann, 251
 high spirits of, 208
 impatience of, 217–20, 232–33
 journal of, 186, 198–99, 200–201,
  202–3, 204, 208, 212, 214, 217–20,
  228, 232–33, 239, 270, 286, 309
 and life after Shangri-La, 304,
  308–9, *308*
 machismo of, 207
 manhood display of, 188
 maturity of, 286–87
 in media, 224–25
 military experience of, 110–14
 resourcefulness of, 109
 and respect and admiration for 1st
  Recon troops, 205, 235, 254, 289,
  307
 in search and rescue mission, 148–51,
  162–67, 173–75, 181–90, 239–42
 sense of humor of, 228–29
 and shell necklace, 276–77
 show of force by, 198–99, 284
 in trek to survivors' camp, 200–203
 undisciplined early years of, 107–10

Walter, C. Earl, Sr., 107–12, *111*, 114,
  144, 145, 148, 151, 232, 309
Walter, Sally Holden, 110, 112, 188,
  220, 226, 308–9
Wamena, Papua New Guinea, 300–
  302, *302*
Wandik, Gilelek, 169–70
Wandik, Helenma, 100, 125, 126, 128,
  133, 196–97, 238, 303, 348
Wandik, Nalarik, 125
Wandik, Sinangke, 133
Wandik, Tomas, 237
Wandik, Wimayuk "Chief Pete," 127,
  131–39, 159, 302, 320
 bond between Margaret and, 136,
  138, 172
 curiosity of, 190
 and departure of westerners,
  236–38
 flexibility of, 134
 as friend of survivors, 140, 169–70
 in handshake with McCollom, 132
 as tribal leader, 133–34, 177
Wandik, Yaralok, 125, 126, 133, 157,
  201
Wandik, Yunggukwe, 136–37
 pig of, 125, 157, 210, 214, 303, 351
War Department, U.S.:
 condolence telegrams of, 214–15
 Public Relations office of, 314
warfare:
 as basis of Native New Guinean
  society, 27, 30, 82, 117–22, 123,
  128–29, 184, 198, 201, 238, 283,
  301
 native vs. modern, 27, 118, 122,
  129–30
weapons:
 modern, 129–30, 183–84, 198–99,
  298
 Native New Guinean, 87, 88–89,
  103, 128, 131, 177, 183–84, 185,
  200, 269, *288*

Weber, Melvyn, 56
Westmoreland, William, 257
Whitney, Courtney, 142–44, 349–50
Wilhelmina, Mount, 45, 84
Winchell, Walter, 27
women:
   Native New Guinean, 87, 116, 118,
      120, 121, 122, 123, 170, 198, 202,
      230, 231, 270–71
   in World War II, 96–97; see also
      Women's Army Corps (WACs)
Women's Airforce Service Pilots
   (WASPs), 97
Women's Army Corps (WACs), 2, 5, 7,
   11–13, 60
   aboard Gremlin Special, 35–37, 96
   in Hanna's funeral, 304
   at Hollandia, 5, 5, 12, 13–16,
      96–98
Women's Auxiliary Ferrying Squadron
   (WAFS), 97
wooden crosses, 210, 213, 214, 297

World War I, 11, 20, 40, 55, 111, 213,
   257
World War II, 1, 5, 33, 248
   American casualties in, 3
   in Europe, 37–38, 97, 260–61
   German surrender in, 7
   Japan in, 8, 11–12
   in Pacific, 8, 11, 24, 106, 111–12,
      260, 268
   women in, 96–97; see also Women's
      Army Corps (WACs)
Wosi, 184, 198, 199, 201
Wright brothers flight, 257

Yali tribe, 117, 124–27, 129, 139, 184,
   197, 357
   survivors' camp near, 124–40, 155–
      57, 167–72, 176–80, 190–203,
      214, 216–20, 224–31, 240–42
Yank, 271

Zuckoff, Mitchell, 303, 309, 351